On the Shoulders of Giants

This book presents eleven classic papers by the late Professor Suzanne Scotchmer with introductions by leading economists and legal scholars. The book introduces Scotchmer's life and work; analyzes her pioneering contributions to the economics of patents and innovation incentives with a special focus on the modern theory of cumulative innovation; and describes her pioneering work on law and economics, evolutionary game theory, and general equilibrium/club theory. The book also provides a self-contained introduction for students who want to learn more about the various fields Professor Scotchmer worked in, with a particular focus on patent incentives and cumulative innovation.

Stephen M. Maurer is Adjunct Professor Emeritus of Public Policy at the University of California at Berkeley. A long-time friend and colleague of the late Professor Scotchmer, he coauthored eight articles and book chapters with her from 1999 to 2014. Trained as a lawyer, Maurer specializes in innovation, antitrust, and science policy. He is the editor and coauthor of *WMD Terrorism* (2007) and the author of *Self-Governance in Science* (2017).

Econometric Society Monographs

EDITORS:
Jeffrey Ely, *Northwestern University*
Donald W. K. Andrews, *Yale University*
The Econometric Society is an international society for the advancement of economic theory in relation to statistics and mathematics. The Econometric Society Monograph series is designed to promote the publication of original research contributions of high quality in mathematical economics and theoretical and applied econometrics.

OTHER TITLES IN THE SERIES:
G. S. Maddala, *Limited dependent and qualitative variables in econometrics*, 9780521241434, 9780521338257
Gerard Debreu, *Mathematical economics: Twenty papers of Gerard Debreu*, 9780521237369, 9780521335614
Jean-Michel Grandmont, *Money and value: A reconsideration of classical and neoclassical monetary economics*, 9780521251419, 9780521313643
Franklin M. Fisher, *Disequilibrium foundations of equilibrium economics*, 9780521378567
Andreu Mas-Colell, *The theory of general equilibrium: A differentiable approach*, 9780521265140, 9780521388702
Truman F. Bewley, Editor, *Advances in econometrics – Fifth World Congress (Volume I)*, 9780521467261
Truman F. Bewley, Editor, *Advances in econometrics – Fifth World Congress (Volume II)*, 9780521467254
Hervé Moulin, *Axioms of cooperative decision making*, 9780521360555, 9780521424585
L. G. Godfrey, *Misspecification tests in econometrics: The Lagrange multiplier principle and other approaches*, 9780521424592
Tony Lancaster, *The econometric analysis of transition data*, 9780521437899
Alvin E. Roth and Marilda A. Oliviera Sotomayor, Editors, *Two-sided matching: A study in game-theoretic modeling and analysis*, 9780521437882
Wolfgang Hardle, *Applied nonparametric regression*, 9780521429504
Jean-Jacques Laffont, Editor, *Advances in economic theory – Sixth World Congress (Volume I)*, 9780521484596
Jean-Jacques Laffont, Editor, *Advances in economic theory – Sixth World Congress (Volume II)*, 9780521484602
Halbert White, *Estimation, inference and specification*, 9780521252805, 9780521574464
Christopher Sims, Editor, *Advances in econometrics – Sixth World Congress (Volume I)*, 9780521444590, 9780521566100
Christopher Sims, Editor, *Advances in econometrics – Sixth World Congress (Volume II)*, 9780521444606, 9780521566094
Roger Guesnerie, *A contribution to the pure theory of taxation*, 9780521629560
David M. Kreps and Kenneth F. Wallis, Editors, *Advances in economics and econometrics – Seventh World Congress (Volume I)*, 9780521589833
David M. Kreps and Kenneth F. Wallis, Editors, *Advances in economics and econometrics – Seventh World Congress (Volume II)*, 9780521589826
David M. Kreps and Kenneth F. Wallis, Editors, *Advances in economics and econometrics – Seventh World Congress (Volume III)*, 9780521580137, 9780521589819
Donald P. Jacobs, Ehud Kalai, and Morton I. Kamien, Editors, *Frontiers of research in economic theory: The Nancy L. Schwartz Memorial Lectures, 1983–1997*, 9780521632225, 9780521635387
A. Colin Cameron and Pravin K. Trivedi, *Regression analysis of count data*, 9780521632010, 9780521635677

On the Shoulders of Giants
Colleagues Remember Suzanne Scotchmer's
Contributions to Economics

EDITED BY
Stephen M. Maurer
University of California at Berkeley

CAMBRIDGE
UNIVERSITY PRESS

CAMBRIDGE
UNIVERSITY PRESS

University Printing House, Cambridge CB2 8BS, United Kingdom

One Liberty Plaza, 20th Floor, New York, NY 10006, USA

477 Williamstown Road, Port Melbourne, VIC 3207, Australia

314-321, 3rd Floor, Plot 3, Splendor Forum, Jasola District Centre, New Delhi - 110025, India

79 Anson Road, #06-04/06, Singapore 079906

Cambridge University Press is part of the University of Cambridge.

It furthers the University's mission by disseminating knowledge in the pursuit of education, learning and research at the highest international levels of excellence.

www.cambridge.org
Information on this title: www.cambridge.org/9781107131163
10.1017/9781316443057

First published 2017

A catalogue record for this publication is available from the British Library

Library of Congress Cataloging in Publication data
Names: Scotchmer, Suzanne, honoree. | Maurer, Stephen M., editor.
Title: On the shoulders of giants : colleagues remember Suzanne Scotchmer's contributions to economics / edited by Stephen M. Maurer.
Description: New York : Cambridge University Press, 2017. | Series: Econometric society monographs ; 57
Identifiers: LCCN 2017014553 | ISBN 9781107131163 (Hardback) | ISBN 9781107578968 (Paperback)
Subjects: LCSH: Scotchmer, Suzanne. | Economists–United States. | Law–Economic aspects–United States. | BISAC: BUSINESS & ECONOMICS / Econometrics.
Classification: LCC HB119.S36 O6 2017 | DDC 330.092–dc23
LC record available at https://lccn.loc.gov/2017014553

ISBN 978-1-107-13116-3 Hardback
ISBN 978-1-107-57896-8 Paperback

Deborah F. Minehart's contribution to this volume does not purport to reflect the views of the US Department of Justice.

For Suzanne

Contents

Contributors

Reiko Aoki, Japan Fair Trade Commission, Tokyo, Japan.

Robert M. Anderson, Department of Economics, University of California at Berkeley, USA.

Eddie Dekel, Department of Economics, Northwestern University, USA, and Berglas School of Economics, Tel Aviv University, Israel.

Nisvan Erkal, Department of Economics, University of Melbourne, Australia.

Joseph Farrell, Department of Economics, University of California at Berkeley, USA.

Jeffrey L. Furman, Questrom School of Business, Boston University, USA.

Nancy Gallini, Vancouver School of Economics, University of British Columbia, Canada.

Neil Gandal, Berglas School of Economics, Tel Aviv University, Israel.

Joshua Gans, Rotman School of Management, University of Toronto, Canada.

Bronwyn H. Hall, Department of Economics, University of California at Berkeley, USA.

Carol Adaire Jones, Environmental Law Institute, Washington DC, USA.

Michael L. Katz, Haas School of Business, University of California at Berkeley, USA.

Stephen M. Maurer, Goldman School of Public Policy, University of California at Berkeley, USA.

Deborah Minehart, Economics Analysis Group, US Department of Justice, Washington DC, USA.

Fiona E. Murray, Sloan School of Management, Massachusetts Institute of Technology, USA.

Arthur J. Robson, Department of Economics, Simon Fraser University, British Columbia, Canada.

Pierre Regibeau, Charles River Associates and Imperial College, London, UK.

Pamela Samuelson, Berkeley Law School, University of California at Berkeley, USA.

Paul Seabright, Toulouse School of Economics and Institute for Advanced Study in Toulouse, Toulouse, France.

Chris Shannon, Department of Economics, University of California at Berkeley, USA.

Carl Shapiro, Haas School of Business, University of California at Berkeley, USA.

Scott Stern, Sloan School of Management, Massachusetts Institute of Technology, USA.

Heidi Williams, Department of Economics, Massachusetts Institute of Technology, USA.

Brian Wright, Department of Agricultural Economics, University of California at Berkeley, USA.

Junjie Zhou, National University of Singapore, Singapore.

Preface

Prof. Scotchmer always said that the only thing an academic really has is time. But for her there wasn't enough. She died at Berkeley after a brief illness on January 30, 2014. She was sixty-four.

It happened in the middle of the afternoon. The next morning I visited her home departments in Economics, Law, and Public Policy to tell them what had happened. From there the news spread across the planet like ripples on a pond. In our Digital Age the echoes came back at the speed of light – the first email responses from Berkeley within an hour, then Boston in the afternoon, Japan that evening, and France overnight. By week's end the messages had mounted into the hundreds.

At first the messages expressed grief and condolences. But that was transient and soon other sentiments appeared. The first was sorrow for the community, which was bound to be poorer and less fun without her. The second took the form of academic obituaries, in which even experts struggled to put her many contributions in perspective. The third was the bittersweet realization that so much of her research agenda remained to be done, an open invitation for bright scholars to finish what she had started.

Three months later, Berkeley Law School tried to satisfy these instincts with a conference to remember and celebrate Prof. Scotchmer's work.[1] Her colleagues came from California and Boston, Israel and Japan. And then something happened that was strange and disconcerting and yet also familiar. Suzanne's friends and colleagues gathered at the reception. We discussed what the speakers had said. We talked about her research style. We admired her contributions. And then we caught ourselves – a little guiltily – smiling. But that awkwardness soon passed. Because in the end we realized we were only doing what she had always wanted. Being glad in each other's company. Enjoying clever ideas. Pushing the work forward. None of us had ever been able to refuse Prof. Scotchmer in life. How could we refuse her in death?

Seven months later the Toulouse School of Economics held its own memorial lecture, followed by two more in 2016 and 2017. As I write, a fourth is planned with no end in view. Because, as one TSE faculty

---

1 "Innovation and Intellectual Property: A Tribute to Suzanne Scotchmer's Work," Berkeley, California (May 1, 2014).

member hesitantly told me, they feel that she belonged to them too. Well yes. Who could doubt it?

The Berkeley and Toulouse gatherings felt very right – a way for the community to pay its respects and say goodbye. But they also let world-class experts look back, assess the health of their disciplines, and argue about the best way forward. The talks were so good, in fact, that nobody wanted to stop. The idea for this book followed immediately.

The usual ambivalence applies. None of us thinks that this book is a fair trade for Suzanne. But we also think that she would understand. Suzanne loved scholarship and, especially, the craft of writing. This is what we have to give.

I said that Prof. Scotchmer did not have enough time, but time runs out for everyone. What matters is that she packed the time she did have with life and laughter and work. And besides, she would have been impatient to see us grieving. Better to go on learning, and loving, and celebrating our subject.

Stephen M. Maurer
Berkeley, California – July 2017

Acknowledgments

We thank the publishers listed below for graciously allowing us to reprint the following:

N. Gallini and S. Scotchmer, "Intellectual Property: When Is It the Best Incentive System?" originally appeared in Adam Jaffe, Joshua Lerner, and Scott Stern (eds.), *Innovation Policy and the Economy* at pp. 51–77 (MIT Press: 2002).

S. Scotchmer, "Standing on the Shoulders of Giants: Cumulative Research and the Patent Law," *Journal of Economic Perspectives* 5(1): 29–41 (American Economic Association: Winter 1991).

J. Green and S. Scotchmer, "On the Division of Profit in Sequential Innovation," *RAND Journal of Economics* 26(1): 20–33 (John Wiley & Sons: Spring 1995).

T. O'Donoghue, S. Scotchmer, and J. Thisse, "Patent Breadth, Patent Life, and the Pace of Technological Progress," *Journal of Economics & Management Strategy* 7: 1–32 (John Wiley & Sons: 1998).

S. Maurer and S. Scotchmer, "Profit Neutrality in Licensing," *American Law and Economics Review* 8(3): 476–522 (Oxford University Press: 2006).

P. Samuelson and S. Scotchmer, "The Law and Economics of Reverse Engineering," *Yale Law Journal* 111: 1575–1663 (Yale Law Journal: 2002).

M. Schankerman and S. Scotchmer, "Damages and Injunctions in Protecting Intellectual Property," *RAND Journal of Economics* 32(1): 199–220 (John Wiley & Sons: Spring 2001).

J. Farrell and S. Scotchmer, "Partnerships," *Quarterly Journal of Economics* 103(2): 279–297 (Oxford University Press: 1988).

B. Ellickson, B. Grodal, S. Scotchmer, and W. R. Zame, "Clubs and the Market," *Econometrica* 67(5): 1185–1218 (The Econometric Society: 1999).

E. Dekel and S. Scotchmer, "On the Evolution of Attitudes towards Risk in Winner-Take-All Games," *Journal of Economic Theory* 87(1): 125–143 (Elsevier: 1999).

S. Scotchmer, "Audit Classes and Tax Enforcement Policy," *American Economic Review: Papers and Proceedings* 77(2): 229–233 (American Economic Association: 1987).

Edna St. Vincent Millay, excerpt from "Dirge Without Music," from *Collected Poems*. Copyright 1928, © 1955 by Edna St. Vincent Millay and Norma Millay Ellis. Reprinted with the permission of The Permissions Company, Inc., on behalf of Holly Peppe, Literary Executor, The Edna St. Vincent Millay Society. www.millay.org.

CHAPTER 1

Introduction

Stephen M. Maurer

We have given the world our passion
We have naught for death but toys.
W. B. Yeats[1]

This is a happy book.

Some readers, particularly those who knew the late Prof. Scotchmer, will immediately understand – she would have said "feel in their bones" – why this book is so unapologetically joyful. Tragedy was foreign to her nature. She was too busy living. Every few months she would stop in mid-sentence, pause for an instant, and say: "We are so lucky. We lead such privileged lives."

She never changed her mind.

**

Prof. Scotchmer would not want a sentimental book. Her work exists and always will. She would not want us to waste our time, or be distracted from pushing our subject forward.

But that is no objection here. Prof. Scotchmer's papers have much to teach, and her work is not complete. There is nothing sentimental about wanting new readers to see her work whole, or take it further. This book is an investment in the future.

Our first purpose, then, is to introduce her work as completely as we can. This is not a textbook, and we have not paraphrased. We want readers to encounter Prof. Scotchmer's work directly. That said, our authors have worked hard to make the process as rewarding as possible. First-time readers will be told how each article fits into the wider topic, preview the main arguments, and learn which lessons to watch for. Returning readers can compare their impressions against what our experts

---

1 W. B. Yeats, "Upon a Dying Lady," *The Wild Swans at Coole* (London and New York: Macmillan, 1919). Prof. Scotchmer knew and admired the lines.

have said. In both cases, we hope readers will indulge in a theorist's disciplined daydreams: linger over some short phrase and let it expand. Check Suzanne's statement against your own reasoning, look for counter-examples, invent and answer questions for yourself. More often than not, you will find a few paragraphs later that she has traveled the path already. Above all, indulge your curiosity. Most readers will come to this book knowing Prof. Scotchmer's innovation research. They will not be disappointed. But we hope they will read further to see how she deployed the economist's characteristic tools in other fields. Club theory is so very interesting.

Our second purpose is intellectual history. It is not surprising that most economists prefer pushing their subject forward to recording the past. Even so, topics like innovation theory are only invented once. Readers can be excused for wanting to know what it felt like to be part of the communities that pioneered the subject at Harvard and Berkeley and Toulouse.

Our third and final purpose is forward looking. Prof. Scotchmer never thought that the economics profession was reserved for geniuses and heroes. It is mostly for ordinary people, and that is its charm. We think that many economists will be interested to hear something about Prof. Scotchmer's work habits, or why she chose some research paths and not others. Careful readers will see how much remains to be done. Here's hoping they extend the work.

**

Part I ("Threads in the Tapestry") begins with recollections of Prof. Scotchmer's characteristic style and habits of mind. Before any specific line of research, there is the primordial alchemy of how she turned the experience of living into models. One broad hint is that Prof. Scotchmer was never far from practicalities. The idea that "real life" and abstract thought could be divorced did not make sense to her, if only because thought and practical action feed each other. So we will be drawn to her personal life at times: you cannot understand her otherwise.

Parts II and III ("Cumulative Innovation" and "Law and Economics") present the principal milestones in Prof. Scotchmer's long investigation of intellectual property ("IP").[2] The centerpiece, inevitably, is her "Giants" paper. Most readers will already know "Giants" for having introduced the "cumulative innovation problem," i.e., the fact that many technologies build on earlier inventions. This chain is bound to break down unless IP

---

2 Readers may also want to consult Prof. Scotchmer's own elegant recapitulation of cumulative innovation in *Innovation and Incentives* (Cambridge, MA: MIT, 2004) as well as her magisterial surveys of innovation theory more broadly in Scotchmer (1998) and Scotchmer and Menell (2007).

finds some way to allocate reward so that each inventor is able to cover her R&D costs.[3] A quarter century later, that would be reason enough to remember "Giants." But in fact the paper lays down a game-theoretic agenda for understanding how IP and antitrust doctrine divide reward. Prof. Scotchmer would spend a decade constructing this edifice, and the rest of her life examining the doctrinal reforms that lawyers need to implement it.

The next three parts remind us that Prof. Scotchmer's passions and contributions did not stop with R&D incentives. Part IV ("Club Theory") recounts her fundamental contributions to general equilibrium theory. Part V ("Evolutionary Game Theory") features her work applying economic logic to the natural world and, more surprisingly, gender inequality. Part VI ("Public Policy") addresses her various public policy papers. The diversity of these chapters is striking in a world where so many academics cling to whichever subject first yielded success. Prof. Scotchmer would have none of this. She was always restless, and when an idea caught her imagination she could not let go.

Finally, Part VII ("Living Legacy") examines how Prof. Scotchmer's work has influenced others. I think she would have liked this. Economics is the work of many hands. Then too, she would have wanted the book to have a forward-looking conclusion.

The book ends with a complete list of publications. Most include URLs and can be downloaded over the Web.

**

Prof. Scotchmer managed her final months, like everything she did, with discipline and grace. Hardly anyone outside the family knew that she was sick. Partly that was her Scandinavian upbringing, a quiet opposition to chaos and wasted motion. But like everything she did, it was also a fully thought-out, personal choice. She didn't need farewells. She had lived her life passionately: she knew that her friends loved her, and they, unmistakably, knew that she loved them. There was nothing unsaid, and nothing left to say.

Her mind was restless to the end. Some of these amusements were nostalgic, returning to pleasures she had known growing up. She beat all comers at Scrabble and calculated the scores impossibly faster than I could. We also did what she used to call "read-alouds," rediscovering Robert Louis Stevenson with *Treasure Island* and then *The Wrecker*[4] with its lovely send-up of an American business school where students bet on a fantasy stock market instead of going to class.

---

3 Prof. Scotchmer later generalized this into a broader class of "ideas models." *See* Erkal, Maurer, and Meinhart, this volume.
4 Robert Louis Stevenson and Lloyd Osborn, *The Wrecker* (London: Cassell, 1892).

On the last day Suzanne was unconscious. Our morning's read-aloud –
"Mrs. Todd's Shortcut"[5] – was a long story about a fearless woman that
I had bought for her the year before. I want to believe that she heard me,
and of course the nurses swear that this is true. But even then my better self
imagined Suzanne watching me, her gray eyes bright with gentle incredu-
lity, asking how I could believe such nonsense.

That afternoon I was in the room talking with a nurse and nurse's aide.
None of us noticed when she slipped away. That, too, was how she wanted
things.

**

The usual disclaimers apply, particularly since Suzanne is no longer here
to correct us. Readers will find that Prof. Scotchmer wrote with uncommon clarity and consistency. Even so, most of us know first-hand what it is
to hear a coauthor exclaim in sudden exasperation, "I didn't mean that at
all." It is practically certain that we have similarly misunderstood Prof.
Scotchmer's ideas in what follows, though I hope only in a few places. We
think she would forgive us. She always came down on the side of trying.

Finally, I should add some notes on editing. Prof. Scotchmer often
wrote with coauthors. While we will use phrases like "Prof. Scotchmer
wrote ..." to describe her papers, this is only a convenient shorthand. To
the contrary: one of Prof. Scotchmer's great gifts was her talent for
coauthorship. This began with a favorite phrase – "coauthorship is hard" –
and ended in articles so seamless that even her coauthors have trouble
remembering who had contributed what. What makes this all the more
remarkable is that the finished papers always end by supplying some
missing piece in Prof. Scotchmer's broader research agenda.

The reprints which follow were published in different journals with
different house rules. I have standardized these. More reluctantly, I have
occasionally cut passages in the interests of space. When I did, my choices
have almost always preserved material that shows Prof. Scotchmer's
thoughts and ideas over her technical virtuosity. In the same vein, I have
reluctantly suppressed the papers' various technical appendices along with
the Clubs paper's "Proofs" section. Since this book is mainly addressed to
economists, I have also eliminated extensive text and hundreds of lawyer-
friendly footnotes from her "Reverse Engineering" paper. My hope is that
the choices will help readers focus on what matters. If not, they can find
the omitted sections on the Web.

There was a time when a book like this would never have called Prof.
Scotchmer by her first name. Today I hardly know what to think. I have
therefore left the choice to each individual contributor. For my own part,
I have tried to use "Prof. Scotchmer" when speaking of her formal

5 Stephen King, *Skeleton Crew* (New York: Putnam, 1985).

intellectual work, while reserving "Suzanne" for more informal and personal memories. Careful readers will see that I am inconsistent.

There are so many people who made this book possible. My special thanks to Eddie Dekel, Suzanne's former student and lifelong colleague. He was always available for detailed and invariably solid advice and this book could never have been written without him. My thanks also to Cambridge University Press's excellent and very patient editor Karen Maloney, along with assistant editors Kristina Deutsch and Kate Gavino. Finally, I want to extend special thanks to Prof. Scotchmer's family – particularly Alan, Judi, and Jaycen Andersen and Roberta Hayes – along with lifelong friends Carl Brodersen and Gale and Sheryl Strohme for reviewing the manuscript and providing indispensable insights into her life. Most obviously, I thank the authors who participated in this collaboration.

**

Prof. Scotchmer used to say, "In the end, all you take with you is your CV." I used to stumble over that sentiment each time she said it, silently objecting that surely you take nothing at all. But now I understand. For Suzanne, life meant being active in the world and making it better. That could not stop with her death: her work and personal example will continue to exert an impact for decades to come. In the meantime, the great pleasure of this project has been to hear her voice. Her papers still teach, and encourage, and inspire. The crisp, precise comments seem to grow each time I read them. Now, through this book and the generosity of my coauthors, she will reach even more readers.

So she was right about that too.

This is a happy book.

PART I

THREADS IN THE TAPESTRY

One of the pleasures of a good theory paper is that the ideas seem to emerge from nowhere. The sources, when they exist at all, are barely more than clippings. More often than not, the reader holds the document in his hands and wonders how anyone could get a paper from such modest hints.

But this is an illusion. Look closely and you will see that the theorist has drawn on more personal resources, some inherited and others carefully cultivated. That is why this chapter begins with the Prof. Scotchmer's life experiences – there is no ignoring her Alaska upbringing – and proceeds to the traits and habits of mind that comprised her signature style as an economist. While none of this "explains" her work, we can at least see the materials she used to construct it. Along the way, economist readers may even find attractive strategies for organizing their own lives.

CHAPTER 2

Alaska

Stephen M. Maurer

It is conventional and logical for a book to start in childhood. The trouble, usually, is that most childhoods – and especially those involving mid-century American scholars – are so dreadfully alike. So we sift through whatever facts we find and ask ourselves which, if any, suffice to explain what followed. The difference, in Suzanne Scotchmer's case, is that the facts are so insistent. After all, how many twenty-first-century economists started their education in a one-room school house? Or spent the first twelve years of their lives in an Alaskan fishing village?[1]

I should say that Suzanne herself would have been skeptical of this approach. Her life was so much about talent and hard work that she would have succeeded no matter where she grew up. Consciously, at least, her family background was mostly visible in the pleasure she took in interacting with Scandinavian colleagues – notably including her extended collaborations with Birgit Grodal (1943–2004) – and, especially, the talks she gave in Finland. As for Alaska itself, she would laugh and say, "Most people think I'm from New York. Actually, I grew up in the wilderness."

The confusion was largely due to an early decision to publish under her then-married name of Scotchmer. She worried that "Andersen" might be common enough to confuse people. Later she recognized that this was a typically Alaskan mistake, and that there weren't enough Andersens in the Lower Forty-Eight to cause a problem.[2]

---

1 Most academics are born to other academics. But some come from such radically different backgrounds that you wonder how they ever imagined the possibility. When the outsider is some Indian or Chinese prodigy – say, Satyendra Bose in physics – this might be order statistics. But there are not nearly enough Alaskans for that argument to work. There is a deep suspicion that Alaska was causal in Prof. Scotchmer's success.

2 The Andersen persona eventually resurfaced in the mid-1990s as the pen name for Suzanne's four creative writing stories. A literary critic would likely argue that the Scotchmer name was a deliberate choice, or "mask." This seems unlikely. I heard Suzanne tell the Scotchmer story several times and have no reason to doubt it. Even so, it was a happy choice for the way she lived her life. Suzanne's great gift of focus meant that she

Origins. Her grandparents had come from Norway and Finland. Like most old-time Alaskans they had started as Goldrushers and, also like most old-time Alaskans, they had failed at it. Judging from some of the Andersen family's surviving Old World silver they must have been solidly middle class and sometimes prosperous. Family lore adds that they were reasonably well educated. At first they settled in Nome. When the Rush ended they moved to Ketichikan.

Suzanne's father Toivo (1910–1991) was the oldest of four children. Toivo was, by all accounts, a genius at fishing, shrewd and self-disciplined and a man who had built his life in deliberate contrast to his alcoholic and occasionally abusive father. He spent most of the Thirties establishing himself as a commercial fisherman. By the early Forties he was coming into his own. That was when he met Margaret Sangder (1911–2005) on a visit to Seattle. The two married after the war and moved to a tiny village called Pelican. Their first child (Alan) was born at the end of '48. Suzanne, the second and final child, arrived on January 23, 1950.

Pelican. You reached Pelican from the sea through a deep inlet bracketed by steep mountains on either side. The town itself was small: even in its heyday the population was hardly more than 150. When Toivo and Margaret arrived it was still raw: the oldest building was just eight years old and the town's *raison d'être* – a cold storage fish plant – had only recently begun operation.[3] Beyond the plant there were houses, a single boardwalked street, and the inevitable boat slips.

The entertainments were both primitive and exotic: hunting and trapping, and picnics and berry-picking, always with a rifle nearby in case of bears. Children took astonishing risks by modern standards, piling into homemade sailboats when they were no more than four or five years old. Suzanne would later recall how her mother yelled at her for crossing the inlet with her inseparable friend, Chris Clauson, in a tiny rowboat. Is it really an accident that Clauson grew up to be a prominent marine biologist – and, after Suzanne, Pelican's leading gift to American universities?

Suzanne would later say, only half in fun, that Pelican was "the Wild West." But it was definitely a place where Tlingit Indians rubbed shoulders with Norwegians who had jumped ship or Americans who did not want to be found. Meanwhile the better element socialized and played cards, skated and hunted in the winter, constantly invented entertainments, and – in Toivo's family – played piano. One citizen had been a professional ice skater. Others were shadowy or alcoholic. One of them,

---

could talk fishing in Alaska and game theory Down South. And always with equal sincerity.

3 For the definitive account of both Toivo and Pelican, see Francis E. Caldwell, *Land of the Ocean Mists: The Wild Ocean Coast West of Glacier Bay* (Edmonds, AK: Alaska Northwest Publishing, 1986), at pp. 127ff.

"Wobblie," was an IWW organizer[4] who had been run out of Seattle after the big General Strike of 1911.

Suzanne loved the place, but nobody could romanticize it. It was too small and simple and you could immediately see how everything worked. To begin with, practically everyone caught fish or supported those who did. And when the big West Coast canneries conspired to push down salmon prices, as they always eventually did, everyone understood and felt the impact personally.

Pelican also bred a certain detachment. To some extent this came with being an Alaskan. Suzanne would recall watching the town's weekly movie and wondering what the endless cities and fancy parties had to do with her life. But there were also divisions within Pelican itself, especially if you were part of a young family. As Suzanne's mother liked to remind her, "There's the church people, and there's bar people, and there's us."

Fishing. World War II had introduced new technologies and dumped them on the market. Much of what Toivo and his friends accomplished lay in inventing new uses for war-surplus radios and navigation electronics. At the same time, they had to install and run this machinery far from home. You could go down to the dock almost any time and see them installing or troubleshooting equipment.

The surprise was that fishing was so cerebral. Toivo thought hard about where the fish were every day, carefully recorded each trip in logs and maps, and then stared at the data until he saw the patterns. This was every bit as abstract as what professors do, except that there were no points for being elegant or cute. He either caught fish or he didn't.

Toivo's most famous achievement lay in discovering a new place to fish.[5] Poring over their charts, Toivo and two friends noticed an area of shallow water called the Fairweather Grounds. Shallow water is often good for fishing, but this particular site was forty miles out to sea and prone to sudden, violent storms. When that happened, a fishing boat would have to make a run for it over the treacherous (and sometimes impassable) sandbars of Lituya Bay. Toivo and his friends made their first trip in 1952. The fishing was good but difficult, and the trio did not return again until war-surplus electronic navigation aids became available "with a little tinkering" in 1954. This time the fishing was astonishing.[6] The sequel was ready-made for the child who would grow up to study innovation theory. No matter how much Toivo and his co-discoverers wanted to keep the location secret, they couldn't stop competitors from watching him unload.

---

4 The International Workers of the World was a radical union founded in 1905. It was particularly strong in the western USA before the First World War. See, e.g., Wikipedia, "Industrial Workers of the World," available at https://en.wikipedia.org/wiki/Industrial_Workers_of_the_World.
5 Caldwell, *Land of the Ocean Mists*, 127ff.
6 Toivo once caught an astonishing 282 king salmon in a single day. Ibid.

Soon other boats were following him into the Gulf until everyone knew the secret.[7] Bad news for the Andersens, but the Fairweather Grounds have supported Alaskan families ever since.

Toivo. Like many 1950s fathers, the memories of Toivo's children seem slightly out of focus: on the one hand, he set high standards, never more so than when his children fell short in fishing or school. On the other, he was always there with toys and stuffed animals and routinely joined in games. One winter he even brought an injured seal home to the family bathtub.[8] Like so many Fifties fathers, he also organized a driving vacation across Canada and on to Florida. For the rest of her life, Suzanne would remember seeing the crowded downtown sidewalks and asking herself the economist's primordial question, "What do all these people *do*?"

Suzanne's love for Toivo is unmistakable in the four memoirs she wrote about life in Alaska.[9] He invariably appears as "Daddy," a quiet but astonishingly capable man whose smile – Suzanne called it his "twinkle" – shines through in old photos. But Toivo and his daughter also shared a stubborn streak that memorably played out in a decades-long argument over whether she could learn to fish or, as Alaskans say, "run gear." Her semi-autobiographical "Smoked Fish," written after Toivo's death, claims that "he thought [the task] beyond a girl's ability." But this may have been literary license in a story whose central joke turns on competence. One Sitka friend who ought to know explains that Toivo, like most fathers in

---

7 IP partisans usually tell this kind of story as a morality play in which the hero is cheated of his "just reward." Prof. Scotchmer was more likely to observe that Toivo's catches in that first year had amply repaid his discovery cost, and he would continue to fish the Grounds – and be lionized by peers – for the rest of his life. As "Giants" explains more carefully, he did not need to receive the full social value of his discovery. For Suzanne's own economic analysis of the fishing industry, see Farrell and Scotchmer (1988), this volume.

8 The story did not end happily and, unlike the usual Disney narrative, the seal died. There was, however, a kind of echo. One day in the early 2000s, Suzanne showed me some baby rats she had found – the mother had been killed in a trap – and she was feeding them milk from an eyedropper. I remember wondering if we were prolonging their suffering, but now I think that she was right. Of course the case was hopeless. But, for the moment, the rats were beautiful and Suzanne had always had a naturalist's eye for the world. And if we could be kind or make them less afraid, what did it matter that the relief was temporary?

9 Suzanne wrote four pieces of creative fiction – "Smoked Fish" (December 1995), "Ghosts of Christmas Past" (December 1996), "Devil's Club Tea" (October 1996), and "Rain" (March 1997). The work is by turns elegiac ("Smoked Fish") and funny ("Rain") and a nearly perfect realization of the Alaskan literary genre that began with Jack London (1876–1916) and Robert Service (1874–1958). It says a great deal for Suzanne's talent that she could write these gems in the space of eighteen months and then move on, never to write another. As in "Giants," the final and seemingly effortless text surely obscures years of thought. It would have helped that Suzanne was passionately interested in contemporary fiction – especially including Penelope Lively, Wallace Stegner, and Ivan Doig – and invariably noticed how their stories were constructed. It was equally typical that, having written the stories, she would never write another. She never repeated herself, and besides there were economics papers to write.

that time and place, had definite ideas about male and female jobs. Suzanne never entirely got over this, and sometimes wondered in all seriousness what her life would have been like running the family business.[10] Given her other successes the irony cannot have escaped her. Even so, Suzanne always recommended creative writing for catharsis,[11] so I think we should take "Smoked Fish" as her final word on the subject. The action starts with Toivo, in his last summer, finally allowing Suzanne to land a fish[12] and ends with the old man's death. By then, however, Toivo himself has left the frame ("unconscious of his own misery") so that the catastrophe falls on his children instead. The scene is powerful precisely because the ancient quarrel no longer means anything.[13]

Sitka and After. Suzanne invariably talked about Pelican as a kind of industrial Eden. But it did have one obvious and fatal defect: there was no high school. So Toivo moved the family to Sitka – still another, more conventionally American Eden – when Suzanne was thirteen. Sitka was not what anyone would call a big city.

By all accounts this was a happy time. Suzanne formed strong high school friendships which she cherished and maintained for the rest of her life.[14] For the most part her friends' memories are what you might expect – that she found math easy, for example, and always finished her assignments far ahead of anyone else. The more interesting thread is that "She was always saying, 'Let's teach ourselves something.'" This sounds a lot like Suzanne's Pelican habits expanding and adapting to a larger and more complicated society. At the same time, her habit of distance persisted. Brother Alan, like most Americans, absorbed a positively encyclopedic knowledge of pop culture.[15] Suzanne did not. This was commendable in the same way that refusing junk food is virtuous. But it also reinforced her tendency to approach American culture as an outsider. While she would be very much part of the economics community, she also never took it for granted or stopped saying what a lucky life she lived.

Sitka was also Suzanne's first exposure to national politics. Not surprisingly for that time and place, her sympathies were mildly Republican and

---

10 Her Alaskan friends treat the notion matter-of-factly, saying "She would have been a good one." Brother Alan smiles – Toivo's twinkle again – and says "She wouldn't have left any for the rest of us."

11 This was a straightforward extension of her invariable advice for doing economic research: "How do you know what you think unless you write it?"

12 This much is certainly true. Whether father and daughter really played the sophisticated game that follows is less clear, though I tend to believe it.

13 Scotchmer (1995).

14 The affection felt on all sides was extraordinary. I was privileged to share this when Suzanne let me tag along to Sitka High's fortieth reunion in 2007.

15 Prof. Scotchmer never saw much point in rock 'n' roll or, for that matter, conventionally intellectual genres like jazz. For some reason I never understood, she insisted on pronouncing Mick Jagger's last name in the German way as "Jaeger."

there is an old family photo that shows her standing beside a poster satirizing the Democratic platform. These early opinions probably did not go any deeper than most teenagers', and would in any case have been reassessed when she went Down South as a college student in the Sixties. Even so, her first thoughts set a pattern. Most academics come from such uniformly liberal backgrounds that party affiliation tends to take on a social dimension by defining who does – and very rarely does not – belong to polite society. Suzanne was impatient of this "us/them" politics to the end of her life, especially when it meant giving professional Democrats an inside track on jobs at Berkeley. For her, the two parties would never be more than the sum of their invariably inconsistent proposals. This did not mean that she lacked passion – to the contrary, that was part of her instinct that public policy research was about much more than supplying jobs for academics. But this passion was never partisan.[16]

One small mystery is that Suzanne formed a fierce interest in UC Berkeley while still in high school. At one level the choice was obvious for a gifted student who would always think twice before moving too far from Alaska.[17] For now, though, the dream was deferred: she enrolled at the University of Washington. This was not very surprising since Seattle has always been Alaskans' go-to destination for big-ticket, sophisticated goods like boats or surgeries. What is slightly more remarkable is that Suzanne initially planned to study physics. That ended when she found out that UW's Economics Department would let her earn her degree in three years.

From Work Habits ... So far I have avoided asking how any of this informed Suzanne's work, but of course that is the point. The safest speculations concern her work habits. Suzanne never lost the fisherman's habit of taking things apart. This could be exasperating for domestic appliances like washing machines. But it also helps explain her extraordinary willingness to learn new programming languages or unfamiliar mathematics when she needed those things. Then again fishermen work for themselves. If you owned a boat, you had to make it pay – but when and how was up to you. For most mid-century Americans the experience of life was framed by mechanical clock time.[18] But in Alaska nobody even

16 Starting in the late 2000s, Suzanne would tell anyone who asked that she was a "single issue voter" who would favor whichever party could control the deficit. This at least leaned Republican, although the GOP would have found her an uncomfortable ally. She invariably added that the problem was hopeless without growth, including a massive increase in immigration.
17 Suzanne herself satirized this reasoning in "Smoked Fish," where her father greets her Harvard economics appointment by exclaiming "You mean you can't get a job in Alaska?" Proximity to Alaska would still be a worry when Suzanne considered offers from East Coast schools in the early 2000s.
18 For a recent introduction to the surprisingly large literature on this subject, see Alexis McCrossen, *Marking Modern Times: A History of Clocks, Watches, and Other Timekeepers in American Life* (Chicago: University of Chicago Press, 2013).

thought of punching a clock, you did the work when you needed to, and had fun with the boat when you didn't. There were no set times, and your mind restlessly returned to whatever problems you had set yourself. That pattern carried over naturally into her life as a professor: she would play at the office and work on vacation, or else she would ride her bicycle to the office at 3 a.m. and return – the brakes had a characteristic rhythmic squeak – in time for breakfast. To her, work *was* play and that was part of what made academics so privileged.

Growing up in the wilderness also fed her sense of community. At one level, she loved economics because the subject delighted her and could make the world better. But her passion also extended to the people who did the activity, and her sincerest wish was always that they would love each other and find insights to push it forward. Anyone who encountered her at conferences will have seen that.

The corollary of her passion was that it was wrong to let time dribble through your fingers like small coins. She *spent* it, preferably strategically and in large denominations. When something was worth doing, she did it immediately. That wisdom showed in everything she did, and never more than when she accepted the Toulouse School of Economics' invitation to visit in the first six months of 2013. A less disciplined or organized scholar would have waited until the fall. But if Prof. Scotchmer had done that she would have entered her final illness in France – and both she and her hosts would have lost their final, happy semester together.

Suzanne's combination of detachment and focus was another asset. These days American society constantly tells us, in Apple's illiterate phrase, to "think different." But of course tropes are insidious so that sooner or later most of us revert to the culturally favored answers. By comparison, Suzanne cared nothing at all for conventional wisdom. This let her consider other, equally attractive assumptions which she would return to over and over – sometimes for years – until every last implication had been worked out.

...To Insights. Suzanne was a materialist in the highest sense of the word. Nothing was mystical, everything could be understood if only you thought hard enough. But I doubt that this understanding extended to her own gifts. Her own, very partial speculation was that her outsider background had encouraged her to take nothing for granted and to notice everything.[19] Of course this was not sufficient, and it was surely

---

19 The most obvious parallel is John Nash, who grew up in rural West Virginia. Cf. Anon., "Notable and Quotable: John Nash," *Wall Street Journal* (May 25, 2015), quoting Nash: "I don't think exactly like a professional economist. I think about economics and economic ideas, but somewhat like an outsider." Prof. Scotchmer did not think outsider status was particularly rare: she used to joke that American academia was full of people who would happily subscribe to *Peasant Magazine*, if only she could find the time to publish such a thing.

more important that Prof. Scotchmer received the best possible education afterward.[20]

A micro-economist could hardly do better than to grow up in a Robinson Crusoe economy. As Prof. Scotchmer frequently said, "I always knew what my family did – we *fished*."[21] And so, except for a few infrastructure providers, did everyone else. But this experience also encouraged an appreciation of markets and how they could fail. Today's mass market cartels are typically so distant from consumers that they are nearly invisible. This means that most micro-economists first encounter monopoly not in life but in theory: despising cartels only comes later and sometimes – most notably in Joseph Schumpeter's case – never happens at all. The difference for Suzanne, who had grown up on stories of the canneries cartel, was that the hatred was visceral. Small wonder that her work returned to antitrust over and over again.

The deeper lesson was that markets, and their capacity for good, depend on institutions.[22] Today, Pelican's fishermen would bring a class action suit against the West Coast canneries or write to their congressmen. But in fact, organizing a co-op had probably been more elegant and effective. The flip side of this history was a melancholy understanding that institutions are fragile. By the time Suzanne left for college, Pelican was entering a long decline. In the end, the town may not last much longer than a human lifetime. At some level, Suzanne felt this frailty of Man's works instinctively. She was fearless in the natural world. Take her to the Sierras and she would gladly step out onto any smooth rock that offered a view. Things were different, though, if the rangers had erected a lookout tower. She would climb that too – of course she would – but there was always a moment of hesitation. City children who visit the wilderness find human-made objects comforting. For Suzanne, who had grown up in Pelican, it was the other way around.

Finally, she never substituted political piety for analysis. Ideology was at best a shortcut for voters who lacked the time to learn the facts and work out logical answers from scratch.[23] Public policy professionals had an obligation to do better. In the end, this was no different from what Toivo had done by poring over charts to catch real fish in dangerous waters.

---

20 One college course stuck in her memory with something like the force of revelation. Prof. Scotchmer often remarked that you really hadn't studied mathematics at all until you had taken real analysis.

21 There may have been a double joke here, since Prof. Scotchmer's family has insisted for generations that the word "fish" connotes salmon, and salmon only. The distinction was blurred by her willingness to admit that one specific cut of halibut – the cheek – was "the food of the gods."

22 Suzanne's favorite example focused on the semester she spent watching Russia try to build post-Soviet capitalism in 1991.

23 See, e.g., Anthony Downs, *An Economic Theory of Democracy* (New York: Harper, 1957), at pp. 98–100.

No worthwhile research was ever really abstract so long as it might lead to new policies and happier lives.

Home. No one, including Suzanne herself, could have predicted what she would have done with a longer life. But she had always been equally at home with fishermen and economists, and that was not about to change. So on the one hand, it is practically certain she would have spent more time in Alaska. Indeed, she had logged one happy trip already learning to run gear aboard her brother's boat, the FV *Sea Haven*.[24] But on the other, she would not have stopped thinking or writing papers. She was restless – this was nothing new – and had talked for years about moving into some branch of economics that she had never thought about before. It is impossible to imagine her having an idea and not developing it.

That future will never happen now. But she did have one last wish – to have her ashes scattered on Sitka Sound. On September 18, 2014 the family honored her request.[25] If you want to, you can go there: the coordinates are 57° 0′ 41″ N, 135° 25′ 36″ W. I think she would like that. Not for herself, of course, but because she would want you to see the place. Alaskans always do.

---

24 Readers can find a digital photo at https://www.law.berkeley.edu/article/professor-and-renowned-scholar-suzanne-scotchmer-dies-at-64/.

25 Four whales waited to one side until the ceremony was over and then circled the boat. There are witnesses and photos to prove it.

CHAPTER 3

Focus

Stephen M. Maurer

I do not know whether Prof. Scotchmer believed in genius. But she did say that it was bad to have heroes, and sometimes she could make admiration sound like a personality defect.[1] My guess is that this opinion was mostly pragmatic. Genius might or might not exist as an empirical matter. But knowing it existed could not possibly help you. Better to use whatever talent you did have and assume that good work will be recognized.[2]

But Prof. Scotchmer did have a quality that was very like genius: when she was interested in a question, she was *really* interested and this could go on for years.[3] It helped that she seldom worked at any defined time or place, but would simply return to whatever topics interested her every few hours. Most of the time you knew when this was happening, and there were recurring signs: She would sketch probability distributions and work through equations, tracing the logic each time from scratch before throwing the paper away. Or she would take walks – "my brain is connected to my feet," she liked to say – that took her miles from campus. Or she would sit very still and think. Even if the problem did not yield at first, the time added up.

I never asked what this felt like. My impression, though, is that she would circle the subject, endlessly looking for a way in. And then, even after she had found one, she would look some more. She used to tell me

---

1 She could, on the other hand, admire people a great deal – for some reason Zvi Grilichas sticks in my mind – and she certainly believed in talent. I never met anyone more matter-of-fact in saying, for example, that this colleague knew more math or even – in at least two cases – was a better economist.

2 I think her private view was that universities really did judge research quality honestly and according to merit – but only after deciding that a candidate was worth considering in the first place. As she angrily exclaimed to one Midwestern university's hiring committee, "There are people who are read and people who are not read."

3 This personal style was slightly at odds with her favorite "Ideas Model" of innovation, which usually treats the arrival rate of ideas as exogenous. The exception to the rule is, tellingly, "Patents in the University" (2013) which relaxes the constraint to posit that funding can increase the flow of ideas even if the content remains unpredictable.

how she had played piano[4] as a young professor at Harvard. Then, one
day, she decided that it was a waste of time and that was when her
academic career began. I did not and do not believe it was that simple,
mainly because it is impossible to imagine a Prof. Scotchmer who did not
delight in economics. But there probably was a moment when she decided
it was time to get serious. The difference was that while most of us have
had such moments, Suzanne could follow through.

The most spectacular product of this gift is, of course, the decade-plus
investigation that leads from "Giants" to *Innovation and Incentives*. The
papers build on each other like bricks slotted into a wall. She does not stop
until she has thoroughly mined her original cumulative innovation insight,
though in the end many of the lessons she discovers hold for older,
Nordhaus-type models as well.[5]

The topics that mattered to her could go on fascinating her for years. Not
all these bets paid off, at least within the time left to her. She thought about
Digital Rights Management, and FRAND clauses, and ASCAP-type
licensing arrangements for years without publishing much.[6] This was itself
a measure of her high standards, since it would have been easy to publish a
mediocre paper along the way. She was still in her office working on one
such topic just weeks before the end, carefully reading and re-reading cases
to work out antitrust's confused and much maligned "essential facilities"
doctrine. So in that case, at least, four years of steady effort produced one
last paper. Characteristically, the work broke out of the usual circle of
arguments in a way that working lawyers find particularly attractive.

There were never deadlines in this work. She would say she was "stuck"
and, after a long time, shift to something else. But that was seldom if ever
the end of her interest. Projects took as long as they needed to.[7]

This tenacity ran too deep to be learned. And indeed, she would
half-apologize for wool gathering as if it was a psychological condition.
There may have been some small truth to that since she could sometimes
become similarly engrossed in topics ranging from Billy the Kid to US
Special Forces in Vietnam[8] to Andrei Sakharov's *Memoirs*.[9] The

---

4 I only heard her once: she played beautifully.
5 This was especially true of her argument that independent invention defenses could tailor
   reward to R&D cost, markedly reducing deadweight loss.
6 But see Park and Scotchmer (2005). The paper explains how DRM fees can be used to
   support a cartelized price for protected content.
7 Even after the paper was published, loose ends were never far from her mind. One day
   I mentioned my puzzlement that patent law, unlike copyright, has no independent
   invention defense. It took her less than a heartbeat to see that an independent invention
   would tie reward to R&D costs, in at least partial compensation for the deep inefficiencies
   she had identified in "Giants."
8 John L. Plaster, *SOG: The Secret Wars of America's Commandos in Vietnam* (New York:
   Simon & Schuster, 1997). In fairness, Suzanne's high school classmate Mike Buckland is
   mentioned at p. 91.
9 Andrei Sakharov, *Memoirs* (New York: Vintage, 1992).

difference was that, unlike her professional interests, these never lasted more than a day or two – the Sakharov fascination for just a single evening. "That," she used to say afterwards, "was my Russian period."

Remarkably, there is still a video where she says what this felt like. The occasion, inevitably, was a talk where she abstracts from her own experience of creativity to think about her "ideas model" of innovation:

> [Y]ou know when you wake up on Saturday morning you think, "Wow there's a good idea. I could work on growth theory," whatever ... What do you do with those ideas? The fact is for most people we throw them away ... Either you don't have the tools to do it, you don't want to make an investment in the literature, you don't have a student who wants to do that topic, most of them you just throw them away. But some of them ... you bank it ... you know you could implement the idea, but you will have to read a lot of literature, you will maybe learn a branch of mathematics you didn't know before, you haven't thought about dynamic optimization for the last five years, you know it's costly. And anyway nobody is thinking about this idea right now but hey, in six years maybe it becomes a topic on the agenda, people are interested, maybe you've learned the skills, the rewards are going to be higher because it's on somebody's agenda, you may pick up this idea again.[10]

Looking back, I still do not know why she picked some topics and not others. There was no predicting. But of course it had to be that way, given that such choices are always at least partially unconscious and instinctual, in the same way that every thinking person experiences creativity. In some cases, at least, she would have been hard-pressed to say why a particular topic interested her.

I am happy to say that this gift of focus performed one final service. Just after Christmas 2013 I found Prof. Scotchmer engrossed in a Netflix documentary called *The West*. She was already ill and, though neither of us knew it, had just over a month to live. But it was a beautiful morning with sunlight streaming through the window, and her pale eyes were shining. The idea that millions of private people would spontaneously set out to settle the West – without planning or resources or compulsion – filled her with wonder. Then I felt it too.

And for the next hour or so we both forgot how time runs out for everyone.

---

10 Video: "Scarcity of Ideas: Use it, Lose It, Or Bank It," 17th Annual Barcelona Lecture, Barcelona Graduate School of Economics (November 10, 2010), Part 4 at 6:30–8:15.
I have made very minor edits for clarity, without, I hope, suppressing Prof. Scotchmer's distinctive voice. Interested readers can watch the original at https://www.youtube.com/watch?v=48ajKsgKdT8. There is something almost confessional when she explains how her mind works. Then again, that is not surprising. For Prof. Scotchmer, good scholarship always began in honesty.

CHAPTER 4

Co-Evolving with Suzanne

Eddie Dekel

I first encountered Suzanne when, as a first-year graduate student, I took her math "refresher" course at Harvard. At the time, I didn't know enough to take full advantage of her presence on the faculty. That only changed after we had both moved to Berkeley in 1986 and I found myself teaching the very same refresher class. Now I could see just how carefully she had thought about the tools that Ph.D. economics students would need and how to present them in an intuitive yet rigorous way. Suzanne's course turned out to be invaluable as I struggled to build my own Ph.D. level course, not just for this particular topic but as a foundation for teaching in general.

Looking back, I see that I have spent much of my academic life following in Suzanne's footsteps, either physically or in spirit. Course materials were just the beginning. Seeing her approach to research and economic reasoning was not just educational – hearing her views helped me form my own style as an economist. Indeed, I see this everywhere I look: how I approach academic publishing, my taste for interdisciplinary work, and even specific work habits like working while walking outdoors.

Conversations with Suzanne were enjoyable yet unpredictable – one idea jumped to another, and there was never any sense that we should limit where the conversation went. For example, our work on evolution began with a conversation about the importance of precedent in legal systems. This freewheeling style was delightful, and suggested an unlimited scope of economic methodology.

Anyone who reads this book will know that Suzanne always approached new topics with one eye on fundamental theory issues and the other on policy. Our work on risk attitudes is an excellent example. Some of our first conversations were about promotions: risk-takers choose projects that are more likely to fail but also – conditional on success – to score higher than competitors. To the extent that different populations have different risk attitudes, this has very real implications for policy. But it also raises the theory question of how evolution could have created males and females with such different risk preferences in the first place. Much of this work was eventually published in Dekel and Scotchmer

(1999),[1] although our section on affirmative action disappeared during the refereeing process. Suzanne eventually developed this direction much further in her later paper on gender in hierarchies.[2]

Our paper argued that, since males of many species participated in winner-take-all environments, which in turn generate evolutionary selection of risk-taking, males will tend to be more risk-taking. This theory led us to study to what extent these winner-take-all environments were prevalent. Suzanne was particularly fascinated by the extreme polygyny of elephant seals – in some colonies, the five most active males copulate with over 400 females. Suzanne's vigilant attitude towards research was present throughout: we debated whether the evolutionary model plausibly suggests why human males will be more risk-taking, whether the issue is important enough to study, and, as always, the potential economic and policy implications.

I also learned a lot from watching Suzanne react to negative referee reports. Perhaps it should have been obvious, but the reports were valuable even when the referee was clearly wrong and confused. After all, our writing had caused the confusion. So instead of just dismissing the comments, we read them even more closely to see how we had led the reviewer to miss or misunderstand our point. This kind of close reading also had a way of making us realize our own confusions. Working with Suzanne enhanced my appreciation of referees and their hard work.

The risk paper grew out of many enjoyable walks in the Berkeley Hills and, especially, the University's Botanical Gardens. I have always loved hiking, but combining work with walks, beautiful views, and wonderful flora – Suzanne loved plants – was a new experience. Suzanne's love for walking and working was a small part of her wider enthusiasm for the outdoors, an enthusiasm that appeared elsewhere in her work. Our discussion of the *Exxon Valdez* disaster and the mechanisms oil companies had set up to respond to such cases led to a joint paper.[3] Her passion on the issue resulted in the fastest article I've ever coauthored.

But her fervor was not limited to any one issue. Her intellectual energy was more like a force of nature – completely integral to her work and, indeed, her identity. It underlay her research approach – she wasn't satisfied unless she found an answer to all the pertinent issues. But it also gave her endless energy: Suzanne grew up fighting to create her identity, and continued to develop her independent path throughout her career.

I am fortunate to have had Suzanne as a friend and colleague. Together we pondered the nearly unlimited research directions available to economists. I delighted in seeing her enthusiasm for combining theory and policy. Most of all, I am grateful to have shared so many happy hours in the beautiful Berkeley Hills.

1 This volume.
2 Scotchmer (2008).
3 Dekel and Scotchmer (1990).

CHAPTER 5

Friend and Colleague

Neil Gandal

I was shocked and saddened to learn that Suzanne passed away. Suzanne was a giant in research. But she was much more than that. She had a great ability to communicate her own passion for knowledge. And no one except for Suzanne could make lectures on mechanism design exciting. A seminar presented by Suzanne was like a good novel. By the end, the audience was as interested in the topic as she was and wanted to go out and learn even more.

I was lucky to have knocked on her door as a graduate student in Berkeley back in the late 1980s. I did not even know her then, but instead of telling me to read three papers and come back in four weeks we talked about an interest we shared – and after a few meetings, we had the foundations of what would turn out to be a joint paper.

Suzanne taught me many important things about the profession: how to write an introduction to a paper, how to present a seminar, how to proof papers (read them aloud word by word), and how to take a break when stuck on a hard proof or concept (by walking in the botanical gardens).

But more than that, Suzanne had an enthusiasm that was contagious. It was hard not to feel good in her presence. She was incredibly energetic and no one worked harder than Suzanne. She also had a healthy sense of humor regarding our profession.

Even if we had not been in contact for some time, we would always pick up as if time had stood still. It was like that when I last saw her in June 2013 in Toulouse. We, of course, took a walk after a long afternoon conference session. We talked a lot, and caught up on life. When I said goodbye, I felt reinvigorated. I will miss her a lot.

CHAPTER 6

Gender

Carol Adaire Jones

Gender was not one of Suzanne's primary topics of research inquiry. The one paper she wrote that explicitly addresses gender in labor markets was published in 2008,[1] though it had been knocking around for a while, and first appeared as a working paper earlier in the decade.[2] But Suzanne came of age as the second wave of feminism was gaining momentum, with energy focused on achieving social equality regardless of gender. In her core, Suzanne had an inalienable belief in the principle of equality based on merit. The inequities in opportunities and in personal treatment she saw around her displeased. At the same time, her analytical mind was irked when she came across sloppy thinking about how to address the problem.

We first met when she joined the Harvard Economics Department as a junior faculty member in 1981, and I was in the final year of completing my Ph.D. The issues of gender equality were alive in academia then, and sadly still are today, thirty-five years later – particularly in many STEM fields, such as economics. Though women represent a substantially larger share of students entering graduate programs in economics today and of graduates hired as faculty, faculty promotions are still subject to a leaky pipeline.[3] Suzanne was a feminist (I can hear her saying, "How could one be anything else?"), though she was not one to engage in identity politics. If anything, she spoke more often of the challenges of her peasant upbringing as a fisherman's daughter in remote Alaska, which left gaps in her knowledge of classical literature and culture. (And also gaps in popular culture: she delighted in telling the story of herself and a friend, as perhaps ten-year-olds, puzzling over the cartoons in the *New Yorker* magazine, which the friend's mother received as a vestige of her previous life on the East coast.) Her family moved from Pelican (pop. 130)[4] to Sitka, the

---

1 Scotchmer (2008).
2 National Bureau of Economic Research Working Paper No. 11213 (2005).
3 CSWEP (2014); Sarsons (2015).
4 https://en.wikipedia.org/wiki/Pelican,_Alaska.

fourth largest place in the state (pop. 3,300),[5] for Suzanne and her brother to go to high school. At the same time, Suzanne was also very clear that the fishing community she grew up in had very stratified gender roles, which vexed her deeply.

She was such a breath of fresh air in the Economics Department, following a dispiriting run of departures of junior faculty women – Janet Yellen had left in 1977, Rachel McCullough in 1979, and Elisabeth Allison a few years later. She was the first of the next wave to come and go in the department. The Economics Department would not tenure its first woman – Claudia Goldin – until 1990. As members of the first Ph.D. entering class with more than one or two women, I and my fellow graduate students fumbled for language to understand and describe our experiences. As more civil rights laws were put in place, we believed the blatant forms of (racial and) sexual discrimination were being addressed. But that turned the focus to understanding more subtle – but pervasive and pernicious – forms of sex discrimination. At MIT, the President appointed Mary Rowe as Ombudsman to address discrimination on campus.[6] Based on her experiences, she articulated the concept of the "rings of Saturn," micro-aggressions that were individually non-actionable but accumulated into a serious negative impact.[7] That resonated with some of us at the campus at the other end of Massachusetts Ave. in Cambridge.

Invisibility was one issue. I remember one eminent senior faculty member in the Economics Department, a man renowned for his empirical analysis, telling me – with an air of certitude – that women students were good, but not the top performers. But of course there was a small numbers problem. When one included top performers over enough years to get a sufficient sample of women, the assertion was simply wrong.

Fortunately, Suzanne had very low susceptibility to verbal micro-aggressions. Of course she did not fit the female stereotype of being less math-y than the men – rather, math was her métier. Along with a piercing intellect, she was charismatic, fascinated with ideas, and passionate about engaging others – anyone – to discuss her ideas, their ideas, anyone else's ideas. She fiercely loved the economics profession and she worked with colleagues around the globe, visiting at over a dozen universities over the years. At the same time, she chafed at the fact that women were not always given the credit they were due, and could be an articulate advocate whether it involved women (including herself) being passed over for professional rewards, or on an interpersonal level, not being heard in mixed groups. Her focus was always on the recognition of merit.

---

5 https://en.wikipedia.org/wiki/Sitka,_Alaska.
6 Rowe is an economist who was (and still is) an adjunct professor at the MIT Sloan School. She retired from her Ombudsman role in 2014.
7 Rowe (1976, 1991).

CHAPTER 7

The Centrality of Theory

Paul Seabright

Suzanne had a strongly pragmatic interest in the world around her that – together with a charming modesty – sometimes cloaked her formidable theoretical intellect. Her powers of observation made conversation a delight, and she often noticed things about people, places or institutions that had escaped others. But if you thought this meant that she would be satisfied with an approach to research that consisted just in the patient accumulation of data points accompanied by a plausible-sounding story, she would soon put you right, firmly though diplomatically.

I remember some seven or eight years ago discussing with her and with Marie Lalanne some of the research Marie and I were doing on gender and professional advancement of top executives. It was not Suzanne's main area of research, though it turned out that she had a paper on it anyway.[1] I had broached the subject with her mainly to benefit from her observations. But as rich and thought-provoking as these were, they were second in importance to her insistence that without an underlying theoretical framework it would be impossible to make sense of the over-abundant evidence.

In particular, she insisted, people have careers, not just jobs. So you can't understand what is happening at any one point in their careers without an understanding of what went on before. You may think you have diagnosed a problem at the senior end of the labor market, say, but you can't be sure that your diagnosis is right until you understand what led individuals to that point in their careers (and that in turn will have been influenced by what they expected to happen to them in the future). That's an important message of her paper, and it was also an important general message of her approach to research, including of course her famous cumulative innovation paper with Jerry Green.[2] The dynamic perspective implies that you have to understand phenomena in terms of their antecedents and their expected consequences. It also implies that the appropriate

---

1 Scotchmer (2008).
2 Green and Scotchmer (1995), this volume at pp. 102–120.

interventions to correct various dysfunctional outcomes may sometimes
need to occur some distance upstream from the outcomes themselves.

I had run into Suzanne briefly on many occasions on the usual academic circuit, in Berkeley, Toulouse and elsewhere, including at one
conference where she responded very patiently and with good grace to a
rather gratuitously point-scoring discussion on my part. But the first time
I got to know her over an extended period was much more recently, when
she and Stephen visited Toulouse for six months shortly before she fell
sick. This was a wonderful opportunity to see how her mind worked, and
to enjoy the way her gift for observation triggered her impish sense of
humor. Her abundant energy and sparkle made her subsequent rapid
illness and death all the more difficult to believe and take in.

A particular highlight of that stay was when my wife Isabelle and
I accompanied her and Steve Maurer to the castles of Peyrepertuse and
Queribus in the foothills of the eastern Pyrenees. These are imposing
constructions from which in theory you can enjoy a magnificent view over
the Pyrenees to Spain on one side, the Mediterranean on another, and
north-westward towards Toulouse on yet another side. In theory. As we
made our way up the hillside from the parking lot towards the fortifications of Peyrepertuse, a large cloud that seemed designed for the purpose
of frustrating our empirical verification of the hypothesis began to shroud
the top of the hill, and by the time we had arrived in the castle visibility
was down to a few yards. When the sky is clear you are supposed to be able
to see from one castle in the Pyrenean chain to another, and it was through
fires lighted along the chain that warnings of threats from the south were
transmitted to the French crown, which had reinforced its control over the
fortifications after the Cathar crusade. But for all we could tell we might
have been in Disneyland. It wasn't until we went online that evening, back
in our hotel, that we could see what the view in theory ought to have been.
It didn't stop the day from being sparklingly fun for all of us, and her
enthusiasm and curiosity from being thoroughly infectious for the
entire party.

Never trust the evidence until you have verified it against theory. A very
fitting conclusion to remember her by.

CHAPTER 8

Choosing a Model

Stephen M. Maurer

Economists can be surprisingly nervous about their enterprise. So it was only natural that Suzanne, who was not nervous at all, would smile when she heard European colleagues insist on calling economics "a science." All the same, the humor pointed to a serious issue. The first step in any successful theory paper is to pick a model. Later, when the paper is successful, the author can usually report logical reasons for her choice. But there is always, inescapably, a question of taste. Does this make economics any less scientific? Plainly not – if anything, physicists are even worse when it comes to endorsing models based on, allegedly, "beauty."[1]

So taste remains mysterious. Still, there are things we can say. Probably the most basic is that Prof. Scotchmer never indulged in the beginner's error of picking models simply because they were solvable, or the more advanced error of choosing assumptions because they are ideologically congenial.[2] Then too, she avoided minutiae. Having learned that some puzzling situation existed, she seldom consulted secondary sources for more detail. Indeed, that would have defeated the theorist's trick of tracing the power of simple assumptions. Instead, she would meditate on how rational people could permit such an odd result to happen. Then, as soon as she could, she would start to write

---

1 Theoretical physicists frequently write papers that generalize from known equations to guess at new ones. Suzanne, who like many economists had thought about going into physics as an undergraduate, found this distinctly odd. Economic models are grounded in definite ideas about how humans behave.

2 None of Prof. Scotchmer's papers shows the slightest evidence of this, and I find it hard to believe that she was ever tempted. To the contrary, she was horrified when Harvard President Larry Summers had to step down after suggesting that women might be less able than men in math and science. This was very much a theorist's reaction. That the premise was probably wrong – indeed, that her own talent argued against it – was no reason to ignore the possibility. Economists were supposed to explore assumptions wherever they led, and flinching betrayed that.

models. This kind of disciplined daydreaming had, of course, been standard among theorists since the nineteenth century.[3]

But these observations mostly tell us how Prof. Scotchmer avoided mistakes. We would much rather know how she came to her successes. Going back to her papers, the source readings – almost always some newspaper story[4] or bestseller[5] or court opinion[6] – are usually limited to a few sketchy facts. By comparison, Prof. Scotchmer's eventual papers tell rich stories – economists always ask "can you tell a story?" – from simple beginnings. This was very close to the novelist's trick of imagining a fictitious world and sitting back to let the characters do what they like.[7] That might sound easy, except that hardly anyone can manage this kind of openness to new and uncontrolled ideas.[8] That Prof. Scotchmer could do this will not surprise anyone who knows her creative writing.[9]

It would be wonderful to track how Prof. Scotchmer used this act of imagination to produce, for example, the "Ideas Model." But the evidence of lesser examples is everywhere. This is particularly obvious in how titles like *Innovation and Incentives*[10] and "Procuring Knowledge"[11] deploy page after page of history. Of course, many innovation books start by telling stories, but in most cases readers can safely skip them. The difference in Prof. Scotchmer's case is that she refused to tell stories

---

3 The traditional mid-twentieth-century approach assumed that "reading the newspaper, and other reports of the economy," combined with the daily business of "buying groceries, insurance, houses, and vacations" gave "the economist ... a range of different 'facts' of the economy." The economist's task was to structure these facts into one body of knowledge, using tools such as the indifference curve. The approach ultimately derives from John Stuart Mill. Floris Heukelom, *Behavioral Economics: A History* (New York: Cambridge University Press, 2014) at p. 19.

4 This is even true of "Giants," which begins by describing newspaper accounts of the Cohen–Boyer patent and Microsoft.

5 Jonathan Harr, *A Civil Action* (New York: Vintage, 1996).

6 See Maurer and Scotchmer (2014).

7 Charles Dickens famously practiced this technique. "Suppose," he told friends, that "I choose to call this a *character*, fancy it a man, endue it with certain qualities; and soon the fine filmy webs of thought, almost impalpable, coming from every direction, we know not where, spin and weave about it until it ... becomes instinct with life." It is telling that Dickens himself referred to the process as "the unfathomable mystery." Shelley Klein, *The Wicked Wit of Charles Dickens* (London: Michael O'Mara, 2002).

8 Yeats captured the problem nicely when he wrote that modern humans are too self-conscious, so that we have lost the "old nonchalance of the hand" and "are but critics, or but half create." "Ego Dominus Tuus," in *The Wild Swans at Coole* (London and New York: Macmillan, 1919).

9 All four stories are available online. See Bibliography at pp. 368–380, below.

10 See Scotchmer (2004b), e.g., at chs. 1 (R&D history), 2.3 (prize design), and 3.6 (laser patents).

11 Maurer and Scotchmer (2004).

unless they taught some pointed and non-obvious lesson which would then show up later in the book's formal models. Probably the best example is *Innovation and Incentives'* extended account of England's eighteenth-century Navigation Prize.[12] Dava Sobel's *Longitude* – and for that matter the average economist – is content to present a dark comedy in which Parliament repeatedly breaks its promises so that our hero/inventor wastes his life building clocks. Prof. Scotchmer cared little for this narrative. Even if it were true, the larger question was what society ought to have received for its money. This led her to "a more sympathetic reading"[13] in which Parliament seeks knowledge but instead receives three hand-built and irreproducible artifacts. Regardless of the prize's literal terms, Harrison's achievement did nothing to protect the fleet.

Was this a good way to proceed? The obvious answer is that it produced results. But there is other evidence. Like many Americans, Prof. Scotchmer loved *The Sopranos*. The difference is that most of us see Tony Soprano's adventures as a joke on cultural expectations – indeed, the action hardly makes sense unless you have seen dozens of gangster movies already. Suzanne, of course, knew this. But that did not stop her from repeatedly asking how the real Mafia must work and what it felt like. This habit could be surprisingly illuminating. I once spent an evening watching Suzanne talk with a distant cousin of mine who had survived the Holocaust. The conventional instinct, carefully inculcated in my family, was that such experiences are inaccessible and unknowable. But Suzanne and my cousin talked long into the night. Later, when my cousin heard about Suzanne's death, she wrote to say that she had never before met anyone who understood what the Holocaust had felt like without having been there.

In the end of course, the stories were just scaffolding. Historians might care – were *supposed* to care – about an inventor's subjective motives. But for a theorist, the only thing that really mattered was logic. Even if the original story turned out to be false, the behavior would eventually surface elsewhere.[14]

I do not know how far to take this. I still do not know if Tolstoy offers valid insights on the Napoleonic Wars, or even whether Prof. Scotchmer's daydreams over the morning paper were more bounded and disciplined

---

12 Scotchmer (2004b), pp. 32–33.
13 Ibid. at p. 33.
14 I once asked Prof. Scotchmer a technical question which she answered with her usual precision before adding matter-of-factly that the same argument was known to David Ricardo. The idea that she could recall this dry detail seemed so impossible to me that, five hours later, I asked her how she could possibly have remembered such a thing from grad school. "Oh, *that*," she laughed. "Ricardo had worked out the theory of rents – he *must* have known that argument."

than the way she wrote short stories. But the more I think of it, the more I see the resemblance. We are all cut off from each other, and lower apes do not bother to work out what their friends think. Humans, uniquely, have evolved brain circuitry to simulate others, the thing that biologists call "a theory of the mind." So maybe Suzanne's extraordinary empathy was a way of knowing after all.

CHAPTER 9

Getting to "Giants"

Joseph Farrell

In the early 1980s, Suzanne was a "mathematical economist." Most academic economists are mathematical, but the term means something more. Ideally it means a focus on those economic questions that seem most likely to be illuminated by intensive use of advanced mathematics. A risk is that it can instead become a focus on how economic questions can showcase one's mathematical pizzazz.

Suzanne was not immune to that risk. As one of the then relatively few female economists who had the mathematical pizzazz – or, more accurately in her case, could pick it up on the fly as needed – she saw a rational career advantage in making that clear to the profession. And I think a more emotional force operated in parallel with that rational one, and outgunned it.

Suzanne's father, Toivo Andersen, was a star ("high-liner") salmon fisherman in southeast Alaska, a background that she described in some of her non-technical writing. Through much of her childhood, Toivo was plainly grooming her brother to succeed him in the business. As Suzanne saw it, Toivo brushed off any idea that she might be capable and interested: she was just a girl. To say that Suzanne was extremely, extremely unhappy about this would be a grave understatement. The emotions were obviously hers, not mine, but I did see them from (decades later still dangerously) close range, and one of Suzanne's burning emotional agendas was to demolish any suspected sexist assumption that some traditionally male activity was beyond her. In her early-1980s professional persona, this meant conquering mathematical economics (primarily club theory).

Yet Suzanne was genuinely interested in economic questions; and she recognized the risk of too much mathematical focus. I like to think that I may have helped reassure her that one can be a micro-economist capable of "mathematical economics" and yet not focus one's energies there. I remember one day, perhaps around 1984, she was especially preoccupied as we hiked in the woods in Lincoln, Massachusetts, and told me at dinner that she wanted to study an actual industry. "Everyone," as she put it (specifically including me), studied economic issues in the information industries. She would study biotech.

Suzanne went to the library and read up on the industry. She emerged talking about "research tools." She couldn't yet explain why she found those interesting, but with hindsight, research tools are all about cumulative innovation: little or no value in themselves, lots of value in enabling subsequent invention. There were controversies around licenses denied, breakdowns in license negotiations, high pricing, and licenses that demanded a share in revenues from subsequent innovation. Some of the inventors of research tools also used them; others were not vertically integrated in that sense: did that make the problems better or worse – and what were the problems anyway? Suzanne was intrigued but, as she liked to say, "baffled." Or perhaps better to say she was baffled and therefore intrigued.

CHAPTER 10

Suzanne in Asia

Reiko Aoki

In the early 2000s I held appointments at both the University of Auckland (New Zealand) and Hitotsubashi University (Tokyo). This gave me the great fun of being Suzanne's colleague and occasional local guide during her semester-long visits Down Under (2002) and to Japan (2004) along with a second, shorter trip to Tokyo in 2008. Auckland and Japan were very different cultures, both from California and from each other. Suzanne took to them completely. It all seemed effortless: if she hesitated, I never saw it. It's hard to know exactly how she could be so natural, but I think it helped that she was so delighted to encounter new people and cultures. This immediately put her hosts at ease too.

I knew that I would learn many things from Suzanne during these visits. Suzanne had already had a great influence on me. I had originally met her in 1988, when I was a new assistant professor at Ohio State. From that first moment, she had treated me as a colleague. I will be forever grateful for that. Everybody who saw her at conferences remembers what great comments she made. But what I appreciated most was that she took time to talk to graduate students, showing us how the profession moved forward by critically evaluating new ideas and then incorporating the best ones. Over the years we stayed in touch. Her most persistent advice was to aim high. She was always happy to see me publish. But if she liked what I had done she would also add, "Why did you publish in that journal? You should have done better."

One of the things she enjoyed most about new cultures was how the experience fed her economic intuition. She was fascinated to find people and institutions behave according to what economic theory suggests. If they didn't, she considered it a challenge and would retrace the logic until she understood what was going on. She respected the fact that everyone and every culture had its own variations on the same basic dynamics.

For her, economics was beautiful. So it was only natural that she made an effort to spread the word. She also felt a special obligation to build the profession itself. Economics in the twentieth century had been led by North America. But Suzanne never gave any indication that she felt that way or was even aware of it. Wherever she visited, she wanted everyone to play and share the fun and beauty of economics. Auckland invited her as part of a Visiting Committee to evaluate its economics department and make strategic recommendations to strengthen it. Suzanne took these assignments very seriously, thinking carefully about our department's strengths and what we could do to build on them. I have heard that some outside advisors treat their visit as a kind of vacation and then write something polite: Suzanne would have considered that unethical! She always said what she thought was best and ignored departmental politics. Of course she never told me about those closed door discussions. Later, though, I got the impression from others that she had been quite dominating, not because she wanted to be but because she spoke her mind fearlessly.

Suzanne's Auckland visit came when she was in the final stages of writing *Innovation and Incentives*. So it was natural that she would give a seminar on the "Political Economy of Intellectual Property Treaties."[1] One of the main things that interested me was how she used historical evidence. Suzanne's talk provided an extensive but concise summary of the history of international intellectual property protection starting with the Paris Convention (1883), which called for national treatment, and the Berne Convention (1886), which introduced the concept of harmonization, though this was at first limited to procedures. She carried the story all the way forward to the then-recent Trade Related Intellectual Property Rights (TRIPS) protocol which had harmonized IP rules on the substance side. The thing which impressed me was that Suzanne did not introduce this history for its own sake or even to argue that recent treaties had "improved" on earlier ones. Instead, she used it as a framework for identifying the main options that policymakers (and economic theorists) could choose from. These included: (a) IP without treaties, which leads to the usual tradeoff between innovation incentives and deadweight loss, (b) national treatment treaties that let foreign firms repatriate profits, (c) national treatment with reciprocity which would let domestic firms collect profits abroad, though possibly with different levels of protection, and (d) harmonization schemes in which each country had the same level of protection. Despite the then-recent history of TRIPS, Suzanne stressed that harmonization was a policy choice and not always desirable. For instance, if one market was sufficiently large, having national treatment without reciprocity could offer sufficient returns to drive R&D while avoiding deadweight loss in the smaller country. According to economists' usual social welfare criteria, it would then be better to let some countries free-ride on their trading partners' innovations. Suzanne also pointed out

---

1 The work was published as Scotchmer (2004a) and later appeared in chapter 11 of *Innovation and Incentives*.

that harmonization treaties tended to expand IP in equilibrium even when public funding would have been more efficient.

One thing I found especially illuminating in Suzanne's Auckland presentation is why IP and international market access agreements need to be coupled, as happened in TRIPS. Developing economies have an incentive to free-ride on the innovation efforts of developed economies and are therefore reluctant to enforce IP rights. On the other hand, developing economies are very eager to export to developed economies. One way for developed economies to obtain IP enforcement is to make this a condition for access to their markets. For example, the US might agree to reduce tariffs (increase quotas) for primary imports in exchange for stronger IP enforcement in Africa.

Of course, I made a point of buying my copy of *Innovation and Incentives* as soon as it was published. I was not disappointed. Most books about IP are anecdotal or analyze small parts of the system in isolation. Here, finally, I could see a clean, first-principles path into not just patents but R&D incentives generally. The economic analysis was to the point, like Suzanne herself, and the level was consistent throughout whether the topic is economic theory, law, or public policy. I immediately saw that a Japanese edition could be very useful. This was particularly true since Suzanne's previous contributions to pure economic theory meant she was already known in Japan and had extra credibility. Talking with Munetomo Ando, who was about to teach a public policy course on innovation, confirmed that a Japanese edition would be particularly helpful to students. However, I also felt that the book could be read by Japanese legal scholars and practitioners, who tend to be less familiar with economic thinking than their US counterparts. I asked Suzanne if I could translate the book, and of course she agreed.

One of the nicest parts of that project was that I was able to write a new chapter on the history of innovation in Japan. Suzanne was delighted to see the familiar IP economics play out in such a different culture, and we talked about the lessons at length. I remember that she was particularly pleased to find that Japan had organized guilds in the eighteenth and nineteenth centuries that controlled technology and innovation, and that Japan, a developing economy at the time, had offered IP protection to foreigners in order to renegotiate an unfavorable trade agreement with Europe during the Meiji era. (This was the same point that Suzanne had argued at Auckland!)[2] Both developments echoed similar history in the West, but almost always with some instructive wrinkle. I am happy to say that the book has sold well, and is particularly popular as a textbook for interdisciplinary courses on innovation.

---

2 Readers can find an English translation at www.ier.hit-u.ac.jp/pie/stage2/Japanese/d_p/dp2006/dp327/text.pdf.

I enjoyed showing Suzanne around Tokyo in 2008. She found basic economic principles in everything. She was particularly amused by the auctions and physical layout of the Tsukiji fish market. I especially remember how she prompted me to ask one of the workers if there were any ascending price auctions. He replied "of course price goes up, lady!" After a while, I figured out that Suzanne was interested for reasons beyond her usual pleasure in visiting new places or watching economics in everyday life. She was an Alaskan, and her family were fishermen. In fact, her brother still shipped fish to Japan. She told me that all her Alaskan friends knew about Tsukiji and would be really impressed that she had seen the place. It was funny to hear this from someone whose own qualifications included making multiple keynote speeches around the world.

We both loved that day, and Suzanne would always mention it every time we spoke. My one small regret was that we arrived too late in the morning to find any products from Alaska.

I wish I had been able to show Suzanne around northern Kyushu, which had been one of the Meiji era's great technology centers for catching up with the West. I sometimes imagine myself trying to answer her questions. And then thinking out loud with her, happily pushing ideas back and forth and putting everything together.

I think she was just beginning to explore Asia. She was scheduled to be a keynote speaker at the Asia Pacific Innovation Conference in December 2013 at Taiwan National University. But that November she sent me an email saying that she had to cancel. She was waiting for some test results, she said, and did not want to risk having to pull out at the last moment. Typical professionalism and considerateness, I thought. Later, when I told her how we had regretted her absence, she wrote back saying how sorry she was to have missed her chance to see Taiwan. That struck me as odd. After all, there would be other chances. Did she know some Taiwanese social norm I didn't? I only realized what she meant a few weeks later.

CHAPTER 11

Thinker, Thesis Advisor, Colleague
Brian Wright

I knew something was wrong when Suzanne told me she could not serve on my doctoral student's exam. In all the years I had known her, she had always agreed to serve on oral qualifying exams whenever she was physically present in Berkeley. And I had served on committees for her students. So I was puzzled. I learned the answer all too soon.

The doctoral committees will be poorer without her. Orals are the place where new economists are launched, or at least get important course corrections. Suzanne felt that responsibility deeply. As a committee member, Suzanne was invariably respectful to the student – totally honest, but always as optimistic as she possibly could be within that constraint. Probably because she spent so much time with Berkeley's law faculty, she favored the Socratic method. I learned a lot watching how she would draw out evidence from some hapless student. Soon everyone, including the student, would begin to see not only that there had been progress, but that much more was possible. Where criticism was necessary she always presented it in a positive way, emphasizing the way forward instead of dwelling on wrong turns, misconceptions, and discarded baggage that belonged to the past.

For talented students she raised the bar. She expected them to perform to her standard. The best became coauthors, and those were very good. So I was surprised to find her somewhere between fury and despair when one of her best students decided to became a consultant. Trying to understand, I could see immediately that there was no class prejudice in this – she knew as well as anyone that it was possible to have a rewarding and socially productive life outside a university. Indeed, I think she would have happily pursued her father's footsteps as a professional salmon fisherman and I have no doubt that she was proud of her father's innovations in that industry. That resonated with me. I had gone off to college thinking I would follow my aunt (and her uncle before her) by learning how to run a complex and risky Australian sheep station. Those kinds of alternative lives – offering substantial autonomy and opportunities for innovation – were surprisingly akin to life at a research university. Either way, though, you owed something to your own talent and the people who had trained you. That meant doing whatever you did as well as possible. For a strong economist, that included finding a job that let you contribute scholarship that would advance the subject.

With her peers, Suzanne was direct. I first met her when she gave a job talk at Yale, on club goods. Years later she cheerfully told me that this was "The worst talk I ever gave." My own clearest memories are, first, that she was obviously highly talented, and second, that at dinner she pronounced that she had learned from Debreu that "You can't do cost benefit analysis." From my point of view it is a pity she did not come to Yale. It would indeed have been fun to have her as a colleague there.

Her intellect was formidable. I am most familiar with the subset of her output that intersects my interests in intellectual property and innovation. Here she was a leader in going beyond the model of stand-alone, "mousetrap" inventions that make no use of prior innovations and are themselves immediately marketable as consumer products. Her great contribution was to show just how quickly "optimal" patent parameters in simple models like Nordhaus (1969) lose their robustness once innovations become inputs to other innovations. This makes the case for patents far more nuanced but also more interesting: licensing becomes much more subtle in a sequential model when the licensees are innovators too.

Newcomers to this work would be well advised to start with Suzanne's *Innovation and Incentives* (Scotchmer, 2004b). The book is a treasure from start to finish. The first chapter (with Steve Maurer) is a classic succinct summary of innovation institutions throughout recorded Western history. The remainder of the book shows the fascinating diversity of models that can help us sort out the economic implications of arcane institutions in this challenging but crucial corner of our profession.

Characteristically, Suzanne insisted that the publisher make the book available online to Berkeley students. It is the only text I use in my advanced undergraduate course, and it remains very current. Students come to recognize that each chapter is loaded with content; close reading is essential. I particularly like to watch juniors, seniors and a smattering of graduate students discover how small, well-crafted models can reshape and extend their understanding. Even today, when several texts on innovation have since been published by major academic presses, there is no useful substitute. (There is no need to elaborate – the interested reader can confirm my diagnosis after fifteen minutes online.) This is not surprising; I see no one in this increasingly crowded field who commands such a breadth of relevant theory, presents key ideas so economically, or can make the combination so consistently interesting to intelligent but inexperienced readers.

Suzanne also left us suggestive ideas for how her insights can be further extended. Her work with Nisvan Erkal[1] distinguishing ideas of different

---

1 Erkal and Scotchmer (2009).

levels of scarcity is a refreshingly new contribution to innovation modeling. I hope it will stimulate further work. Her work with Junjie Zhou[2] on
picking winners in multiple rounds of elimination also deserves attention.

I never collaborated with Suzanne. But she once suggested that it might
be good to explore a dynamic model of optimal innovation incentives
under uncertainty. She wanted to go beyond what I had established about
the relative merits of patents, prizes, and contracts to explore fully efficient
information aggregation. The stumbling block was that she wanted to start
from the assumption that individuals would exchange everything they
knew for a dollar when there was no prospect of higher bids. At the time
I found this a weak if not implausible foundation for what promised to be
a labor-intensive project. Now I see that the destination, not to mention
the trip, could have been interesting.

2 Scotchmer and Zhou (2011).

CHAPTER 12

Every Criticism Is an Opportunity

Junjie Zhou

I first met Suzanne in the winter of 2010. I was a third-year grad student and the occasion was a reading course called Econ 296. There were fewer than six of us and I don't think we expected the instructor to put in much effort. But the first day of class Suzanne told us that she had a practical purpose beyond just teaching innovation theory. "All of you," she said, "are going to be teachers." This meant that, one day soon, we would need to know how to set up a course for ourselves. Over the next few weeks she set an example by posting a highly detailed syllabus, weekly schedule, and reading assignments on the course website.

This was the first time I saw how she did things. Whether it was teaching or writing research articles, her advice was always "Show, don't tell." Econ 296 persuaded me she was right. On the one hand, I used the materials as a student, just as I always had. Now, though, I also saw things from the professor's standpoint, watching Suzanne worry constantly what someone new to the subject (like me!) would want to know, and the most transparent way to say it. The other thing I remember from those first weeks was how welcoming she was and how this made everything easier for students. I especially recall her characteristic smile.

I should not have been surprised, but after a month or so she stopped following Econ 296's brand new syllabus entirely. Well, that was also a learning experience. Topics got as much coverage as they needed – better to learn a few things well than many badly. So long as we spent the time productively, she never worried that we were "behind schedule" or "should be further along." At a more personal level, that class also gave me the chance to do some important "firsts" in my life. I learned how to prepare and deliver a PowerPoint presentation for other economists. I struggled to write down a toy model on my own. And eventually I started to do research with Suzanne.

I could see right away that Suzanne kept a very busy daily schedule. But I also discovered that she was also very generous when students asked for help. I knew enough to see how valuable this was and went to see her regularly during office hours. By the end of the semester Suzanne and

I had started work on a joint project called "Picking Winners in Rounds of Eliminations."[1]

So now I had a research life too. Normally I would walk the endless, mazelike corridors of Berkeley Law School[2] some weekend afternoon (or weekday evening) and knock on the door to Office 342. Then Suzanne would welcome me with her familiar smile and we would start working. Sometimes that meant just staring at each other. Sometimes one of us would write something on the board and then cross it out a few minutes later. Sometimes we paced back and forth in the office. Pretty soon I realized that research could be painful, but also that this was the price of having high standards. I can't remember how many afternoons and evenings we talked about our project before finding the right approach. It was a big number.

I cannot remember a single time when she did not drop what she was doing to talk – enthusiastically! – about our research. We did that constantly wherever we happened to be. We talked while walking along the Garonne River in Toulouse in the dead of winter. We talked pacing back and forth in her small office. We talked in fine French restaurants. We talked in grubby Berkeley coffee houses. But wherever we talked, she never compromised her standards. Once, early on, I sent her a theorem we needed. Not wrong, exactly, but very loose mathematically. As a Ph.D. student in mathematics, I thought that would be good enough for an economics paper! Instead of complaining, she replied by sending back a new and much more rigorous version complete with careful explanations and thoughtfully intuitive Greek math symbols. Show, don't tell! I swore on the spot that I would always write economics papers that anyone with even minimal mathematics training could understand.

Like many new economists, I had trouble on the job market. That was in late 2011. Suzanne probably guessed that might happen; certainly, she had insisted that I apply for some post-doc positions too. Looking back, I should have taken her advice by doing a post-doc before I even applied for tenure track. But sometimes you don't really know how brutal the process can be until you struggle. At any rate I was very depressed, but thanks to Suzanne this didn't last very long. The important thing, she said, was to keep moving forward. She also helped me find a way to visit the Paris School of Economics in 2013. That was especially lucky because it gave me more time to study with Suzanne, who happened to be visiting the Toulouse School of Economics with Steve Maurer that spring. And from there, I eventually accepted a job in Shanghai where I could pursue my research and ... keep moving forward.

---

1 This later led to the paper posted at http://papers.ssrn.com/sol3/papers.cfm?abstract_id=2120974.
2 Steve Maurer tells me that most US law school buildings have the same twisty, disorienting quality. Might this be a deliberate architectural choice?

Just before fleeing to Shanghai, I visited Toulouse to see Suzanne and Steve again. And of course, I was hoping that Suzanne and I could make some progress on a theory paper we were writing, that compared the market outcomes for e-book sites like Amazon against traditional, brick-and-mortar bookstores. As always, we walked, crossing countless bridges and rivers. This time the subject was all things China – the rising number of patents, the different historical dynasties, the current political system, the Chinese Communist Party, and everything under the sun. Along the way, Suzanne pointed to a bridge called *Pont Neuf*, explaining that this meant "*new bridge*" in English. I laughed. "In Shanghai," I said, "everything built before the twenty-first century is considered old."

She had always been interested in China and I was already thinking about finding a way for her to visit in 2014. Neither of us knew that was our last walk together. I think it was better that way. That night Suzanne treated Steve and me to a fancy dinner. I still remember how good the salmon tasted. Then she hugged me and showed me which direction to go for my train, and stood for a long moment watching me leave. I looked back and waved and that was that.

**

The skills you get from grad school are only partly technical. You learn new theory and math your whole life, but this is when you develop research habits.

One of the things you need to understand about Suzanne was that the ideas that appear in her public papers also filled her private thoughts. There was no deep division: she would use personal experience to feed her theory intuition, and then turn around and use theory to organize her own research. Each constantly fed the other. This was especially visible in the advice she gave students about how to do research. One of the Ideas Model's key insights is that the stories we teach children about heroes like Edison and Marconi are much too simple. For industries like biotech or electronics, solitary genius is seldom good enough: you need many cumulative ideas to move forward, and, as she liked to say, these are "widely distributed across the scattered genius of mankind."

For a theoretical economist, just saying these words suggests models faster than you can write them down – ideas are scarce; patent rewards must be large enough to develop each idea in the chain; inventors can use or bank ideas, but never lose them . . . . Anyone who knows her work can immediately appreciate how rich those statements really are. But Suzanne also used the same insights to explain how young economists should build their careers. Because one way to paraphrase the Ideas Model was to say that every human is also a kind of genius. And this is true. Every paper builds on – and is impossible without – earlier references. Every criticism could contain an idea that you would never think of yourself. The more you pay attention, the more "giants' shoulders" you notice and can stand on.

Then I remembered something else that Suzanne told me: "You never know what you think unless you write it down." That's when I started keeping an electronic research diary in my computer. It stores the ideas that flash across my mind, along with the things I read and that others tell me. So now I am banking ideas too, and watching them multiply into papers of my own.

**

Well, those aren't the only things I learned from Suzanne. She was my advisor, friend, and mentor! All the same, I do have one small complaint. Suzanne's "Show, don't tell" is a fine rule. I remember it, and use it, and teach it to my own students every day. But if she were here I think I would tell her that it is incomplete. Some ideas, it turns out, can *neither* be told *nor* shown. Here is my proof. I remember that one day we were working on our "Picking Winners" paper when she made some silly whiteboard error and said, in all apparent seriousness, "After passing a certain age, one can't do calculus." I remember grinning but also thinking that this could never be true for her – and certainly not for me. The other day I was standing at the podium in front of forty-six grad students in my advanced micro class. All of a sudden I looked at formula $(X^x)'$ on the blackboard and my mind went completely blank. Suddenly I thought of Suzanne's smile almost as if she were physically present. "Hey," I said to myself, "she was right about that too!"

CHAPTER 13

Top 10 Work Mantras

Stephen M. Maurer

Prof. Scotchmer was analytical about anything that was important to her, and nothing could be more important than research. Part of that instinct was to tell others what she had learned about the process. Here, David Letterman style, are my "Top 10" favorites among her aphorisms:

10. "How do you know what you think unless you write it down?"
9. "Show, don't tell." (Regarding written and oral presentations.)
8. "Write what you have to say and then stop."
7. "Do whatever helps the reader." (Regarding footnote conventions.)
6. "Don't tell me. I want to figure it out."
5. "In the end, all you die with is your CV."
4. "Teaching is a great way to learn new subjects."
3. "Time is the only asset that any academic has."
2. "If someone kills your idea you should be grateful. Thinking about bad ideas is a waste of time."
1. "We lead such privileged lives."

PART II

INNOVATION THEORY (I):
CUMULATIVE INNOVATION

Anyone who picks up this book will already have realized that Prof. Scotchmer contributed to an extraordinarily diverse group of economic disciplines. Nevertheless, there is no denying that her best-known work focused on innovation. This part recounts her discovery of the cumulative innovation problem and the path-breaking game theory investigations that followed. Part III explores how her later work extended this foundation and extracted increasingly practical recommendations for IP and antitrust reform.

CHAPTER 14

The Giant's Shoulders
Joshua Gans

Prior to the 1980s, there were very few complete models of innovation in economics. To be sure, Ken Arrow had founded the field in 1962 (something he could do even on a bad day) but there had been little progress for a couple of decades. There had also been continual grappling with some basic Schumpeterian questions – namely, what the relationship between innovation and competition was – but it is safe to say that (a) that was unresolved and (b) there was a sense in which that was not a first-order issue.

That changed in the late 1980s with a paper Suzanne Scotchmer coauthored with Jerry Green on sequential innovation (eventually published in 1995), followed up with another in 1996 that really framed the issues of incentives and intellectual property in a new light. What this research line did was see innovation as not just a one-off event but as a cumulative one. Innovations were followed by others. They were combined with one another and also became a ladder of ever increasing improvements. This notion was not new – indeed, Isaac Newton had recognized it when he claimed that his insights came because he had "stood on the shoulders of giants" – but it had never been given its due in economics.

Suzanne Scotchmer was lecturing at Harvard during this critical period. Indeed, one suspects that these notions appeared earlier in those lectures and influenced students such as Philippe Aghion – who built cumulative innovation explicitly into growth models – and Rebecca Henderson whose work examined how the recombination processes and assimilation of radical innovations would impact on organizations and their viability. But for Scotchmer, the immediate challenge was how to think about intellectual property protection.

Prior to that time, the policymaker's choice when it came to things like patents was a tradeoff between incentives to innovate and the deadweight losses associated with patent protection. This suggested that policymakers could work out what the optimal length of a patent should be by balancing these two conflicting objectives. Cumulative innovation posed a stickier set of issues. In this situation, not only were there consumers who would want cheaper access to innovations in the form of products, but follow-on innovators would need that too lest their own incentives to innovate be crimped. Thus, it was not possible for policymakers to simply claim that they were weighing incentives to innovate with stronger patent protection as this was no longer an obvious proposition.

Scotchmer reformulated the problem and posed it as one dealing with how we thought about innovative rewards through the market. A pioneer innovation would enable follow-on innovations and so, to encourage their optimal provision, pioneer innovations should have a claim on the rewards to follow-on innovations. But the problem with this was that follow-on innovations required incentives of their own. You simply couldn't have both. A patent that leveraged into those follow-on innovations may well not encourage more innovation at all. Of course, this meant that the problem could be mitigated by *ex ante* agreements (to the extent you knew who was following on from you) and integration (involving similar issues). But when things were more fluid and there were markets in between, intellectual property protection was not a catchall solution. You would want to narrow patent scope and increase patent length to avoid claiming things that were follow-on innovations that did not reduce the economic life of pioneer ones and do the reverse when that was not the case. You would also want to consider carefully the interaction with antitrust law.

The research that followed on from this pioneering work has defined the economics of innovation since. In particular, it has become critical in framing the policy issues surrounding reach through patent rights. In that debate the general issue associated with cumulative innovation and patent rights was given less formal expression in terms of the notion of the anti-commons. The anti-commons is a situation where, when there are too many claimants to a resource, there are impediments in terms of ensuring that resource is optimally utilized. In this case, the resource comprises the potential innovative efforts of many people, leading to concerns regarding weak incentives. While this appears in the IT and software spaces with work building on other work, the canonical case was in biotech. Specifically, a few years ago the US Supreme Court heard the *Myriad* case where a patent holder on the genes shown to indicate propensity for breast cancer exercised their rights with respect to applications that built on that knowledge – most notably, testing for the gene. The Supreme Court decided against Myriad and opted to restrict patent rights so as to promote cumulative innovation.

The standard, informal theory of harm here is that follow-on innovators, feeling that they cannot easily deal with the patent-holder on the pioneer innovation, decide that the risks are too high to invest and so opt not to do so. To be sure, this 'hold-up' concern is not good for anyone, including possibly the patent rights holder who loses the opportunity to earn licensing fees from applications of their knowledge. Suffice it to say, this has been a big feature of the movement against the current strength and, indeed, existence of the patent system.

One issue, however, was that the evidence on the impact of patents on cumulative innovation was weak. Mostly that was due to the problem of finding an environment where impact could be measured. How do you measure an innovation, measure follow-on innovations or applications or, indeed, the quality of all of this? Then you have to find a situation where there was a natural experiment (a policy change or exogenous source of variation) in the patent system to allow you to examine causality. It is a tall order.

For this reason, all previous attempts concerned intermediate steps – most notably, the impact of patents on citations whether in publications or in patents. This includes work by Fiona Murray and Scott Stern, Heidi Williams and Alberto Galasso and Mark Schankerman. While there is some variation, this work showed, using various clever approaches, that patent protection (or other IP changes) might deter cumulative innovation upwards of 30 percent. That's a big effect and a big concern even if the results were somewhat intermediate.

In 2014, a new paper by Bhaven Sampat and Heidi Williams actually found a way to examine the impact of patents on follow-on innovations themselves. Their setting was to look at precisely the area of the *Myriad* case. They utilized the human genome and the fact that genes that were sequenced could be patented. What's useful about this setting is that the gene itself has a unique identifier that the researchers can use to identify whether it is subject to a patent claim (and indeed a patent application that may be accepted or rejected by the United States Patent and Trademark Office (USPTO)) and then also identify whether that gene was the subject of publications and clinical trials. This is as good as it gets for the measurement of innovation.

But how do you find a way of comparing what happens if there is a patent on a gene sequence versus if there is no patent? After all, there may be no patent because no one thinks that gene is important, which may also be the reason why there is no follow-on research. That means you have to find some relatively independent reason why a patent may exist or not. Sampat and Williams exploit imperfections at the USPTO that can them-selves be identified to obtain that reason. They found that the identity of the patent examiner was useful here as some people could be tough and others lenient. Using that information, Sampat and Williams could not find evidence for a negative effect on cumulative innovation.

What is interesting about this result is that if we read Scotchmer's work carefully we find that it often predicts that patent rights holders will find a way to ensure that follow-on innovators do their innovations and get paid enough to make it worthwhile. The reason is that it is mutually beneficial for follow-on innovation to occur and, in typical Coasian fashion, it works out. To be sure, the follow-on innovators would prefer not to pay the pioneer patent-holder but that is secondary to the issue of whether the innovation actually takes place. The Sampat–Williams evidence suggests that for most patent-holders the pioneer innovations do not end up blocking follow-on innovation – at least not because they happen to have a patent.

Cumulative innovation has spurred two decades of fruitful research that now places it at the forefront of intellectual property policy. We are still working through its implications and nuances but, if we were to take stock right now, the simple basic insights that Scotchmer worked out right at the start remain the first-order issues of the day.

CHAPTER 15

Reimagining Innovation Theory: Suzanne Scotchmer and the Ideas Model

Nisvan Erkal, Stephen M. Maurer, and Deborah Minehart

If you asked Prof. Scotchmer an innovation question, and particularly if it was fundamental, her explanation would almost always begin: "In the Ideas Model ..." These four words went by quickly and were easily overlooked. But when you noticed them you were flattered. Because they showed that Prof. Scotchmer took your question seriously enough to work out the answer from first principles. And the more you thought about it, the more you valued the Ideas Model. Because if you know a subject's first principles you will eventually work out the theory. But first you have to know them.

The key assumption in almost all of Prof. Scotchmer's innovation research was that an innovation requires both an idea and a decision to invest in it. She saw ideas as the primitive in the economy. They represent investment opportunities. What was important in her view was whether these investment opportunities are public or private knowledge (O'Donoghue et al., 1998). If they are public knowledge, then research becomes a race to see which innovator will be the first to fill a known market niche. That outcome might be stochastic, but anyone can invest because everyone knows that the market niche (investment opportunity) exists. The main determinant of success is effort.

However, if ideas (i.e., investment opportunities) are private knowledge, then only the owner of the idea can invest. This was the key aspect of Prof. Scotchmer's "Ideas Model." Probably the best-known example is her models of sequential innovation, which assume that each generation of a technology can only be developed by a single firm. This is because (by assumption) only a single firm owns the idea.

The key thing about the Ideas Model approach is that no two innovators are the same. This immediately emphasizes heterogeneity amongst innovators or, to be more precise, their ideas. This is an important point of departure from what Prof. Scotchmer typically called "knowledge production function models," where investment opportunities are public knowledge (Menell and Scotchmer, 2007). When everyone invests to fulfill the same market niche, whether it is one firm or many firms doing the investment really does not matter. True, adding more firms increases competition and reduces the expected time to innovation. However, the presence of any single firm is not important: we can replace any firm with another and nothing changes. This is definitely not the case in the Ideas Model. Since all firms have different ideas, if we take one firm out of the picture, the possible outcomes change.

Another way of explaining the difference between the two paradigms is in terms of the fundamental question they pose for innovation. In the Ideas Model, the question is: "Which idea or market opportunity is it efficient to invest in?" In the knowledge production function model, the question is: "How much should we invest in this one market opportunity?" Hence, they represent quite different approaches to innovation.

Over the years, Prof. Scotchmer expressed the Ideas Model in many different ways, for example by pointing out that "ideas are scarce" (Menell and Scotchmer, 2007), that they came, as Prof. Scotchmer liked to tell her students, "from the distributed genius of mankind," and that "there is such a thing as 'imagination'" (Scotchmer, 2004, at p. 151). More formally, ideas arrived in pairs (v, c) which required investment by sponsors, consumers, and/or other inventors to develop. Patents were just one institution for incentivizing the required investment and, depending on the circumstances, alternative institutions like prizes or government research might be more efficient (Menell and Scotchmer, 2007; Maurer and Scotchmer, 2004).

Mid-Century Orthodoxy. Like most good insights, the Ideas Model is simple. After all, economics is the science of allocating resources under scarcity. From that standpoint, the notion that ideas are scarce – and can be allocated through markets – is hardly surprising. But in that case, why did the Ideas Model take so long?

It helps to recall some history. Pre-war innovation models literatures had concentrated on the idea that invention depended on fortuitous discovery or an individual's stubborn fascination with some specific problem. The resulting models implied that invention was both non-economic and inelastic (Nordhaus, 1969, at pp. 16–17). To the extent that economic incentives did appear, they simply assumed that R&D investment would occur automatically when firm profits fell below some specific level or factor prices changed (Menell and Scotchmer, 2007, at p. 1478).

To this point economic models, to the extent that they existed at all, assumed that R&D occurred within a single black box. This view was increasingly challenged by the rise of large commercial "invention factories" in the late nineteenth and early twentieth centuries (Anon., n.d.; Gertner, 2012) which specialized in turning basic knowledge into commercial projects. This broke the black box apart by recognizing that a second group of actors – university researchers – had to make enough basic discoveries to "keep the pipeline full" (Geiger, 2004). That said, getting ideas from universities to the people who developed them seemed simple enough: given that basic discoveries could not be patented, anyone could potentially exploit them. The real challenges were almost entirely downstream in the commercial sector. Given that applied research was expensive and failure-prone, only the largest corporations could fund enough projects to diversify risk. Celebrated mid-century examples included General Electric and, especially, Bell Labs.

The idea that commercial R&D consisted of large industrial labs developing university discoveries was eventually formalized in Prof. Arrow's foundational paper on R&D incentives, which argued that "the only way" to manage R&D risk within the private enterprise system is to conduct "research by large corporations with many products going on, each small in scale compared with the net revenue of the corporation," so that "the corporation acts as its own insurance company" (Arrow, 1962, at p. 616). However, Arrow was careful to note that large corporate laboratories could be avoided through alternative institutions like research contracts, research institutes, and joint ventures (ibid. at pp. 624–625). Nordhaus seemed to close this loophole by invoking empirical evidence that the optimum size of inventive teams had grown over time (Nordhaus, 1969, at p. 17). This vastly simplified the problem of getting ideas from universities to those who developed them. So long as R&D was housed within a handful of large labs, the pipeline only had to reach a few players for "everyone" to know everything.

World War II seemed to vindicate this logic. Every major power had recognized the main technical possibilities for atomic bombs, radar, jet engines, computers and the like. Despite this, most had failed to develop them. The lesson seemed to be that, as MIT's Vannever Bush emphasized, progress was mostly a matter of money. This meant that a permanent extension of wartime R&D support could accelerate civilian products as well (Bush, 1945). This new orthodoxy was backed by massive increases in science funding.

The assumption that the main source of scarcity in the economy was resources instead of ideas also became the basis for many postwar economic models. This is already evident in Nordhaus's (1967, 1969) seminal theory of patent incentives, which sought to formalize the tradeoff between deadweight loss and consumer welfare which had been understood and debated in a qualitative way – often with considerable sophistication – since Victorian times (Menell and Scotchmer, 2007, at p. 1477). Here the focus was plainly on investment incentives rather than scarcity of ideas. Indeed, Nordhaus largely ignored the distinction between public and private knowledge, pointing to contemporary empirical research suggesting that many inventive ideas were "awaiting exploitation" so that progress mainly depended on firms' readiness to "exploit their pool of unused inventions when the time comes" (Nordhaus, 1969, at p. 10). This opened the door to a large literature with a focus on the adequacy of incentives to invest in public R&D opportunities, and not on how firms come to those ideas in the first place. This line of thinking was further developed and reached its definitive form in, for example, Loury (1979), Lee and Wilde (1980), and Reinganum (1981, 1982, 1985).

The Ideas Model. Prof. Scotchmer came to the Ideas Model gradually. The process almost certainly started with newspaper accounts of how firms in the then-new biotech and software industries continually built on each other's ideas. These are already mentioned in Scotchmer and Green (1990). However, "Giants" (1991) pushes these same software and biotech examples much harder. In the cumulative innovation model, progress *only* proceeds one firm at a time. This, however, can only happen if racing is suppressed. Prof. Scotchmer explains this by pointing out that the same biotech and software firms that inspired her model are invariably obsessed with secrecy. Firms cannot race unless they know that an idea exists. However, secrecy is only effective where ideas are rare. As Menell and Scotchmer (2007) remark, "If Ideas are scarce, then racing is not an issue" (ibid. at p. 1498).

Following this thought ultimately led Prof. Scotchmer to the Ideas Model. The model first appears in her work on cumulative innovation (see, e.g., Green and Scotchmer, 1995; O'Donoghue et al., 1998). Prof. Scotchmer later developed the Ideas Model in other directions so that most of her innovation theory papers after 2000 contain some version of the insight. We close by describing three particularly creative examples, although interested readers will have no trouble finding additional instances in, for example, Scotchmer's (2004) exhaustive survey or Gandal and Regibeau's (this volume) discussion of open source.

Managing Option Value of Inventions. Prof. Scotchmer's model of cumulative innovation focused on the extreme case where R&D ideas occur to just one firm at a time. But ideas in many technologies are substitutes. This observation creates a natural way of capturing creativity using the economic concept of scarcity. Specifically, creative minds are the owners of rare ideas which are hard to replace. Hence, we can use the scarcity of substitute ideas as a measure of an idea's value (Erkal and Scotchmer, 2011). This immediately opens deep questions about which ideas society should fund, or indeed whether it might sometimes be better to wait for the arrival of cheaper ideas that will serve the same purpose. This option value problem was new to innovation theory, and explains why scarce ideas need higher rewards, and also why sponsors should adjust rewards upward if no ideas are forthcoming.

University Research. Prof. Scotchmer routinely emphasized that the flow of ideas was a "primitive" in her model that no government could influence. However, she also knew that Congress had passed the Bayh–Dole Act on the opposite assumption that IP incentives would encourage universities to produce more ideas. Prof. Scotchmer's "Patents in the University" (2013) filled this gap by developing an Ideas Model where the flow of ideas is proportional to funding even though the specific ideas are still unpredictable. The paper finds that Bayh–Dole models can indeed increase the flow of ideas, but only if universities (a) prefer research to other goals, or (b) cannot adjust their overhead fees so that patent revenues crowd out grant support. The paper also identifies a deep tension between Bayh–Dole incentives and the traditional rule that basic research cannot be patented. The basic intuition is that unpatented discoveries attract racing. This implies that commercial firms earn zero profit in expectation so that the university can earn nothing from licensing (Scotchmer, 2013).

Policy Implications. The choice between the Ideas Model and Production Function approaches ultimately turns on our belief about how ideas originate. This has deep implications for policy. In the Ideas Model, the decentralization of ideas across multiple inventors makes the patent system a useful vehicle for funding R&D. Any firm, any actor, can have access to the patent system to successfully commercialize their private ideas. By comparison, a world where R&D opportunities are known to all makes competing mechanisms more attractive. This is especially true of taxpayer-funded schemes, such as prizes or government procurement, that avoid deadweight loss (Menell and Scotchmer, 2007, at p. 1478).

At the same time, the Ideas Model also strengthens the case for antitrust. Schumpeter's famous defense of monopoly capitalism implicitly assumes that innovation is a matter of raising money. This suggests that society can profitably trade short-run deadweight loss for growth. This argument is much less compelling in the Ideas Model, where eliciting widely scattered ideas is at least as important as developing them. Here, a world of small, one-idea firms will often be quicker to develop and disclose ideas than large corporate labs that develop a handful of candidates while leaving most ideas perpetually on the shelf.

CHAPTER 16

N. Gallini and S. Scotchmer, "Intellectual Property: When Is It the Best Incentive System?" (2002)

INTRODUCTION   NANCY GALLINI

"The best way to have a good idea is to have lots of ideas"
Dr. Linus Pauling, Nobel Prize in Chemistry (1954)
and Nobel Peace Prize (1962)

Suzanne Scotchmer was a perfect example of her "cumulative research" paradigm. She processed new ideas quickly and cleverly; developed the most promising ones into insightful innovations; shared them in conferences and conversations with colleagues who built upon them and inspired her with their ideas ... and then a new cycle of intellectual growth would begin once again. However, she did *not* resemble her paradigm in one way. Her ideas seemed anything but "scarce." Her sparks of imagination arrived frequently at a very high rate and she readily shared them with her colleagues, that is, if they were up to the challenge of joining her for a brisk "stroll" up into the Berkeley Hills.

Some of Suzanne's influential ideas are reviewed in the accompanying paper, which we wrote a decade after her insight on cumulative research in "Giants" (Scotchmer, 1991) and Scotchmer and Green (1990). Our paper was an attempt to sort through the virtues and deficiencies of the patent system relative to other simple mechanisms (e.g., prizes, auctions, and contracts), as informed by the literature. At the time, the press was increasingly hostile to intellectual property ("IP"), especially following the Supreme Court's *State Street* decision upholding business method patents (US Federal Circuit, 1998). The criticism was hard to ignore, but Suzanne never seemed to let popular opinion, or even her own previous findings, influence her thinking. Rather, she would let her theory skills – and, by then, deep knowledge of real institutions – take her in whatever direction they chose.

I do not know the original inspiration that directed Suzanne to her cumulative research insight. But by the time she wrote "Giants," she was asking a basic question that would fascinate her throughout her career: *Where do innovations come from?* Strikingly, "Giants" announces an equally simple but fundamentally important answer: "From previous innovations." This observation, followed by Suzanne's exploration into the theory of cumulative research, transformed the economics of innovation. It replaced Nordhaus's (1969) discrete, single-invention framework with a new paradigm in which complementary innovation builds upon previous discoveries. It differed sharply from the case of substitutes for a single invention, in which follow-on innovation duplicates or imitates the patented invention (see, e.g., Klemperer, 1990; Gilbert and Shapiro, 1990; Gallini, 1992). Merges and Nelson (1989) had also explored the idea that innovation flows from previous knowledge, but that did not become part of the canonical economic model until Suzanne provided us with a theoretical framework for analyzing it. In sections III and IV of our paper, we review the recent literature on optimal patent design, respectively for the single invention and cumulative research cases.

But Suzanne recognized that new innovators need more than just previous discoveries and ample R&D resources. They also must have an *idea*, that is, "an act of imagination" for a new product (Scotchmer, 1991) or a "concept" for an improvement over current product (O'Donoghue, Scotchmer, and Thisse, 1998 [this volume]). *Ideas* became a "primitive" in her models. In contrast, the literature tended to treat ideas and innovations as indistinguishable; that is, everyone knew the possibilities up front and so the social planner's problem was reduced to deciding which ideas (equivalently, innovations) to invest in and who should do the work. But in Scotchmer's analysis, ideas arrive randomly and possibly infrequently and an idea became an innovation when the R&D investment was made. At the time of deciding which or whether any *known* projects should be undertaken, the planner had no way of knowing what new ideas might become available in the near future or who would receive them.

These two fundamental insights – cumulative research and the random arrival of ideas – can have a significant impact on the planner's decision of whether or not to innovate. To see this, consider the Nordhaus-type model in which innovation activity is determined by R&D investment. Then, the decision problem for a social planner is straightforward: Develop an innovation i if and only if $v_i > c_i$, where v_i is the value of innovation i and c_i is the R&D cost of turning an idea into an innovation. Now suppose there are two related innovations $i = 1, 2$. In the case of sequential innovation in which the two ideas are complementary, the planner's decision rule becomes: Develop *both* innovations if and only if $v_1 + v_2 > c_1 + c_2$. That means, in contrast to Nordhaus, the first invention should sometimes be developed even if $v_1 < c_1$. Alternatively, suppose the ideas are substitutes that arrive randomly at rate λ. Then, if $v_2 - c_2 > v_1 - c_1 > 0$, and λ is high (ideas arrive frequently), it may pay to hold out for the more efficient second technology and not develop the first even if $v_1 > c_1$.

Given her deep understanding of where innovations came from, Suzanne naturally asked *How can society bring them about?* As noted above, Suzanne and I began our paper at a time when IP incentives were being routinely criticized. But the criticism against IP was incomplete: the relevant question was whether patents were inferior to any realistic alternative or, as Suzanne liked to say, *"Compared to what?"* This became the second fundamental question that motivated much of Suzanne's research over the past two decades, a question that is especially natural to someone whose career was grounded in game theory and mechanism design. And so, Suzanne spent much of her effort, following "Giants," searching for optimal incentive mechanisms that would produce socially efficient rates of innovation. This included both a decision ("which scarce ideas should be developed?") and a delegation problem ("who should develop the ideas and at what rate of investment?").

Gandal and Scotchmer (1993) had already taken an important first step in this agenda. In their analysis of research joint ventures, they considered a setting that includes both asymmetric information (heterogeneous firms have private information on their research efficiencies) and moral hazard (investment levels of firms are not observable). They showed that a menu of fixed fee contracts with firm-specific prizes can optimally solve the delegation problem by producing truthful information about relative efficiencies and efficient rates of investment. Although in theory their mechanism is superior to simpler policies, in practice it could be difficult to implement.

With that, Scotchmer turned her attention to more conventional mechanisms for promoting innovation – prizes, procurement, and patents – with particular focus on IP. As reviewed in section II of our paper, the optimal mechanism depends on what is observable to the researcher and planner and verifiable by the courts. Again, suppose each idea is represented by (v, c), where v is the value of the project and c is the R&D cost. Then, if delegation is the only problem such that v is known but there are multiple researchers with unknown costs c_i, an auction can select the most efficient firm. In the case of a single researcher, a simple prize equal to v will generate efficient innovation, provided that the researcher can protect herself against moral hazard on the part of the planner. In contrast, when c is known but v is not, a contract of c could work as long as the social planner is able to verify v to prevent moral hazard on the part of the researcher. With multiple researchers, the social planner can use an auction-plus-patent-buyout scheme to elicit the social value of a project that can then be paid to the researcher

(Kremer, 1998). The message here is that for patents to be justified, both v and c must be unobservable to the social planner. Furthermore, as already noted in Gandal and Scotchmer (1993), neither IP nor prizes will be dominated by other mechanisms in more complex environments. More generally, neither alone can aggregate information that is decentralized among firms, and neither will be completely effective at delegating research effort efficiently (Minehart and Scotchmer, 1999).

Following on that theme, Scotchmer (1999a) presents an important analysis of optimal patent design in an environment in which both v and c are unobservable. She found, somewhat surprisingly, that it looks very much like the current patent renewal system, existing in the USA, Canada, and Europe. In particular, the optimal mechanism is a menu of contracts (F, T), which allows firms to choose longer patent lives T for higher fees F. Under certain conditions, she finds that the mechanism compels owners of higher-valued projects to select longer patents at higher fees. An important message from her paper and related literature is that when the social planner cannot verify either v or c, IP can be justified in the form of a patent renewal system that screens for high-valued, high-cost projects (Scotchmer, 1999). Similarly, Cornelli and Schankerman (1999) justify IP but in a model where R&D productivity of firms is heterogeneous and unobservable. In their model, a patent renewal system increases investment, and therefore the value of innovations by higher productivity firms.

Importantly, Scotchmer (1999) also adds a second message that the patent system can be adapted to different environments and technologies, without the need to write multiple statutes. This research is important in thinking about the patent system, which is typically viewed as a blunt instrument for satisfying the needs of innovators in diverse sectors. Here, Scotchmer showed how patent policy is more adaptable to different environments and technologies. Rather than legislating different levels of protection according to subject matter, the idea here is to design a system that is nuanced, according to choices by innovators acting on their private information.

That said, these analyses only applied to single, isolated inventions. In light of Suzanne's pioneering work on cumulative innovation, she next naturally asked: *What does optimal patent policy look like in a cumulative, sequential framework?* With that question, Scotchmer launched into an in-depth, game-theoretic analysis of the IP system with close attention to the legal details, to understand how it can better align private with social incentives. Scotchmer explored the IP system with great fervor, generating a breathtaking array of ideas in economic theory, law and practice which, when taken together, comprise the most valuable and influential contributions to the economic theory on optimal patent design, with emphasis on patent breadth. I address these ideas further in Chapter 18.

Adam Jaffe, Joshua Lerner, and Scott Stern (eds.),
Innovation Policy and the Economy
2002, pp. 51–77

Intellectual Property: When Is It the Best Incentive System?

Nancy Gallini, *University of Toronto*
Suzanne Scotchmer, *University of California, Berkeley*

Executive Summary

Intellectual property is not the only mechanism used in the American economy for rewarding R&D. Prizes and contract research of various types are also common. Given the current controversies that swirl around intellectual property policies, we review the economic reasoning that supports patent and other intellectual property over the alternatives. For those economic environments where intellectual property is justified, we review some of the arguments for why it is designed as it is. We focus particularly on the issue of how broad awards should be and how much protection should go to the original inventor (as opposed to those who subsequently improve the invention). We emphasize that the ideal design of an intellectual property system depends on the ease with which rightsholders can enter into licensing and other contractual arrangements involving these rights.

I. Introduction

Intellectual property is the foundation of the modern information economy. It fuels the software, life sciences, and computer industries, and pervades most other products we consume. Although most inventors consider it essential, it is currently under attack by some academics and policymakers. One complaint is that intellectual property rewards inventors beyond what is necessary to spur innovation. Another is that intellectual property is a drag to innovation, rather than a spur, since it prevents inventions from being used efficiently, especially in creating further innovations. A third complaint is that some inventions should not be protected at all but, instead, be supported by public sponsors.

Controversies over what should constitute intellectual property swirl around business methods, computer software, research tools in the biomedical industry, and genetic sequences. However this is not new; controversies have swirled around every new technology in the twentieth century. A sampler might include the question of whether player piano rolls should receive copyright protection, whether purification of chemical compounds constitutes "invention" for purposes of patent law, and whether mathematical algorithms such as public key encryption should be patentable. Technologies that fall outside the subject matter of patents and copyrights have sometimes received *sui generis* protections, such as computer chips under the Semiconductor Chip Protection Act.

For all these technologies, the same questions arise: Are there natural market forces that protect inventors so that formal protections or other incentives are not necessary? If not, is intellectual property the best incentive system, or would the technology more appropriately be developed by a public sponsor and offered freely in the public domain? How should intellectual property be designed so as to minimize deadweight loss due to monopoly pricing without undermining incentives to innovate?

Our objective in this paper is to review what economists have said about incentive schemes to promote R&D, including intellectual property. While we focus on environments in which other forms of protection are not available, we note that other protections can obviate the need for any formal reward system. For example, encryption offers the potential to protect digitally distributed products such as music, movies, and software, even in the absence of intellectual property (National Research Council 2000). In the realm of databases, for which formal protections have been mandated in Europe and proposed in the U.S. Congress, vendors are protecting their data with both clever business strategies and technology (Maurer 1999, Maurer and Scotchmer 1999). In markets with network effects, there may be natural barriers to entry, so that a vendor may capture the entire market even without formal protection (Farrell 1995). And, of course, trade secrecy can be an important protection, especially when firms devise clever nondisclosure agreements that enable them to license without leaking the secret to unauthorized users (e.g., see Anton and Yao 1994). In some of these examples, the alternative protection involves social costs that could be avoided by formal intellectual property. But if not, the case for intellectual property may be weak.

In section II, we compare intellectual property with alternative incentive schemes. Without losing the thread of the paper, the reader who is only interested in the design of intellectual property (as opposed to other incentive schemes) can skip the last three subsections of section II. In section III we review optimal design issues for intellectual property, especially the question of patent breadth, and in section IV we turn to the special problems that arise when innovation is cumulative. In section V, we summarize the arguments for and against intellectual property. We comment on whether the design recommendations of economists can actually be implemented, and argue that intellectual property regimes should be designed so that the subject matter of each one has relatively homogeneous needs for protection.

II. Alternative Mechanisms for Rewarding Innovation

Competitive markets may not be conducive to innovation, for a reason that was well articulated by Arrow (1962). Inventions are *information*, and information is a public good. An invention such as a wireless palmtop is a combination of tangible embodiments and an intangible idea, as well as information about how to manufacture it. Typically, both the information and the tangible embodiments are costly to the inventor, but only the tangible components are costly to a rival. Without some sort of protection or reward, the inventor will therefore be at a market disadvantage relative to rivals, and will possibly be dissuaded from investing.

Arrow explained why some incentive scheme is needed, but not *which* scheme. Many schemes have been used in practice. In the seventeenth century, for example, a prize was offered in France for developing a workable water turbine (Reynolds 1983, p. 338). For about a century in the same era, a prize was outstanding for developing a method to calculate longitude at sea (Sobel 1995). In the modern era, R&D is sponsored to a large extent by government grants. According to the National Science Foundation (2000), in 1998 about 30% of U.S. research was funded by the Federal government. These examples raise the following question: In what environments are there better incentive schemes than intellectual property?

We shall use the term *intellectual property* (IP) to mean an exclusive right to market an invention for a fixed time period. It includes copyrights, patents, plant patents, protection under the Plant Variety Protection Act, and other *sui generis* types of protection. By a *prize* we mean a payment funded out of general revenue that is made to a researcher conditional on delivering a specified invention. Prizes can either be tailored individually to firms, depending on their efficiency characteristics, or can be offered symmetrically to any firm that wants to compete, just as a patent is. By *procurement*, we mean a mechanism to solve the problem of getting an invention at minimum cost, in a timely manner, or otherwise efficiently (e.g., Laffont and Tirole 1986, 1987). A simple procurement mechanism would be an auction for the right to be paid when the invention is delivered.

A form of procurement commonly used in government-sponsored research appears, on its face, to be a fixed-price contract. For example, the National Institutes of Health give funding in advance for projects that are described in the proposals. Funds are not withheld if the output is not delivered, since the idea of the contract is to pay costs as they accrue. If such funding were a one-time event for each researcher, researchers might be inclined to "take the money and run." This moral hazard problem is overcome because future grants are contingent on previous success. The linkage between previous success and future funding seems even more specific in the case of the National Science Foundation. Fixed-price contracts thus operate much like prizes, with the wrinkle that a researcher must convince his sponsor in advance that his output might be worthy of a prize. For this purpose, his reputation might suffice, and in some cases, much of the research has already been completed.

We begin our analysis with a benchmark. When both the costs and values of innovations are publicly observable to both firms and a public sponsor, IP is not the best incentive scheme. A better scheme is for a public sponsor to choose the projects with the largest net social benefits, and pay for them on delivery, using funds from general revenue. With IP, projects are funded out of monopoly profits. Monopoly pricing is equivalent to taxing a single market, which is generally thought to impose greater deadweight loss than the broad-based taxation that generates general revenue. Thus, to justify intellectual property, there must be some type of asymmetric information about the costs and benefits of research programs.

We first make some comparative remarks about intellectual property, prizes, and procurement contracts. These remarks are much in the spirit of Wright (1983), who gave the first formal treatment of how asymmetric information should inform our choice among incentive mechanisms. In the subsections that follow, we then show that these three mechanisms can generally be improved upon.[1]

IP has an obvious defect as well as obvious virtues. The defect is the deadweight loss due to monopoly pricing. The virtues are several. Most importantly, if the costs and benefits of R&D investments are known only to firms, and not to government sponsors, firms will use their superior knowledge to screen investments. A sponsor does not need to decide in advance which investments are meritorious. An investor knows that he will be punished by the market if he does not invest wisely. Another obvious virtue is that the prospect of valuable IP might elicit higher levels of effort than those generally associated with sponsored research. For example, much has been made of the human genome project, whose completion was accelerated by a private firm hoping to win IP rights on gene sequences. Finally, an IP system imposes the costs of an invention on its users. In other incentive mechanisms, the costs are borne more generally by taxpayers. Taxpayers might rightfully revolt if asked to bear the cost of developing, say, computer games.

Lest these advantages of IP be overstated, however, we note that prizes have many of the same virtues. If an investment's prospective value is known to the sponsor (or defined by the sponsor, as in the case of military wares), the sponsor can screen projects himself. A prize system then seems superior to IP. It avoids deadweight loss, and can be as good as IP at motivating effort.

Moreover, IP will not work as an incentive mechanism unless third parties can observe at least some aspects of value. A rightholder must be able to defend his right against potential infringers. He must be able to prove in court that his intellectual property meets the standard for protection, and that an alleged infringer is marketing a product that falls within the breadth of his claims. Aspects of the invention's value must therefore be observable ex post, although typically at the high cost of litigation and discovery.

The ex post observability requirement will typically impose less cost under an IP system than under a prize system. Under an IP system, the costs of discovery are incurred only if there is litigation. In contrast, for a prize, costs would have to be incurred for every invention in order for the sponsor to set a payment commensurate with the value.[2] Therefore, our distinction is not really between observability and nonobservability, but rather on whether the value is known to the sponsor without incurring cost. The most natural example is when the sponsor defines the value of the invention himself, as in military procurement.

Recently the World Health Organization and the World Bank have suggested prizes for developing vaccines that would not be developed or might not be widely enough distributed under a system of proprietary rights. The problems are great: how to assess whether a vaccine merits a prize; how to ensure that the prizes are not given prematurely before higher-quality vaccines are brought forward; how to ensure that the prizes are actually given, when it is easy to manufacture reasons to withhold them. Prizes can also be organized so that worthy projects need not be identified in advance, but administering the prize then becomes particularly burdensome. The problems are particularly acute where innovation is cumulative. See Kremer (2000) for a thoughtful and detailed analysis of how such a system might work.

Unlike IP, a procurement contract would typically not be offered to all comers. Instead there would be a negotiation phase in which the procurement officer tries to sort out which firm(s) are more efficient, and only offers the "prize" to those firms. A mechanism that allows such flexibility is more effective by definition than a prize offered to all comers. As for prizes, the sponsor must identify worthy projects. For traditional government procurement, such as for fighter jets, this is automatic. For medical research, the sponsor may solicit open-ended proposals, which entails administrative cost. In addition, the negotiation required for procurement might be politically infeasible as well as costly.

In the next subsections, we investigate optimal incentive mechanisms in specific research environments, with a view toward understanding how optimal mechanisms relate to IP, prizes, and simple reimbursements. We focus on environments in which no alternative mechanisms for protection (private or market) are available, and on single inventions that do not lead to future innovations. Following Scotchmer (1999b), we stylize the allocation problem as having three facets, which are intertwined. The first is the *decision problem*: should a project be undertaken? The second is the *delegation problem*: by which firms, or how many, and at what rates of investment? The third is the *funding problem*: Can the deadweight loss of monopoly pricing be avoided?

The Problem of Aggregating Information

To solve the decision, delegation, and funding problems jointly, all the information that is decentralized among firms may have to be aggregated. IP, prizes, and simple procurement mechanisms such as fixed-price contracts and auctions cannot aggregate information, and are therefore flawed at the outset.

To see this, consider a well-defined project, such as funding an AIDS vaccine or developing a supersonic transport. Suppose that there are two potential researchers, $i = 1, 2$, and that each researcher i has an efficiency parameter c_i for this project, interpreted as the cost of success. The product will have a common value v regardless of which firm develops it, and each firm has a signal v_i of this value. The underlying value will typically be determined by the extent of demand or anything else that affects monopoly profit and social welfare. Because each v_i is a noisy signal of an underlying common value, it is natural to suppose that the signals $\{v_1, v_2\}$ are correlated. It is less obvious whether the cost parameters $\{c_1, c_2\}$ would be correlated. We shall assume that they are independent draws from a known distribution.

To make an efficient investment decision, each firm would like to know the other firm's signal. For example, a firm with a low signal of value, $v_1 = L$, might invest if it knew the other firm had a high signal of value, $v_2 = H$, but not otherwise. But neither the value nor its best estimate is known ex ante to the other firm, since neither can observe the other's signal.

The importance of aggregating information is revealed in the following special case in which both the costs and the signals take on binary values: $c_i \in \{l, h\}$, $v_i \in \{L, H\}$. Suppose that the first-best, full-information rule for allocative efficiency is that the project should be undertaken unless (1) both firms have high costs, regardless of the signals of value or (2) both firms have low signals of value, regardless of costs. The project should be undertaken by a single firm if (3) at least one firm has low cost and at least one firm has a high signal of value, or (4) both firms have high cost and both have high signals of value.

Suppose $(c_1, v_1) = (l, L)$. Firm 1 should invest if $(c_2, v_2) = (h, H)$ but not if $(c_2, v_2) = (h, L)$. Without knowing firm 2's information, firm 1 could not make an efficient decision. Such could be the case under a patent system. Firm 1 may fail to invest because it is pessimistic about value ($v_1 = L$), and firm 2 may fail to invest because its costs are too high ($c_2 = h$). If the firms could share their information, firm 1 would invest based on firm 2's propitious information about the market. To some extent, the firms should be able to learn each other's private information by observing each other's investments. However, even if the firms know each other's costs, they might get stuck in an inefficient, but self-reinforcing, equilibrium where each invests because the other is investing, and each incorrectly thinks the other has a high signal of value (or vice versa) (Minehart and Scotchmer 1999). When the firms have different, unobservable costs, the difficulties of making inferences from investment behavior are compounded. A firm that invests could be doing so either because it has low cost or because it has very propitious private information about the market. The observing firm cannot distinguish between these two cases.

Neither IP nor prizes nor simple procurement mechanisms (e.g., auctions) can cope with the problem of aggregating information. Scotchmer (1999b) describes a procurement mechanism that bears little resemblance to auctions, prizes, or IP, but can achieve as good an outcome as when the signals of value are known, provided the firms' signals of value are correlated.[3] While the mechanism described will delegate efficiently, it may not be realistic given the constraints of government procurement. The mechanism might entail payments from firms to the government, or payments to firms that are not asked to invest. Such payments would be difficult to enforce.

The problems with the efficient procurement mechanism may explain the use of prizes, IP, and simple procurement mechanisms, but, under the conditions presented in this example, no one has studied their relative merits as second-best mechanisms. In order to identify the relative merits of the simple schemes and other more realistic mechanisms, we now consider the decision and delegation problems separately.

The Delegation Problem

We isolate the problem of optimal delegation by assuming that the sponsor already knows the optimal decision, namely, to invest. That is, the sponsor knows the value of the project and that it exceeds the cost of delivery, but it does not know which firm(s) is (are) more cost efficient. Optimal delegation has two components: choosing the most efficient firm or group of firms, and motivating the firm(s) to invest at efficient rates.

If the sponsor faced only a problem of selecting the more efficient firm(s), then the delegation problem would be easy to solve, e.g., by auctioning the right to invest. In contrast, IP and prizes could lead to inefficiency. If the market has room for only one firm, there is no reason to suppose that the lower-cost firm will be the entrant, especially when the relative efficiencies of the firms are not publicly observable.

But even an auction will not perform well when there is also a problem of inciting the right amount of effort, so that the invention is delivered in a timely manner. The appropriate rate of progress is key to the economics of R&D: How much additional cost should be tolerated in return for a higher rate of progress?

A firm's willingness to accelerate invention at higher total cost depends on the prize it will receive, conditional on delivering the product. Thus the size of the prize determines the rate of investment. However the optimal size of prize (and the optimal rate of investment) depend both on the researcher's "efficiency" and on his efficiency relative to other firms. For an inefficient firm, the optimal rate of investment may be zero if it is possible to delegate to a more efficient firm, but positive if the other firm is even less efficient. Thus, the problem is to tailor prizes both to the firms' individual efficiencies and to their relative efficiencies.

Gandal and Scotchmer (1993) study this problem, and show that the sponsor should offer a menu of options with both fixed fees and firm-specific prizes.[4] The menu serves two purposes: it gets the firms to reveal their relative efficiencies, and, once the contracts are awarded, it gets the firms to invest at the efficient rates. The difficulty is in the coordination: each firm's efficient rate depends on both firms' efficiency parameters. A simple patent or prize system, where the IP or prizes are not tailored to the firms' relative efficiency, will not ensure that only the most efficient firm(s) invest, or at the efficient rates. And a simple fixed-price contract may not create incentives to invest fast enough, even if the contract is auctioned to the more efficient firm.

The message here is that, even when the value of the prospective invention is known prior to the investments, optimal procurement requires a mixture of prizes and fixed payments, rather than a pure prize system, a patent system, or an auction. Simple mechanisms can be resurrected as best in very simple contexts. An auction performs well when the only issue is to choose the most efficient firm, but there is no issue of eliciting the right amount of effort. A simple prize performs well when there is a single firm qualified to undertake the research. If the prize is set equal to the social value, the firm will have the same objective function as society and will invest efficiently. Since the best simple mechanisms are different for different simple contexts, it is no surprise that complicated research environments with several firms call for mechanisms that combine instruments.

In the next section we focus on the optimal decision problem, assuming that the value of the innovation is unknown. In order to avoid the problem of optimal delegation, we also assume there is a single potential researcher.

The Decision Problem

We have just pointed out that if there is a single firm qualified for the research program, the optimal mechanism is a prize set equal to the social value. The firm's private incentives are then aligned with social incentives. However, to set such a prize, the sponsor must know the social value in advance or observe it ex post. Since IP automatically reflects the social value, at least to some extent, IP looks like an attractive alternative to a prize when the social value is unobservable. We now investigate whether this justification for IP holds up.

Kremer (1998) proposes a system to create a prize equal to the social value, even when the sponsor cannot observe it in advance. His proposal involves IP, but avoids deadweight loss by turning a patent into a prize. He proposes that the patent authority take possession of the patent, and auction it to the highest bidder, assuming that every firm can observe the value ex post. The rules of the auction are that with very small probability the patent will actually be sold to the highest bidder, and otherwise the invention will be put in the public domain. Firms will bid the true value, hence revealing it. The social value is estimated from the revealed private value, and the inventor receives a prize equal to the social value, paid out of general revenue. He will thus invest if the social value exceeds his cost, as is efficient.[5]

Another scheme to avoid deadweight loss is proposed by DeLaat (1996). To illustrate his idea in a very simple model, suppose that a potential R&D project is described by a pair (c, v), where c is the cost, which is observable to the sponsor, and v is the value, which is not. But if the cost c is observable to the sponsor, he can ask the researcher to report the prospective value v, and then give a fixed-price contract to reimburse the cost c if and only if the prospective value exceeds the cost. Since the researcher earns zero profit whatever he reports (he is only reimbursed the cost), he will report the value truthfully to the sponsor, who will make the efficient decision whether to invest. Thus, IP is unnecessary.

But this scheme only seems credible if (contrary to the premise) the value of the invention is observable ex post, or if the sponsor can verify that the researcher is investing exactly as he promised (as deLaat assumes explicitly).[6] If not, the researcher could use the contract money for other purposes and deliver a shoddy product; there is a disabling problem of moral hazard, which IP could overcome.

Nevertheless, we can conclude from the arguments of Kremer and deLaat that if either cost or value is truly observable to a sponsor, there may be a better mechanism than IP. Consistent with this view, Scotchmer (1999a) justified patents by assuming that the cost and value are both unobservable. A similar interpretation can be made for Cornelli and Schankerman (1999). The latter present a model where the value of an invention is endogenous to the firm's investment effort, which, in turn, depends on an unobservable efficiency parameter. In effect, neither cost nor value is observable to the sponsor. Thus it is hard to see how any mechanism short of IP could be effective. Since the value of the patent increases with the value of the invention, a patent system gives the firm at least some incentive to spend more resources to create a product of greater value. Cornelli and Schankerman show how this incentive can be increased by using a patent renewal system.

The patent renewal system is a menu of options (F, T), where F is a payment from the patentholder to the sponsor and T is a patent life.[7] The fee F increases with the patent life, and might start out negative (a subsidy). The patentee can then "buy" a longer patent life by paying renewal fees. The value of the patent automatically increases with the value of the invention, but increases more for higher-value inventions, since those are the ones that will be renewed in return for fees. Thus the incentive to develop higher-value products is compounded.

Scotchmer (1999a) derives the renewal system as a multidimensional screening mechanism for ideas, (c, v), where both are unobservable. Again, it is the higher-value ideas that will be renewed the longest, compounding their value. Thus the cost c that firms are willing to bear may go up faster than linearly with the value of the innovation, v.

As mentioned, the renewal system could start with subsidies, which are then reduced as firms pay fees in return for a longer patent life. Subsidies are advocated by Shavell and van Ypersle (1998) on grounds that they are a more efficient way to reward innovators than IP. Subsidizing low-value innovations allows the protection on high-value innovations to be shorter (thus reducing the deadweight loss), without jeopardizing incentives to innovate.

The problem with subsidies, of course, is that they may be exploited by opportunistic firms, which could collect the subsidy and either not invest or produce something worthless. To avoid this problem, subsidies, like their close kin, prizes, must be contingent on some aspect of the resulting invention, such as its value. Thus it seems reasonable to suppose that subsidy schemes will not be used if the invention's value or success cannot be verified ex post. But then we have a contradiction. If subsidies are possible, it must be because some aspect of value is observable ex post. If so, IP should not be used at all, since prizes (rewards, fixed-price contracts) dominate. IP and prizes can serve the same screening function, and can motivate firms to the same levels of effort, but prizes avoid the deadweight loss. Consistent with this caveat, renewal schemes seen in practice do not provide for subsidies. (See Calandrillo (1998) for a broader set of criticisms of subsidies.)

In conclusion, IP can be justified in two ways. First, it can be justified as a screening mechanism to encourage investment in high-value projects, which may also have high cost. Second, it can be justified as a means to increase the rate at which firms invest, either to increase value or to accelerate progress. Without a means to link prizes to social value, there is no alternative to achieve these results. These virtues of IP should be weighed against the aggregation problems described earlier when more than one firm is capable of the research.

Assuming that, in a second-best analysis, IP would prevail, we now ask how the right should be designed. We have already discussed the benefits of a renewal system. But how broad and long should protection be?

III. Optimal Design: The Case of a Single Innovation

Perhaps the most influential work on patent design was that of Nordhaus (1969), who explained why patents (or other IP) should have finite length. If the sole concern is to encourage innovation, then IP should last forever. And if the sole concern is to avoid deadweight loss that occurs through proprietary prices, then IP should not exist at all. A finite length of protection balances these two concerns. Longer protection would encourage more innovation, but only by prolonging the deadweight loss on inventions that would be made anyway.

Nordhaus's simple framework spawned a large literature on the design of IP with consideration of patent races, imitation by rivals, technology licensing, and how the design question changes when technology is cumulative. In this section we focus on the design question of breadth (also called scope), which occupied considerable journal space in the 1990s. In the next section we turn to sequential or cumulative research, where breadth plays a different role.

We begin with Gilbert and Shapiro (1990; GS) who introduced the notion of patent scope into the Nordhaus analysis. They define patent scope as the price p that the innovator is able to charge for the product that embodies the innovation. Thus a patent policy is (T, p), where T is the patent life. While such a definition is far removed from what a court might use, the analysis that arises from using it is still informative, as discussed below. Maximizing social surplus over all combinations (T, p) that yield enough revenue to cover the cost of research, GS find that optimal patent length is infinite, with the patent scope set at the level that just covers R&D investment.[8] That is, the optimal design is for the patent to be narrow and long.

Gallini (1992) reversed this design conclusion in a model where patent breadth determines the ease of entry into the protected market. She defined scope technologically, as the cost K that rivals must incur to imitate the invention without infringement. Thus a patent policy is a pair (T, K). The lower price that results from narrow scope arises from rivals' attempts to "invent around" the patent, rather than from some type of regulatory or antitrust action, as assumed by GS. In contrast to GS, the innovator's profit does not strictly increase with patent life, since a long patent life will encourage imitation (hence competition) before the patent expires. An increase in patent life provides incentives for wasteful imitation but not for productive innovation.

For a given imitation cost K, a sufficiently long patent will attract imitators, resulting in oligopoly pricing instead of monopoly pricing. Conversely, for a given patent life T, a sufficiently narrow scope will attract entrants. Patent life and scope are complementary in that both instruments must be increased or reduced to achieve most efficiently the required reimbursement to the innovator.

With imitation, the social cost of a patent may have two components: deadweight loss and the cost of imitation. The optimal patent policy minimizes these costs. Gallini shows that the optimal design is to avoid entry entirely by making the patent broad and short, in contrast to that proposed in GS. That is, the patent should be just long enough to generate the required revenue for the monopolist patentholder, and broad enough to prevent imitation.

However, this reversal depends on an assumption about licensing (or, rather, its absence). In the Gallini model, if the patent is too long or too narrow, the innovator is assumed to sit back passively and watch imitators erode her market share. Maurer and Scotchmer (1998; MS) point out that the duplicative waste could be avoided voluntarily through licensing rather than by adjusting patent policy, which can again reverse the optimal design. Whatever the market outcome without licensing, the innovator and potential entrants can achieve the same market outcome (price and number of entrants) through a licensing agreement with appropriate royalties and other fees. Since both the innovator and potential entrants can jointly save the imitation costs, they prefer licensing to imitation. The innovator can do even better by fine-tuning the number of entrants.

An important point of agreement among GS, Gallini, and MS is that a narrow patent reduces market price. However, their arguments differ. GS have in mind some sort of regulatory mechanism; Gallini argues that the price reduction will occur through duplicative entry; and MS argue that the price reduction will occur through licensing to prevent duplication. In addition, the analyses of social cost differ, leading to different prescriptions about optimal length and breadth. Since GS do not recognize imitation costs, they simply ask whether the deadweight loss of monopoly pricing is smaller with a long patent and low price, or with a short patent and high price. Gallini argues that if the social cost includes the cost of imitation, the optimal policy should be aimed at avoiding it. MS argue that the imitation costs will not be borne in practice if licensing is available, so that the GS type of analysis is restored.

It is worthwhile expanding on why licensing will lower the market price, by considering what would happen if there were a single potential entrant. The latter situation was analyzed by Gallini (1984), who first pointed out that licensing can prevent entry. With a single potential entrant (or a fixed number), the optimal licensing strategy is to sustain the profit-maximizing (monopoly) price with high royalties, and to share the revenues by using other fees. The licensor has an incentive to keep the market price high regardless of the cost of imitation. In contrast, in the argument above, the licensor is worried about imitation by nonlicensees as well as by licensees; there is always an unlicensed potential entrant. The patentholder commits to a low market price precisely to reduce the attractiveness of entry by nonlicensees, who can be numerous and unidentifiable ex ante. This point stresses the significance of potential entry to the welfare analysis of licensing and, therefore, to the optimal design of IP.

The foregoing discussion shows that private contracting can dramatically alter the optimal design of patents, and that public and private instruments may be complementary in reducing social costs. Patent scope governs the market price in the proprietary market, and licensing prevents wasteful imitation. In this environment where goods are homogeneous, licensing determines the design of patent policy: If licensing is available, a case can be made for narrow and long patents; if licensing is not available, the analysis points to patents that are broad and short.

Licensing may not occur for a variety of reasons, in which case we need a more thorough investigation of the relative merits of the GS and the Gallini arguments, in broader economic environments than they address. Such an analysis has been provided by Denicolò (1996). He explains that narrow (and long) or broad (and short) patents depend on the concavity or convexity, respectively, of the relationship between social welfare and postinnovation profit. Situations in which relatively short broad patents are optimal include costly imitation; Cournot duopoly with constant marginal costs; and horizontally differentiated firms and linear transportation costs, as in Klemperer (1990).

We now turn to cumulative innovation in which subsequent research activity is directed toward the development of improvements or applications of a previous innovation.

IV. Optimal Design: The Case of Cumulative Innovation

In the above discussion, IP is designed for isolated innovations that may be imitated. In reality, research is cumulative. Innovations build upon each other, and subsequent research activity is directed toward improvements or applications of previous discoveries. This fact changes the problem of patent design in interesting and complex ways.

The first and most fundamental complexity, articulated by Scotchmer (1991), is that early innovators lay a foundation for later innovations. The later innovations could not be made without the earlier ones. So that the first innovator has enough incentive to invest, she should be given some claim on profit of the later innovations; otherwise, early innovators could be underrewarded for the social value they create. This is particularly evident in the case of a research tool for which all the social value resides in the innovations it facilitates. If the innovator could not profit from the later products, she would have no incentive to create the tool. The incentive problems are particularly vexed in the case of *creative destruction*, discussed by Schumpeter (1943): an innovator's descendants can actually become the instruments of his destruction.

The Shumpeterian perspective highlights an important problem that arises in the cumulative context: that of dividing the profit between innovators in a way that respects their costs. If, for example, only one pot of money is available for distribution between two innovators and most is allocated to the first firm, the second inventor 's incentive for research is reduced, and vice versa. Green and Scotchmer (1995) argue that because of the difficulties in dividing profit, patent lives will have to be longer than if the whole sequence of innovations occurred in a single firm. Ex ante licensing – licensing before investments are made – is a way of mimicking the latter outcome. As in the case of a single invention, the availability of private contracting influences the optimal patent scope when innovation is cumulative (see below).

Cumulativeness changes the design instruments that are relevant to the length of protection. The statutory life can be irrelevant when a non-infringing substitute, such as an improvement, can displace a protected product. What matters is the effective life, that is, the time until the noninfringing substitute appears (Scotchmer 1991; O'Donoghue, Scotchmer, and Thisse 1998 (OST)). The effective life is determined by patent *scope* or *leading breadth*, which is interpreted as the minimum quality improvement that avoids infringement. As in the case of costly imitation discussed above, the effectiveness of patent life as an instrument for R&D may be limited when subsequent innovation can undermine profitability.

Finally, cumulativeness makes a third instrument – the minimum standard for protection, or minimum inventive step – relevant to the optimal design of IP. For copyrighted works the standard for protection is low (as is the breadth of protection), while for patents, the patentability standard (or novelty requirement) can be quite stringent. In our discussion of isolated inventions above, we assumed that the invention was protectable, since there would be no incentives to innovate if there were no IP or other incentive instruments. But in the cumulative context, patentability on second-generation inventions is less essential, since an innovation can be protected by an exclusive license on a previous patent it infringes, rather than by its own patent. Leading breadth and the standard for patentability together determine the level of "forward protection" each innovation has.

Several arguments favoring both weak and strict standards for IP protection have been advanced. Scotchmer and Green (1990) argue with caution for a weak standard (a weak "novelty requirement"), so that firms are encouraged to disclose every small bit of progress. While these disclosures could speed up invention by giving a technological boost to competitors, Scotchmer and Green warn that the weak novelty requirement could also encourage firms to choose trade secrecy over patents. In contrast, a tightening of the standards for patentability can encourage firms to be more ambitious in the improvements they attempt to develop (O'Donoghue 1998) or can direct their investments toward more socially useful inventions (Eswaran and Gallini 1996). Even when the standard for protection does not reorient research efforts, it can affect the division of profit among sequential researchers. Scotchmer (1996) argues that the strictest novelty requirement (no protection) on second-generation products would tilt the joint profit of a sequence of innovations in favor of earlier innovators without jeopardizing second-generation advances. A second-generation product can be protected by an exclusive license on the infringed patent of the earlier generation. Denicolò (2000a, b) makes a case for a patent policy with a weak patentability standard and narrow leading breadth. In a model in which firms race for the first and second-generation patents, he shows that tilting profits in favor of earlier innovators might only encourage a socially wasteful patent race at the stage of basic research and underinvestment in the second stage.

Although the complexities of cumulativeness seem to defy clear, unqualified design implications, one lesson is clear: The optimal design of IP depends importantly on the ease with which rights holders can contract around conflicts in rights. Contracting is especially relevant to the question of breadth, which determines the likelihood that a follow-on innovation will infringe a prior patent.

A danger of IP that has been debated from its inception to the present (see Machlup and Penrose 1950) is that IP can stifle innovation and slow progress. Merges and Nelson (1990) link this danger to breadth, using examples from the aircraft, radio, and pharmaceutical industries to argue for narrow patents. An earlier example concerned steam engines. James Watt refused to license his patents for improvement, with the result that there was a flood of pent-up invention when his patents expired in 1800 (Derry and Williams 1993, p. 324).

In contrast, Kitch (1977) argues that broad patents are socially beneficial precisely *because* they stimulate further developments. Scotchmer (1991) and Green and Scotchmer (1995) take the same point of view, but focus on how ex ante contracting affects division of profit. With ex ante contracting, the role of breadth is not to determine whether subsequent products are made (they will be made if they add to joint profit), but rather to determine how the profit is divided. This theme is also carried forward in later papers, e.g., Merges (1998, 1999), Scotchmer (1996), Lemley (1997) (who compares how copyright and patent doctrines respectively treat the possibility of blocking), O'Donoghue, Scotchmer, and Thisse (1998), and Schankerman and Scotchmer (2001). Matutes, Regibeau, and Rockett (1996) and Chang (1995) argue for broad patents even without assuming that ex ante contracts can be made.

To some extent, broad patents are also supported by the arguments of O'Donoghue, Scotchmer, and Thisse (1998), who study breadth in a model with an infinite sequence of improved products (quality ladder). If patents are relatively narrow, the effective life of each patent ends when a noninfringing improvement arrives, and is thus endogenous. But if the patent is broad, then the statutory life is also the effective life: Every subsequent innovation on the quality ladder infringes during the statutory life and must be marketed under license. To achieve the same rate of progress under both regimes, the effective patent life with a narrow patent must be longer than the (effective) statutory life with a broad patent. Broad, short patents are more efficient at rewarding innovators along the quality ladder, because less of the total profit in the system accrues to high-value innovations that would be made in any case, and more goes to the innovators who need additional incentives.

Thus, with some caution, we can extract from the literature a case for broad (and short) patents. Broad patents can serve the public interest by preventing duplication of R&D costs, facilitating the development of second-generation products, and protecting early innovators who lay a foundation for later innovators. However, these benefits disappear if licensing fails. Heller and Eisenberg (1998) argue that licensing will likely fail when researchers must negotiate multiple licenses, as now occurs in the biomedical industry. Mazzoleni and Nelson (1998) caution that these transaction costs may limit the use of contracts for coordinating innovations that follow from a broad patent.

Another problem with licensing is that it can lessen competition both in innovation markets[9] and in product markets. It thus raises antitrust issues, even in the simpler context where there is no cumulative aspect. One of the difficult issues is determining whether an ex ante merger of research activities through licensing is efficient or inefficient from a social perspective. On the efficiency side, ex ante licensing can enable firms to avoid duplicated costs and to delegate efficiently, much as discussed in section II. But on the inefficiency side, ex ante licensing can retard progress, e.g., by nullifying the acceleration that would otherwise come from a patent race. See Gilbert and Sunshine (1995) for a discussion of these issues.[10]

The cumulative context raises another issue. Above we focused on the salutary effects of licensing, namely that ex ante licensing can ensure investment in infringing follow-on products that would add to joint profit. Turning this argument on its head, licensing can stifle noninfringing follow-on products that would *detract* from joint profit. Gallini and Winter (1985) analyze a situation where a potential competitor is licensed ex ante in order to dissuade him from investing in a noninfringing cost reduction that would have lowered prices in the market. Such licensing clearly reduces product market competition relative to what the Congress apparently intended in designing patent law. If such licensing occurred ex post to prevent production of the cost-reducing innovation after it had been developed, it would presumably be an antitrust violation. Chang (1995) analyzes precisely that type of ex post collusion and advocates a strict antitrust rule against collusion. For a discussion of how principles of competition policy might be formulated to distinguish ex ante licensing that is procompetitive from that which is anticompetitive, see Scotchmer (1998).

Besen and Maskin (2000) argue that if firms do not license in a way that takes full advantage of their IP, e.g., because of antitrust restrictions, then licensing may reduce industry profits below those available without licensing, and the broad patents that support such licensing are counterproductive. In this sense, Besen and Maskin's paper is consistent with the above observation that impediments to contracting may strengthen the case for narrow patents.

In light of these qualifications, what conclusions can we make for patent design in the cumulative context? One interpretation is that, when research is cumulative, relatively broad patents may be efficient if ex ante contracting is available. However we prefer to be cautious; the jury is still out.

What is conclusive is the importance of private contracting. Whether property rights are helpful or counterproductive in encouraging innovation depends on the ease with which innovators can enter into agreements for rearranging and exercising those rights, as constrained by the rules of antitrust law.

V. Conclusions

In the past two decades, academic interest in the economics and law of intellectual property has exploded. The renewed interest has been fueled by controversies surrounding new technologies, by international agreements, and by changes in the nature of protection, e.g., see Mazzoleni and Nelson (1998). It is generally thought that IP rights have been strengthened, but there is also evidence that some forms of IP, in particular, patents, have previously been ineffective (Cohen et al. 2000). Contrary to the apparent intent, strengthening of IP is thought by some commentators to impede research rather than to promote it (Heller and Eisenberg 1998). In this environment, economists have had much to say about both the optimal design of IP and the advisability of substituting other incentive mechanisms.

Although it comes as no surprise that a property system has defects, we hope we have illuminated some offsetting virtues, and some circumstances where other mechanisms, such as prizes, fixed-price contracts, and auctions can dominate. Our main conclusions on the effectiveness of intellectual property are that:

1. IP is probably the best mechanism for screening projects when value and cost are not observable by the sponsor, since the private value of IP reflects the social value, and firms automatically compare some measure of value with the cost of innovation. In addition, IP encourages firms to accelerate progress, since the reward is conditional on success. Prizes could serve the same purposes if the size of the prize could be linked to the social value but without the deadweight loss of monopoly pricing.
2. Neither IP nor prizes can aggregate the information that is decentralized among firms, and neither will be completely effective at delegating research effort efficiently. A procurement system that restricts prizes to certain firms, or differentiates prizes according to firms' relative efficiencies, can improve on a simple prize system or patent system, but then there must be an ex ante negotiation to select the favored firms.

For circumstances where IP is justified, we asked how the property right should be designed. Every IP regime has provisions on length, breadth, and the standard for protection. The economics literature on design of IP concerns the appropriate choice of these provisions. The optimal length, breadth, and standard for protection depend on the economic environment, e.g., the shape of the demand curve, the rate at which improvements to existing technologies are developed, or the relative costs of sequential innovators.

How much flexibility is there in designing IP rights differently for different economic environments? In fact, there is a lot of flexibility. Different IP regimes are targeted at different subject matter, and the subject matter is an important defining aspect of the IP regime. Copyright has traditionally been targeted at literature, other printed matter, and art. Patents have traditionally been targeted at manufactured items. The subject matters of *sui generis* laws typically have been very specific, e.g., the Plant Patent Act, the Plant Variety Protection Act, the Semiconductor Chip Protection Act, and the proposed database legislation.

The IP regimes that cover different subject matter are noticeably varied in the three important features: length, breadth, and standard for protection. On the matter of length, copyrights last essentially forever, patents last 20 years, and chip protection lasts 10 years. On the matter of breadth, copyright protection is restrained by fair use exemptions and by the fact that the underlying "ideas" are not protected; patents have the doctrine of equivalents; and copying of chips is allowed for some uses but not others. We thus believe that it is incorrect to criticize the economic design arguments on grounds that, in IP, "one size fits all." While we do not think it would be appropriate to define new IP regimes for every small category of technology, we wish to emphasize that the Congress can exercise as much flexibility as it wishes, and that courts also have some flexibility.

Each IP regime should cover subject matter with similar needs for protection, especially if heterogeneous needs cannot be remedied by courts. Many controversies arise because of heterogeneity within IP regimes. For example, business methods probably do not need the strong protection provided by the Patent Act, even though such protection is appropriate for other patentable subject matter. A new regime could have been created for business methods, but protection under the Patent Act could alternatively be weakened through the courts' interpretation of novelty and nonobviousness.

Finally, there are the design recommendations themselves. We have not been specific in this review about the exact ways in which length, breadth, and standards for protection should reflect the economic environments, and refer the reader to the underlying papers for more detail. Instead, we have emphasized a message of a different sort: the optimal design of the property right should depend on whether firms contract with others for the use of their protected innovations. With fluid contracting, policies that otherwise would be inefficient may be optimal. For example, licensing can avoid wasteful imitation, making an otherwise inefficient narrow patent optimal. In the cumulative context, there is a danger that broad patents will inhibit future innovators from making product improvements. But with contracting, the patentholder can profit from, instead of being threatened by, new improved products, and will ensure that they arise even if infringing. The most striking message of the literature is that IP and private instruments may be complementary in reducing social costs from an overreaching or insufficient protection regime.

However, contracting also has the potential to undermine competition in ways that were not anticipated or approved by the Congress when designing IP. Contracting that we have not covered includes cross-licensing and patent pools. We have also not discussed joint ventures and other alliances for avoiding litigation, duplicated efforts, and holdups. A recurring theme, especially evident in these contexts, is that despite the efficiencies that contracting can ensure, contracting may also facilitate anticompetitive behavior. See Hall and Ziedonis (2001), Shapiro (2000), Denicolò (2000a,b). To understand whether the property system is too strong, too weak, or necessary at all requires us to understand the incentives for contracting, and its potential anticompetitive consequences.

Notes

1 For example, in the environment discussed by Wright (1983), none of the three mechanisms is optimal. The first best can be achieved with a mechanism similar to the one mentioned in note 3 below.
2 Prizes might also require enforcement. John Harrison's longitude prize was delayed for decades while the prize committee attempted to prove that astronomical solutions were superior to his clock. Harrison eventually sought redress in Parliament, and was partially rewarded.
3 She suggests a two-part procedure. The sponsor first asks the firms to reveal their information on value and then, if warranted, employs the best procurement mechanism to delegate to the least-cost firm(s). Following Cremer and McLean (1988), it is costless to get the firms to reveal their correlated information on value. They are asked to report their signals of value, and then rewarded if they agree and punished if they disagree. Due to the correlation, an equilibrium is to report truthfully, and the payments can be chosen so that each firm makes zero expected profit.
4 A related problem is studied by Bhattacharya et al. (1998). Instead of assuming that firms have different efficiency parameters, they assume that firms have different knowledge about the cost of achieving an innovation. If the knowledge is revealed, then all firms have the same cost. Their mechanisms also use payments conditional on delivery (prizes).
5 We caution, however, that the Kremer scheme is efficient only if there is a single researcher. A prize equal to the social value could easily attract other firms to a race in which the firms overinvest (Loury 1979). Not only is there a problem of

overinvesting, but inefficient firms as well as efficient firms may invest. This is the problem avoided by the more complex procurement mechanism discussed above, where prizes are tailored to the firms' relative efficiency in order to make sure that the investment effort is undertaken by the more efficient ones.

6 In deLaat's model, the sponsor chooses the "size of the invention," which is observable, given the firm's report of the market size (value), which is unobservable to the sponsor. DeLaat assumes that the sponsor can verify which invention is made, but not the market conditions (e.g., demand) for the invention.

7 For recent empirical investigations of how firms exercise their option to renew, and implications for the values of innovations, see Lanjouw (1997) and Schankerman (1998).

8 The intuition for this result can be found in the familiar economic principle that underlies Ramsey pricing. Ramsey pricing solves the problem of maximizing consumer surplus in multiple markets subject to the constraint that revenues cover cost. The solution is to set prices below monopoly prices so that the markup of price in each market is inversely proportional to the elasticity of demand in each market. In the patent problem, the different time periods are parallel to different markets, and since the demands are assumed to be constant over time, the markup of price over cost in each period is identical.

9 See the U.S. Department of Justice-Federal Trade Commission Antitrust Guidelines for the Licensing of Intellectual Property (1995) for a discussion of innovation markets.

10 One of the thorny questions that arise is whether competition policy should view licensing practices more leniently than otherwise if incentives to innovate are at stake. See Gallini and Trebilcock (1998) for a discussion of this issue.

References

Anton, J., and D. Yao. 1994. "Expropriation and Inventions-Appropriable Rents in the Absence of Property Rights." *American Economic Review* 84(1): 191–209.

Arrow, K. J. 1962. "Economic Welfare and the Allocation of Resources for Invention," in Universities-National Bureau of Economic Research Conference. Series, *The Rate and Direction of Economic Activities: Economic and Social Factors*. Princeton: Princeton University Press.

Besen, James, and Eric Maskin. 2000, January. "Sequential Innovation, Patents and Imitation." Working Paper no. 00–01. MIT.

Battacharya, S., C. D'Aspremont, and L.-A. Gerard-Varet. 1998. "Knowledge as a Public Good: Efficient Sharing and Incentives for Development Effort." *Journal of Mathematical Economics* 30: 389–404.

Calandrillo, Steve. 1998. "An Economic Analysis of Intellectual Property Rights: Justifications and Problems of Exclusive Rights, Incentives to Generate Information, and the Alternative of a Government-Run Reward System." *Fordham Intellectual Property Media and Entertainment Law Journal* 9: 301–348.

Chang, H. 1995. "Patent Scope, Antitrust Policy, and Cumulative Innovation." *RAND Journal of Economics* 26: 34–57.

Cohen, Wesley M., Richard R. Nelson and John P. Walsh (2000), "Protecting their Intellectual Assets: Appropriability Conditions and Why U.S. Manufacturing Firms Patent (or Not)," National Bureau of Economic Research Working Paper 7552.

Cornelli, F., and Mark S. Schankerman. 1999. "Patent Renewals and R&D Incentives." *RAND Journal of Economics* 30(2).

Cremer, J., and R. P. McLean. 1988. "Full Extraction of the Surplus in Bayesian and Dominant Strategy Auctions." *Econometrica* 56(6): 1247–57.

De Laat, Eric A. A. 1996. "Patents or Prizes: Monopolistic R&D and Asymmetric Information." *International Journal of Industrial Organization* 15(3): 369–90.

Denicolò, V. 1996. "Patent Races and Optimal Patent Breadth and Length." *Journal of Industrial Economics* 44: 249–265.

Denicolò, V. 2000a. "Two Stage Patent Races and Patent Policy." *RAND Journal of Economics* 31: 488–501.

Denicolò, V. 2000b. "Combination of Competing Patents and Antitrust Policy." Working paper. Department of Economics, University of Bologna.

Derry, T. K., and Williams, Trevor I. 1993. *A Short History of Technology: From Earliest Times to A.D. 1900.* Mineola, NY: Dover.

Eswaran, M. and N. Gallini. 1996. "Patent Policy and the Direction of Technological Change," *RAND Journal of Economics* 27(4): 722–746.

Farrell, J. 1995. "Arguments for Weaker Intellectual Property Protection in Network Industries." In Brian Kahin ed., *Standards Policy for Information Infrastructure.* 368–377. Cambridge, MA: MIT Press.

Gallini N. T. 1984. "Deterrence by Market Sharing: A Strategic Incentive for Licensing." *American Economic Review* 74: 931–41.

Gallini, N. T. 1992. "Patent Length and Breadth with Costly Imitation." *RAND Journal of Economics* 44: 52–63.

Gallini, N., and M. Trebilcock. 1998. "Intellectual Property Rights and Competition Policy – A Framework for the Analysis of Economic and Legal Issues." In R. Anderson and N. Gallini, eds., *Competition Policy and Intellectual Property Rights in the Knowledge-Based Economy.* Industry Canada Research Series, University of Calgary Press: 17–64.

Gallini, N. T., and R. Winter. 1985. "Licensing in the Theory of Innovation." *RAND Journal of Economics* 16: 237–52.

Gandal, N., and S. Scotchmer. 1993. "Coordinating Research through Research Joint Ventures." *Journal of Public Economics,* 51: 173–93.

Gilbert, R., and C. Shapiro. 1990. "Optimal Patent Length and Breadth." *RAND Journal of Economics* 21: 106–12.

Gilbert, R., and G. C. Sunshine. 1995. "Incorporating Dynamic Efficiency Concerns in Merger Analysis: The Use of Innovation Markets." *Antitrust Law Journal* 63: 569–602.

Green, Jerry, and Suzanne Scotchmer. 1995. "On the Division of Profit in Sequential Innovation." *RAND Journal of Economics* 26: 20–33.

Hall, B. H. and R. Ham Ziedonis. 2001. "The Patent Paradox Revisited: An Empirical Study of Patenting in the U.S. Semiconductor Industry, 1979–1995," *RAND Journal of Economics* 32(1): 101–128.

Heller, Michael A., and R. S. Eisenberg. 1998. "Can Patents Deter Innovation? The Anticommons in Biomedical Research." *Science* 280: 698–701.

Kitch, E. W. 1977. "The Nature and Function of the Patent System." *Journal of Law and Economics* 20: 265–90.

Klemperer, P. 1990. "How Broad Should the Scope of Patent Protection Be?" *RAND Journal of Economics* 21: 113–30.

Kremer, Michael. 1989. "Patent Buyouts: A Mechanism for Encouraging Innovation." *Quarterly Journal of Economics* 113: 1137–67.

Kremer, Michael. 2000. "Creating Markets for New Vaccines." Conference Paper, Innovation Policy and the Economy. Cambridge, MA: National Bureau of Economic Research.

Laffont, J.-J. and J. Tirole. 1986. "Using Cost Observation to Regulate Firms." *Journal of Political Economy* 94: 614–41.

Laffont, J.-J. and J. Tirole. 1987. "Auctioning Incentive Contracts." *Journal of Political Economy* 95: 921–937.

Lanjouw, J. 1998. "Patent Protection in the Shadow of Litigation: Simulation Estimations of Patent Value." *Review of Economic Studies*. Vol. 65, 671–710

Lemley, M. A. 1997. "The Economics of Improvement in Intellectual Property." *Texas Law Review* 75: 989.

Loury, G. C. 1979. "Market Structure and Innovation." *Quarterly Journal of Economics* 93:395–410.

Machlup, Fritz, and Edith Penrose. 1950. "The Patent Controversy in the Nineteenth Century." *Journal of Economic History* 10(1): 2.

Matutes, C., P. Regibeau, and K. E. Rockett. 1996. "Optimal Patent Protection and the Diffusion of Innovation." *RAND Journal of Economics* 27: 60–83.

Maurer, S. 1999. "Raw Knowledge: Protecting Technical Databases for Science & Industry." Report commissioned by the National Academy of Sciences. www.nap.edu/html/proceedings_sci_tech/appC.html

Maurer, S. M., and S. Scotchmer. 1998. "The Independent Invention Defense in Intellectual Property." John M. Olin Working Paper no. 98–11. Boalt School of Law, University of California, Berkeley.

Maurer, S. M., and S. Scotchmer. 1999. "Database Protection: Is it Broken and Should We Fix it?" *Science* 284: 1129–1130.

Mazzoleni, Roberto, and Richard R. Nelson. 1998. "The Benefits and Costs of Strong Patent Protection: A Contribution to the Current Debate." *Research Policy* 27: 273–84.

Merges, R. P. 1998. "Antitrust Review of Patent Acquisitions: Property Rights, Firm Boundaries, and Organization." In Robert D. Anderson and Nancy T. Gallini, eds., *Competition Policy and Intellectual Property Rights in the Knowledge-Based Economy*. Calgary: University of Calgary Press.

Merges, R. P. 1999. "*Intellectual Property Rights, Input Markets and the Value of Intangible Assets.*" Working Paper. Berkeley: University of California.

Merges, R. P., and R. R. Nelson. 1990. "On the Complex Economics of Patent Scope." *Columbia Law Review* 90(4): 839–916.

Minehart, D., and S. Scotchmer. 1999. "*Ex post* Regret and the Decentralized Sharing of Information." *Games and Economic Behavior* 27(1): 114–131.

National Research Council. 2000. *The Digital Dilemma: Intellectual Property in the Information Age Committee on Intellectual Property Rights and the Emerging Information Infrastructure, Computer Science and Telecommunications Board*. Washington DC: National Academy Press.

National Science Foundation. 2000. *Science and Engineering Indicators 2000*. www.nsf.govIsbeIsrsIseind00Iframes.htm

Nordhaus, W. 1969. *Invention, Growth and Welfare: A Theoretical Treatment of Technological Change*. Cambridge, MA: MIT Press.

O'Donoghue, T. 1998. "A Patentability Requirement for Sequential Innovation." *RAND Journal of Economics* 29: 654–67.

O'Donoghue, T., S. Scotchmer, and J. F. Thisse. 1998. "Patent Breadth, Patent Length and the Pace of Technological Progress." *Journal of Economics and Management Strategy* 7: 1–32.

Reynolds, T. 1983. *Stronger than a Hundred Men: A History of the Vertical Water Wheel*. Baltimore: Johns Hopkins Press.

Schankerman, M. 1998. "How Valuable is Patent Protection? Estimates by Technology Field." *RAND Journal of Economics* 29: 77–107.

Schankerman, M., and S. Scotchmer. 2001. "Damages and Injunctions in Protecting Intellectual Property." *RAND Journal of Economics* 32: 199–220.

Schumpeter, J. 1943. *Capitalism, Socialism and Democracy* London: Unwin University Books.

Scotchmer, S. 1991. "Standing on the Shoulders of Giants: Cumulative Research and the Patent Law." Symposium on Intellectual Property Law. *Journal of Economic Perspectives*, 5(1): 29–41.

Scotchmer, S. 1996. "Protecting Early Innovators: Should Second-Generation Products Be Patentable?" *RAND Journal of Economics* 27: 322–31.

Scotchmer, S. 1998. "R&D Joint Ventures and other Cooperative Arrangements." In *Competition Policy and Intellectual Property Rights in the Knowledge-Based Economy*, R. Anderson and N. Gallini, eds. Industry Canada Research Series. University of Calgary Press: 203–22.

Scotchmer, S. 1999a. "On the Optimality of the Patent Renewal System." *RAND Journal of Economics* 30, 181–196.

Scotchmer, S. 1999b. "*Delegating Effort in a Common Value Project.*" IBER Working Paper no. E99–266. Berkeley: University of California.

Scotchmer, S., and J. Green 1990. "Novelty and Disclosure in Patent Law." *RAND Journal of Economics* 21:131–46.

Shapiro, C. 2000. "Navigating the Patent Thicket: Cross Licenses, Patent Pools, and Standard-Setting." Working Paper. Berkeley: University of California Competition Policy Center. Working Paper No. CPC00–11. Now published in *Innovation Policy and the Economy*, Vol. 1, MIT Press, 2001. Adam B. Jaffe, Josh Lerner, and Scott Stern, eds.

Shavell, S., and T. van Ypserle 1998. "*Rewards versus Intellectual Property Rights.*" Olin Discussion Paper no. 246. Harvard University.

Sobel, D. 1995. *Longitude: The True Story of a Lone Genius Who Solved the Greatest Scientific Problem of His Time.* New York: Walker.

U.S. Department of Justice and Federal Trade Commission. 1995. *U.S. Department of Justice-Federal Trade Commission Antitrust Guidelines for The Licensing of Intellectual Property.*

Wright, B. 1983. "The Economics of Invention Incentives: Patents, Prizes and Research Contracts." *American Economic Review*, 73, 691–70.

Afterword: Extending the Paradigm to Open Source

Neil Gandal and Pierre Regibeau

Suzanne's deepest contribution to intellectual property (IP) theory was undoubtedly her analysis of sequential innovation (Scotchmer, 1991, 1996, 2010; Green and Scotchmer, 1995). It is no exaggeration to say that her insights into the cumulative aspects of innovation rejuvenated the entire field. At the same time, Suzanne's work was always characterized by great rigor and thoroughness of thought. While her work frequently focused on patents, she knew that any advantages or disadvantages were relative and had to be compared against possible alternative incentives like prizes or contract research. (See Gallini and Scotchmer, 2002 [this volume]; Maurer and Scotchmer, 2004.) The problem, as she emphasized in *Innovation and Incentives*' first chapter, is that these alternative mechanisms are surprisingly few in number. Small wonder, then, that she would be fascinated when open source methods of organizing software R&D promised to expand the toolbox.

Open source first became popular during the dot.com boom of the Nineties and is still widely used today. The basic idea is that source code is licensed, i.e., made available free of charge to all interested parties; furthermore, users have the right to modify and extend programs. Some open source collaborations also use so-called GPL licenses which require any further development that uses the project's source code to itself be publicly available. But open source presents a puzzle. From the point of view of traditional IP theory, it is hard to see why innovators would ever voluntarily give up the right to patent their innovations. Given her own work, Suzanne would also have taken a particular interest in asking how efficiently open source allocates reward across sequential innovations.

Economists spent much of the early 2000s exploring the incentives problem. The earliest insights focused on individuals, stressing that volunteers could receive material benefits for joining open source collaborations. This might include, for example, signaling expertise that could lead to enhanced employment opportunities (e.g., Lerner and Tirole, 2002). This has led to a large literature on the motivation of programmers and the types of licensing employed in open source projects. (For a selective survey see Fershtman and Gandal, 2011a.) Later, as commercial firms became more involved in open source projects, economists realized that individual incentives were only a partial explanation. This led to explanations in which open source provided benefits that could not be achieved using traditional IP models of innovation, most notably since public domain code encouraged users to find and solve problems (bugs) quickly. This, however, begged the question of why users would help manufacturers debug their products in the first place. That seemed to send the inquiry back to individual incentives. Then too, why would manufacturers agree to free debugging if the price was a total loss of protection against imitation?

Maurer and Scotchmer (2006b) were among the first to examine this issue. Many proprietary firms, it turns out, use a mixed-source business model in which some products are distributed under traditional licenses while others are distributed as open source. For example, West and Gallagher (2006) point out that open source development is equivalent to "pooled" R&D, which implies cost savings. In the same spirit, firms share code to test software, fix bugs, and to make improvements (see Rossi and Bonaccorsi, 2005). Finally, there may be spillovers in R&D, which arise from the sharing of code. Fershtman and Gandal (2011b) find empirical support for the existence of such knowledge spillovers in SourceForge data.

It was practically inevitable that Suzanne would extend these ideas to sequential innovation. Scotchmer (2010) uses a typically simple and elegant model to show that open source development can be privately preferable to traditional IP. Unlike the rest of her sequential innovation papers, she argued that economic actors might not know their place in the innovation order, i.e., that it is often unclear who will be the first innovator. This was yet another variant on her characteristic "Ideas Model" approach of asking what happens when technical progress depends on contributions from multiple independent contributors. (See Erkal, Maurer, and Mine-hart, this volume.)

The results were surprising. Following Suzanne's earlier work on sequential innovation, one would have expected the first innovator to choose proprietary innovation over an open source license in order to capture surplus from the second innovation. However, this strategy would not be optimal for the industry as a whole. In Suzanne's model, this is because the costs of the second innovators are not observable before the second innovation is realized. This means that claiming IP in the first innovation can sometimes make R&D into the second invention unprofit-able. Total profits would therefore be higher if the first innovation used GPL.

So far, the model is similar to Polansky (2007) who argues that the first innovator has an incentive to commit to the GPL in order to avoid *ex post* hold-up that reduces the incentives for follow-on innovation. However, this implied that the decision to adopt GPL depended entirely on the first mover's private interest in escaping hold-up. The crucial difference in Suzanne's model was that firms could not know *a priori* whether they were first or second movers. This meant that the benefits of the GPL influence both agents. The result is that the GPL is always chosen in Suzanne's model but only sometimes in Polansky's. In fact, the GPL is adopted even where the first mover would prefer a proprietary regime. So, in a sense, firms' ignorance about the order of sequential innovation makes the innovation process more efficient than it would be otherwise. This is, of course, equivalent to saying that innovation occurs across multiple inde-pendent actors, i.e., that the world fits the Ideas Model paradigm.

These differences between Scotchmer (2010b) and Polansky (2007) have testable implications that have yet to be investigated. In particular, we would expect the GPL to be more prevalent in fast-moving industries with many participants where Suzanne's "veil of ignorance" assumption is most likely to be valid. Empirical studies of this issue will shed important light on how often the Ideas Model applies and, indeed, whether the GPL is desirable in the first place. In closing, it is important to note Suzanne was never convinced that GPL improved welfare compared to, say, giving users unrestricted access to code (Maurer and Scotchmer, 2006b, at pp. 302–304). Perhaps it will be possible to address this point as well empirically.

CHAPTER 17

Suzanne Scotchmer, "Standing on the Shoulders of Giants: Cumulative Research and the Patent Law" (1991)
and
Jerry Green and Suzanne Scotchmer, "On the Division of Profit in Sequential Innovation" (1995)

INTRODUCTION MICHAEL L. KATZ AND
CARL SHAPIRO

This section introduces two of Suzanne's papers on the subject of cumulative innovation, "Standing on the Shoulders of Giants: Cumulative Research and the Patent Law" (1991) and "On the Division of Profit Between Sequential Innovators" (1995), the latter written jointly with Jerry Green. During this same time frame, she also published two closely related papers not reprinted here: "Novelty and Disclosure in Patent Law" (1990), again writing with Jerry Green, and "Protecting Early Innovators: Should Second-Generation Products be Patentable?" (1996).

From the vantage point of today, it is hard to appreciate the lack of prior art and the novelty of this line of research at the time of its writing. Moreover, it can be easy to lose sight of the work's importance. Today, we take it for granted that cumulative innovation occupies a central role in the current paradigm for research regarding intellectual property rights. That was not true in the early 1990s, and Suzanne's work is largely responsible for putting cumulative innovation on the research map.

It is useful to put her contribution in perspective. Economists and historians studying technological change had long recognized that innovations build upon each other. Indeed, the title of Suzanne's (1991) paper is drawn from Sir Isaac Newton's famous acknowledgment that "If I have seen far, it is by standing on the shoulders of giants." So, as Suzanne would have been the first to acknowledge, her contribution lay less in recognizing the importance of cumulative innovation than in pioneering the rigorous exploration of its implications for patent law and innovation policy more generally.

During the 1980s, economists harnessed the tools of game theory to better understand the role that patents and patent licensing play in promoting innovation. Early in the decade, models of patent races showed how patents could over-reward innovation. (See, e.g., Dasgupta and Stiglitz, 1980.) By the middle of the decade, these models had been generalized to include the possibility that the loser of the patent race would imitate the winner's product with a non-infringing version or enter into a patent license with the winner, both of which could affect the first innovator's investment incentives. (See, e.g., Katz and Shapiro, 1987; Reinganum, 1989 [literature survey].) It was also recognized that the research efforts of one firm could complement the efforts of rivals due to technological spillovers. (See, e.g., Spence, 1984; Katz, 1986.) In terms of public policy, economists also explored the effects of patent length and breadth on the first innovator's financial returns and social welfare. (See, e.g., Gilbert and Shapiro, 1990; Klemperer, 1990.)

Critically, these game-theoretic models focused solely on the incentives surrounding a single innovation. This is understandable, because one must walk before one can run.

But Suzanne insisted that we do better. She forced us to think deeply about how the rewards provided to one inventor affect the incentives of *subsequent* inventors to conduct R&D building on the discovery of the first. She emphasized that the initial and subsequent innovations all contribute to the creation of value. In other words, the efforts of the different generations of innovators are complementary. Considering all inventors' incentives in this way led to the fundamental insight that there is no allocation of intellectual property rights that can allocate to each of two (or more) complementary innovators 100 percent of the social value created by its innovation. (The statement assumes that no R&D subsidies are available, since we are talking about the patent system, not public funding of R&D or a "prize" system. Suzanne studied prize systems extensively in her other writings.) Suzanne emphasizes this conundrum in "Giants":

> A system of property rights that might seem natural would be to protect the first innovator so broadly that licensing is required from all second generation innovators who use the initial technology, whether in research or in production. But such broad protection can lead to deficient incentives to develop second generation products. (Scotchmer, 1991 [this volume])

We can also frame Suzanne's contribution in another way. Economists had long recognized and studied the social costs associated with strong intellectual property rights (e.g., a patent monopoly) as an example of the deadweight loss associated with any monopoly: the lack of competition leads to higher prices, lower output, and thus less adoption of the patented technology compared with a technology in the public domain. Framed this way, the potential downside of strong intellectual property rights takes the form of a traditional deadweight loss triangle. By contrast, posing the question in terms of cumulative innovation changes this analysis in three important and related ways:

- The narrative is no longer about a virtuous innovator whose returns may be reduced by later imitators when intellectual property protection is too weak. The narrative is instead about two innovators, one of whom happens to come after the other. The first innovator is not the only one who generates positive spillovers for other innovators and benefits for consumers.
- The deadweight loss associated with reduced adoption of the initial innovation is not merely a triangle but rather a trapezoid: to the extent that the second innovator is unable to capture the consumer benefits generated by consumption of the products embodying both innovations, its derived demand for a license to the first innovation does not fully reflect the social benefits of licensing that innovation. Stated another way, if one believes that innovation is under-rewarded, adding monopoly inputs (in the form of a patent license) to the obstacles facing innovators is more worrisome because their efforts are already under-rewarded.
- Examining the effects of intellectual property rights on cumulative innovation opens up a wide range of issues to be modeled regarding the relationships between early and later innovators. Depending on when the earlier and later innovators become aware of each other and can interact, there are many possible relationships into which they may enter, including vertical integration, licensing contracts, or a hybrid form, such as a research joint venture.

Suzanne specialized in the rigorous analysis of formal economic models. But her work was also marked by careful attention to important market institutions, including private contracting and public policy. For example, her 1995 paper with Jerry Green considers a wide range of contractual relationships between the initial and follow-on innovators, and she focused her analyses on specific features of the intellectual property system, such as patent breadth and the novelty requirement. Indeed, she spent fall 2000 as Scholar in Residence at the Court of Appeals for the Federal Circuit to learn more about how these issues are dealt with in practice.

Suzanne was asking about various aspects of the patent system well before most other economists who use game-theoretic models were doing so. The line of research she spurred, with its focus on complementary innovations and the recognition that overly strong intellectual property rights can *stifle* rather than promote innovation has also helped to advance patent law in the United States. The Supreme Court has long recognized this issue when someone has attempted to patent a law of nature. Indeed, in 1843, rejecting the broad claim in Samuel Morse's patent application for the telegraph covering the use of "electro magnetism, however developed for marking or printing intelligible characters, signs, or letters, at any distances," the Court stated that

> For aught that we now know, some future inventor, in the onward march of science, may discover a mode of writing or printing at a distance by means of the electric or galvanic current, without using any part of the process or combination set forth in the plaintiff's specification. His invention may be less complicated – less liable to get out of order – less expensive in construction, and in its operation. But yet, if it is covered by this patent, the inventor could not use it, nor the public have the benefit of it, without the permission of this patentee. (US S. Ct., 1853, at 112–113)

In 2012, the Supreme Court reiterated this long-standing interpretation of patent law:

> "Phenomena of nature, though just discovered, mental processes, and abstract intellectual concepts are not patentable, as they are the basic tools of scientific and technological work." *Gottschalk v. Benson*, 409 U. S. 63, 67 (1972). And monopolization of those tools through the grant of a patent might tend to impede innovation more than it would tend to promote it. (US S. Ct., 2012, at 1293; see also US S. Ct., 2014)

Suzanne's contribution – and the work that has since built on it – gives us a framework in which to think about these issues broadly and coherently. The tradeoffs between creating incentives for initial innovators and subsequent ones arise in many settings besides the patentability of natural laws, and there are many policy issues beyond whether an initial innovation is patentable or not.

Finally, although extremely important in its own right, cumulative innovation is just one example of the broader phenomenon of complementary innovation. Complementarity can sometimes involve one innovation following another. But contemporaneous innovations can also come together to create value. For example, better batteries, better wireless communications, and better data storage and processing interact positively to make smartphones more valuable.

Developments over the past twenty-five years in the economics literature have proven the importance of cumulative innovation and complementary innovations both in theory and for practice. Examples include the analysis and legal treatment of patent thickets, standard-essential patents, patent pools, cross-licensing, and patent portfolios.

Sir Isaac Newton understood well the importance of cumulative innovation, but it took Suzanne Scotchmer to pull the economics literature in that direction some twenty-five years ago. Since that time, many have stood on her shoulders.

Journal of Economic Perspectives,
Vol. 5 No. 1 (Winter, 1991): 29–41

Standing on the Shoulders of Giants: Cumulative Research and the Patent Law

Suzanne Scotchmer*

Sir Isaac Newton himself acknowledged, "If I have seen far, it is by standing on the shoulders of giants." Most innovators stand on the shoulders of giants, and never more so than in the current evolution of high technologies, where almost all technical progress builds on a foundation provided by earlier innovators. For example, most molecular biologists use the basic technique for inserting genes into bacteria that was pioneered by Herbert Boyer and Stanley Cohen in the early 1970s, and many use a technique for causing bacteria to express human proteins that was pioneered at Genentech. In pharmaceuticals, many drugs like insulin, antibiotic, and anti-clotting drugs have been progressively improved as later innovators bettered previous technologies. Computer text editors are similar to one another, as are computer spreadsheets, in large part because innovators have inspired each other. An early example of cumulative research was Eli Whitney's cotton gin, which was quickly modified and improved by other innovators who seriously curtailed his profit.[1]

Most economics literature on patenting and patent races has looked at innovations in isolation, without focusing on the externalities or spillovers that early innovators confer on later innovators. But the cumulative nature of research poses problems for the optimal design of patent law that are not addressed by that perspective. The challenge is to reward early

* Suzanne Scotchmer is Professor of Public Policy, University of California, Berkeley, California.

1 Eli Whitney was very generous in disclosing details of his gin to other innovators, even beyond what was required by patent law. Other innovators patented improvements, but after much litigation the new patents were held to infringe Whitney's underlying patent. Whitney and his partner did not recover sufficient damage awards to compensate them for their litigation and the time that it took to enforce the patent. For an extensive discussion, see Jeanette Mirsky and Allan Nevins, *The World of Eli Whitney* (Macmillan Co. 1952). Klemperer (1990) also discusses the cotton gin.

innovators fully for the technological foundation they provide to later innovators, but to reward later innovators adequately for their improvements and new products as well. This paper investigates the use of patent protection and cooperative agreements among firms to protect incentives for cumulative research.

The Available Tools

The breadth of patent protection is a key consideration in the incentives to innovate. Patent applicants protect themselves against competition from derivative products by claiming broad protection. Patent law would provide no protection at all if it did not protect against trivial changes, like color or size. The allowable breadth of claims is determined by patent examiners and the judiciary. If broad protection is granted, then a derivative or second generation product will likely infringe the prior patent, so a license on the original patent is required to market it. If patent protection is narrow, then many derivative products and applications can be patented and marketed without infringement.[2] We might be tempted to conclude that broad protection encourages firms to find fundamental technologies but discourages them from seeking out second-generation applications and derivative products. However, these two conclusions may be inconsistent, since proper incentives to find fundamental technologies may require that the first patent-holder earn profit from the second generation products that follow. There will be no such profit if no second-generation products follow.

Patent protection would be an unnecessary policy tool if the government had the same information about the costs and benefits of individual research projects as firms have. In that case, the government could simply select the research projects that would be socially efficient and commission research from the lowest cost firms. However, the government will generally have less information than firms,[3] and I will therefore assume that the length and breadth of patent protection and other aspects of the government's policy toward R&D cannot depend on firms' private information about their expected costs.[4]

Given that the length and breadth of patent protection cannot depend on the expected costs of an R&D project, the only way to ensure that firms undertake every research project that is efficient is to let the firms collect as revenue all the social value they create. Otherwise, some projects that are

---

2 U.S. patent protection is broader than that in most other countries, particularly Japan, partly due to the "doctrine of equivalents," which can broaden protection beyond the claims in the patent according to similarity of function.

3 Wright (1983) discusses the private information of firms as the main justification for patent protection, rather than using prizes or contracts as incentive instruments.

4 A policy of reimbursing costs to the successful innovator would not be adequate, since a project that was a "good bet" at the beginning might nevertheless fail.

socially desirable will not be undertaken. If an innovation is a reduction in the cost of producing a good, then the social value is the saved costs. If the innovation is an improvement to a product, the social value is the difference in consumers' willingness to pay for the improved and unimproved products. When research firms collect all the social value as profit, households still benefit, but in their capacity as shareholders rather than as consumers.

But there are at least two problems with allowing research firms to collect all the social surplus as profit (or as much as possible). First, strong patent protection leads to socially inefficient monopoly pricing. Second, firms in a patent race may overinvest in research if the patent is worth more than the (minimum) cost of achieving it. (Loury, 1979). This problem is related to the problem of the commons: An increase in one firm's rate of investment transfers some probability of becoming a patentholder from the other firms to itself. Because of this transfer, all firms might overinvest.[5] These points are well-recognized in the R&D literature.

When an initial innovation facilitates later ones, as is the case with basic research, another issue arises. Part of the first innovation's social value is the boost it gives to later innovators, which can take at least three forms. If the second generation could not be developed without the first, then the social value of the first innovation includes the incremental social surplus provided by the second generation products. If the first innovation merely reduces the cost of achieving the second innovation, then the cost reduction is part of the social surplus provided by the first innovation. And if the first innovation accelerates the development of the second, but at the same cost, then its social value includes the value of getting the second innovation sooner.

Because of these externalities provided to later innovators, developing the first innovation may be efficient even if its expected cost exceeds its value as a stand-alone product. First innovators will have correct incentives to invest only if they receive some of the social surplus provided by second generation products. But at the same time, enough profit must be left for the second innovators so that they will invest if investing is efficient. This essay asks how close patent incentives can come to accomplishing that goal.

A premise in much of what follows is that firms other than the first innovator should participate in the development of second generation products. Since the first innovator might not have expertise in all applications, more second generation products are likely to arise if more researchers have incentives to consider them. In this view, contrary to the premise of much of the patent race literature, creativity is largely serendipitous. Not every R&D firm sees the same opportunities for new products.

---

5 But Gandal and Scotchmer (1989) show that prior agreements among firms that would otherwise race can overcome the incentive for overinvestment, even if their research costs are private information. When such prior agreements are allowed, the firms will invest at the efficient rates if and only if the private value of the patent is equal to the social value.

However, outside research firms can integrate with initial patentholders in at least two ways: the firms can form cooperative ventures to research and develop new products, and they can form licensing agreements after products have been developed and patents have been awarded. I will call these two types of contracts prior agreements and licenses, respectively. Prior agreements permit firms to share the costs, as well as the proceeds, of research.[6] Licenses are negotiated after research costs are sunk and patents have been awarded. Both types of agreements can increase profit by improving efficiency and possibly by reducing product market competition. Although many authors have discussed cooperation in research, they have not focused, as I will, on how the breadth of patent protection and cooperation among research firms work together in protecting incentives to innovate. In this view of how incentives to innovate are protected, a key role of patent protection is that it sets bargaining positions for the prior agreements and licenses that will form, and therefore determines the division of profit in these contracts.

Patent Protection and Licensing

A system of property rights that might seem natural would be to protect the first innovator so broadly that licensing is required from all second generation innovators who use the initial technology, whether in research or in production. But such broad protection can lead to deficient incentives to develop second generation products. When the licensing agreement is negotiated after a patent has been granted, research costs have already been sunk. The bargaining surplus to be split between the first and second innovators at that time is the incremental market value of the second product, *not* net of research costs. A second innovator who cannot market the next generation product without a license has a very weak bargaining position. If the second innovator does not get all the surplus being bargained over, he will earn only a fraction of the new product's market value and presumably only a fraction of its social value, and this fraction may be less than the cost of developing it. Hence the incentive for an outside firm to develop second generation products can be too weak.[7] Under such broad patent protection, the incentive for the first innovator to develop a second generation product will be stronger than for an outside firm (provided the first innovator has expertise to develop the new product, and thinks of it), since the first innovator will earn the entire incremental profit.

6 Prior cooperation in research has been treated leniently by antitrust law and the authorities. For example, the National Cooperative Research Act (1984) established that joint ventures are not per se illegal, but will be treated according to a "rule of reason." The Act also reduced damages in civil suits from treble to single, provided the firms follow the proper notification procedure. Perspectives on this act are discussed in the symposium on "Collaboration, Innovation and Antitrust" in the Summer 1990 issue of this journal.
7 See Green and Scotchmer (1990) for an elaboration of this idea.

As well as offering deficient incentives for second innovators, broad patent protection might inefficiently inflate incentives for the first solution. In licensing agreements, the first innovator will earn a share of the market value of each infringing later product. If the first innovation reduces the cost of achieving later innovations, but is not the only possible vehicle to achieve them, the first innovator's share should not exceed the cost reduction. If it does, the first innovator will be overrewarded.

In what follows I explore two solutions to these defective incentives. The remainder of this section investigates what happens if the first innovator's patent protection is narrowed so that a different enough second generation product does not infringe and thus can be marketed without a license from the first innovator. In the following section, I investigate prior agreements in which the second innovators can "sell" their ideas to the first innovator or integrate with the first innovator. Neither solution is perfect, as we shall see.

The inadequacies of narrowing patent protection are most easily exposed if we first suppose that first and second generation products do not compete in the market, although second generation products build on the first generation technology; for example, many new pharmaceuticals that are therapies for different illnesses all build on a few basic techniques of bio-engineering. Second innovators cannot have excessive incentive to invest, since they cannot earn more than consumers' willingness to pay in the markets they serve. Licensing from the first innovator would transfer away some of the second innovators' revenue and hence reduce their incentive to invest. To provide efficient incentives to the second innovator, society should protect the first innovation so narrowly that a new product never infringes and therefore second innovators never have to license. But such a scheme does not sufficiently reward the first innovator, since the first innovator does not profit from the cost reduction conferred on the second innovators.

The first innovator's incentive to invest becomes still weaker under narrow patent protection if the second generation product is a substitute for the first. Competition between the two patent-holders would erode their joint profit, transferring some of the social surplus of the combined innovations to consumers. As an example, suppose that the second generation product is a superior version of a drug, and that the two patent-holders compete on price. Then the second generation product will survive in the market and its price will equal the difference in consumers' willingness to pay for the two drugs plus the marginal cost of producing the drug. In this outcome, the second innovator earns as profit exactly the incremental social value of the newer drug, while the first innovator's profit falls to zero.

Such profit erosion could be mitigated if the antitrust authorities permitted collusive pricing among patentholders who would otherwise compete. For example, licensing with per-unit royalties can lead to collusive outcomes, since the royalty raises the licensees' private production cost and therefore keeps the equilibrium price high.[8] In ordinary antitrust law, collusion through licensing would violate the spirit of the Sherman Act and subsequent legislation. But where incentives to innovate are at stake and where later technology builds on an earlier technology, such collusion allows the first innovator to profit from the externality conferred on later innovators. Of course, firms would be tempted to exploit any leniency by the antitrust authorities in contexts where incentives to innovate are not at stake. This problem should not be minimized.

There is something quite general that economists can say about the combined effects of patent law with licensing: No such policy can achieve fully efficient incentives, even if society permits collusive licensing between patent-holders who would otherwise compete and the firms jointly collect all the social surplus as profit. This is essentially because of "double marginalization." To give the second innovator an incentive to invest whenever social benefits exceed R&D costs, the second innovator must earn the entire social surplus of his innovation. But to compensate the first innovator for the externality or spillover she provides, she too must earn part of this surplus. It is impossible to give the surplus to both parties.[9]

When both first and second generation products are developed, the division of profit between the two innovators depends on the breadth of patent protection. To see this, assume that there is a random component to the outcome of a research project, so that when a research firm invests in a second generation product, it does not know whether its product will infringe the prior patent. The breadth of the prior patent determines the probability that the second generation product will infringe. If the second product turns out to infringe, the second innovator must license and this will force him to share the profit of the improvement with the first innovator. The second innovator is in a better position if its product turns out not to infringe, since the second innovator can profitably compete with the prior patentholder in the market. Thus, if breadth of the first patent could be interpreted to depend on the expected costs and benefits of a second generation product, we could ensure that the second innovator's expected profit would be zero. If not, some second generation products will be stymied even though they would contribute positively to social welfare, and the second innovators who invest will typically make positive profit.

To summarize, the "natural" system of property rights – requiring every later innovator to license any underlying technology – will on average give deficient incentives for outside firms to develop second generation products. This is because the second product infringes and therefore the second

---

8 If royalties are permitted, then licensing is similar to permitting the initial patent-holder to buy up the patents on later products that use the initial technology.

9 Green and Scotchmer (1990) argue this in a model where the second innovation would be impossible without the first innovation. It is also true in the less drastic case when the first innovation merely reduces the cost of achieving the second innovation.

innovator must transfer some of the innovation's revenue to the first innovator by licensing. If the first innovator can be relied upon to develop all second generation products, this would not matter. Second, no system of narrower patent protection and licensing can give the right incentives to both the first innovator and other firms that develop improvements, even if collusive licensing among noninfringing products were allowed. The latter result depends on my premise that the breadth of an underlying patent cannot be separately tailored to the costs and benefits of each second generation product.

In the next section, I ask to what extent these inadequacies of patent protection and licensing can be overcome by prior agreements reached before some or all of the patents have been obtained. Incentives with licensing are defective mainly because firms negotiate after all costs have been sunk and patents have been issued. A prior agreement integrates the potential second innovator into the firm of the first innovator before investing in the second innovation. Such prior agreements can indeed guarantee efficient investment in second generation products, but cannot perfectly solve the incentive problem unless the negotiation is before *all* costs are sunk, including the costs of the first innovator, or unless the first innovator has all the bargaining power.

Prior Agreements

Prior agreements among research firms are often called research joint ventures. Joint ventures presumably form to increase the joint profit of the members, but they do not necessarily increase social welfare, since the cooperation is among firms only and does not include consumers.[10] Joint ventures increase profit both by providing incentives to the members to invest more efficiently, and by finding ways to transfer social surplus from consumers to firms. The greater efficiency might result from exploiting economies of scale (Katz, 1986), from sharing technological know-how (Bhattachearya, Glazer and Sappington, 1988), or from undoing the inefficiencies of a patent race (Gandal and Scotchmer, 1989).

One solution to the incentive problem would be to integrate all possible innovators into one firm before even the first innovator has invested. Then, provided the integrated firm gets most of the social surplus from the joint innovations, it should invest (close to) efficiently. Although research firms do not know with certainty what projects they will think of after the first generation technology has been developed, they have expectations about the possible benefits and costs of such projects. Provided that all

---

10 The Coase theorem would conclude that bargains increase the joint welfare of all the parties. Thus, if consumers and firms could jointly cooperate, prior agreements would inevitably benefit both groups. But since some of the parties are excluded – namely consumers – there is no guarantee that prior agreements increase total welfare.

researchers have similar expectations, an agreement negotiated before the first investment could ensure that the first innovation is undertaken if and only if efficient, where efficiency is defined relative to the prior judgments about costs and benefits. But the more serendipitous is the discovery of second generation products, and the more difficult it is to include all potential second innovators, the less feasible such an agreement seems. I therefore consider the more limited prospects when integration occurs after the first innovation. The difficulties in transferring profit to the first innovator are clearest if we assume that the innovators can jointly collect all the social surplus as profit, provided they do not compete in the market.

After the first patent has issued, a potential second innovator could approach the first patent-holder with an idea for an improvement or new product, and suggest they share both the costs and proceeds of research. Such an agreement can increase joint profit by increasing investment in profitable second generation products and by preventing market competition among firms that would otherwise own competing patents. If patent protection is broad, without this prior agreement the second innovator could have deficient incentive to invest, as explained above. With a prior agreement, the initial patent-holder can agree to share both the costs and the proceeds of the second innovation, and will do so whenever benefits exceed costs.

Prior agreements are a social improvement over licensing because they can improve incentives to invest in second generation products, whatever the breadth of patent protection. With licensing, the breadth of patent protection serves two purposes: It determines investment in second generation products and determines how the firms' joint expected profits will be divided. With prior agreements, the breadth of patent protection serves one purpose instead of two: The two innovators have an incentive to invest efficiently in second generation products whatever the breadth of patent protection. The breadth of protection determines only the bargaining positions, hence the division of profit.[11]

Whether a prior agreement can provide efficient incentives for the first investment as well as the second depends on two factors: How much social surplus must be transferred from the second innovator to the first (how big the externality is), and the second innovator's bargaining power. A second innovator who has a strong bargaining position will earn positive profit in a prior agreement, thus limiting how much social surplus the first innovator can collect. The second innovator's bargaining position is strongest if there is a high probability the second innovation will not infringe and if the second generation product is itself patentable. The second innovator will

---

11 On the other hand, approaching the first innovator with the idea for the second innovation might give away the idea of the potential second innovator, and thereby undermine its bargaining position. The law has remedies for this problem, but presumably they do not work perfectly.

also have a strong bargaining position if no other firm is capable of developing the second generation product.

To bid the second innovator's profits to zero, it is not necessarily enough that each potential second innovator has many competitors. Suppose the second generation product is itself patentable and that that firm will develop the improved product and have an exclusive license on the initial patent. Despite this agreement, the parties will be forced to negotiate with any other firm that gets the improvement first since they could not duplicate the second invention without infringement. Anticipating this, potential second innovators might not bid away their profit in trying to make an agreement with the first innovator. (Scotchmer, 1990).

Some authors who have written on research joint ventures have pointed out that firms' incentives to cooperate at the research stage depend partly on whether the members can also collude in using the resulting patents (Ordover and Baumol, 1985; Katz, 1986; d'Aspremont and Jacquemin, 1988; Choi, 1989). My discussion has assumed they can, and that such collusion is an important way to protect incentives to innovate. It would be difficult to implement a rule that permitted the consolidation of property rights through a prior agreement only if the eventual patents would otherwise be infringing. When research outcomes are random, patent authorities cannot know whether an R&D project will result in new technology that infringes an earlier patent.

Conclusion

A main conclusion of this essay is that it is misleading to ask how broad patent protection should be without simultaneously asking whether research firms can integrate or otherwise cooperate. Similarly, it is misleading to ask how leniently society should treat cooperation among research firms without simultaneously asking how broad patent protection should be. Prior agreements have the advantage of leading to more efficient investment in second-generation products. But if the patent authorities disallow collusive licensing of patents that are noninfringing, they might also want to disallow prior agreements. A prior agreement merges the interests of the two firms whether or not the patents would be non-infringing, and could circumvent the antitrust authority's desire to force competition. Of course, competition has a disadvantage where incentives to innovate are at stake: It erodes the joint profit of the firms, which undermines at least one firm's incentive to invest in R&D when such investment is efficient.

There are no simple conclusions to draw about the optimal breadth of patents. It is not necessarily optimal to protect the first innovation so broadly that every derivative or second generation product infringes. If prior agreements are disallowed or ineffective for some reason, then broad patent protection could discourage the development of second generation products, as explained above. And if the first innovator does not expect to profit by licensing to second generation inventors, broad protection could inhibit the first innovation as well, thus undermining the entire research line.

Broad protection might also be undesirable when prior agreements are allowed. To encourage researchers to invest in second generation products, the first innovator might have to make prior agreements with firms that have bargaining power. Their bargaining power derives from the fact that, without an agreement, they might have a credible threat not to invest, and from patentability of the second generation product. Because of their bargaining power, they may get a share of the bargaining surplus. Suppose patent protection is narrowed enough so that second innovators will invest without a prior agreement, but their profit is kept low. This would increase the first patent-holder's profit, as may be necessary to compensate the first innovator for the externality or spillover conferred on second innovators.[12]

Patent law is limited in its instruments: The main ones are the patent life and the breadth of protection.[13] The private value of patent protection is linked to the social value of the technology through market demand, but is not linked to firms' research costs. The optimal rule for the breadth of a patent can only use information that is available to patent examiners and courts.[14] Thus, the patenting rule can depend on observable aspects of discovered technologies, but not on prior expectations regarding techno-logical outcomes and costs of research. This restriction greatly reduces the effectiveness of patent law in protecting incentives.

Before investing in a second generation technology, the researcher must evaluate the probability that the new technology will not infringe the prior patent. This probability depends on the breadth of the prior patent and on the distributions of possible outcomes of the second investment. The probability of infringing the first patent is lower if the distribution of outcomes places greater weight on outcomes that lie outside the allowed claims of the first patent. A project with low probability of infringing will look more profitable to the second generation researcher than a project

---

12 See Green and Scotchmer (1990) for an elaboration of this argument.
13 Of course, details like priority rules also matter. Everywhere except the United States, a disputed patent issues to the first applicant. In the United States, a disputed patent issues to the first inventor, regardless of when application occurs. See Scotchmer and Green (1990) for a discussion of the incentive effects of these two rules. The anomalous American rule is now being reconsidered.
14 Except for Wright (1983), authors have not focused explicitly on what information is available to patent authorities. Gandal and Scotchmer (1989), Green and Scotchmer (1990), Klemperer (1990) and Scotchmer and Green (1990) assume that patent protection cannot depend on costs. Klemperer (1990) and Gilbert and Shapiro (1990) assume that the breadth of patent protection can depend on aspects of market demand. Green and Scotchmer (1990) assume that the breadth of patent protection can depend on the level of previous technical advance.

that places greater prior weight on outcomes that infringe the first patent. But both projects could have the same expected social value if the expected costs of one project were sufficiently higher than the other. The patent policy should equally encourage two projects with the same social value, but that cannot be accomplished with a patent rule that depends only on technological outcomes.

A disadvantage of narrow patent protection that I have not yet discussed is that it might discourage first innovators from patenting and disclosing their technologies. Patent law requires disclosure for the same reason that innovators dislike it: it is the vehicle by which technical knowledge is passed from the patenting firm to its competitors.[15] The first innovator would rather develop second generation products than let other firms develop them, since that would be more profitable. As a consequence the first innovator could hold the product off the market until it develops the more valuable second generation products, or it could market the first product and rely for protection on the law of trade secrets, which does not require disclosure, but also does not protect against independent invention.

The first innovator's incentive to patent the initial technology depends on: (i) the profitability of marketing the first technology prior to the development of second generation products; (ii) the extent of disclosure that patenting entails;[16] (iii) the ease with which the technology can be reverse-engineered if marketed but not patented; and (iv) the breadth of patent protection. The incentive not to patent is especially strong when patent protection is narrow, since a second generation product is then more likely to damage the first innovator's profit.

The problem of cumulative research is especially acute when the first technology has very little value on its own, but is a foundation for valuable second generation technologies. Even with licensing, the first innovator might not capture the full social value that it facilitates and may have deficient incentive to invest. This is presumably why governments fund basic research. The branches of government that fund research are not those that set patent policy, and the decision to support basic research

15 The disclosure requirement in section 112 of the patent law states that "the specification shall contain a written description ... in such full, clear, concise, and exact terms as to enable any person skilled in the art ... to make and use the same ..." Scotchmer and Green (1990) show that a leading firm might not want to patent a patentable technology even if this means holding it off the market until the next innovation in order to avoid reverse engineering.

16 Disclosure of some technologies, such as chemical compositions, teaches competitors much that is valuable. For example, after the basic material of superconductors was disclosed, many other researchers developed aspects of it (*The New York Times*, January 2, 1989, p. 34). Disclosure of other technologies, like bio-engineered proteins, gives away much less that it useful to competitors, and therefore innovators will not fear disclosure as much.

might be interpreted as a recognition that patents and licensing are inadequate.

Governments have taken different views of whether publicly sponsored research should also be patentable. The U.S. government permits and even encourages patenting of results from government sponsored research; for example, the Boyer-Cohen patent. In contrast, the British government forbade the Cambridge Molecular Biology Lab from patenting monoclonal antibodies in the mid-1970s. Permitting patents on government sponsored research rewards successful innovators twice, once through government funding and again through the patents.

I have focused in this essay on how to divide joint profit among innovators when one innovator's technology builds on another's. I have not focused on the length of patent protection as a policy tool. My simplifying assumption that the innovators can jointly get all the social surplus as profit if they do not compete in the market essentially means that the patent continues forever. When owners of noninfringing patents cannot collude through licensing, a noninfringing second generation product will undermine the profitability of the first patent, and this may happen before the end of the patent life. Mansfield (1984) surveyed research firms and found that the effective lives of most patents are much shorter than the stipulated 17 years. In the extreme case where a second product is an improved version of the first, the effective length of the first patent may simply end when the second product is introduced. The effective patent life is determined directly by its breadth, since the breadth determines how long it takes until this happens. On the other hand, when second generation products serve different markets, as when consumers have different tastes and a second generation product is a variant that serves a different set of consumers, length and breadth can be chosen independently, although the monopoly power conferred by a patent may be eroded over the patent's life as similar but noninfringing products are invented.

Gilbert and Shapiro (1990) and Klemperer (1990) have discussed breadth of patent protection in the context of single innovations without focusing on the problem of dividing profit among sequential innovators. In their conceptualization, breadth and length are substitute ways to provide a fixed profit to a single innovator, and they ask what combination of length and breadth minimizes the cost of monopoly distortions. They do not ask how large the fixed profit should be and therefore do not focus on how to preserve incentives to innovate. The prescription for patent breadth that comes out of that perspective may well conflict with the prescription for patent breadth that comes from considering incentives to innovate when research is cumulative.

It appears that patent policy is a very blunt instrument trying to solve a very delicate problem. Its bluntness derives largely from the narrowness of what patent breadth can depend on, namely the realized values of the technologies. As a consequence, the prospects for fine-tuning the patent system seem limited, which may be an argument for more public sponsorship of basic research.

☐ *Prepared for the Symposium on Intellectual Property Law, funded by the RAND Corporation and the John P. Ohlin Foundation, which took place in Washington DC on October 24, 1989. I thank Stan Besen, Joe Farrell, Jerry Green, Leo Raskind, Steve Salop, Carl Shapiro, Eugene Smolensky, Joe Stiglitz, and Timothy Taylor for useful comments. I thank Lucette Decorde for her able research assistance and the NSF, Grant SESE 89 09503, for financial support.*

References

d'Aspremont, C., and A. Jacquemin, "Cooperative and Noncooperative R&D in Duopoly with Spillovers," *American Economic Review*, 1988, *78*, 1133–1137.

Bhattacharya, S., J. Glazer, and D. Sappington, "Motivating Exchange of Knowledge in R&D Ventures: First-Best Implementation," Bell Communications Research, Technical Memorandum, 1988.

Choi, Jay P., "An Analysis of Cooperative R&D," mimeo, Dept. of Economics, Harvard University, 1989.

Gandal, N., and S. Scotchmer, "Coordinating Research Through Research Joint Ventures," GSPP Working Paper #171, University of California, Berkeley, 1989.

Gilbert, Richard and Carl Shapiro, "Optimal Patent Length and Breadth," *The RAND Journal of Economics*, 1990, *21*, 106–112.

Green, J., and S. Scotchmer, "*Antitrust Policy, the Breadth of Patent Protection and the Incentive to Develop New Products*," GSPP Working Paper #171 (revised), University of California, Berkeley, 1990.

Jacquemin, A., "Cooperative Agreements in R&D and European Antitrust Policy," *European Economic Review*, 1988, *32*, 551–560.

Katz, M., "An Analysis of Cooperative Research and Development," *The RAND Journal of Economics*, 1986, *17*, 527–543.

Klemperer, Paul, "How Broad should the Scope of Patent Protection Be?" *The RAND Journal of Economics*, Spring 1990, *21*, 113–130.

Loury, Glenn C., "Market Structure and Innovation," *Quarterly Journal of Economics* 1979, *XCIII*, 395–410.

Mansfield, Edwin, "R&D and Innovation: Some Empirical Findings," in Griliches, Zvi ed., *R&D, Patents and Productivity*. Chicago: University of Chicago Press for the National Bureau of Economic Research, 1984.

Ordover, Janusz, and William J. Baumol, "Antitrust for High-Technology Industries: Assessing Research Joint ventures and Mergers," *Journal of Law and Economics* 1985 *XXVIII*, 331–331.

Scotchmer, S. "Protecting Early Innovators: Should Accessory Products, Bundled Improvements and Applications Be Patentable?," GSPP Working Paper #183, University of California, Berkeley, 1990.

Scotchmer, S., and J. Green, "Novelty and Disclosure in Patent Law," *The RAND Journal of Economics*, 1990, *21*, 131–146.

Wright, Brian, "The Economics of Innovation Incentives: Patents, Prizes and Research Contracts," *American Economic Review*, 1983, 73, 619–707.

RAND Journal of Economics,
Vol. 26 No. 1 (Spring, 1995): 20–33

On the Division of Profit in Sequential Innovation

Jerry R. Green*

and

Suzanne Scotchmer**

In markets with sequential innovation, inventors of derivative improvements might undermine the profit of initial innovators through competition. Profit erosion can be mitigated by broadening the first innovator's patent protection and/or by permitting cooperative agreements between the initial innovators and later innovators. We investigate the policy that is more effective at ensuring the first innovator earns a large share of profit from the second-generation product it facilitates. In general, not all the profit can be transferred to the first innovator, and therefore patents should last longer when a sequence of innovations is undertaken by different firms rather than being concentrated in one firm.

1. Introduction

Knowledge and technical progress are cumulative in the sense that products are often the result of several steps of invention, modification, and improvement. Indeed, the "development" aspect of "research and development" can be as commercially important as the "research." But when

* Harvard University.
** University of California, Berkeley.

   A previous version of this article circulated under the title "Antitrust Policy, the Breadth of Patent Protection, and the Incentive to Develop New Products." We thank the National Science Foundation, grant nos. SES-88-09107 and SES-89-09503, for financial support. We thank Nancy Gallini for very useful comments that much improved this article. We also thank Joe Farrell, Neil Gandal, two anonymous referees, conference participants at the C.E.P.R. conference on Industrial Organization held in May 1992 in Barcelona, and seminar participants in Toulouse.

innovation occurs in two stages, the first innovator may have insufficient incentive to invest. First, competition between improved products could undermine the original innovator's profit. Profit erosion could be so severe that the original research could be unprofitable, and that could stymie the entire line of technology. But even when derivative products are not direct competitors to the first product – e.g., when they are "applications" of the first product that serve unrelated markets – the first innovator might have deficient incentive to invest. This is because the social value of an early innovation includes the net social value of the applications it facilitates. If the first innovator does not collect that value as profit, he might not invest even if the combined profit of the innovations exceeds the combined costs.

Incentives to innovate are protected overall by granting a sufficient patent life. Nordhaus (1969) argued that patent lives should be finite, even though some R&D might be deterred, in order to reduce monopoly distortions on average. In this article we are concerned not only with the total profit earned by the innovators, but also with the division of profit. For example, it is useless to ensure that a sequence of two innovations is jointly profitable if all the profit goes to the second innovator and the first innovator cannot cover his costs. In that case neither the first nor second innovation would be invented.

In Section 2 we specify a model that we use to investigate the division of profit. For simplicity we assume that after the first innovation is made, the idea for each derivative improvement occurs to only one firm, which is uniquely capable of developing it at a cost. The first innovator can profit by selling his product in the market, by licensing his patent to second-generation innovators after their innovations are achieved, or by sharing profit in *ex ante* agreements to develop second-generation products. At the end of the article we comment on whether our conclusions are robust to these assumptions.

Using this model we investigate the complementary roles of patent length and breadth. The breadth determines how profit is divided in each period of the patent, and the length determines the total profit that is collected by the firms jointly. The division of profit in each period depends on whether the second product infringes the first patent. If a second patent infringes, the second innovator must license, which transfers profit from the second innovator to the first. Because the breadth of the first patent determines whether a product infringes, it thus determines the division of profit. If the division of profit is too unfavorable to one innovator or the other, the patent must last a long time to ensure that the less-favored innovator covers his costs. Our object is to investigate how the patent breadth should be chosen to keep the patent life as short as possible.

In Section 3 we make a general point about patent life that is independent of the breadth: the patent should last longer when R&D takes place in several firms than if it is concentrated in one firm. If R&D is concentrated in one firm, the patent should last just long enough to cover total costs. But with two firms, such a short patent life would place a severe demand on the division of profit: each researcher would have to earn exactly enough revenue to cover his own costs. We show that this will typically not happen, and in fact the second innovator will make positive profit whatever the patent breadth. Therefore, the incentive to undertake basic research will inevitably be too weak if the patent life provides only zero total profit.

Nevertheless, our objective is to make the patent life as short as possible. This can be done by finding ways to transfer profit from the second innovator to the first. In Section 4 we ask how the patent breadth should be chosen in order to do this. We give circumstances in which the first patent should be very broad so that all second-generation products infringe, and other circumstances in which this is not the best policy.

Our conclusions about optimal patent policy rely on certain assumptions about what types of licensing agreements the firms can make. Licensing agreements can occur at two stages: *ex ante*, which is before the second innovator invests in the improvement or application, and *ex post*, which is after the improvement or application is achieved. The difference is in whether the second innovator has sunk his costs at the time of the negotiation. We stress in this article that *ex ante* licensing has an important advantage over *ex post* licensing: it can ensure that the innovators invest in the improvement or application if and only if it would increase their joint profit.[1] *Ex ante* agreements may have a second advantage for the firms as well: without an *ex ante* agreement, the firms might become *ex post* competitors.

The question of what kinds of licensing agreements should be allowed is only slightly murkier than the question of what types are in fact allowed under current antitrust law. Although we think our maintained hypotheses in Sections 2 to 4 are reasonable, we point out in Section 5 that they are not the only ones imaginable. In Section 5 we turn our attention to the optimal design of antitrust policy, again with a view toward trying to understand what policies divide profit in such a way that patent life can be relatively short. In Section 6 we present our conclusions.

2. The model

We call the quality of the first product x, and the quality of the second-generation product $x + y$, so that y represents the size of the improvement. These qualities are related to consumers' willingness to pay. We assume that if the first product alone is marketed as a monopoly, the monopolist earns revenue $\pi_x(T)$ when the patent lasts a period T, and if the improved product is marketed by a monopolist, the revenue is $\pi_{x+y}(T)$. If the two

---

1 Thus we study the mirror image of the problem studied by Gallini (1984), who showed how *ex ante* licensing can prevent a competitor from inefficiently duplicating an invention. In both cases *ex ante* licensing can remedy an investment decision that would decrease the joint profit of the two firms. See also Spence (1984).

products compete, the revenues are respectively $\pi^c_x(T)$ and $\pi^c_y(T)$, and we assume (reasonably) that $\pi^c_x(T) \leq \pi_x(T)$ and $\pi_{x+y}(T) \geq \pi^c_x(T) + \pi^c_y(T)$. These profits increase with T. To reduce notation, we often omit the argument T.

A special case used in Propositions 3 and 5 below is when

$$\pi_{x+y} = \pi_x + \pi^c_y = \pi^c_x + \pi^c_y.$$

This circumstance can arise in at least two ways. In the first, the entire commercial value of the basic research resides in the second-generation products, as when each second generation product is an "application." Then it is reasonable to assume that $\pi_{x+y} = \pi^c_y$ and $\pi_x = \pi^c_x = 0$. For example, the first invention might be laser technology, which has no direct value to consumers, and an application might be laser surgery. The two innovations are linked only through the fact that the first one facilitated invention of the second one. In the second circumstance, the two innovations are not close substitutes because they serve different markets. For example, a surgical device for humans might generate, as a spin-off, a surgical device for pets.

After the first product is patented, a firm called firm 2 gets an "idea" for an improved product, and this idea is described by (y, c_2) drawn from the distribution (G, H) known to everyone prior to the first investment. The investment in the first product (with quality x) must be made before the "idea" for the second product (with quality $x + y$) or the identity of the second firm is known. Although both y and c_2 are unknown at the time of the first investment, some of the uncertainty will typically be resolved prior to the second investment. Below we consider two possibilities: (i) that all the uncertainty is resolved, so that the prospective second innovator knows both the value and cost of the improvement when he makes his investment decision, and (ii) that only the cost is resolved, but the value is still uncertain.

For simplicity we will assume that little time elapses between the innovations, so that both patents begin and end at the same time. Relaxing this assumption would complicate the model without yielding substantially different conclusions. The firms will decide whether to invest in the idea according to a game described below. First, however, we discuss what would be efficient.

Efficiency. The social value of entry by firm 1 has two parts. First, there is the social value of the first innovation of quality x, which might be marketed with no further improvements, and second, there is the option value of a potential application or improvement y by firm 2. Even if the social value of the first product alone does not exceed its costs, the possibility of a valuable second-generation product(s) might justify the investment. However, the social value that accrues from the two products depends on the market structure in which they are marketed. The social surplus (profit plus consumers' surplus) is different if the products are sold by one monopolist than if the differentiated products compete in the market. Below we permit the two innovators to join their interests in an *ex ante* agreement, and they will typically find this profitable. Therefore we can assume that *ex ante* agreements always occur in equilibrium and that the two goods will be sold jointly by a monopolist for the duration of the patent. They will jointly earn $\pi_{x+y}(T)$ if both x and y are invented. The improvement y will be invented if $\pi_{x+y}(T) - \pi_x(T) - c_2 > 0$.

We assume that if the first patent is profitable for some T, investing in it is efficient; investment is efficient if $\pi_x(T) - c_1 + E_{G,H} \max \{[\pi_{x+y}(T) - \pi_x(T) - c_2], 0\} > 0$. This is because the monopolist's profit is no greater than the social surplus. Consumers collect some surplus even during the patent life, and their surplus continues beyond the patent life.

Patent breadth. The patent breadth is a value y^* with the interpretation that if the subsequent innovator discovers a product of quality $x + y$, with $y \geq y^*$, then this product is deemed not to infringe the patent. If $y < y^*$, then this product will infringe. In U.S. patent law, patent claims will be upheld by the examiners and the courts only if the applicant invented the claimed technologies, and if they satisfy "novelty" and "non-obviousness." Although these tests refer to scientific and technical considerations, and not to economic values, our model uses the latter as a proxy.[2]

Antitrust rules. There are two stages in our model at which an agreement between sequential innovators could be reached. The first is when the second innovator gets his idea for the improved product before he has sunk costs. We call this an *ex ante* license or *ex ante* agreement. A second opportunity arises after the costs of the improved product have been sunk and the resulting product infringes. We call this an *ex post* license. We do not permit agreements between firms prior to the first innovation. Although such agreements could achieve first-best incentives for research in our model, they would be difficult to negotiate; prior to invention of the first technology, it is difficult for the first innovator to identify the firms that will think of second-generation products.

2 See Merges and Nelson (1990, 1992), Merges (1992a, 19921b), Matutes, Regibeau, and Rockett (1990), and Chang (1995) for discussions of how to interpret these clauses. A more fully elaborated model would have the scientific "novelty" (n) of the improvement distributed jointly with its economic value (y). A product would be noninfringing if it were sufficiently novel, $n > n^*$, irrespective of y. If we reinterpret y in our model as $E(y|n)$ and if y and n were positively correlated, then a higher n^* cutoff translates into a higher $E(y|n)$ and hence a higher y^*. However, Chang (1995) argues that whether or not the patent law insists on a cutoff policy, in the special case of unit demand and Bertrand competition, incentives are better under a patent policy in which either very trivial or very important innovations are deemed to infringe.

3. The division of profit

Figure 1 shows the order of decisions and payoffs. If firm 1 does not invest, nothing further happens and both firms get zero profit. If the first product is developed, firm 2 has its "idea" (y, c_2) for an improved product. The two firms could then make an *ex ante* agreement in which they share both the cost c_2 and the incremental revenue $\pi_{x+y} - \pi_x$ of the improved product. If they do not form this agreement, firm 2 must decide whether to invest c_2 and develop the product alone.

Figure 1 shows the defect of using only *ex post* licensing as a way to encourage research. Suppose we ignore the opportunity for an *ex ante* agreement. If the second product infringes, but the second innovator invests anyway, *ex post* he will bargain with the first patentholder over the incremental profit of the improvement, $\pi_{x+y} - \pi_x$ but not over the sunk research costs c_2. We assume each firm earns half the bargaining surplus. Because firm 2 earns only $\frac{1}{2}(\pi_{x+y} - \pi_x) - c_2$, investment in

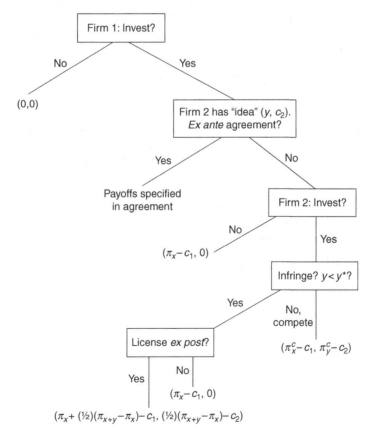

Figure 1 On the Division of Profit between Sequential Innovators

second-generation products may be deterred even if such investments add to the firms' joint profits and are efficient. We could bolster the second firm's incentive to invest by ensuring that the second innovation never infringes (e.g., $y^* = 0$), but then another problem arises. The first innovator's profit is eroded through competition, and, anticipating this, the first innovator might not invest.

Ex ante agreements (before investing c_2) can help solve these problems. Neither firm would agree to less profit in the *ex ante* agreement than it would get by forgoing the agreement and doing whatever would happen instead. What would happen without an *ex ante* agreement determines the "threat points" for the *ex ante* agreement. We assume that in the *ex ante* agreement each firm will receive its threat-point profit plus one-half the bargaining surplus that the *ex ante* agreement makes available. *Ex ante* agreements can ensure that the second investment is undertaken whenever it adds to joint profit (and is therefore efficient). However, we show in the following proposition that if the patent life provides zero joint profit $(\pi_{x+y} - (c_1 + c_2) = 0)$, then the first innovator will have deficient incentives to invest. Therefore the patent life must be longer when the two stages of R&D are undertaken in different firms than when concentrated in one firm.

Proposition 1. Given T, firm 1's profit is never more than π_{x+y} $(T) - (c_1 + c_2)$, and for the some second-generation products it is less.

Proof. First suppose that firm 2 would enter even if there were no *ex ante* agreement. There are two cases: $y > y^*$ and $y < y^*$. If $y > y^*$, so that the second innovator could compete *ex post* with the first innovator, the threat points for the *ex ante* agreement are $(\pi^c_x - c_1, \pi^c_y - c_2)$. Our assumption that firm 2 would enter means that $\pi^c_y - c_2 > 0$. The extra profit the firms earn by making an *ex ante* agreement, hence the bargaining surplus, is the profit available by avoiding *ex post* competition, namely $\pi_{x+y} - (\pi^c_x + \pi^c_y) > 0$. Splitting the surplus, their profits in the *ex ante* agreement are $(\pi^c_x - c_1 + \frac{1}{2}(\pi_{x+y} - (\pi^c_x + \pi^c_y)), (\pi^c_y - c_2 + \frac{1}{2}(\pi_{x+y} - (\pi^c_x + \pi^c_y))$. Because $\pi^c_x < \pi_{x+y} - \pi^c_y$, the profit earned by firm 1 is

$$\frac{1}{2}\left(\pi_{x+y} + \pi^c_x - \pi^c_y\right) - c_1 < \frac{1}{2}\left(2\pi_{x+y} - 2\pi^c_y\right) - c_1$$
$$= \pi_{x+y} - c_1 - \pi^c_y < \pi_{x+y} - (c_1 + c_2).$$

That is, firm 1 earns less than the full joint profit.

Suppose now that firm 2 would enter without an *ex ante* agreement and $y < y^*$. Firm 2 could not compete with firm 1 *ex post*. An *ex post* license would enable them to bring an improvement to market and sell it at joint profit π_{x+y}. The *ex ante* agreement provides the same joint profit as entry with *ex post* licensing, and because there is no surplus to split, the division of profit will be the same as with *ex post* licensing. The bargaining surplus for the *ex post* license is $\pi_{x+y} - \pi_x$. Splitting this surplus equally, the profits of the firms in both an *ex post* license and an *ex ante* agreement are

$$\left(\pi_x - c_1 + \tfrac{1}{2}\left(\pi_{x+y} - \pi_x\right), \tfrac{1}{2}\left(\pi_{x+y} - \pi_x\right) - c_2\right).$$

The circumstance only arises if $\tfrac{1}{2}(\pi_{x+y} - \pi_x) - c_2 \geq 0$, or $\tfrac{1}{2}\pi_x \leq \tfrac{1}{2}\pi_{x+y} - c_2$. Thus the profit earned by firm 1 is

$$\tfrac{1}{2}\pi_{x+y} + \tfrac{1}{2}\pi_x - c_1 \leq \pi_{x+y} - (c_1 + c_2).$$

Contrary to what we have assumed so far, firm 2 might not enter without an *ex ante* agreement: e.g., if the product would infringe ($y < y^*$), and profit would seriously be eroded by *ex post* licensing. Firm 2's profit with *ex post* licensing, $\tfrac{1}{2}(\pi_{x+y} - \pi_x) - c_2$, might be negative. If firm 2 would not enter absent an *ex ante* agreement, the bargaining surplus is the incremental profit $\pi_{x+y} - \pi_x - c_2$ provided by the improvement if it is positive, so the profits in the *ex ante* agreement are

$$\left(\pi_x - c_1 + \tfrac{1}{2}\left(\pi_{x+y} - \pi_x - c_2\right), \tfrac{1}{2}\left(\pi_{x+y} - \pi_x - c_2\right)\right).$$

Because the two firms' profits sum to $\pi_{x+y} - (c_1 + c_2)$, and because firm 2's profit is greater than or equal to zero (and for some products will be positive), firm 1's profit is no greater than $\pi_{x+y} - (c_1 + c_2)$.

This completes the proof, as we have exhausted all the cases.

Q.E.D.

The three cases considered in the proof show why the second innovator has bargaining power, so that the first innovator cannot collect all the profit. First, if the second product will not infringe, the first innovator is threatened with profit-eroding *ex post* competition, as well as the inability to collect royalties on the new product. Second, if the product infringes but its incremental benefits are large relative to its costs, the second innovator may find it profitable to invest even though he must negotiate licensing fees *ex post* after his costs are sunk. He will not give away more profit in the *ex ante* agreement than is available by declining the *ex ante* agreement in favor of *ex post* licensing. And third, if the second innovator has an exclusive ability to develop the product, he might have a credible threat not to do so unless he gets a positive fraction of the incremental profit.

4. Optimal patent breadth

In the case of isolated inventions, it would be optimal, if possible, for the patent life to be just long enough to cover the costs of R&D.[3] But Proposition

---

3 This is true so long as R&D costs are "lump sum" and there is no issue of distorting flow rates of investment. See our discussion in Section 6.

1 shows that this principle does not apply when two stages of innovation are undertaken by different firms, because not all the profit can be transferred to the first innovator. If the patent life is just long enough to cover total R&D costs ($c_1 + c_2$), the first innovator will in general not enter because he could anticipate negative profit. Nevertheless, the more profit we can transfer to the first innovator, the shorter is the patent life required to stimulate research. It is therefore of interest to investigate the policies regarding patent breadth and the antitrust policy toward licensing that contribute to the goal of transferring profit from the second innovator to the first.

Turning first to the optimal breadth of the first patent, we ask whether it is best to implement the natural and straightforward policy of setting $y^* = \infty$ so that improved products and applications automatically infringe the orignal patent. So far we have assumed that firm 2's "idea" is a realization (y, c_2), which means that all the uncertainty about the benefits and costs are resolved before investing. In this circumstance it turns out that $y^* = \infty$ is the best policy because it minimizes firm 2's profit in the *ex ante* agreement. To see this, first consider ideas (y, c_2) such that $\frac{1}{2}(\pi_{x+y} + \pi_x) - c_2 < 0$ (so that firm 2 would not enter without an *ex ante* agreement if the product infringed), and $\pi^c_y - c_2 \geq 0$ (firm 2 would enter without an *ex ante* agreement if the second product did not infringe). Firm 2 gets $\frac{1}{2}(\pi_{x+y} - \pi_x - c_2)$ in the *ex ante* agreement if the product infringes, and $\frac{1}{2}(\pi_{x+y} - (\pi^c_y - \pi^c_x)) + (\pi^c_y - c_2)$ if not. Firm 2 is worse off if the product infringes because

$$\frac{1}{2}\left(\pi_{x+y} - \pi_x - c_2\right) < \frac{1}{2}\left(\pi_{x+y} - \pi^c_x - c_2\right) + \frac{1}{2}\left(\pi^c_y - c_2\right)$$
$$= \frac{1}{2}\left(\pi_{x+y} - \left(\pi^c_x + \pi^c_y\right)\right) + \left(\pi^c_y - c_2\right).$$

Now consider ideas (y, c_2) such that firm 2 would not enter without an *ex ante* agreement, even if its product did not infringe. Then firm 2 gets the same profit in the *ex ante* agreement whether or not the product infringes, because the firms split the same surplus *ex ante* in both cases. Finally, consider ideas (y, c_2) such that firm 2 would enter whether or not the second product infringed. The profit the firms would split in the case of infringement would be $\pi_{x+y} - \pi_x$, and in the case of noninfringement it would be $\pi_{x+y} - (\pi^c_x + \pi^c_y)$. Therefore, in the *ex ante* agreement, firm 2 gets $\frac{1}{2}(\pi_{x+y} - \pi_x) - c_2$ in the case of infringement, and $\frac{1}{2}(\pi_{x+y} - (\pi^c_y + \pi^c_x)) + (\pi^c_y - c_2)$ in the case of non-infringement. Because

$$\frac{1}{2}\left(\pi_{x+y} - \pi_x\right) - c_2 < \frac{1}{2}\left(\pi_{x+y} - \pi^c_x + \pi^c_y\right) - c_2$$
$$= \frac{1}{2}\left(\pi_{x+y} - \left(\pi^c_y + \pi^c_x\right)\right) + \left(\pi^c_y - c_2\right),$$

firm 2 gets more profit if its product does not infringe. Thus, for all ideas (y, c_2), firm 1 is better off in the *ex ante* agreement if firm 2's product infringes. Therefore:

Proposition 2. *If all the uncertainty on y and c_2 is resolved prior to investment in the second product, the best patent breadth is $y^* = \infty$.*

It is intuitive that the best way to protect firm 1's profit is to give firm
1 a broad patent. But curiously, this is not necessarily true when the
only uncertainty on c_2 has been resolved. To take the extreme case,
suppose that an "idea" is (G, c_2); firm 2 knows how much it must invest,
but it does not know at the time of investment how valuable the
outcome will be. In this case, firm 2 cannot make a different entry
decision for every y, conditional on c_2. However, the optimal breadth
may now be finite, as shown in Proposition 3. The condition that
$E_G \frac{1}{2}(\pi_{x + y} - \pi_x) - c_2 \leq 0$ for all c_2 in the support of H means that if
the firm must license *ex post* for sure, it would never enter without an *ex
ante* agreement. We have already interpreted the assumption that $\pi_{x + y}
= \pi_x + \pi_y^c = \pi_x^c + \pi_y^c$; it could be either the special case where the second-
generation product is an application, or the special case where the
second-generation product is a spin-off product that serves an unrelated
market.

The intuition behind Proposition 3 is that a very broad patent can give
firm 2 a credible threat not to enter, because it knows that with high
probability its profit will be eroded through *ex post* licensing. This credible
threat enables firm 2 to bargain *ex ante* for half the incremental value of
the new product. If the first patent is narrower, there is some possibility
that firm 2's product will turn out to be noninfringing, which raises the
expected profit from entering without an *ex ante* license. A narrower
patent can overcome firm 2's credible threat not to enter, while keeping
firm 2's expected profit less than half the incremental value of the new
product.

Proposition 3. Suppose firm 2's "idea" is (G, c_2). Suppose further
that $E_G \frac{1}{2}(\pi_{x + y} - \pi_x) - c_2 \leq 0$ for all c_2 in the support of H, and
that $\pi_{x + y} = \pi_x + \pi_y^c = \pi_x^c + \pi_y^c$. Then the optimal patent breadth is
finite, $y^* < \infty$.

Proof: If firm 2 enters in the absence of an *ex ante* agreement, its expected
profit is

$$\int_{y*}^{\infty} \pi_y^c \, dG + \int_0^{y*} \frac{1}{2}(\pi_{x+y} - \pi_x) dG - c_2 = \int_{y*}^{\infty} \pi_y^c \, dG + \int_0^{y*} \frac{1}{2}\pi_y^c \, dG - c_2.$$

We can assume that $E_G \pi_y^c - c_{2L} > 0$, where c_{2L} is the smallest c_2 in the
support of H; otherwise no policy will induce entry of firm 2, and there is
no problem to solve. Because $E_G \frac{1}{2}\pi_y^c - c_{2L} < 0 < E_G \pi_y^c - c_{2L}$, there is $y^{**}
< \infty$ that satisfies

$$\int_{y^{**}}^{\infty} \pi_y^c dG + \int_0^{y^{**}} \frac{1}{2}\pi_y^c \, dG - c_{2L} = 0.$$

For all projects with $c_2 > c_{2L}$, the patent breadth y^{**} provides the same benefit to firm 1 as $y^* = \infty$, namely max $\{\frac{1}{2}(E_G \pi^c_y - c_2), 0\}$. (Without an *ex ante* agreement, firm 2 would not enter, and therefore, in the *ex ante* agreement, the two firms split $E_G \pi_y^c - c_2$). For the project with cost c_{2L}, firm 1 earns more profit with y^{**} than with $y^* = \infty$, the bargaining surplus is $E_G\pi^c_y - c_{2L}$. With the breadth y^{**}, there is no longer a bargaining surplus to be split, because firm 2 would invest even without an *ex ante* agreement and earn zero profit, which is less than $\frac{1}{2}(E_G \pi^c_y - c_{2L})$. Thus the policy y^{**} transfers more profit to firm 1 than the policy $y^* = \infty$.

Q.E.D.

5. Antitrust policy

Our main objective has been to study patent policy, and to show the important role of patent breadth in setting threat points for negotiating licensing agreements between sequential innovators. By setting the threat points, the patent breadth determines the division of profit in each period and affects the minimum paetnt length required to stimulate R&D.

A subsidiary issue, which cannot be studied in depth without more structure than we have imposed on our model, is what types of licensing agreements the antitrust authorities should allow. So far we have taken the antitrust policy as fixed. We have assumed that *ex post* licensing is possible only if the second product infringes. This excludes *ex post* collusive licensing between innovators who would otherwise compete in the market. We have also assumed that *ex ante* agreements are not always legal. There is a slight inconsistency here in that the firms are allowed to collude by forming agreements *ex ante* even when such collusion would be prohibited *ex post*. Our first task in this section is to explain these assumptions, and our second task is to shed some light on the optimal design of antitrust policy.

The antitrust authorities would presumably allow *ex post* collusion only if it was necessary *ex ante* to encourage R&D; otherwise they would prohibit it in order to protect consumers. To justify collusion *ex post*, the antitrust authorities would have to reason that without the assurance of *ex post* permission to collude, the firms would not have invested. The problem of verifying this circumstance *ex post* seems daunting, especially because firms have incentive to misrepresent. Once R&D is done, the antitrust authorities might easily want to protect consumers rather than compensate firms for their sunk costs of R&D.

Contrast this with the problem of giving *ex ante* permission to collude: the firms might argue that they will not invest without an *ex ante* agreement because *ex post* competition between them will erode their profit.

Such an argument might be more credible if it is made before costs are sunk rather than after. In addition, it is unknown *ex ante* whether the second product will infringe; if it does, the firms will end up merging their interests *ex post* anyway, and there is no consumer loss due to the *ex ante* agreement. These considerations might make the antitrust authorities more lenient. In addition, the firms' opportunity to merge their interests *ex ante* will reinforce the antitrust authorities in their skepticism about collusive licensing *ex post*. If petitioned by opportunistic firms *ex post*, the antitrust authorities could reasonably reply that if the firms had truly been worried about profit-eroding competition, they should have petitioned to merge their interests *ex ante*.

Although we believe that our assumptions about contracting opportunities are reasonable and might reflect current policy, the arguments we have just made are not unassailable, and it is therefore of interest to consider the optimal design of antitrust policy. What types of licensing *should* be legal? *Ex ante* and not *ex post*? *Ex post* and not *ex ante*? *Ex ante* only when the second product would infringe? It is obvious that at least one type of licensing should be permitted. Otherwise no firm would ever invest in an infringing second-generation product (because he could not bring it to market), and this would impede progress if firms have specialized abilities.

We first consider *ex post* licensing, assuming that *ex ante* licensing is legal. It is hard to imagine that the authorities would prohibit such licensing, because they would reason that an infringing product could not come to market without a license. However, this argument is flawed if firms can license *ex ante* instead of *ex post*. When *ex ante* licensing is available, the only role of *ex post* licensing is to shift the threat points of the *ex ante* agreement. The possibility of *ex post* licensing does not affect the total profit that is available to the firms, but only the division of it.[4] It turns out that the possibility of *ex post* licensing favors the first innovator because it may take away firm 2's credible threat not to enter, which reduces his bargaining power in an *ex ante* agreement. (The argument is similar to the argument above in Proposition 3.) To show this, we return to the assumption that firm 2's "idea" is a realization (y, c_2), although a similar argument applies when an "idea" is (G, c_2).

Proposition 4. Assume *ex ante* licensing is legal. For any patent breadth, the first innovator earns greater profit if *ex post* licensing is permitted than if not.

Proof. We need to show that for a given T and y^*, the possibility of *ex post* licensing increases firm 1's profit in the *ex ante* agreement and decreases

---

4 Horbulyk (1991) shows how *compulsory* licensing, which affects the terms of the *ex post* licensing agreement, can have a further salutary effect on the threat points. In his model the compulsory fee is fixed in advance by the authorities.

firm 2's profit. We divide our analysis into three cases. The first case is when the second product does not infringe ($y > y^*$). Then *ex post* licensing is irrelevant, and the firms' profits in an *ex ante* agreement are the same whether or not *ex post* licensing is legal. The second case is when the second product infringes ($y < y^*$), but firm 2 would not enter without an *ex ante* agreement even if licensing were legal (and *a fortiori* would not enter if licensing were not legal). Then the firms' profits with an *ex ante* agreement are respectively the same whether or not licensing is legal. The only case where *ex post* licensing matters for dividing the profit *ex ante* is when the second product infringes ($y < y^*$) and firm 2 would enter if *ex post* licensing were legal, but not otherwise: i.e., when $\frac{1}{2}(\pi_{x+y} - \pi_x) - c_2 > 0$. When *ex post* licensing is prohibited, the firms' profits with no agreement would be $(\pi_x - c_1, 0)$, and with an *ex ante* agreement they would be

$$\left(\pi_x - c_1 + \tfrac{1}{2}\left(\pi_{x+y} - \pi_x - c_2\right), \tfrac{1}{2}\left(\pi_{x+y} - \pi_x - c_2\right)\right).$$

When licensing is legal, the firms' profits with *ex post* licensing would be $(\pi_x - c_1 + \frac{1}{2}(\pi_{x+y} - \pi_x), \frac{1}{2}(\pi_{x+y} - \pi_x) - c_2)$. Hence, firm 1's profit is greater when licensing is legal than when it is not.

Q.E.D

A more troublesome question is whether *ex ante* agreements should be permitted given that *ex post* licensing is permitted. The consequence of permitting *ex ante* agreements is that for the duration of the patents the products are sold by a single monopolist who earns profit $\pi_{x+y}(T)$. If *ex ante* licensing were prohibited, and if the second product infringed, then the two products would compete in the market and earn $\pi^c_x(T)$ and $\pi^c_y(T)$ instead of the longer $\pi_{x+y}(T)$. Although the per-period profit of firms is then smaller, the per-period customers' surplus is larger. To compensate firms for smaller per-period profit, the patents must be longer, but lengthening the patent hurts consumers.

With no more structure on the model than we have so far imposed, it is impossible in general to say whether it is better to force competition for a longer period or permit collusion for a shorter period. Nevertheless, we can identify at least one important circumstance in which *ex ante* agreements should clearly be allowed. The next proposition says that when the second-generation product is an application of a basic technology (rather than an improvement of it), allowing *ex ante* agreements permits a shorter patent life while not affecting per-period monopoly distortions. Therefore, *ex ante* agreements improve social welfare.

Proposition 5. *Suppose that second-generation products are applications of the first technology, which has no value as a stand-alone product, that is, $\pi_{x+y} = \pi^c_y$. Then whatever the patent breadth, ex ante licensing improves social welfare.*

Proof. The per-period monopoly distortions are the same whether the license is *ex ante* or *ex post*, or whether the second product is noninfringing and marketed with no license. In all these regimes, the second product is marketed by a monopolist, and the first product does not compete with it. *Ex ante* agreements increase social welfare because they can ensure that the second product is developed (which improves utility even though there are monopoly distortions), and they can increase the profit of the first innovator. If the patent life is such that firm 2 would enter without an *ex ante* agreement (whether or not the second product is infringed), then the *ex ante* agreement will not change either the monopoly distortions or the firms' profits and is irrelevant. But if the second innovator would not enter (either because the patent life is so short that $\frac{1}{2}(\pi^c_y(T) - c_2) < 0$ or because *ex post* licensing is illegal), then if $\frac{1}{2}(\pi^c_y(T) - c_2) > 0$, *ex ante* agreements will ensure that the investment is made, and will also increase the first innovator's profit. Thus, permitting *ex ante* agreements never decreases social welfare, and for some T increases social welfare.

Q.E.D.

The unresolved question is for the case that the two products compete, e.g., the second is an improved version of the first, or they are horizontally differentiated. To address this case we would need more structure in our model. By assuming the same structure of preferences and the same type of competition as Kemperer (1990) assumes, we might be able to infer whether *ex ante* agreements should be allowed. However, we do not wish to adopt additional structure, as our other conclusions do not require it.

An intermediate policy between always allowing or always disallowing *ex ante* licensing is to allow a complete *ex ante* merger of interests when the second product would infringe the first patent, but not otherwise. If the second product would likely not infringe, assume that the firms can agree *ex ante* to share costs c_2, but must compete *ex post* in the market.[5] Of course, such a rule would be hard to interpret unless all the uncertainty about the second product ("y") were resolved before investing in it, because it would not be known whether the product would infringe. For purposes of discussion we will assume that the uncertainty is largely resolved. If it were known that the second product would infringe, then the division of profit in the *ex ante* license would be as discussed above. If it were known that the second product would not infringe, there would be no *ex ante* agreement to share costs. If $\pi^c_y(T) - c_2 > 0$, the second firm would enter without an agreement, and then there is no reason for the

---

5 Such a rule would be in the spirit of the literature following d'Aspremont and Jacquemin (1990), in which firms are allowed to cooperate in R&D but required to compete *ex post* in the market. In that literature, R&D reduces unit costs of production, and there are positive spillovers between firms in reducing costs. Firms will cooperate to exploit those spillovers even if they must compete *ex post*.

agreement, because it cannot increase both firms' profits. If $\pi^c_y(T) \quad c_2 < 0$ so that the second firm would not enter without some cost sharing, then, because $\pi^c_x(T) - \pi_x(T) < 0$, it follows that $(\pi^c_x(T) + \pi^c_y(T)) - \pi_x(T) - c_2 < 0$. The latter is the increment to profit that the firms would jointly earn investing in the second product, and they will therefore not invest. If *ex post* competition were not required, then the incremental joint profit would be $\pi_{x+y}(T) - \pi_x(T) - c_2$, which might be positive even when $\pi^c_y(T) - c_2 < 0$.

Thus, forcing firms to compete except in cases of infringement undermines the joint profit the two firms can collect. In order to ensure a fixed profit for the first innovator, the patent must last longer when *ex post* competition is required in cases of noninfringement than when the firms can always merge their interests through *ex ante* licensing. The welfare considerations are similar to those discussed above: it might be better to prevent collusion and let the patent last longer rather than to permit collusion for a shorter period. Our model does not have enough structure to address this issue.

We conclude this section with a remark on the interaction between patent policy and antitrust policy. In general, optimal patent policy should depend on what contracts the firms are permitted to make or are likely to make. A patent policy that assumes firms will license *ex ante* could be counterproductive if there were obstacles to such agreements, such as asymmetries in information, that would make contracts difficult to negotiate. For example, for the case that all uncertainty on y is resolved prior to the second investment, we concluded that if *ex ante* licensing is available, the first patent should be so broad that all second products infringe it. This is not the optimal policy if *ex ante* agreements are prohibited. Suppose that $\frac{1}{2}(\pi_{x+y}(T) - \pi_x(T) - c_2) < 0$ for all products. Then prohibiting *ex ante* agreements would ensure there would be no investment in second-generation products. A better patent policy would be to make some second-generation products noninfringing.[6]

6. Conclusion

We have studied the interaction between patent breadth and antitrust policy in a simple model designed to focus attention on the division of profit between sequential innovators, and to see how the division of profit depends on patent breadth and on the opportunities for cost-sharing

---

6 If the high-value second products would be invented but not the low-value products, then one might want to make only the low value products noninfringing. Chang (1995) discusses such a policy, although it might be hard to reconcile with patent law. We have assumed that patent breadth must be a "cutoff" policy y^* such that only products with $y > y^*$ are noninfringing.

through licensing. Despite the simplicity of the model, we believe that some of our propositions are very robust.

Ex ante agreements have the potential to increase the expected profits of both parties without inhibiting later research, but even with *ex ante* agreements, the first innovator cannot collect all the profit from second-generation improvements. This conclusion, which derives primarily from the fact that the second innovator has bargaining power, seems quite general, and it has a clear consequence for patent length: in order to give sufficient incentive for basic research, patents must last longer when cumulative innovation is undertaken by different firms than when both generations of research are concentrated in the same firm.[7] In the latter case, there is no problem of dividing profit.

In the model presented here, the sequential innovators will always form *ex ante* agreements, and the roles of *ex post* licensing and patent breadth are to set "threat points" for such agreements. We concluded that the possibility of *ex post* licensing has a salutary effect on the first innovator's profit in *ex ante* agreements. We would have been quite disturbed to reach the opposite conclusion, because *ex ante* agreements might not occur for a variety of reasons not discussed here, and then *ex post* licensing is necessary to bring improved products to market. We were less conclusive about the circumstances in which *ex ante* agreements should be legal, except in the (not uncommon) case where second-generation products are applications of a basic technology. In that case, *ex ante* agreement unambiguously serves the public interest. As to the breadth of patent protection, we have shown circumstances in which the first patent should be broad, but other circumstances in which a broad patent reduces the first innovator's profit because it increases the later innovator's bargaining power. It does this by giving the later innovator a credible threat not to undertake a profitable investment unless the first innovator is willing to share the costs. Counterintuitively, the first innovator can be better off with a narrower patent when the patent's life is fixed.

Except for the qualifications in Section 5, the premise behind all these conclusions is that it is desirable to mimimize the patent life in order to minimize the duration of monopoly distortions. We should notice, however, that minimizing the patent life could have a distortionary effect not yet discussed: It could reduce the rates of R&D investment as in the extensive patent race literature based on the Poisson process. Our model avoids this issue because R&D investments are lump sum. However, if the

---

7 If the sequential patents could have different lengths, and if the lengths could depend on the costs of R&D, then all the profit could be transferred to the first innovator. However, patent law has no provision for patent length to reflect R&D costs, and in any case, for such a scheme to work, the length of the patent on the initial innovation would have to be different for each second-generation product. See Scotchmer (1991a, 1991b, forthcoming) for further discussion.

rates of investment were endogenous, our model would face the same tradeoff as any other patent race model: by reducing the patent value (patent life), one reduces the rate at which firms find it optimal to invest, and this could be inefficient. (This issue is discussed in Loury, 1979; Nordhaus, 1969; Dasgupta and Stiglitz, 1980; and Gandal and Scotchmer 1993.) In this richer model, the optimal patent life must consider the effects both on rates of investment and on monopoly distortions.

For completeness, it is worth noting that our main result on patent life would follow if we were concerned with rates of R&D investment as well as with minimizing monopoly distortions. To take the extreme case, let T^* be the patent life that elicits efficient rates of investment in the first stage of innovation with a fixed number of firms, possibly one, when each first-stage firm is capable also of developing the second product. Compare this with what happens if the two stages take place in different firms. By our argument in Section 2, the second-stage firms will collect some of the joint profit, and therefore each firm at the first stage races for a smaller reward. The firms will therefore reduce their rates of investment. To restore the efficient rates of investment, the patent life (patent value) must be increased.

One might worry that the conclusions of this article depend critically on the fact that a unique firm can develop the improvement or application. Although it is easy to imagine that a single firm has the idea or capability for the improvement or application, it is also easy to imagine that the idea leaks out, and that several firms might compete for an *ex ante* license for the same improvement or application. Such competition should aid the first patentholder in capturing profit. However, Scotchmer (1991b) argues that even in that case the first innovator cannot capture all the profit. The firm that receives the *ex ante* license might nevertheless find itself in a race. If another firm achieves the improvement first, the license becomes less valuable because two firms now hold blocking patents on the improved product. We are therefore back to bilateral bargaining, and this possibility will reduce each firm's willingness to pay for an *ex ante* license.

Finally, we reiterate that patent length and breadth play a diffferent role when innovation is cumulative and *ex ante* agreements are available than when they are not. In the models of Gilbert and Shapiro 1990) and Klemperer (1990) there is only one innovator, and the authors study the question of whether it is better to provide a fixed amount of profit by granting a long, narrow patent or a short, broad one. Broadening the patent increases the per-period profit earned by the innovator. In the Gilbert and Shapiro model this is because a broader patent permits the innovating monopolist to charge a greater markup. In the Klemperer model it is because a broader patent prevents competitors from selling close substitutes. In our model the per-period joint profit of the firms is fixed because the sequence of innovators will act like a joint monopolist. The role of patent breadth is not to determine the *level* of per-period profit, but rather its *division* betweeen sequential innovators. It does this by establishing the bargaining positions of sequential innovators who might end up holding blocking patents if they did not agree *ex ante* to license. If one looks only at the first innovator, then it follows from Proposition 3 that for a fixed patent life, narrowing his patent would increase his profit, contrary to what happens in the models of KIemperer and Gilbert and Shapiro.

References

CHANG, H. F. "Patent Scope, Antitrust Policy, and Cumulative Innovation," *RAND Journal of Economics*, Vol. 26 (1995), pp. 34–57.

DASGUPTA, P. AND STIGLITZ, J. "Uncertainty, Industrial Structure, and the Speed of R&D." *Bell Journal of Economics*, Vol. 11 (1980), pp. 1–28.

D'ASPREMONT, C. AND JACQUEMIN, A. "Cooperative and Noncooperative R&D in Duopoly with Spillover." *American Economic Review*, Vol. 80 (1990) pp. 641–642.

GALLINI, N. T. "Deterrence by Market Sharing: A Strategic Incentive for Licensing." *American Economic Review*, Vol. 74 (1984), pp. 931–941.

GANDAL, N. AND SCOTCHMER, S. "Coordinating Research through Research Joint Ventures." *Journal of Public Economics*, Vol. 51 (1993), pp. 173–193.

GILBERT, R. AND SHAPIRO, C. "Optimal Patent Length and Breadth." *RAND Journal of Economics*, Vol. 21 (1990), pp. 106–112.

GREEN, J. AND SCOTCHMER, S. *"Antitrust Policy, the Breadth of Patent Protection and the Incentive to Develop New Products."* H.I.E.R. Working Paper, Harvard University, December 1989.

HORBULYK, T. M. *"Compulsory Licensing of Innovation and the Incentives for Cumulative Research."* Mimeo. University of Calgary, 1991.

KLEMPERER, P. "How Broad Should the Scope of Patent Protection Be?" *RAND Journal of Economics*, Vol. 21 (1990), pp. 113–130.

LOURY, G. C. "Market Structure and Innovation." *Quarterly Journal of Economics*, Vol. 93 (1979), pp. 395–410.

MATUTES, C., REGIBEAU, P., AND ROCKETT, K. E. *"Optimal Patent Protection and the Diffusion of Innovation."* Mimeo, Department of Economics, Northwestern University, December 1990.

MERGES, R. P. "Uncertainty and the Standard of Patentability." *High Technology Law Journal*, Vol. 7 (1992a), pp. 1–70.

——.*"On Limiting or Encouraging Rivalry in Technical Progress: The Effect of Patent Scope Decisions,"* Center for Law and Economics Studies Working Paper no. 72, Columbia University, 1992b.

MERGES, R. P. AND NELSON, R. R. "On the Complex Economics of Patent Scope." *Columbia Law Review*, Vol. 90 (1990), pp. 839–916.

—— AND ——.*"On Limiting or Encouraging Rivalry in Technical Progress: The Effect of Patent Scope Decisions,"* Center for Research in

Management, Consortium on Competitiveness and Cooperation, Working Paper no. 92–8, University of California, Berkeley, 1992.

NORDHAUS, W. D. *Invention, Growth and Welfare.* Cambridge, Mass: MIT Press, 1969.

SCOTCHMER, S. "Standing on the Shoulders of Giants: Cumulative Research and the Patent Law." *Journal of Economic Perspectives,* Vol. 5 (1991a), pp. 29–41.

—— "*Protecting Early Innovators: Should Second Generations Products be Patentable?*" Graduate School of Public Policy Working Paper no., 183, University of California, Berkeley 1991b.

—— "Patents as an Incentive System." *Proceedings of the 1992 World Congress of the International Ecomoics Association,* Paris, forthcoming.

SPENCE, A. M. "Cost Reduction, Competition, and Industry Performance." *Econometrica,* Vol. 52 (1984), pp. 101–121.

CHAPTER 18

Ted O'Donoghue, Suzanne Scotchmer, and Jacques Thisse, "Patent Breadth, Patent Life, and the Pace of Technological Progress" (1998)

INTRODUCTION NANCY GALLINI

Suzanne's IP theory papers on cumulative research address a host of policy levers, from the breadth and duration of patent protection to the remedies that courts provide for infringement to the constraints that antitrust places on licensing agreements. Throughout Suzanne's analysis, patent breadth was central. Together, her papers in this area provide what is arguably the most important and influential theoretical analysis of patent breadth in economics.

The following paper by O'Donoghue, Scotchmer and Thisse ("OST") provides a good example of these contributions. It recognizes two distinct components of patent breadth – *leading* and *lagging* – and the implications of each on incentives to innovate. In this essay, I outline the way in which OST fits into the evolution of Suzanne's wider insights on patent breadth, beginning with Green and Scotchmer (1995), and the influence her ideas have had on subsequent theoretical, empirical, and policy research.

Patent Breadth and Life

The single-invention R&D model of Nordhaus (1969) explored only one policy lever – patent life or duration – as a means of encouraging R&D. In the decades that followed, researchers began to examine models with entry by firms duplicating the invention or imitating it with differentiated substitutes. This naturally led to examination of a second policy lever: patent breadth. But this analysis was developed in models that effectively retained the conventional framework of the discrete, one-time invention. (See, e.g., Klemperer, 1990; Gilbert and Shapiro, 1990; Gallini, 1992.)

Suzanne's framework, starting with Scotchmer and Green (1990) and "Giants" (1991), was very different. The new paradigm – inspired by modern knowledge-based companies such as biotechnology, telecommunications, and consumer electronics – saw innovation as a cumulative research process in which inventions build on previous research and discoveries. In her analysis, sequential ideas are complementary or vertically related. For example, an entrant could provide an application of the pioneer's basic research or improve on the first generation technology, rather than simply supply a competing imitation as in the earlier models. This new focus shifted the central inquiry from *"What should be the reward?"* to *"How should the reward be divided among the (possibly numerous) R&D stages to encourage efficient innovation?"* The latter question was first addressed in the elegant sequential framework of Green and Scotchmer (1995). In this paper, the question "How should the reward be divided?" turned out to be equivalent to: *How broad should the pioneer's patent be?* Their answer: Patent breadth should be set at the level that maximizes the return to the pioneer, after compensating the second firm for research costs, so as to shorten patent duration and therefore minmize deadweight loss. That level will depend, in turn, on the ease with which researchers can contract around conflicts in IP rights through licensing agreements.

Green and Scotchmer allowed the pioneer firm to renegotiate its property rights through two types of licensing: *ex ante* licensing (negotiated prior to the second firm making its R&D investment) and *ex post* licensing (negotiated after the R&D investment is sunk). It is here that patent breadth plays a distinct role from patent duration: it sets the "threat points" in the negotiations that will divide the pie; patent life then determines the size of the reward. This framework also crucially introduces the concept of *leading* breadth, which allows the pioneer to charge royalties on its invention when used to develop subsequent improvements; effectively, this form of breadth gives the pioneer property rights on future innovations. When breadth is *leading*, as in Green and Scotchmer, it can have important implications for *ex ante* licensing. There, *ex ante* licensing can *facilitate* the development of a new, productive innovation. However, when breadth can only cover imitations of the pioneer's invention (called *lagging* breadth in OST) as in the previous literature, then *ex ante* licensing can *deter* the development of improvements (e.g., Gallini-Winter, 1985).

Suzanne and coauthors would further develop this *lead/lag* distinction in OST and beyond to arrive at important policy insights (*infra*). Returning to the above question, what is the patent breadth (or threat point) that will give the pioneer the larger piece of total surplus? Green and Scotchmer show that typically the best patent–antitrust policy is typically one that grants broad patent rights and allows unrestricted *ex ante* licensing. That way, the pioneer can negotiate with the subsequent innovator, ensuring sufficient compensation for its research investment as well as a share of the additional surplus from the improvement. Since this policy yields a greater flow of profits to the pioneer, it also leaves consumers with greater surplus by reducing the time before inventions enter the public domain. Importantly, broad patents are *not* introduced to motivate innovation per se – long, narrow patents would provide the same reward – but rather to shorten patent life by giving the pioneer a larger piece of the per-period pie.

But here is the wrinkle: broad patents may not always be the best because of an interesting economic subtlety. The pioneer may, in fact, be better off when patents are *both* narrow *and* shorter. The reason – counter-intuitively – is that the pioneer sometimes finds that a narrow patent actually *increases* its bargaining power. Here is why: If patents were broad, the second inventor could credibly threaten not to innovate unless the pioneer agreed *ex ante* to split the cost of its research. In contrast, a narrow patent can sometimes undercut the second inventor's threat by making it profitable to develop the improvement even if *ex ante* negotiations fail. The net result is that a narrow patent can leave more surplus with the pioneer while simultaneously rewarding consumers with a shorter patent life. This important impact on optimal patent design highlights a crucial departure of the sequential innovation paradigm from the traditional one-time innovation model, in which broad patents could never disadvantage a pioneer researcher.

So, a deep message of Green and Scotchmer (1995) is that *the effectiveness of IP depends importantly on the ease with which innovators can contract around conflicts in their property rights.* This (optimistically) suggests that private contracting can complement public policy levers in reducing social costs of patents by allowing the patent-holder to profit from potential competition. Related to this, Acemoglu and Ackcigit (2006) find in a general equilibrium framework that a state-dependent patent policy in which stronger protection is given to leaders along with licensing so that followers can "catch up" provides increased incentives for cumulative innovation and contributes to growth. Although the drivers in the partial and general equilibrium models differ, the results are strikingly consistent in recommending strong patents for leaders and licensing to facilitate follow-on research.

The trouble, of course, is that contracting can also suppress competition by restricting entry. Importantly, IP policy should not be viewed in isolation as simply a matter of property rights provided by the patent system and enforced by the courts. Instead, its social impact also depends on private contracting (as limited by antitrust policy and contract law) and transaction costs in bargaining. This insight requires policymakers to look beyond Nordhaus's one-time innovation model to a multi-temporal/multi-innovation/multi-institutional framework that considers antitrust and IP together.

Lagging and Leading Patent Breadth

As noted above, leading breadth protects against improvements while lagging breadth protects against imitations. These have very different strategic and social implications for *ex ante* licensing. OST unites both effects within a single theoretical framework for a sequence of improvements.

OST compares two possible patent policies: (a) infinite patent life with finite leading breadth and (b) finite patent life with infinite leading breadth. (Lagging breadth protection is assumed in both cases.) They show that optimal patent protection should include some degree of leading *and* lagging patent breadth; otherwise innovation rewards can be seriously reduced when the "hit rate" of better ideas obsoletes earlier products. In that case, the *effective* patent life will fall short of the statutory one. In comparing the two patent regimes, the case of finite breadth and infinite *statutory* life is more efficient in reducing R&D costs. Although it would also require a higher *effective* patent life to generate the same rate of innovation as an infinitely broad patent, it would be socially preferred in the absence of any market distortions. But when reality is introduced through static inefficiencies, a tradeoff arises between lower R&D costs for the narrow (but long) patent and the lower market distortions in the broad (but short) regimes. As in Green and Scotchmer, broad patents can be advantageous in reducing market distortions from delays in the diffusion of quality innovations, although at higher R&D costs. This paper is an important contribution to the literature, in recognizing the distinct roles of these two forms of breadth for informing policy. Moreover, it highlights that statutory patent life as a policy lever for encouraging research may be ineffective in industries with rapid technological turnover.

OST has also been useful in providing a framework for theorists seeking to extend the basic sequential innovation paradigm. For example, Hopenhayn et al. (2006) extend the OST analysis in search of the best mechanism among patents, prizes, and "buyouts." Their optimal mechanism includes a patent buyout, selected by the patentee in advance, and paid by the follower in order to commercialize its improvement. Effectively, the required buyout must satisfy a predefined quality threshold and, therefore, can be interpreted as a measure of "patent breadth." In practice, this mechanism is a form of compulsory licensing. Since the driving force in this model is the buyout payment (patent breadth), with *effective* patent life defined by the time it takes for a follower to achieve the quality threshold, the mechanism provides a generalization of the polar case in OST of a fixed breadth/infinite life policy. Hopenhayn et al (2006) also parallels Scotchmer (1999) on the patent renewal system. In the latter paper, prospective patentees are offered a menu of patent lives and fees – a longer life can be chosen for a higher fee – whereas Hopenhayn et al. allows patentees to choose from a menu of patent breadths in return for a buyout fee paid by later entrants. (See also Hopenhayn-Mitchell, 2001). This literature provides creative ways in which an otherwise uniform patent system can be nuanced by giving privately informed researchers the opportunity to self-select into different degrees of patent protection.

Patent Breadth and Patentability

Suzanne also examined the relationships between patent breadth and the standards for attaining a patent in the first place. Prior to Scotchmer (1996) economists had conflated these two patent levers: if patents were very broad, then the literature seemed to suggest that an infringing invention would not be sufficiently novel to merit a patent. Yet, legally, the concepts are distinct: patentability is governed by "novelty" and "non-obviousness" standards, whereas infringement is governed by the "doctrine of equivalents." Scotchmer asked: *To what extent is this legal distinction between breadth and patentability also distinct for purposes of economic analysis?*

Scotchmer (1996) showed that this formal legal distinction does have important economic consequences. She argued that, provided *ex ante* exclusive licenses are available, denying patents on a follow-on invention can increase a pioneer's bargaining power. This permits shorter patent lives without stifling future products. To see this, suppose the first patent is moderately broad and the inventive step is weak so that the follow-on firm can get an infringing patent. The threat points in this case will be duopoly with litigation, which could give the pioneer a smaller return. Injunction rules also impact the reservation profits since the follower faces a threat of being closed down. If that firm can counter-sue with an invalidity claim, then the reservation profit of the pioneer will also be lower, and incentives to negotiate higher. That is, legal rules affect firms' incentives to cooperate as well as to innovate and litigate.

However, if impediments to *ex ante* licensing exist, then second-generation innovation can indeed be compromised so that a weaker patentability standard could be better even when patent duration must be increased to maintain adequate rewards. This provides yet another instance of Green and Scotchmer's observation that *When R&D is decentralized among many firms rather than concentrated in one, patents must last longer to sufficiently compensate for R&D investment.* Another reason for allowing patents on second-generation innovations is to reduce delays between the basic and follow-on innovations, where expected delays might be taken as prima facie evidence that the second product was "non-obvious" and thus deserving of a patent. Of course, if patentability depended on delays, firms could strategically delay investments in order to qualify for patents.

Scotchmer develops these ideas further in *Innovation and Incentives* (2004). In particular, she explains that an invention can be patentable and infringing (e.g., novel improvements), non-patentable but not infringing (prior art), infringing and non-patentable (imitations), or patentable and non-infringing (blockbuster advances). She emphasized that even where patentability and non-infringement generate equivalent total profits, the division of rewards can be different. For example, if patents are narrow, the pioneer will prefer the follow-on invention to be patented, even if this gives the later inventor more bargaining power, because it avoids having to face multiple followers. On the other hand, a pioneer who receives a broad patent will typically prefer a restrictive patentability standard, since it increases the flow of profits while allowing for a shorter duration.

Patent Breadth and "Fair Use"

Suzanne was masterful at applying economics to legal principles. In this subsection I touch on her work involving "fair use" non-patent tools. In this research, Scotchmer consistently comes down on the side of the alleged infringer. In particular, Maurer and Scotchmer's paper on independent invention (2002) identifies conditions under which a follow-on researcher should be allowed to independently invent without fear of reprisal from an infringement suit, unless impediments to licensing are too great and duplication costs are too low. They show that such a provision will be efficient when *ex ante* licensing is available, in which case the pioneer can set a sufficiently low royalty to discourage firms from engaging in wasteful duplication. The threat of independent invention, therefore, encourages the pioneer to make its invention available. That reduces the price and unproductive duplication and costs from patent races. As in Scotchmer's earlier work, the idea that public and private levers are interdependent in achieving efficient outcomes is central to their analysis.

Samuelson and Scotchmer (2002, this volume) suggest how proposals for new IP rights should be designed with respect to reverse engineering. They analyze the law and economics of the 1998 Digital Millennium Copyright Act, which prohibited tools circumventing systems that protected digital copyrighted works, along with the Semiconductor Chip Protection Act of 1984. They recommend a form of limited reverse engineering that would permit valuable incremental innovation, noting that information-based industries are less protected by the costs and time to reverse engineer, compared to traditional manufacturers. They also warn that rules "protecting the protections" through technology can lead to excessive rights relative to that available through conventional IP rights. In allowing followers to learn the state of the art by recreating it, they contend, reverse engineering can be viewed as consistent with the social contract of IP of disclosure for protection.

Scotchmer also favored exemptions from infringement challenges for individuals using patented research tools for non-commercial research or experimental purposes (Scotchmer, 2004). Relatedly, Maurer and Scotchmer (1999) also contributed to the debate on databases. In 1996 Europe enacted broad, copyright-type protection for databases and insisted that the USA. and Canada do the same. Maurer and Scotchmer argued that the extensions would constrain research in the sciences, reducing the viability of non-profit databases and hampering free communication between scientists. Finally, while not a fair use provision, it is worth noting that she made a persuasive case for open source, noting that it can be more profitable than proprietary licensing when researchers operate under a "veil of ignorance," unaware in advance which of them will be the leader (Scotchmer, 2010).

Connecting the Pieces

So what do all of Scotchmer's findings imply about optimal patent breadth? As noted above, Scotchmer argued for broad patents to pioneers (Green and Scotchmer, 1995 [this volume]) and strict patentability standards for follow-on researchers (Scotchmer, 1996) in her earlier research, but then later argued for greater flexibility in *fair use* provisions for subsequent researchers (Maurer and Scotchmer, 2002; Samuelson and Scotchmer, 2002) which would narrow the breadth of the pioneer's patent. These results, at first glance, may seem to be at odds or even signal a change of heart towards the patent system. In fact, closer examination reveals that the two sets of results are entirely consistent, based on fundamental principles, and point to a clear, concise recommendation for optimal patent design.

To see this, first note that Scotchmer's earlier results on broad patents call for a commensurate reduction in patent length. Broad patents are optimal, not because they give the patentee more rents, but because they keep the monopoly period as short as possible. That is, Scotchmer believed the patent system should provide no more reward than is needed to stimulate productive innovation that otherwise would not occur. As OST points out, broad, short patents can be valuable in reducing delays in the diffusion of more efficient inventions. Moreover, it is important to note that *ex ante* licensing plays a powerful role in determining the optimality of broad patents; without it, the results could be reversed. Second, the earlier and later results pertain to qualitatively different types of breadth. The earlier results relate to broad (and short) *leading* breadth on improvements, whereas the fair use provisions refer to *lagging* breadth on duplications.

So, what does this imply for patent policy? While Scotchmer was careful not to be too prescriptive, her research collection is sufficiently rich to yield important policy recommendations. Combining the two streams of research suggests that – when *ex ante* licensing is possible – patent life should be broad and short on the upside (leading breadth) but narrow and long on the downside (lagging breadth). This is implementable by giving the pioneer a relatively short patent life against all subsequent inventions, followed by an additional term solely against imitators/duplicators with limited fair use exemptions. However, if *ex ante* contracts are not available, as empirical studies have found in some industries (see next section), then the results are reversed: leading breadth should be narrow and duration long, and lagging breadth should be broad and duration short since independent invention could stifle R&D incentives of the pioneer. Again, the recurring theme is evident: that patent policy depends critically on the interplay between private contracting, IP and antitrust policies, and other institutions.

Recent Empirical Studies

A central tenet of Scotchmer's research is to recognize that if firms can contract around their property rights, then many of the hold-up problems of patents can be overcome. That is, if *ex ante* contracting is available (low transactions costs of negotiating, flexible antitrust rules), then patents should facilitate future innovation since contracting allows firms to reorder their property rights to extract gains from trade (Heller and Eisenberg, 1998). This of course raises the question: *What if licensing fails?* Hold-up problems can easily arise if researchers cannot license with each other. (See, e.g., Green and Scotchmer, 1995 [this volume].)

One extension of the Green–Scotchmer case in which basic research leads to new applications or improvements involves situations in which the first-stage (upstream) innovation generates multiple essential inputs for a second-stage (downstream) one. In this case, an anti-commons problem arises if follow-on researchers are required to negotiate and pay royalties on stacking licenses (Heller and Eisenberg, 1998). Such problems are prevalent in standardized products in telecommunications and consumer electronics. In this case, licensing agreements in the form of patent pools can mitigate the problem and reduce impediments to future innovation from previously granted patents. (See, e.g., Shapiro, 2001; Lerner and Tirole, 2004; Gallini, 2014, and the references therein.)

In theory, this scenario has a relatively clear solution that combines broad patents with private contracting. In reality, negotiation costs can be prohibitive, rendering private agreements infeasible; innovation can be complex, requiring hundreds of components, many of which are protected by patents with overlapping claims; or the players with whom one must negotiate may not be known, especially if they are far afield in unrelated industries. In these situations, researchers can find themselves entangled in a patent thicket. (Other reasons that contracting may fail are asymmetric information, differences in valuations of the innovations, or antitrust restrictions on cooperation between competing firms.) The denser the thicket, the greater will be the incentive to patent defensively, thereby making it prohibitive for prospective innovators to enter. Licensing cannot rectify this problem if overlapping patents cannot be collected into useful bundles or potential researchers cannot be identified.

This discussion naturally leads to the following empirical question: *Are patents helpful or harmful to sequential innovation?* Scotchmer's work suggests that patents should help innovation when sequential researchers can negotiate contracts *ex ante*. Conversely, patents can impede follow-on research where transaction/negotiation costs are high or strict antitrust rules prevent agreement. Inspired by Scotchmer's research, these hypotheses were put to the test in several clever and important empirical studies (see Furman et al., this volume). I mention a small subset to illustrate the empirical relevance of Scotchmer's research.

To get a sense of the "thicket industries" where bargaining failures are likely to be pervasive, Hall et al. (2013) constructed a measure of "patent thickets" and found that they occur in industries deemed complex (by other measures), and that they do indeed impact negatively on new entry. In another study, Galasso and Schankerman (2015), while not examining thickets per se, ask more directly if awarding patents blocks follow-on research. They find that patents significantly block research in traditionally complex and fragmented industries: computers and communications, electronics, and medical instruments (including biotechnology). Moreover, blocking occurs by patents owned by large firms and, when they are invalidated, small firms can innovate, and follow-on research increases by 50 percent on average. These results are also supported in Murray and Stern (2007) who show that patents lead to a 10–20 percent reduction in citations from follow-on scientific research. Similarly, Williams (2013) shows a 20–30 percent effect from a contract law-based form of IP that protected genes sequenced by Celera between 2001 and 2003 when the company was able to sell its data for substantial fees and required firms to negotiate licensing agreements for any resulting commercial discoveries. At that time it was known that Celera's genes would be sequenced by the public effort and be in the public domain by 2003. In contrast, a more recent study by Sampat and Williams (2015) on gene patents in the USA finds that patents have not impeded scientific researchers and diagnostic test developers. It appears that in this market, problems in negotiating licenses were surmountable, but patents neither encouraged nor discouraged follow-on research.

While more empirical research is needed, the consistent empirical results so far allow some speculation. The evidence suggests that pharmaceuticals, mechanical and chemicals – non-complex industries – are less likely to suffer from bargaining failure. That is, patents have not been a deleterious constraint on follow-on research and commercial products, suggesting that private contracting has been able to create incentives for both early and follow-on research. With these theoretical and empirical advances, the literature appears to have gone full circle from establishing benefits of patents for stand-alone innovation (Nordhaus), to identifying their costs in cumulative research environments (Scotchmer and coauthors), to resurrecting their potential benefits if Coase-like negotiations are available to "undo" impediments of patents, at least in "non-thicket" industries. Along the way, the models have become more realistic and we have acquired a much deeper understanding of innovation processes for informing IP policy.

Concluding Reflections

Scotchmer pioneered the now well-accepted paradigm of cumulative research for understanding the impact of IP, antitrust, and related mechanisms and institutions on innovation incentives. Her insights regarding the critical role that licensing between firms can play has been particularly valuable in opening the door to studying new and richer interactions between IP and antitrust policy levers, the courts, and private incentives for innovators to research, litigate, and cooperate. This has been a dramatic improvement over the single-invention model and continues to pay dividends in the form of a growing theoretical, empirical, and policy literature in the law and economics of innovation.

Through her prolific writings, Scotchmer has arguably given us the best exposition on patent breadth, particularly because she cared about how this patent lever might interact with other policy levers, legal rules, antitrust and related institutions to adjust reward to socially efficient levels. In her world, IP (particularly patent breadth) provided threat points for dividing the gains from sequential progress rather than providing protection from imitators. Scotchmer also recognized that IP was not always the best mechanism, but given its firm roots in the US Constitution, it was here to stay. The good news is that other institutions (antitrust, contracts, courts) are also here to stay, and could potentially interact with it to improve innovation incentives.

If Suzanne were reading this review, I have no doubt that she would challenge some (many) of my interpretations and speculations, in her typically persuasive deep and articulate manner. Like many others, I came to expect that from her at every seminar, conference, and café conversation. We will miss those discussions and anticipating her next provocative idea. But we can look forward to the creative work from the next generations of economists and legal scholars who will continue to build upon her rich intellectual legacy.

Journal of Economics & Management Strategy,
Vol. 7 No. 1 (Spring, 1998): 1–32

Patent Breadth, Patent Life, and the Pace of Technological Progress

Ted O'Donoghue
Department of Economics
Cornell University
414 Uris Hall
Ithaca, NY 14853

Suzanne Scotchmer
Department of Economics and Graduate School of Public Policy
University of California
Berkeley, CA 94720

Jacques-François Thisse*
C.O.R.E.
UniversitéCatholique de Louvain
Louvain, Belgium

In active investment climates where firms sequentially improve each other's products, a patent can terminate either because it expires or because a noninfringing innovation displaces its product in the market. We define the length of time until one of these happens as the effective patent life, and show how it depends on patent breadth. We distinguish lagging breadth, which protects against imitation, from leading breadth, which protects against new improved products. We compare two types of patent policy with leading breadth: (1) patents are finite but very broad, so that the effective life of a patent coincides with its statutory life, and (2) patents are long but narrow, so that the effective life of a patent ends when a better product replaces it. The former policy improves the diffusion of new products, but the latter has lower R&D costs.

1. Introduction

When technology grows cumulatively, there may be a large discrepancy between the social value of an innovation and the profit collected by the innovator. On one hand, the innovation may be very valuable because it has spillover benefits for future innovators. On the other hand, future innovators are a competitive threat. Each innovator fears that his profit flow will be terminated by invention of an even better product.

In such an environment the statutory life of a patent may be irrelevant. In this paper we introduce the notion of *effective patent life*, which is the expected time until a patented product is replaced in the market. We argue that effective patent life depends on patent breadth as well as on statutory patent life, since patent breadth determines which products can replace the patented product. We investigate the optimal design of patents, given that breadth helps determine effective life.

There is at least some evidence that effective patent lives are short. Mansfield (1984) reports from survey evidence that in some industries 60 percent of patents are effectively terminated within 4 years, which is considerably less than the statutory life of 17 years. This finding was corroborated by Levin et al. (1987), who reported (Table 9) that almost all

* We thank the France/Berkeley fund for financial support. For useful discussion we thank Paul-Emmanuel Piel and seminar participants at U.C. Berkeley, the NBER Workshop on Patent Policy, July 1995, the June 1996 Strasbourg conference on Innovation sponsored by NBER and CNRS, and the University of Minnesota.

patents are duplicated within five years. Further evidence of short effective patent lives comes from patent renewal data: Schankerman and Pakes (1986) conclude that European patents lose on the order of 20 percent of their value per year, and Pakes (1986) reports that only 7 percent of French patents and 11 percent of German patents are maintained until the patent expires (see also Pakes and Schankerman, 1984). Lanjouw (1993) presents a more disaggregated model of how German patents become obsolete, and concludes that fewer than 50 percent are maintained more than ten years.

Of course, a discrepancy between effective and statutory patent lives is not inevitable: it vanishes if patents are very broad so that every subsequent innovation in a product line infringes on every unexpired patent in that product line. We are led to the following design question: Should patents be long-lived but narrow, so that they effectively expire at an endogenous time when a better product is made? Or should they be relatively broad but short-lived, so that the effective patent life coincides with the statutory patent life? It turns out that the two policies are not equivalent, even if both lead to the same rate of innovation. To sustain a given rate of innovation, the effective patent life in the first policy must be longer than the effective (statutory) patent life in the second policy, which exacerbates the inefficiencies due to market power.

To study this question, we must have a stylized understanding of patent law. We propose that there are at least two types of patent breadth: *lagging* breadth and *leading* breadth. We propose that lagging breadth protects against competition from products inferior to the patented product, and leading breadth protects against competition from products with higher quality. We show that lagging breadth alone may provide insufficient incentives for investment even when the statutory patent life is very long, and we show how leading breadth can extend effective patent life and stimulate R&D.

We realize that leading breadth seems prima facie untenable on the basis that it gives property rights on qualities (products) that the patentholder did not invent. We address this question at some length in the conclusion. For the moment we simply observe the implication of our analysis: Without some form of leading breadth, the effectiveness of the patent system to promote innovation is seriously impeded.

To isolate the questions of interest, we study a particularly simple investment environment where the rate of turnover in the market has an exogenous component, namely, the rate at which firms have *ideas* for improved products. An innovation requires both an idea and a decision to invest in it. The R&D literature has studied two types of research environments: those where opportunities for investment (i.e., ideas) are public knowledge, and those where opportunities for investment are private knowledge. When an investment opportunity is public knowledge, then firms may race for the patent. Since patent races have been well studied elsewhere [see Reinganum (1989), or O'Donoghue (1996) for patent races on quality ladders], we assume that ideas are private knowledge, so that a single firm has the opportunity to invest in each one. This is essentially the assumption of Nordhaus (1969) and the recent literature with two stages of innovation, e.g., Green and Scotchmer (1995). Each firm makes a single decision, which is whether or not to invest in a given investment opportunity.

As in all investigations of optimal patent policy, our conclusions involve a tradeoff between the rate of innovation and monopoly distortions. Broad patents may accelerate innovation, but since infringing improvements must be licensed, broad patents concentrate market power by consolidating quality improvements in the hands of one firm. Consolidation increases the quality gap between firms in the market, and leads to an inefficiency due to delayed diffusion. To show this, we use an axiomatic model of the output market based on the natural-oligopoly model of Gabszewicz and Thisse (1980) and Shaked and Sutton (1983).

Our main conclusions are:

- Patent breadth – in particular, leading breadth – can increase the rate of innovation by increasing the effective patent life, and without it, the rate of innovation may be seriously suboptimal.
- A specified rate of innovation can be achieved with either (1) a patent of infinite length and modest leading breadth, or (2) a patent with infinite leading breadth and modest length. The former is more efficient in minimizing R&D costs, but the latter is more efficient in minimizing the costs of delayed diffusion.

Although our notion of leading breadth is similar to the notion of patent breadth used in the two-stage models of Green and Scotchmer (1990, 1995), Scotchmer (1991, 1996), Chang (1995), Cheong (1994), Chou and Haller (1995), Matutes et al. (1996), Schmitz (1989), and Van Dijk (1996), we investigate a different issue. The two-stage models focus on how patent breadth operates via infringement and licensing as a vehicle to transfer profit from applications of a technology to its inventor. The time between innovations is assumed for convenience to be zero, and the statutory patent life determines the total profit while the breadth determines its division. [See in particular Green and Scotchmer (1995), Scotchmer (1991, 1996), Chou and Haller (1995).] With repeated innovation the division of profit between first and second innovators is not the focus, since every innovator will be in both positions. Instead the focus is how to increase total profit while minimizing monopoly distortions.

Tandon (1982), Gilbert and Shapiro (1990), Klemperer (1990), Gallini (1992), and Denicolò (1996) have addressed optimal patent breadth in the context of one-time innovation, where broader patents permit a shorter patent life. Broader patents increase static inefficiencies, but with a shorter life the inefficiencies terminate sooner. In contrast, when innovation is cumulative the patent breadth and patent life must work together to achieve an adequate *effective* patent life, which is an additional consideration.

In Section 2 we present a simplified model with homogeneous tastes, and expose the potential deficiencies of a patent system without leading breadth. In Section 3 we show how leading breadth can extend effective patent life and stimulate R&D, and we compare the two types of policy with leading breadth outlined above. In Section 4 we introduce oligopoly distortions by introducing heterogeneity in tastes and studying the natural-oligopoly model. This permits us to investigate which type of policy is least distortionary from the consumers' point of view. Section 5 investigates leading breadth in the natural-oligopoly model, and Section 6 concludes with a discussion of how the model described here reflects patent law.

2. A Model with Homogeneous Tastes

We first consider a simple output market with homogeneous tastes and no static inefficiency. This simple model allows us to illustrate why lagging breadth can lead to suboptimal investment, and how leading breadth can stimulate R&D. In later sections we introduce oligopoly distortions due to heterogeneous tastes.

2.1 Innovation

Innovation determines what qualities are technologically feasible at any given time (but patent law may restrict the qualities that are available to a given firm). We assume there is an infinite sequence of innovations described by $(\Delta_1, \Delta_2, \ldots \Delta_i, \ldots)$, and qualities are given by $q_i = q_{i-1} + \Delta_i$, where Δ_i is the i th innovation (see Figure 1). After innovation i, any quality $q \leq q_i$ is technologically feasible.

We assume there is a Poisson process with parameter λ that determines the rate at which firms collectively receive ideas for improvements, with each idea received by a single random firm. We assume that there are a large number of firms, so that a firm is unlikely to be its own successor.

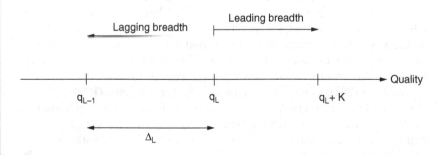

Figure 1

In fact, for simplicity we assume that a firm's probability of being its own successor is zero; the next firm to get an idea will be a different firm.[1]

An *idea* is a pair (Δ, c), where Δ is the quality improvement facilitated by investment and c is the cost. If the firm pays the investment cost, the idea becomes an *innovation*, namely an increment to the previous maximum quality. If the firm does not pay the investment cost, the idea is lost. For simplicity, we assume that every idea has the same investment cost c, but that the quality improvement Δ is distributed (conditional on having an idea) according to a stationary distribution F with support in $\mathbb{R}_+$ and density f. Our assumption of constant investment costs is a proxy to mean that costs are distributed independently of Δ.

2.2 Patent Instruments

The premise, of course, is that the government cannot tell firms which ideas to invest in. Instead, the government has a limited set of policy tools that can create incentives to invest.

We consider three policy tools concerning patents: patent length, lagging breadth, and leading breadth. The statutory patent life is the number of years, T, until the product can be marketed by competitors. To define lagging and leading breadth, suppose that a quality q_i is patented. Leading breadth is a number $K > 0$ such that any firm producing a quality in the interval $(q_i, q_i + K)$ (qualities higher than the patented quality) would *infringe* the patent, which means for our purposes that such a quality cannot be produced without a license. By lagging breadth, we mean a protected zone of qualities lower than the innovator's quality with the same infringement interpretation. See Figure 1. We assume that all innovations are patentable, whether they infringe another patent or not.[2]

2.3 Output Market

In this section and the next we assume that all agents purchase one unit of the good, and have the same willingness to pay for quality, i.e., their preferences are $q - p$, where q is the quality and p is the price. We refer

---

1 This assumption is for analytical ease. In the basic model of this section and the next, this assumption will be irrelevant: Whether a firm invests in a given idea is independent of whether that firm had the previous idea. In the natural-oligopoly model of Sections 4 and 5, market incumbents are less likely to invest than outside firms; however, the qualitative nature of our results for outside firms (i.e., leading breadth can increase the incentive to invest) also holds for market incumbents.

2 A fourth policy instrument is whether an innovation is patentable, whether or not it infringes. See O'Donoghue (1997) for a discussion of this additional policy instrument in the context of an infinite stream of innovation, and Scotchmer and Green (1990), Scotchmer (1996), and Luski and Wettstein (1995) for discussions in the context of two stage innovation.

to this model as *homogeneous tastes*. Firms compete on price, so if a firm produces quality q_i and the highest quality produced by a rival is q_{i-1}, then the price will be $p = q_i - q_{i-1}$. Hence, if the i th innovator can protect the entire quality increment Δ_i facilitated by his innovation, then he can charge price Δ_i. We assume that the market has size one, so that the flow of profit is equal to the price.

The social value of an innovation Δ is Δ/r (where r is the discount rate), since it becomes the base for all future quality improvements, and its incremental value lasts forever. Let Δ^{opt} be the minimum idea such that all ideas $\Delta \geq \Delta^{\mathrm{opt}}$ should optimally become innovations. Then Δ^{opt} satisfies $\Delta^{\mathrm{opt}}/r = c$.

The *rate of innovation* when all ideas become innovations $\Delta \geq \underline{\Delta}$ is defined by

$$\Phi(\underline{\Delta}) \equiv \lambda \int_{\underline{\Delta}}^{\infty} \Delta \, \mathrm{dF}. \tag{1}$$

The rate of innovation is the arrival rate of ideas, λ, multiplied by the expected innovation size conditional on having an idea. The socially optimal rate of innovation is $\Phi(\Delta^{\mathrm{opt}})$.

2.4 The Limits of Lagging Breadth

Perhaps the most natural type of patent breadth is lagging breadth, since it protects against imitation of a product that has already been invented. In contrast, leading breadth grants property rights on qualities that have not been invented by the patentee. We now point out that lagging breadth alone provides insufficient incentives for R&D.

To make the most favorable case for lagging breadth, we assume that it protects the entire quality gap between the patented quality and the previously patented quality. Hence, flow revenue for the i th market incumbent is Δ_i, , and lasts until the next innovation. Since the i th innovation creates flow welfare Δ_i, it follows that each innovator appropriates the entire flow of social benefit he created, but only during his incumbency.

To make the case for lagging breadth even more favorable, we assume that the statutory patent life is infinite. However, the flow of profit ends when the $(i + 1)$st innovation occurs. If firms invest in ideas $\Delta \geq \underline{\Delta}$, the arrival rate of innovations is

$$\Gamma(\underline{\Delta}) \equiv \lambda[1 - F(\underline{\Delta})], \tag{2}$$

and the net discounted profit for the i th innovator is $\Delta_i/[r + \Gamma(\underline{\Delta})] - c.$[3]

---

3 If the flow of profit Δ lasts for length t, the discounted profit is $\Delta(1 - e^{-rt})/r$. If the duration t is distributed according to a Poisson process with arrival rate Γ (which is $\lambda[1 - F(\Delta)]$

The profitability of an idea Δ to a given firm depends on the investment strategy of future firms, since their investment strategy determines the effective patent life.

An *equilibrium without leading breadth* is Δ^* such that $\Delta^*/[r + \Gamma(\Delta^*)] = c$, and all ideas $\Delta \geq \Delta^*$ become innovations.

The equilibrium rate of innovation is $\Phi(\Delta^*)$, where Φ is defined in equation (1).

Proposition 1 (Without Leading Breadth, Firms Underinvest in R&D): *The equilibrium rate of innovation is suboptimal, that is, $\Phi(\Delta^*) < \Phi(\Delta^{\mathrm{opt}})$.*

Proof. The result follows because Δ^* satisfies

$$\frac{\Delta^*}{r + \lambda[1 - F(\Delta^*)]} = c,$$

and Δ^{opt} satisfies $\Delta^{\mathrm{opt}}/r = c$; hence $\Delta^* > \Delta^{\mathrm{opt}}$.

The intuition for Proposition 1 is that discussed in the introduction: Even though patent life is infinite and each innovator can fully appropriate the flow benefits of his innovation during his market incumbency, the patent effectively terminates when another firm invents a better product. To emphasize this intuition, we define *effective patent life* as the expected length of time for which an innovator remains the incumbent. Without leading breadth (but with infinite statutory patent life), the effective patent life is $1/\Gamma(\Delta^*)$.[4] In the next section, we ask how leading breadth can extend effective patent life and stimulate R&D.

3. The Role of Leading Breadth

Our contribution in this section is to show how leading breadth can stimulate R&D by increasing effective patent life. The intuition is as follows: With leading breadth $K > \Delta^*$, the effective patent life can be longer than $1/\Gamma(\Delta^*)$, because any innovation $\Delta \in (\Delta^*, K)$ infringes the previous patent and therefore does not terminate that patent. The objective is to elicit investment in infringing innovations $\Delta < \Delta^*$, thus increasing the rate of innovation. A longer effective patent life makes an infringing innovation more profitable by extending the length of time it can be licensed to the market incumbent.

---

above), it has probability density $\Gamma e^{-\Gamma t}$, $t \in [0, \infty)$. Hence we have $\int_0^\infty [\Delta(1 - e^{-rt})/r]$ $\Gamma e^{-\Gamma t} dt = \Delta/(r + \Gamma)$.

4 If the length of market incumbency, t, is distributed according to a Poisson process with arrival rate Γ, then the expectation of t is $1/\Gamma$.

We consider two types of patents with leading breadth: (1) patents with finite leading breadth and infinite patent life, and (2) patents with infinite leading breadth and finite patent life. Under the first type of policy, the effective patent life is determined endogenously by when a sufficiently better product is invented. Infinite patent life is a proxy for a long, finite patent life, where an innovator's monopoly power is more likely to end because a better product is invented than because the patent expires. Under the second type of policy, the effective patent life is the statutory patent life T.

Formally, *a patent policy with leading breadth* is $(K, T) \in \mathbb{R}_+ \times \mathbb{R}_+$. The previous section without leading breadth investigated the policy $(0, \infty)$. We now consider policies (K, ∞), $0 < K < \infty$, and (∞, T), $0 < T < \infty$. Infringing innovations will be licensed to the market incumbent, and they increase the incumbent's market power by increasing the gap between the quality he sells and the previous patented quality. If a market incumbent with patented quality q_i and market gap (price) Δ_i licenses an innovation Δ, the new quality gap (price) will be $\Delta_i + \Delta$, and the quality he sells will be $q_i + \Delta$.

Leading breadth elicits investment in infringing innovations that will be licensed. Both policies (K, ∞) and (∞, T) create larger market gaps than would occur without leading breadth, but the gap does not grow forever. Under the policy (K, ∞), licensed innovations eventually stop accumulating when a noninfringing improved product appears in the market. Under the policy (∞, T), licensed innovations eventually stop accumulating because older patents expire.

The incentives for R&D depend on how profit is shared in licensing negotiations. Without specifying a bargaining game, we make three assumptions about how profit is shared:

Assumption 1: When a firm receives an idea for an infringing improvement, it can bargain with an infringed patentholder without giving away the idea.

An alternative assumption would be that bargaining takes place after the innovator has invested c in developing the improvement. Then the bargaining surplus would exclude costs c, which are sunk. *Ex post* bargaining would discourage some innovations, hence reduce investment, but would not change the nature of our conclusions. Our assumption makes the arguments simpler.

Assumption 2: The incremental profit facilitated by an infringing innovation is divided in a licensing agreement such that the owner's share is nonincreasing in the number of infringed patents.

This assumption holds for familiar bargaining solutions such as Nash bargaining, and means that the bargaining power of the infringing innovator does not increase if he faces more opponents.

Assumption 3: The parties to a licensing agreement divide the incremental profit so that each one receives a nonnegative share.

3.1 Finite Leading Breadth

We now consider the patent policy (K, ∞).

Under a policy (K, ∞), an innovator with a noninfringing innovation will remain the market incumbent until the next noninfringing innovation, and may license infringing innovations in the interim. Innovations $\Delta \geq K$ are noninfringing. If $K < \Delta^*$, then leading breadth has no effect. Assuming that $K \geq \Delta^*$, the arrival rate of noninfringing innovations is $\Gamma(K) \equiv \lambda[1 - F(K)]$. The effective patent life is thus $1/\Gamma(K)$, and the effective patent life increases with K.

The effect of leading breadth on the rate of innovation turns on which *infringing* ideas will become innovations, since those are the ideas $\Delta < \Delta^*$ that would otherwise not become innovations. Assuming $K > \Delta^*$, it is immediate that all ideas $\Delta \geq K$ will become innovations. These ideas are noninfringing, and if they are profitable without leading breadth, then they are even more profitable when leading breadth is granted, since leading breadth increases the effective patent life.

An infringing innovation Δ contributes increment Δ to the market incumbent's flow of profit. The profit surplus created by licensing is therefore $\Delta/[r + \Gamma(K)] - c$, and Assumption 1 implies that investment occurs if this surplus is nonnegative. (See footnote 3 above for the calculation.)

For $K \geq \Delta^*$, an *equilibrium under policy* (K, ∞) is Δ^K such that $\Delta^K(K)/[r + \Gamma(K)] = c$ and all ideas $\Delta \geq \Delta^K(K)$ become innovations.

The equilibrium rate of innovation is $\Phi(\Delta^K(K))$, where Φ is defined in equation (1).

Proposition 2 (Under Policies (K,∞), the Limit Rate of Innovation as K Becomes Large is Optimal): *The equilibrium rate of innovation $\Phi(\Delta^K(K))$ is increasing in K, and $\lim_{k\to\infty}\Phi(\Delta^K(K)) = \Phi(\Delta^{\mathrm{opt}})$.*

Proof. $\Phi(\cdot)$ and $\Delta^K(\cdot)$ are both decreasing, so $\Phi(\Delta^K(K))$ is increasing in K. Using the definition of equilibrium, as $K \to \infty$, $\Delta^K(K) \to \Delta^{\mathrm{opt}}$. The result follows.

3.2 Infinite Leading Breadth

Now suppose the patent policy is (∞, T). Under a policy (∞, T), every future improved product infringes until expiration of the patent. Hence, the effective patent life is identical to the statutory patent life T.

To understand how licensing operates in this case, consider an innovation at time t. If patents have infinite leading breadth and patent length T, the innovation at time t infringes all patents issued between $t - T$ and t, and the innovator must reach licensing agreements with their owners. Further, any innovation made between t and $t + T$ will infringe the patent issued at time t, and licenses will be negotiated with those innovators. Every patent goes through the following life cycle: In early life it infringes prior patents, in midlife it is both infringing and infringed, and in late life subsequent patents infringe it.

We are not specific about which firm is the seller at any given time, e.g., the seller might be the latest innovator or the owner of the oldest unexpired patent. The division of profit can be negotiated independently of who is the actual seller. The parties to the negotiation are the prospective innovator and the owners of unexpired patents. As in the previous section, the incentive to invest in an idea Δ depends only on the surplus profit that the innovation would create, and not on the specific licensing fees.

The profit surplus has two components: (i) the direct addition to output market profits, and (ii) the incremental claims on subsequent innovations that are patented between t and $t + T$. These are the first and second terms of equation (3) below. An innovation Δ contributes increment Δ to market profits for the entire life of its patent. Hence, part (i) has discounted value $\Delta(1 - e^{-rT})/r$.

Part (ii), which is $L(\cdot)$ below, will depend on the history of innovation, since profit on subsequent infringing innovations will be shared in a way that reflects the number of infringed patents. We let H be the set of possible patenting histories. A specific history $h \in H$ describes the dates and sizes of all previous quality improvements. The dates of all previous patents and the patent length T determine the number of infringed patents at any time t. The number $L(T, h)$ describes expected claims on innovations invented between t and $t + T$ facilitated by the patent at time t when the history is h; that is, claims that could not otherwise be made on future innovations. Assumption 2 implies that $L(T, h) > 0$ for all $T > 0$, $h \in H$.

The profit surplus of an innovation Δ is therefore

$$\Delta\frac{1 - e^{-rT}}{r} + L(T, h) - c. \tag{3}$$

An equilibrium under policy (∞, T) is a set of values $\{\Delta^T(T, h), h \in H\}$ such that for each $h \in H$, $\Delta^T(T, h)(1 - e^{-rT})/r + L(T, h) = c$ and all ideas $\Delta \geq \Delta^T(T, h)$ become innovations.

The rate of innovation under policy (∞, T) is defined by

$$\lambda\int_H\left(\int_{\Delta^T(T, h)}^{\infty} \Delta df\right)dG(h; T) \equiv \int_H \Phi(\Delta^T(T, h))dG(h; T). \tag{4}$$

The equilibrium induces a probability distribution on histories, described by elements of H. That is, at a random time t, there is a probability distribution on the dates of previous innovations, which we shall refer to by a cumulative distribution function $G(\cdot; T)$.

Proposition 3 (Under Policies (∞, T), the Limit Rate of Innovation as T Becomes Large Is No Smaller than Optimal): *Suppose that for each $h \in H$, $L(T, h)$ converges to a nonnegative limit as T becomes large. Then for each $h \in H$, $\lim_{T \to \infty} \Phi(\Delta^T(T, h)) \geq \Phi(\Delta^{\text{opt}})$.*

Proof. This follows from (3) because $L(T, h) > 0$ and hence $\lim_{T \to \infty} \Delta^T(t, h)) \geq \Delta^{\text{opt}}$.

3.3 Comparison of the Two Policies with Leading Breadth

We have shown in a model with homogeneous tastes that both types of policy with leading breadth can extend effective patent life and stimulate R&D. However, they are not equivalent, as they may have different R&D costs. In addition, different effective patent lives may be required to support the same rate of innovation. The latter will be important in the next section, where we introduce heterogeneous tastes and oligopoly distortions.

Proposition 4 (Comparison of the Policies with Leading Breadth): *Suppose two policies (K, ∞) and (∞, T) induce the same rate of innovation. Then:*

1. *Policy (∞, T) has a shorter effective patent life, or $T < 1/\Gamma(K)$.*
2. *Policy (K, ∞) has lower total R&D costs.*

[Proof omitted – ed.]

Proposition 4(1) states that to achieve a specified innovation rate, the effective patent life under a policy (K, ∞) must be longer than under a policy (∞, T). Alternatively stated, if the effective patent life under (K, ∞) were the same as the statutory patent life T, then the policy (K, ∞) would induce a smaller rate of innovation. This might seem paradoxical, since policies with the same patent lives should generate more or less the same total profit. Hence the difference in the amount of investment must be traceable to how the profit is distributed.

In the policy (∞, T), patents eventually expire, so that a prospective innovation causes future innovations to be infringing in periods when they would otherwise be noninfringing. By causing them to be infringing, the patent creates claims against them that were not available to the previous patentholders. The profit of these infringing innovations is shared with the infringed patentholder through licensing, represented by the licensing surplus $L(\cdot)$.

Compare with the alternative policy (K, ∞). The marginal idea $\Delta^K(K)$ that determines the innovation rate is always an infringing idea. An infringing idea does not create claims against future innovations that are not already owned by the previous patentholder, since the previous patent lasts forever. The surplus on infringing ideas that is shared through licensing accrues to the owners of noninfringing ideas, who collect a large share of the total profit. But it is the willingness to invest in infringing ideas, not noninfringing ideas, that determines the rate of innovation, and the infringing ideas receive a small share of total profit. In contrast, the policy (∞, T) makes no such clear distinction between infringing and noninfringing ideas.

Although the policy (∞, T) can sustain a specified rate of innovation with a shorter patent life, Proposition 4(2) states that it may have the offsetting disadvantage of higher R&D costs. The intuition for Proposition 4(2) is as follows. The minimum acceptable idea under the policy (∞, T) is stochastic (it depends on the history h), so sometimes ideas with low D may be undertaken, whereas other times higher-valued ideas are forgone. Costs can obviously be cut by investing once in 2Δ rather than twice in Δ, and this is why the common minimum value $\Delta^K(K)$ leads to lower total costs, conditional on a fixed innovation rate.

If all quality innovations reach all consumers instantly and demand is inelastic, policy (K, ∞) is clearly better than policy (∞, T): (K, ∞) has lower R&D costs, and the longer effective patent life is irrelevant, since there are no consumer losses due to market distortions. But with static inefficiencies, a longer effective patent life reduces consumer welfare. That is the topic of the next two sections.

4. Oligopoly Distortions

The purpose of the previous section was to isolate the role of leading breadth in extending effective patent life and stimulating R&D. We therefore studied a model with no market distortions once the innovations had occurred. The only inefficiencies were that the rate of innovation could be too low, and R&D costs could be unnecessarily high. We showed that R&D costs would be higher in the policy (∞, T) than in (K, ∞).

We now show that market distortions can change our conclusions in two ways: Lagging breadth alone might *over*reward R&D so there is too much innovation, and the market distortions might be more onerous in the policy (K, ∞) than in (∞, T), and thus overturn its cost advantage.

4.1 The Output Market

To develop these points we introduce heterogeneity in tastes into the above model. This gives us the natural-oligopoly model of Gabszewicz and

Thisse (1980) and Shaked and Sutton (1983). In order not to be distracted by details of the output market, we first take an axiomatic approach to how the market operates, and then point out in Appendix C [omitted – ed.] how the axioms follow from the natural-oligopoly model. An inefficiency arises because consumers have heterogeneous tastes for quality, and as a result do not all consume the highest-quality product, even though that would be efficient. Instead, the consumers with lower willingness to pay for quality consume a lower-quality product. Quality improvements are diffused to the whole market only after a delay.

Our axioms pertain to the output market once the qualities of the potential entrants are fixed by innovation and patents:

1. Competition in the output market allows exactly two firms to earn positive profit at any point in time, a *market leader* with a higher quality product denoted q_H, and a *market follower* with a lower quality product denoted q_L.
2. Each consumer consumes one unit of the product at each point in time, but the quality purchased improves as innovation occurs. Consumers have preferences $\theta q - p$, where $\theta \in [\theta_0, \theta^0]$. They thus differ in their willingness to pay for product quality, and in the outcome of market competition, they separate into two groups that do not change over time. A group of size n_L with lower willingness to pay for quality always purchases from the current market follower, and a group of size n_H with higher willingness to pay for quality always purchases from the current market leader.
3. Define the *quality gap* as $\Delta \equiv q_H - q_L$. The two firms in the market each earn profit that is a linear function of the quality gap. We let $\pi_H \Delta$ and $\pi_L \Delta$ refer respectively to the equilibrium profits of the firms with higher quality and lower quality, where π_L and π_H are constants with $\pi_H > \pi_L$.
4. Let B represent the sum of all consumers' willingness to pay for a unit increase in quality, and let ℓ, represent the portion of that willingness to pay attributable to the n_L consumers who purchase the lower-quality product. Then the flow welfare when the market qualities are q_H, q_L is $B_{qH} - \ell \Delta$.
5. The flow of profit $\pi_H \Delta$ that accrues to the higher-quality firm is no greater than the summed willingness to pay of its customers, $(B - \ell)\Delta$. Hence, $B - \ell > \pi_H$.

Axiom 1 is the main conclusion of the natural-oligopoly model. When consumers differ in their willingness to pay for quality, there can be more than one firm in the market, but there is room for only a finite number of firms. With appropriate specification of parameters, as discussed in Appendix C [omitted – ed.], there is room for exactly two firms. Axiom 2 reflects the division of consumers among firms in the natural-oligopoly model. The profit functions in Axiom 3 are the outcome of price competition in the natural-oligopoly model when there is a flow cost to market participation. Axiom 4 reflects that each consumer's utility is linear in the quality consumed.

4.2 Lagging Breadth in the Natural-Oligopoly Model

We begin our analysis of the natural-oligopoly model by reinvestigating what happens with complete lagging breadth and infinite patent life, but no leading breadth.

In the natural-oligopoly model, the i th innovator earns payoffs in two periods: as market leader just subsequent to the innovation, when it collects flow profit $\pi_H \Delta_i$ and as market follower after the next innovation, when it collects flow profit $\pi_L \Delta_{i+1}$. After subsequent innovations, the firm is displaced from the market. Hence, if future firms invest in ideas $\Delta \geq \underline{\Delta}$, the net discounted profit for the i th innovator is

$$\prod (\Delta, \underline{\Delta}) \equiv \frac{\pi_H \Delta}{r + \Gamma(\underline{\Delta})} + \frac{\pi_L \Delta^e (\underline{\Delta})}{r + \Gamma(\underline{\Delta})} \left(\frac{\Gamma(\underline{\Delta})}{r + \Gamma(\underline{\Delta})} \right) - c, \tag{5}$$

and $\Gamma(\cdot)$ is the arrival rate of innovations and is defined by $\Gamma(\underline{\Delta}) = \lambda[1 - F(\underline{\Delta})]$ [as in equation (2)]. The expectation function Δ^e is defined by

$$\Delta^e (\underline{\Delta}) \equiv \frac{1}{1 - F(\underline{\Delta})} \int_{\underline{\Delta}}^{\infty} \Delta dF.$$

The first term of (5) is the discounted flow of profit as market leader, which lasts until the innovator is displaced as market leader by the next innovation (see footnote 3). The second term is the discounted flow of profit after the innovator becomes the market follower. During the period as follower, the innovator's profit is determined not by his own quality increment Δ_i, but by the quality increment of his successor, which has expected value $\Delta^e(\underline{\Delta})$. Discounted from when it begins, the flow profit $\pi_L \Delta^e(\underline{\Delta})$ has discounted expected value $\pi_L \Delta^e(\underline{\Delta})/[r + \Gamma(\underline{\Delta})]$, which reflects that the flow of profit ends when a third innovation occurs. $\pi_L \Delta^e(\underline{\Delta})/[r + \Gamma(\underline{\Delta})]$ is multiplied by $\Gamma(\underline{\Delta})/[r + \Gamma(\underline{\Delta})]$ because the flow of profit begins when the innovator is displaced as market leader by the next innovation.[5]

It is convenient in this section to make explicit in the definition of equilibrium that the minimum profitable idea Δ^* depends on λ. An *equilibrium without leading breadth* is

---

5 If the value $v \equiv \pi_L \Delta^e (\underline{\Delta})/(r + \Gamma(\underline{\Delta}))$ is received at time t, the discounted value is ve^{-rt}. As in footnote 3, t has probability density Γe^{-rT}, $t \in [0, \infty)$, so $\int_0^{\infty} (ve^{-rt})\Gamma e^{i\Gamma t} dt = v\Gamma/(r + \Gamma)$.

$$\tilde{\Delta}^*(\lambda) = \begin{cases} \Delta' & \text{if} \quad \Pi(\Delta',\Delta') = 0, \\ 0 & \text{if} \quad \Pi \geq 0, \end{cases} \bigg\} \Gamma(\Delta)$$

where it is understood that $(\cdot, \cdot)$ depends on λ. All ideas $\Delta \geq \tilde{\Delta}^*(\lambda)$ become innovations.

We first point out that the natural-oligopoly model creates a "foot-in-the-door effect": Since firms earn profit as market follower in addition to their profits as market leader, there is an added incentive to invest. The profit an innovator will earn as market follower will depend on the size of the next innovation, which could be large. As a result, firms may invest in small ideas simply as a means to secure a market position. The following example shows that the minimum profitable idea can even be $\Delta = 0$, which is clearly inefficient, since $\Delta = 0$ provides no consumer value.

Example (Foot-in-the-Door Effect):

Suppose that $\Delta^e(0) = 1$, $c = 1$, $\lambda = 0.5$ (so ideas occur on average every 2 years), $r = 0.1$ and $\pi_L = 1$.[6] Then $\pi(0, 0) > 0$, so firms will invest in all ideas.

In this example, firms invest in ideas that yield zero flow profit as market leader because the expected future profits as market follower are sufficient to cover R&D costs. The foot-in-the-door effect implies that firms might overinvest in R&D even without leading breadth.[7] But when λ is high so that market incumbency is short, firms must make high profit as both market leader and market follower in order to cover their costs. As a result, for high λ, investment will be suboptimal despite the foot-in-the-door effect.

Figure 2 summarizes how the equilibrium $\Delta^*(\cdot)$ depends on λ. The parameter $\hat{\Delta}$ is defined by $\pi_H \hat{\Delta}/r - c = 0$ and represents the equilibrium cutoff if an innovator remained market leader forever. The following lemma is proved in Appendix A [omitted – ed.].

Lemma 1: $\hat{\Delta}^*(0) = \hat{\Delta}$, and $\Delta^*(\cdot)$ is either nondecreasing or U-shaped.

To compare equilibrium with optimal investment we must characterize optimal investment. The following welfare expression $W^*(\Delta)$ is derived in Appendix B [omitted – ed.]:

$$W^*(\Delta) \equiv \frac{\Gamma(\Delta)}{r} \left[\frac{B}{r} \Delta^e(\Delta) - \frac{l}{r + \Gamma(\Delta)} \Delta^e(\Delta) - c \right].$$

---

6 [footnote omitted – ed.]

7 A separate reason for excess investment in R&D is that patent races speed up investment. See Reinganum (1989) for a summary of the patent-race literature. A related idea is what the endogenous-growth literature calls the "business stealing effect" [see Aghion and Howitt (1992), Grossman and Helpman (1991), and Romer (1994)].

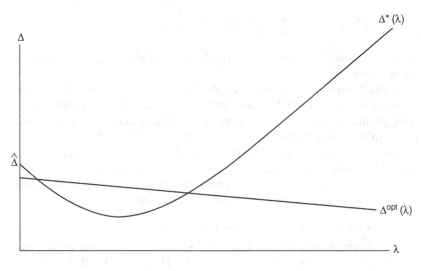

Figure 2

This expression assumes for simplicity that the initial market gap is 0, but we point out in Appendix B [omitted – ed.] that our propositions remain intact if the initial market gap is positive. A simple (but slightly misleading) intuition for the expression is as follows.

The bracketed factor is the expected value of each innovation. There are $\Gamma(\underline{\Delta})$ innovations per unit time, and we divide by r to allow for all the innovations in the infinite future. The first bracketed term represents the expected social benefit of a quality increment if it is received by all consumers immediately. The increment to welfare flow $B\Delta^e(\underline{\Delta})$ is divided by r to reflect that it lasts forever, since the quality increment becomes a foundation for future quality increments. From this value we subtract the loss due to the delay in diffusing the quality increment to consumers with low willingness to pay. Using the reasoning in footnote 3, the second term captures the expected discounted value of losing flow welfare, $\ell\Delta^e(\underline{\Delta})$ until the next innovation. Finally we subtract off the cost of the innovation.

Let $\tilde{\Delta}^{\text{opt}}(\lambda)$ represent the maximizer of W^* (which depends on λ). That is, $\tilde{\Delta}^{\text{opt}}(\lambda)$ is the minimum idea that should optimally become an innovation, recognizing that each innovation reaches the low-willingness-to-pay consumers only after the subsequent innovation. Our objective in calculating this second-best type of optimum is to compare the second-best optimum with equilibrium. The following is easily verified:

Lemma 2: $\tilde{\Delta}^{\text{opt}}(0) < \hat{\Delta}$, and $\tilde{\Delta}^{\text{opt}}(\cdot)$ is decreasing.

In Figure 2, the foot-in-the-door effect appears where $\Delta^*(\lambda) < \Delta^{\text{opt}}(\lambda)$. It can only occur for low hit rates λ of ideas. If the hit rate of ideas is high, then investment without leading breadth is always deficient, just as in the simple model with homogeneous tastes. This is the content of the following proposition:

Proposition 5 (In the Natural-Oligopoly Model, If Ideas Are Frequent Then Firms Underinvest without Leading Breadth): *Suppose tastes are heterogeneous. There exists λ^* such that $\tilde{\Delta}^*(\lambda) < \tilde{\Delta}^{\text{opt}}(\lambda)$ for all $\lambda \geq \lambda^*$.*

Proof. $\tilde{\Delta}^*(\cdot)$ is continuous and $\lim_{\lambda \to \infty} \tilde{\Delta}^*(\lambda) = \infty \cdot \Delta^*(\lambda) < \Delta^{\text{opt}}(\lambda)$. Given this, the result follows directly from Lemmas 1 and 2.

Thus if the hit rate of ideas is high, lagging breadth is inadequate in the natural-oligopoly model despite the foot-in-the-door effect. We now investigate whether leading breadth can solve this problem by prolonging effective patent life as in the model with homogeneous tastes.

5. Leading Breadth in the Natural-Oligopoly Model

The premise of this section is that ideas are frequent (λ is high) and firms underinvest in R&D without leading breadth. To stimulate R&D, we reconsider the two policies (K, ∞) and (∞, T) considered in Section 3. We first describe the equilibria with these policies, pointing out that leading breadth plays the same role in the natural-oligopoly model as in the model with homogeneous tastes. However, the natural oligopoly model introduces a static inefficiency.

In what follows, we suppress the argument λ from $\tilde{\Delta}^*$, assuming λ is large enough to warrant leading breadth.

5.1 Finite Leading Breadth

Under the policy (K, ∞), an innovator with a noninfringing innovation becomes the market leader, and will maintain this position until the next noninfringing innovation. In addition, the innovator may license infringing innovations while market leader. Unlike in the model with homogeneous tastes, the next noninfringing innovation does not terminate the innovator's flow of profit. Instead the innovator becomes market follower, and earns a second flow of profit until the subsequent noninfringing innovation.

As before, we define the *effective patent life* as the expected time between noninfringing innovations, namely $1/\Gamma(K)$.[8]

As with homogeneous tastes, we focus on $K \geq \tilde{\Delta}^*$, since otherwise K has no effect. As before, the effect on the rate of innovation turns on how K

---

8   The length of time that a noninfringing innovation earns profit under the policy (K, ∞), is actually longer than this, since the innovator also earns profit as market follower. However, this is not true of infringing innovations. It is investment in infringing innovations that determines the rate of innovation.

affects the profitability of infringing ideas $\varDelta < K$. All ideas $\varDelta > K$ will become innovations, since K extends effective patent life relative to no leading breadth, and thus increases the profitability of noninfringing innovations.

An infringing innovation $\varDelta$ contributes an increment $\pi_H \varDelta$ to the market leader's flow of profit until the next noninfringing innovation. However, an infringing innovation does not add any anticipated profit from becoming market follower. The market leader will eventually become market follower whether or not he licenses the infringing improvement. In addition, his profit when market follower depends on the size of the noninfringing innovation that displaces him, and not on the quality of the product he sells, hence not on the accumulation of licensed improvements. Thus, the profit surplus created by licensing is

$$S^K(\varDelta, K) \equiv \frac{\pi_H \varDelta}{r + \Gamma(K)} - c,$$

and investment occurs if this surplus is nonnegative.

In the natural-oligopoly model, an *equilibrium under policy* (K, ∞) is

$$\tilde{\varDelta}^K(K) = \left\{ \begin{array}{c} K \text{ if } S^K(K, K) \leq 0 \\ \varDelta' \text{ if } S^K(K, K) > 0 \text{ and } S^K\left(\varDelta', K\right) = 0 \end{array} \right\}$$

such that all ideas $\varDelta \geq \tilde{\varDelta}^K(K)$ become innovations. Since S^K is increasing in its first argument, the equilibrium $\tilde{\varDelta}^K(K)$ is unique.

The basic intuition for how the policy (K, ∞) can extend effective patent life and stimulate R&D is identical to that in Section 3, and we do not repeat the argument. Our main discovery regarding the policy (K, ∞) in the natural-oligopoly model is that a small amount of leading breadth can retard R&D relative to no leading breadth at all ($K = 0$). This is perhaps counterintuitive, but can be explained as follows.

Without leading breadth, the marginal innovation is noninfringing, and the innovator stands to profit both as market leader and as market follower. The foot-in-the-door effect (which results from the profit as market follower) may elicit investment. In contrast, with leading breadth the marginal innovation infringes the prior patent. The foot-in-the-door effect is absent, as reflected in the fact that when $K = \tilde{\varDelta}^*, S^K(\varDelta, K) < \Pi(\varDelta, \tilde{\varDelta}^*)$. The marginal innovation is less profitable when it infringes the prior patent and must be licensed.

Proposition 6 (Small Leading Breadth Can Retard R&D): *Suppose tastes are heterogeneous.*

1. *$\tilde{\varDelta}^K(K) = \tilde{\varDelta}^*$ for all $K \in [0, \tilde{\varDelta}^*]$.*
2. *There exists $K^* > \tilde{\varDelta}^*$ such that the rate of innovation and social welfare are strictly larger for $K = 0$ (no leading breadth) than for any $K \in (\tilde{\varDelta}^*, K^*)$.*

Proof. 1: If $K < \tilde{\Delta}^*$, then leading breadth does not affect any ideas that firms would invest in.

2: Recalling Figure 2, consider two cases: $\hat{\Delta} \geq \tilde{\Delta}^*$ and $\hat{\Delta} < \tilde{\Delta}^*$. In the first case, take any $K^* > \tilde{\Delta}^*$, since $\tilde{\Delta}^K(K) \geq \hat{\Delta}$ for all K. In the second case, we have $S^K(\tilde{\Delta}^*, \tilde{\Delta}^*) < \Pi(\tilde{\Delta}^*, \tilde{\Delta}^*) = 0$. Since S^K is increasing in its second argument, there exists a unique $K^* > \tilde{\Delta}^*$ such that $S^K(\tilde{\Delta}^*, K) = \Pi(\tilde{\Delta}^*, \tilde{\Delta}^*)$, which implies $\tilde{\Delta}^K(K) = \tilde{\Delta}^*$. For any $K \in (\tilde{\Delta}^*, K^*)$, $S^K(\tilde{\Delta}^*, K) < 0$, and $\tilde{\Delta}^K(K)^* > \tilde{\Delta}^*$, since S^K is increasing in its first argument. Hence, the rate of innovation is smaller for any $K \in (\tilde{\Delta}^*, K^*)$ than for $K = 0$.

Social welfare is smaller for any $K \in (\tilde{\Delta}^*, K^*)$ than for $K = 0$ because not only is there less innovation, but in addition low-θ consumers receive innovations with a longer lag than without leading breadth.

5.2 Infinite Leading Breadth

Suppose the patent policy is (∞, T), so the effective patent life is identical to the statutory patent life T. The analysis of this policy is essentially identical to the case of homogeneous tastes in Section 3, and we will omit much of it.

Under policy (∞, T), there will be a market follower who makes positive profits; however, market-follower profit is not a consideration when a firm decides whether to invest in an idea. Unlike under the policy (K, ∞), a patentholder will not necessarily become market follower when he ceases to be market leader. Under the policy (K, ∞), the previous market leader's patent is still valid when his product is supplanted in the market. Since no other firm can market his product, he becomes market follower. Under the policy (∞, T), the market follower produces the highest-quality product whose patent has expired. But since the patent has expired, there is no reason to believe that its inventor will market it. We therefore assume that a random firm is the market follower.[9]

The profit surplus is therefore the same in the natural-oligopoly model as in the homogeneous-tastes model, except that the increment to the

---

9 If each patentholder enjoyed a period as market follower, our main conclusion regarding relative effective patent lives would be strengthened. Since every innovation then becomes even more profitable under the policy (∞, T), the same rate of innovation can be sustained with an even shorter patent life T. The market for the low-quality product should be competitive, since the relevant patent has expired. In our formulation, this market is competitive in the sense of free entry– given the flow cost of market participation (see Appendix C [omitted – ed.]), entry would not be profitable. If there were no cost of market participation, then the price of the low-quality product would be driven to zero. In that case, market-leader profits are still linear in the quality gap, so the qualitative results are unchanged. However, the magnitude of market-leader profits is smaller, undermining the effectiveness of policy (∞, T). For policy (K, ∞), this issue does not arise, since the market follower owns a valid patent.

market leader's flow profit is $p^H \Delta$ instead of Δ. Hence, investment occurs if the following surplus is nonnegative:

$$S^T(\Delta, T, h) \equiv \pi_H \Delta \left(\frac{1 - e^{-rT}}{r} \right) + L(T, h) - c.$$

In the natural-oligopoly model, *an equilibrium under policy* (∞, T) is a set of values $\{ \tilde{\Delta}^T(T, h), h \in H \}$, such that

$$\tilde{\Delta}^T(T, h) = \left\{ \begin{array}{l} \Delta' \text{ if } S^T \left(\Delta', T, h \right) = 0 \text{ and } \Delta' > 0, \\ \quad 0 \text{ if } S^T(0, T, h) \geq 0, \end{array} \right\}$$

and, conditional on a history h, all ideas $\Delta \geq \tilde{\Delta}^T(T, h)$ become innovations. Since S^T is increasing in its first argument, the equilibrium values $\{ \tilde{\Delta}^T(T, h), h \in H \}$ are unique.

The intuition for how policy (∞, T) can stimulate R&D in the natural-oligopoly model is identical to that in the model with homogeneous tastes.

5.3 Delayed Diffusion

In the model with homogeneous tastes we showed that both policies (K, ∞) and (∞, T) can stimulate R&D, but conditional on having the same rate of innovation, policy (K, ∞) has lower total R&D costs. This result is driven by the fact that under (K, ∞) the equilibrium cutoff is constant, while under (∞, T) it is stochastic. Clearly, this result will hold in the natural-oligopoly model as well. The inefficiency introduced by heterogeneous tastes is on the consumer side, and it comes in the form of delayed diffusion.

In the natural-oligopoly model, not all consumers consume the highest-quality product. Although every innovation eventually reaches every consumer, there is a lag before it reaches the consumers with relatively low willingness to pay for quality. Under policy (K, ∞) the expected lag is the expected time between noninfringing innovations, and under policy (∞, T) the lag is the statutory patent life T. Under either policy, a longer lag increases the social cost of delayed diffusion.

In Section 3, we showed that to induce the same rate of innovation, policy (K, ∞) must have a longer effective patent life than policy (∞, T). With homogeneous tastes, effective patent life is irrelevant for social welfare. In the natural-oligopoly model, however, the longer effective patent life of policy (K, ∞) leads to a higher cost of delayed diffusion.

To compare the cost of delayed diffusion in the two policies, we need a welfare expression for each. The welfare expressions defined below, W^K for the policy (K, ∞) and W^T for the policy (∞, T), represent the expected social benefits (excluding costs) of the infinite streams of innovations:

$$W^K(K) = \frac{\Gamma(\tilde{\Delta}^K(K))}{r}\left(\frac{B}{r}\Delta^e\left(\tilde{\Delta}^K(K) - \frac{\ell}{r+\Gamma(K)}\Delta^e(\tilde{\Delta}^K(K))\right)\right)$$

or $\quad W^K(K) = \frac{\lambda}{r}\left(\frac{B}{r} - \ell\frac{1}{r+\Gamma(K)}\right)\int_{\tilde{\Delta}^K(K)}^{\infty}\Delta dF;$ (7)

$$W^T(T) = \int_H \frac{\Gamma(\tilde{\Delta}^T(T,h))}{r}\left[\frac{B}{h}\Delta^e(\tilde{\Delta}^T(T,h)) - \ell\left(\frac{1-e^{rT}}{r}\right)\right.$$

$$\left. \Delta^e(\tilde{\Delta}^T(T,h))\right]dG(h;T)$$

or $\quad W^T(T) = \frac{\lambda}{r}\left[\frac{B}{r} - \ell\left(\frac{1-e^{rT}}{r}\right)\right]\int_H\left(\int_{\Delta^{-T}(T,h)}^{\infty}\Delta\,dF\right)dG(h;T).$ (8)

In each case the social benefit of an innovation, which would be $(B/r)\Delta$ if all consumers received it immediately, is reduced by the expected delay until it reaches the consumers with lower willingness to pay. The reasoning is analogous to that behind W^* in Section 4. (See also our comments in Appendix B [omitted – ed.].)

Proposition 7 [Conditional on the Rate of Innovation, Policy (∞, T) Has Lower Costs of Delayed Diffusion than Policy (K, ∞)]: *Suppose tastes are heterogeneous, and that two policies (K, ∞) and (∞, T) have the same rate of innovation. Then $W^K(K) < W^T(T)$.*

Proof. The rates of innovation are the same if and only if

$$\int_{\Delta^{-K}(K)}^{\infty}\Delta dF = \int_H\left(\int_{\Delta^{-T}(T,h)}^{\infty}\Delta dF\right)dG(h;T).$$ (9)

Equation (9) and the equilibrium conditions imply $(1 - e^{-rT})/r < 1/[r + \Gamma(K)]$. The proof for the natural oligopoly is identical to the proof for homogeneous tastes in Proposition 4(1). In addition, equation (9), in conjunction with equations (7) and (8), implies $W^T(T) > W^K(K)$ if and only if $(1 - e^{-rT})/r < 1/[r + \Gamma(K)]$. The result follows.

The intuition for Proposition 7 is straightforward. Given that the effective patent life required to sustain a given rate of innovation is greater in (K, ∞) than in (∞, T), the delay is longer before low-willingness-to-pay consumers receive quality improvements, so it should be no surprise that the costs of delayed diffusion are greater.

6. Discussion

Our main observation in this paper is that the profitability of R&D depends on the effective patent life, and that effective patent life is determined not only by statutory patent life but also by patent breadth.

Unless there is some sustained advantage to entering the market, such as occurs in the natural-oligopoly model (the foot-in-the-door effect), lagging breadth alone will not provide sufficient incentives for R&D. We compared two remedies with leading breadth: (1) infinite patent life with finite leading breadth and (2) finite patent life with infinite leading breadth. In the first policy, effective patent lives are endogenous to the leading breadth and the hit rate of ideas. In the second policy, effective patent lives coincide with statutory patent lives, and both are immune to the hit rate of ideas. We showed that the first policy is superior in reducing R&D costs (conditional on the rate of innovation), while the second policy has a shorter effective patent life, and therefore reduces the market distortions.

We conclude with a few remarks on patent doctrine in order to put our observations into perspective. The fundamental protection of a patent is that other firms are barred from using the patented technology without the patentholder's consent. This is as straightforward as the law can be, but many controversies arise regarding the technologies that can be covered by the patent. The US patent statute does not refer to patent breadth, except implicitly in how claims are limited by the enabling disclosure, and in the requirements of novelty and nonobviousness. These requirements mean collectively that the claimed technologies must differ substantially from "prior art." The disclosure requirement is a test of whether the patentee actually invented the technologies claimed.

For the context of cumulative innovation it seems plausible that an innovator "invented" all the qualities between the previous state of the art and his new improved state of the art, and therefore (in our terms) complete lagging breadth seems justifiable under the law. However, there are at least two ways to think about leading breadth. Perhaps the most straightforward is to say that every subsequent improvement uses the previous technologies, and hence infringes for the duration of the previous patents. This interpretation would support the policy with infinite leading breadth and finite patent life.

But another interpretation is to say that since previous patentholders have not invented the superior qualities, it is unreasonable to give them effective patent protection against all such products; hence leading breadth is by its nature untenable. In our model, such an interpretation might support the policy with long patent life and finite patent breadth, where effective patent lives are terminated by noninfringing innovations. A small amount of leading breadth might be justified under the "doctrine of equivalents." [See, for example, Merges and Nelson (1990).]

The patent recommendation in this paper is that leading breadth should be granted when the hit rate of ideas is high; that is, there is an exogenous force toward rapid turnover in the market. Of course one must ask what the patent authorities must observe in order to implement such a policy. The main consideration is how quickly an innovator would lose his market position in the absence of such protection. However, such considerations are not part of the patent statute, and one could even see how the patent authorities might reach the opposite conclusion: An active investment climate can be seen as prima facie evidence that ideas are "obvious" and therefore not protected at all. We point this out in order to emphasize that the effectiveness of patent law in supporting research is seriously impeded by the fact that it does not refer to costs or market structure in how patent protection is circumscribed.[10]

References

Anderson, S., A. de Palma, and J.-F. Thisse, 1992, *Discrete Choice Theory of Product Differentiation*, Cambridge, MA: The MIT Press.

Aghion, P. and P. Howitt, 1992, "A Model of Growth through Creative Destruction," *Econometrica*, 60, 323–352.

Chang, H. F., 1995, "Patent Scope, Antitrust Policy and Cumulative Innovation," *The RAND Journal of Economics*, 26 (Spring), 34–57.

Cheong, I., 1994, "Invent or Develop? On Sequential Innovation and Patent Policy," Mimeograph, Department of Economics, Princeton University.

Chou, T. and H. Haller, 1995, "The Division of Profit in Sequential Innovation Reconsidered," Working Paper E95–02, Department of Economics, VPI & State University.

Denicolò, V., 1996, "Patent Races and Optimal Patent Breadth and Length," *The Journal of Industrial Economics*, 44, 249–265.

Gabszewicz, J. J. and J.-F. Thisse, 1980, "Entry (and Exit) in a Differentiated Industry," *Journal of Economic Theory*, 22, 327–338.

Gallini, N. T., 1992, "Patent Policy and Costly Imitation," *The RAND Journal of Economics*, 23 (Spring), 52–63.

Gilbert, R. and C. Shapiro, 1990, "Optimal Patent Length and Breadth," *The RAND Journal of Economics*, 21 (Spring), 106–112.

Green, J. and S. Scotchmer, 1995, "On the Division of Profit in Sequential Innovation," *The RAND Journal of Economics*, 26 (Spring), 20–33.

Grossman, G. M. and E. Helpman, 1991, "Quality Ladders in the Theory of Growth," *Review of Economic Studies*, 58, 43–61.

Klemperer, P., 1990, "How Broad Should the Scope of Patent Protection Be?" *The RAND Journal of Economics*, 21 (Spring), 113–130.

---

10 For a broader discussion of the deficiencies of patent law, see Scotchmer (1991, 1996).

Lanjouw, J., 1993, "Patent Protection in the Shadow of Infringement: Simulation Estimations of Patent Value," Mimeograph, Department of Economics, Yale University.

Levin, R. C., A. K. Klevorick, R. R. Nelson, and S. G. Winter, 1987, "Appropriating the Returns from Industrial Research and Development," *Brookings Papers on Economic Activity*, 3 (Special Issue), 783–831.

Luski, I. and D. Wettstein, 1995, "An Optimal Patent Policy in a Dynamic Model of Innovation," Discussion Paper 95-3, Monaster Center for Economic Research, Ben Gurion University of the Negev, Beer Sheva.

Mansfield, E., 1984, "R&D and Innovation: Some Empirical Findings," in Zvi Griliches, ed., *R&D, Patents and Productivity*, Chicago: University of Chicago Press for the National Bureau of Economic Research.

Matutes, C., K. E. Rockett, and P. Regibeau, 1996, "Optimal Patent Protection and the Diffusion of Innovation," *The RAND Journal of Economics*, 27 (Spring), 60–83.

Merges, R. P. and R. R. Nelson, 1990, "On the Complex Economics of Patent Scope," *Columbia Law Review*, 90(4), 839–916.

Mussa, M. and S. Rosen, 1978, "Monopoly and Product Quality," *Journal of Economic Theory*, 18, 301–317.

Nordhaus, W., 1969, *Invention, Growth and Welfare*, Cambridge, MA: MIT Press.

O'Donoghue, T., 1996, "Patent Protection When Innovation Is Cumulative," Ph.D. Thesis, Department of Economics, University of California.

O'Donoghue, T., 1997, "A Patentability Requirement for Sequential Innovation," Northwestern University, Math Center Discussion Paper No. 1185.

Pakes, A., 1986, "Patents as Options: Some Estimates of the Value of Holding European Patent Stocks," *Econometrica*, 54, 755–785.

Pakes, A. and M. Schankerman, 1984, "The Rate of Obsolescence of Patents, Research Gestation Lags, and the Private Rate of Return to Research Resources," in Zvi Griliches, ed., *R&D, Patents, and Productivity*, Chicago: University of Chicago Press, 73–88.

Reinganum, J., 1989, "The Timing of Innovation: Research, Development and Diffusion," in R. Schmalensee and R. D. Willig, eds., *Handbook of Industrial Organization*, Amsterdam: Elsevier, 849–908.

Romer, P., 1994, "Increasing Returns and Long-Run Growth," *Journal of Political Economy*, 94, 1002–1037.

Schankerman, M. and A. Pakes, 1986, "Estimates of the Value of Patent Rights in European Countries During the Post–1950 Period," *Economic Journal*, 96, 1052–1076.

Schmitz, J. A., Jr., 1989, "On the Breadth of Patent Protection," Mimeograph, State University of New York at Stony Brook.

Scotchmer, S., 1991, "Standing on the Shoulders of Giants: Cumulative Research and the Patent Law," *Journal of Economic Perspectives*, Symposium on Intellectual Property Law, Winter, 29–41.

Scotchmer, S., 1996, "Protecting Early Innovators: Should Second Generation Products be Patentable?" *The RAND Journal of Economics*, 27, 117–126.

Scotchmer, S. and J. Green, 1990, "Novelty and Disclosure in Patent Law," *The RAND Journal of Economics*, 21 (Spring), 131–146.

Shaked, A. and J. Sutton, 1983, "Natural Oligopolies," *Econometrica*, 51, 1469–1483.

Tandon, P., 1982, "Optimal Patents with Compulsory Licensing," *Journal of Political Economy*, 90, 470–486.

Van Dijk, T., 1996, "Patent Height and Competition in Product Improvements," *Journal of Industrial Economics*, 44, 151–167.

Top 10 Insights About Intellectual Property

Stephen M. Maurer

Prof. Scotchmer built her work insight by insight. Results, once achieved, were seldom discarded but became stepping stones to the next problem. At the same time, her prose is so compact that it can be hard to keep the various tenets firmly in mind. Here, David Letterman style, is my Top 10 list of the insights that supported Prof. Scotchmer's vision of IP theory. While I think that her own list would have been similar, careful readers of *Innovation and Incentives* (Scotchmer, 2004b), for example, could reasonably disagree:

10. Government procurement would be an ideal funding mechanism if ideas were not so widely distributed (Scotchmer, 1991; Menell and Scotchmer, 2007, at p. 1477). The great virtue of IP is that it is inherently decentralized and provides coordination where central planners may not even know that an R&D opportunity exists.

9. Patent rewards operate differently for stand-alone inventions, research tools, and improvements to preexisting technology (Scotchmer, 1991; Menell and Scotchmer, 2007, at p. 1477). For example, owners of stand-alone and improvement patents can usually deploy a combination of fixed and unit royalties to cartelize product markets. This option does not exist for research tools.

8. The IP reward depends on *both* a property right *and* whichever business model the inventor selects to exploit it. The former is governed by IP law, the latter by antitrust. It is impossible to analyze

reward problems without considering both bodies of law simultaneously.

7. IP provides a powerful incentive for prioritizing investment and weeding out bad ideas. Economists almost always analyze IP using concepts borrowed from the theory of the firm. They should pay more attention to mechanism design.

6. IP does little to aggregate information across firms (Scotchmer, 1998). This means that R&D tasks may not be delegated to the most efficient firms, or even the right number of firms (Menell and Scotchmer, 2007, at p. 1477). Additional instruments including government-sponsored research, tournaments, and joint ventures can often improve coordination compared to IP alone.

5. IP theory depends sensitively on the research environment. This crucially includes whether investment opportunities are universally known ("production function models") or scarce ("ideas models"). (Scotchmer, 1991 [this volume]; Menell and Scotchmer, 2007, at p. 1477.)

4. Courts find it nearly impossible to measure R&D costs directly (Scotchmer, 1998). This forces patents to set up payments based on the full social value instead. The resulting overpayment aggravates the social waste generated by deadweight loss and racing (Scotchmer, 2004a, at p. 151). Independent invention and reverse engineering defenses offer important levers for managing this problem (Maurer and Scotchmer, 2002; Samuelson and Scotchmer, 2002).

3. Patents are "a very crude incentive with pernicious side effects" (Scotchmer, 1998). Other incentives can be more efficient depending on the circumstances (Menell and Scotchmer, 2007, at p. 1531).

2. Innovation is seldom a one-off process. Many products are instead developed through "cumulative innovation" by successive independent inventors (Scotchmer, 1998). Patents must divide profit so that, at a minimum, each successive contributor covers her costs (ibid.).

1. The saving grace of IP is that every invention funded with intellectual property creates a Pareto improvement. The main defect of patents is deadweight loss. (Menell and Scotchmer, 2007, at p. 1477; but see Kremer, 1998 [patent buyouts].)

PART III

INNOVATION THEORY (II):
LAW AND ECONOMICS

American law schools have treated "Law and Economics" as a distinct academic discipline for more than forty years. In the abstract, the reason seems obvious. However much we appreciate the beauty of economics, society only gets full value from its investment in IP theory when academic insights are used to improve existing institutions. This necessarily includes applying sophisticated theory to real statutes and case law. The trouble, in practice, is that the boundary between economics and law is so deep. This means that the great majority of "Law and Economics" papers can be reliably categorized as "mostly economics" or "mostly law." Even today, very few papers combine theory with legal doctrine on anything like an equal footing.

We have seen that Prof. Scotchmer's cumulative innovation work was based on the premise that any satisfactory theory had to address the complex "legal details" that allocate reward across successive inventors. By the early 2000s, she began extending this approach to other IP and antitrust topics. The result was a new kind of paper in which "Law" and "Economics" alternate from one section to the next. The power of this new approach encouraged her to tackle doctrinal problems that had defied judges' best efforts for decades.

CHAPTER 19

The Long Journey: From Models to Legal Doctrine

Stephen M. Maurer

Every theorist spends her life looking for models that are rich enough to surprise but simple enough to solve. One of the things that made Prof. Scotchmer's work so distinctive is that she found some of her best models in legal doctrine.

Cumulative Innovation Theory. Prof. Scotchmer's earliest papers on tax enforcement, crime, and contingent fee agreements (this volume, Part VI) used simple models that suppressed the messy detail of real legal systems. This level of abstraction is typical of the Law and Economics literature and, in this case, helped to identify the tradeoffs that almost any legal system would face. But it also discarded information about the problems that real systems had encountered. Law professors routinely mine statutes and case law in search of interesting policy questions. But for a theoretical economist, taking on the complexity of learning – much less modeling – real legal doctrines must have seemed daunting.

Despite this, Prof. Scotchmer made the investment. At the time, she would have had at least three reasons to take this path. The first and most obvious was her interest in patents. By the late Eighties, economists had taken simple models about as far as they could. New insights would require richer models. The second was that law followed carefully designed, explicit rules. This was a broad hint that litigation could be fruitfully modeled through game theory. Finally, and somewhat more speculatively, recent history had shown that economists could gain important intuition by reading cases and other legal materials. Indeed, economists' decade-long infatuation with racing models had begun with University of Virginia law professor Edmund Kitch's celebrated observation that real patent cases often involve multiple independent teams working on the same invention (Kitch, 1977). While economists certainly would have come to this insight eventually, the intuition came much faster to someone who constantly read court opinions. While Kitch's article contains little or no dynamics – indeed, it does not even mention racing – economists quickly filled in the blanks.

I do not know how conscious this strategy was. But there is no denying that Prof. Scotchmer dove much deeper into the nitty-gritty of IP law than any economist before or since, or that her models were spectacularly convincing. Her first paper already set the pattern by modeling patent law's "non-obviousness" and "first-to-file" rules (Scotchmer and Green, 1990). It shows how these seemingly arcane terms increase patent owners' bargained-for reward – and society's deadweight loss – compared to simple models in which innovation is a one-off activity. The fact that legal doctrine could be so convincingly reduced to an extended form game must have greatly encouraged her. At the same time, it came at the cost of a very steep learning curve. This was especially visible in Scotchmer and Green's (1990) incorrect claim (p. 131) that "The legal requirements of 'novelty' and 'nonobviousness'" related not just to whether a patent would be granted, but also "determined how different a subsequent innovation must be in order not to infringe." Fortunately this confusion turned out to be harmless for the paper's reasoning and Prof. Scotchmer quickly discovered the nuance. Indeed, she eventually followed the clue to point out how divorcing eligibility ("leading breadth") from infringement ("trailing breadth") would create a useful new policy lever (O'Donoghue, Scotchmer, and Thisse, 1998 [this volume]; Scotchmer, 2004b, at pp. 146–149).

Prof. Scotchmer's next paper, "Giants" (Scotchmer, 1991 [this volume]) announces the cumulative innovation agenda that would dominate her research for the following decade. Famously, it maps the efficiency problems that arise when IP tries to share reward across successive inventors. But "Giants" limits itself to a generic choice between "narrow" and "broad" patents. This deliberate generality is informative because it shows that cumulative innovation issues are deeper than any particular choice of rules. At the same time, the obvious next step was to ask *which* rule does the best job of balancing innovation against deadweight loss. Here, the usual theorist's trick of inventing and exploring hypothetical rules was doomed to failure – there were simply too many choices, none of which was obviously better than the rest. So, instead, Scotchmer turned to the rules that legislators and judges had actually designed. Apart from its obvious relevance to policy, this may also have reflected the usual economist's instinct that evolved institutions tend to be at least approximately rational.

Green and Scotchmer (1995) (this volume) began this work by presenting a formal game theory analysis of improvement patents, albeit with the conventional game-theoretic shortcut of assuming that each firm receives half the bargaining surplus. Schankerman and Scotchmer (1999) (this volume) complete the project by showing how damages and injunctive relief rules actually divide the surplus.

Prof. Scotchmer's growing knowledge of doctrine also helped her spot previously overlooked policy levers. She had already emphasized in "Giants" that the patent system would be much more efficient if judges could tune each patent owner's reward to his expected R&D costs. But these costs were normally invisible to courts. Despite this, she managed to find a partial solution in a piece of legal trivia: copyright – unlike patent law – permits "independent invention," so that future authors are free to create similar works so long as no actual copying takes place. Extending this defense to patents, she argued, would tune rewards to R&D costs (Maurer and Scotchmer, 2002). The reason, following "Giants," is licensing. At least in principle, introducing the defense would allow parties who had been denied a license under existing patents to order their engineers to re-invent it in so-called "clean rooms" that had been swept clear of all references to the original invention. Given that inventing something a second time is costly, this new threat point would persuade the patent owner to license the original invention after all. Better yet, if this happens often enough, the royalty rate will eventually be bid down to the otherwise unobservable cost of R&D (ibid.). This marked a significant advance over La Manna et al. (1989), who had warned that legislators who adopted the defense would have to extend patent duration to compensate for the erosion of per-period rewards. In Scotchmer's telling, the "eroded" reward provided otherwise unavailable information that policymakers could use to reduce deadweight loss. Best of all, the mechanism improved efficiency not just for cumulative innovation but also Nordhaus models.

Characteristically, Prof. Scotchmer saw this as much more than an interesting thought experiment. Granted that a pure independent invention defense faces practical problems – most obviously, latecomers will be tempted to use the patent teachings while feigning ignorance – narrowed versions could minimize these risks. Scholars have emphasized that the defense is especially likely to be practical where the independent invention takes place before the original patent becomes public. (See, e.g., Shapiro, 2006; Vermont, 2006; Lemley, 2007.)

Learning Curves and Collaborations. Writing papers that treat law and economics with equal sophistication required a large personal investment. For an economic theorist, just finding the law was not sufficient since many standard judicial formulations are opaque or awkward to model. Instead, she had to invent crisp paraphrases that lawyers would find compelling. Prof. Scotchmer would continue to develop this skill, alone and with colleagues, for the rest of her life.

She approached the task with her customary fearlessness, or more accurately delight. Echoes can still be found in the tutorials she left for economists, including her "Primer for Nonlawyers on Intellectual Property" (Scotchmer, 1994b, at pp. 65–93) with its detailed advice (pp. 92–93) on how to do legal research. It helped that her own research instincts were well suited to legal problems, most obviously her knack for returning over and over again to hard problems – a tangled court opinion, say – until she saw a pattern. The habit helped free her from the folkloric – and often misleading – received wisdom that sometimes grows up around famous cases. For example, most law professors have been socialized to paraphrase the *Terminal Railroad* case (US S. Ct., 1912) as a dispute over how many railroads could use St. Louis's only bridge across the Mississippi River. But when Prof. Scotchmer went back to read the original opinion, she discovered that there had actually been *three* bridges which the defendants had purchased seriatim and then cartelized. This helped her to recover the Court's original (and fruitful) insight that the Sherman Act's concern for competition must be tempered by the need to preserve economies of scale. Modern theories of the case that stress leveraging miss this logic entirely. (See, generally, Maurer and Scotchmer, 2014).

It helped that lawyers and economists tended to share certain thought patterns. This was most visible in Prof. Scotchmer's lawyer-like enthusiasm for inventing and debating underlying principles that would "harmonize" apparently disparate judicial rulings. Though superficially surprising, the exercise was almost inevitable for someone who was already steeped in the mathematician's characteristic obsession with clarifying logical foundations. At the same time, the principles she invented were very different from those a lawyer would have come to. Most obviously, they were invariably phrased in the language of economics, for example by suggesting that the legality of reverse engineering should depend on whether the copyist did more than rent-seeking (Samuelson and Scotchmer, 2002 [this volume]) or arguing that the case for antitrust relief was much less compelling where cooperation between rivals promised significant scale economies (Maurer and Scotchmer, 2014).

The next natural step was to pursue more intense collaborations through coauthorship. Here the main examples are her work with Samuelson (2002), Maurer (2002), and Menell (2007). These required significant learning on both sides – and not just because, as Prof. Scotchmer liked to say, "coauthorship is hard." Arriving at paraphrases that were simultaneously realistic and definite enough to model could easily consume months of back-and-forth discussion. At the same time, arguing over equivalent paraphrases also had a way of forcing unexamined assumptions to the surface. These are particularly visible in the extensive case analyses that Prof. Scotchmer wrote for Maurer and Scotchmer (2014).

One small surprise was that Prof. Scotchmer was willing to suggest nut-and-bolts legal reforms as enthusiastically as any lawyer. Indeed, she sometimes spotted doctrinal issues that even the professionals had missed. Writing in the mid-1990s, Federal Circuit Chief Judge Helen Nies had famously argued that "[a] substitution in a patented invention cannot simultaneously be both nonobvious and insubstantial [under the doctrine of equivalents]" (*Roton Barrier, Inc.* v. *Stanley Works*, 79 F.3d 1112 at 1128 [Fed. Cir. 1996]). This, however, depended on a hidden assumption that the "doctrine of equivalents" and "non-obviousness" standards were identical. The thought appealed to the conventional lawyers' instinct for limiting the proliferation of standards. By comparison, Prof. Scotchmer's economic training convinced her that it was important to preserve as many independent policy levers as possible. From this standpoint, identifying non-obviousness with the "doctrine of equivalents" served no purpose. (See Scotchmer, 2004b, at pp. 84–88.)

Reforming Legal Doctrine. By the early 2000s Prof. Scotchmer's decade-plus inquiry into cumulative innovation was winding down. Never sentimental about sunk costs, she might have walked away from law at this point. Instead, she began experimenting with a new type of paper that was neither law review nor economic theory, but instead combined aspects of both to attack law's hardest problems.

This new departure coincided with much deeper ties to the legal community. Here the most spectacular example was her 2002 stint as the Federal Circuit's first (and so far only) Scholar in Residence. Colleagues still recall how she would return to Berkeley excited by what she had learned – but then shake her head and add, "You won't believe what some of these people think." Further outreach included semester-long visiting appointments to the Law Schools at the University of South California (2007) and New York University (2008) and a permanent appointment to Berkeley Law School in 2008. Faculty at all three institutions remember that she was a strong believer in community, who was always ready to talk through the day's legal puzzles in every possible venue from hallway conversations to formal seminars.

These interactions plainly helped her to notice new economic theory problems to study. Probably the clearest example is Scotchmer (2010), which took contemporary debates over the Supreme Court's decision in *Bilski* v. *Kappos* [US Supreme Court (2010)] as a motivating problem to rethink traditional rules against patenting basic science. The paper sharpens the point by identifying a deep tension in the Bayh–Dole premise that patent incentives can be used to accelerate further discovery: since unpatented discoveries can be developed by anyone, all university licenses are non-exclusive and will therefore command zero royalties in expectation.

She also moved beyond economic theory to write for lawyers directly. The earliest installment was her reverse engineering paper with Prof. Samuelson (Samuelson and Scotchmer, 2002 [this volume]). This extended the basic logic of her independent invention work by arguing that the legal rules for reverse engineering should depend on copying costs. Contrary to most theory papers, this economic logic was cast in plain English that judges could use to decide cases.

Prof. Scotchmer was also struck by the fact that so many famous doctrinal problems had persisted for decades and, in some cases, centuries. Not only did the law remain chaotic, but new law reviews added very little to reforms suggested fifty years before. In these cases, at least, it was reasonable to think that ordinary legal reasoning methods had run out of steam. At the same time, many of these problems (particularly in IP and antitrust law) had a large economics component. This made it reasonable to think that better economic analyses could break the impasse. Prof. Scotchmer therefore began writing papers that paired sophisticated legal reasoning with formal economic models. The bottom line, in each case, was that the paper had to be useful to practitioners. This implied, among other things, respecting precedent. Rather than invent her own policy goals, she took what judges said as given. The same went for the court's factual findings about what had happened. But that still left the very large category of judicial reasoning and, in particular, the often careless or garbled economic arguments that explained how the judge's ruling was supposed to further the law's purpose. That became her focus.

The first such project, Maurer and Scotchmer (2007), uses formal models to rationalize the classic Supreme Court cases defining when patent licenses are and are not acceptable under the Sherman Act. Prof. Scotchmer's last paper – completed less than a month before her death – similarly revisits the *Terminal Railroad* problem of deciding when antitrust law should permit and even force rivals to share assets (Maurer and Scotchmer, 2014). Characteristically, she leaves no legal or economic tool off the table. On the one hand, Prof. Scotchmer uses rigorous models to show how various generic license terms affect competition. On the other, she carefully addresses the best-known US and European cases, showing how the modern tendency to analyze essential facilities in terms of leveraging theories has forgotten the Supreme Court's original purpose of reconciling competition with the need to preserve scale economies.

We will never know how far Prof. Scotchmer would have taken this agenda. Her style was still evolving, and she would certainly have refined it further. But the goal was always to be directly useful to judges and lawyers. She would have been especially pleased to know that the American Antitrust Institute would posthumously honor her essential facilities paper as the "Best Section 2 Article of 2014."

CHAPTER 20

M. Schankerman and S. Scotchmer, "Damages and Injunctions in Protecting Intellectual Property" (1999)

INTRODUCTION STEPHEN M. MAURER

This paper provides a particularly nice illustration of how Prof. Scotchmer used game theory to investigate the legal rules that divide reward across successive inventors. In this sense, it represents one of the last milestones along the long economic theory agenda from "Giants" (1992) to *Innovation and Incentives* (2004). Yet I recall that, even at the time, Prof. Scotchmer did not describe the paper that way. Instead, she called it an effort to sort out American law's famously incoherent "lost royalties" doctrine.[1] This explicitly legal purpose looked forward to a new research agenda that would use economic tools to attack hard legal problems.

Despite this, Prof. Scotchmer probably did not anticipate just how convincingly this agenda would speak to legal scholars and judges. Most theory papers focus on high level concepts like "reward size," "deadweight loss," or "patent breadth." But working lawyers hardly ever discuss IP this way. Instead, they let these bottom line variables percolate up from dozens of smaller arguments over this statute or that judge-made rule. The difference, in the mid-Nineties, was that Prof. Scotchmer had begun constructing game theory models that operated at this same level of abstraction. In her hands, at least, IP theory and law finally possessed a common language.

The Paper. Schankerman and Scotchmer (1999) appeared at a time when the post-"Giants" agenda was already well advanced. By then, Prof. Scotchmer had modeled the first-to-file, non-obviousness, and doctrine

---

1 *Georgia-Pacific Corp.* v. *United States Plywood Corp.*, 318 F. Supp. 1116 (S.D.N.Y. 1970). One measure of the case's incoherence is that it tells judges to estimate damages based on a grab bag of *fifteen* factors. The problem, of course, is that no human mind can possibly do such a thing. Instead, judges usually emphasize whatever factors validate their preexisting prejudices.

of equivalents[2] rules that decide what lawyers call "infringement," i.e., whether the defendant owes money to earlier inventors. But this still left the obvious question of just how much money (or relief) was owed.

The authors sort out the problem for so-called "research tools" in which the first generation invention provides a platform for commercially saleable, second generation products. Most economists then and now would have imagined just two possibilities, "damages" and "injunction." But this is not enough for Scotchmer and Schankerman, who dig into patent relief with the kind of precision one normally expects from law professors. This leads to a nuanced account in which damages and injunctions are limited by two separate defenses ("laches" and "estoppel") that depend on the parties' behavior, and especially the first inventor's delay in bringing suit. They also note that "damages" have historically been implemented in two distinct ways. Before World War II, US patent law had measured damages by asking what the infringer had earned in breaking the law ("unjust enrichment"). Since then, however, patent law has instead awarded patent-holders the profits they would have earned but for the infringement ("lost royalties"). Despite some judicious simplifications, most IP lawyers find the paper's stylizations remarkably lifelike.[3]

The rest of the paper presents extended form games that investigate how cumulative patents divide the IP reward. As usual, the answer depends on market structure. The authors provide detailed analyses for situations where the first patent is a research tool required to make the second generation products (section 3), is not essential but only saves R&D costs (section 4), and must be combined with other tools to reach the final result (section 5). Section 6 investigates the "blocking patent" scenario in which the first generation inventor races to develop the product against potential infringers. Section 7 presents a general model that can be applied to still other contexts where the natural use of patents includes licensing.[4]

Three Lessons. The bottom line of these investigations is that the old, unjust enrichment rule is (a) more favorable to plaintiffs in the research tool scenario, but (b) less favorable for scenarios where the first and second generation products compete. But the fact that unjust enrichment sometimes

---

2 O'Donoghue, Scotchmer, and Thisse (1998). This volume at pp. 130–155, *supra*.
3 I did some supporting research for this paper, and can still recall long arguments about how to paraphrase the judge-made rules for injunctions and damages. As a lawyer, straying from the exact treatise language made me nervous. Today, looking back, I find that I can't remember which paraphrases I argued over and which seemed fine from the outset. That seems like the right result.
4 Following "Giants," the inquiry is narrowly focused on asking how legal rules influence royalty amounts during licensing. This is itself markedly different from the usual law and economics paper, which almost always asks how litigants settle cases.

reduces the first inventor's recovery casts doubt on Congress's postwar decision to rewrite patent damages. After all, "Giants" had argued that efficient allocation rules should normally maximize returns to the first generation inventor. At the time, it was hard to know what to do with this observation – since neither damages measure was clearly superior to the other, the article's advice was indeterminate. More recently, however, legal scholars have begun to argue that patent law should be interpreted to make *both* forms of relief available so that patent owners could select whichever measure offered the highest reward.[5] Following Scotchmer and Schankerman, this step would unambiguously improve welfare.

Scotchmer and Schankerman also find a second difficulty in the modern rule. In order to award lost royalties, courts must find evidence of what willing licensees paid for similar inventions in the past. But this is circular. After all, these past royalties were themselves negotiated against the amounts that the patent owner could have realized by bringing a lawsuit. This suggests that many different lost royalty rewards are stable in equilibrium.[6]

Finally, Schankerman and Scotchmer point out that unjust enrichment damages can be so large that the second inventor never develops her product at all. When this happens, the patent owner receives higher returns by negotiating against the threat of injunction. The surprise is that weakening injunctive relief by giving the infringer more laches and estoppel defenses can actually increase returns to the patent owner. The reason, following Green and Scotchmer (1995), is that the second inventor can no longer credibly threaten to abandon the project. This reduces her bargaining power so that she recovers a smaller share of total royalties. Here, Scotchmer and Schankerman make a potentially transformative suggestion for legal doctrine. Lawyers have long interpreted laches and estoppel by asking when delay is "unfair" to the infringer. Reinterpreting the defenses as a "policy instrument"[7] for allocating reward would make doctrine much more determinate, most notably by introducing the authors' very concrete and non-intuitive observation that the defenses should be stronger when (a) the patent owner is large or cash-rich, or (b) the second generation invention has limited sales potential.[8]

Bridging the Gap. Congress has continuously debated, and occasionally passed, wide-ranging patent reform for more than a decade now. Despite

5 Roberts (2010). Unjust enrichment and lost profits damages are already available side-by-side for copyright and design patents (ibid.).
6 This means, among other things, that the relative ranking of lost royalties and unjust enrichment recoveries is sometimes indeterminate. This happens, for example, for cost-saving inventions (Part IV).
7 Schankerman and Scotchmer (1999), *infra* at p. 194.
8 Ibid. at p. 174.

or perhaps because of this attention, most proposals remain distressingly *ad hoc*. Consider the so-called "patent trolls" issue, which claims that many Silicon Valley patents cover trivial discoveries and, in any case, are too broad. As I write, Congress is actively considering a variety of reforms including ratcheting up pleading standards, cutting back pre-trial discovery, limiting appeals, and changing to a "losers pay" attorneys fees rule.[9] All of these rules would surely reduce the number of trolls. But as Prof. Scotchmer would immediately point out, they will also make it harder for first generation inventors to recover. So no one really knows what these proposals would do on net, and Congress is uneasy, and Congress is right to hesitate.

In the meantime we have this outwardly conventional game theory paper. Who knew that reforming damages law could unambiguously improve cumulative innovation? That "lost profit" damages are path-dependent? Or that laches and estoppel offer potentially powerful policy instruments? A theory paper, yes, but with a practical core. You can't help wondering. Congress pays for so much research. Why don't they read it?

RAND Journal of Economics,
Vol. 32 No, 1 (Spring, 2001): 199–220

Damages and Injunctions in Protecting Intellectual Property

Mark Schankerman[*]
and
Suzanne Scotchmer[**]

We investigate how liability rules and property rules protect intellectual property. Infringement might not be deterred under any of the enforcement regimes available. However, counterintuitively, a

9 See, e.g., J. C. Boggs, Jennifer H. Burdman and William J. Sauers, "Debate on Patent Reform Legislation Continues in Congress: What You Need to Know," Bloomberg – BNA, available at www.bna.com/debate-patent-reform-n17179934625/.

 * London School of Economics and CEPR: m.schankerman@lse.ac.uk.
** University of California, Berkeley and NBER: scotch@socrates.berkeley.edu
      We are grateful to the Sloan Foundation and National Science Foundation for financial support and to the managers, scientists and lawyers in biotechnology firms who provided valuable information about the biotechnology industry and its legal context. We thank two anonymous referees and the Editor for very constructive comments, Stephen Maurer for guidance on legal issues and other helpful comments, and also Rebecca Eisenberg, Rob Merges, Lynn Pasahow, Brian Wright, and participants at the NBER conference on The Patent System and Innovation (January 1999) and Institute of Economics, University of Copenhagen.

credible threat of infringement can actually benefit the patentholder. We compare the two doctrines of damages, lost profit (lost royalty) and unjust enrichment, and argue that unjust enrichment protects the patentholder better than lost royalty in the case of proprietary research tools. Both can be superior to a property rule, depending on how much delay is permitted before infringement is enjoined. For other proprietary products (end-user products, cost-reducing innovations), these conclusions can be reversed.

1. Introduction

Rights to intellectual property are protected in two ways: by court orders to enjoin infringement, and by holding the infringer liable for damages. Injunctions intervene directly to stop infringement, whereas liability intervenes indirectly by making the infringement unprofitable. Under U.S. law, there are two liability doctrines that might determine damages. The first is that the infringer must reimburse the property owner's "lost profits," and the second is that he must disgorge his "unjust enrichment." We study the deterrence effects of damage rules and injunctions and their effect on a patentholder's profit.

Our main interest is in intellectual property that would normally be licensed, in particular, research tools. Examples include the Cohen-Boyer patent on the technology for inserting foreign genetic material into bacteria, the Genentech patent on a technology for getting foreign genes to "express," the PCR technology for replicating DNA in test tubes, gene guns, and recent suppression technologies that cause gene sequences to become inactive. The salient feature of such property is that it is efficient to let firms other than the patentholder use it. It would thus normally be licensed, and the relevant notion of "lost profit" includes lost royalties.

Two of our main, and somewhat surprising, conclusions are that

(i) infringement is not necessarily deterred under either liability doctrine, and
(ii) the patentholder might *prefer* an enforcement regime that leads to infringement, absent a license.

Under the unjust-enrichment doctrine, an infringer must disgorge his ill-gotten gains, leaving him with zero profit. Whether such a rule would deter infringement depends on other aspects of the legal environment. If an infringer might escape liability entirely, e.g., by failure of the patentholder to detect infringement, then he might not be deterred from infringement under the doctrine. But if he would incur additional costs in litigation, such as lawyers' fees or punitive damages, he will more likely be deterred.

Deterrence can be even harder to ensure under the lost-profits doctrine. If the sole use of the intellectual property would be licensing, then the measure of "lost profits" is entirely lost royalties. The lost-profit (lost-royalty) doctrine leads to the following circularity: On one hand, prospective damages determine the maximum license fee that a licensee would pay. On the other hand, the presumed license fee determines the damages. License fees and prospective damages are equal and self-reinforcing.[1] We argue that many license fees and damages may be consistent with the doctrine, but the prospective damages will not deter infringement. License fees that more than exhaust the available profit could not arise in equilibrium and therefore could not be "lost royalty."

But, counterintuitively, a failure to deter infringement might benefit the patent-holder. Consider a research tool whose sole profit will come from licensing. Ultimately, both the patentholder's and the licensee's (or infringer's) profit will come from selling a proprietary product that the tool will facilitate. If the enforcement regime deters infringement, it gives the potential licensee a credible threat not to develop the product, depriving both parties of profit. Hence, the licensee has a "holdup" threat for the value of the product, and this strengthens his bargaining position for a license. Compare this outcome with a damage regime that would not deter infringement. If infringement is a credible threat, the patentholder would not agree to license terms that give him less profit than he could get by refusing the license, letting the infringement go forward, and collecting damages *ex post*. If the expected damages are high enough (but not so high they deter infringement), these terms can be more attractive to the patentholder than those he would negotiate if the potential licensee could credibly threaten to deprive him of the product.

Injunctions are an alternative enforcement regime to liability. The patentholder can sue to enjoin an infringing use before an infringer has brought his new product to completion. However, deterrence by injunction can undermine profit in the same way as deterrence by the threat of high damages. Once an infringement is enjoined, the infringer has a credible threat not to develop the profitable product, and this gives him holdup power over the patentholder.

In studying these enforcement regimes, we take the view that infringement will never occur in equilibrium. If infringement is truly tempting, then the firms will license to avoid it, especially if the infringement would lead to inefficient use of the intellectual property. The only role of damages

---

1 Leitzel (1989) discusses a similar circularity for contract damages: He proposes to avoid circularity by defining "reasonable" damages as the socially efficient damages. This would not work in our context, where "reasonable royalty" is based on a hypothetical negotiation between the two parties in which the outcome may not be socially efficient. For a recent example in the context of copyright fair use, *see A.G U. v. Texaco*, 60 F.3d 913 (2d Cir. 1994).

and injunctions is to set "threat points" for negotiating licenses. The terms of each license are negotiated in the shadow of what would happen otherwise, and in this way, the enforcement regime determines how profitable the patent is for its owner.

For most intellectual property, infringement of a patent reduces the patentholder's and infringer's joint profits, relative to licensing. For example, a cost-reducing innovation that is licensed with royalties will generate more profit to the patentholder and licensee jointly than if an infringer adopts the cost-reducing innovation without paying royalties. Competition without royalties will reduce the market price. In contrast, infringement of a research tool will not typically reduce the patentholder's and infringer's joint profit even though it deprives the patentholder of his just reward. The profit arises from a proprietary product that is developed with the tool, and the profit available from that product does not typically depend on whether it accrues solely to an infringer, or whether part of the profit is paid back to the patentholder through license fees.

It turns out that this difference in profit dissipation matters for the relative attractiveness of the two damage rules. For research tools we conclude that

(i) a wide array of damage measures may be consistent with the lost profit (lost royalty) doctrine of damages, and infringement would not be deterred, absent a license.
(ii) damages under the unjust-enrichment doctrine are unique. If infringement would be deterred under that doctrine, then the two liability doctrines cannot be ranked. If infringement would not be deterred under the unjust-enrichment doctrine, that doctrine is generally more profitable to the patentholder than the lost-profit (lost-royalty) doctrine.
(iii) a right to enjoin infringement is more profitable to the patentholder than liability under the lost-royalty doctrine, even when both are available. However, injunctions are not an improvement if they must be invoked "too soon" or "too late" as governed by the *doctrine of laches*, discussed below.

These conclusions are in part reversed for other licensed intellectual property, such as product innovations or cost-reducing innovations, where infringement would lead to profit dissipation. For those we conclude that

(i) damages under both doctrines are unique. Infringement is unambiguously deterred under the lost-profit doctrine.
(ii) the lost-profit doctrine and unjust-enrichment doctrines are equally profitable to the patentholder if infringement is deterred under both doctrines, but otherwise unjust enrichment is less profitable to the patentholder.

In legal parlance, damages are awarded under a "liability rule" and injunctions are sought under a "property rule." These rules have been discussed at length in the legal literature for other types of property. Calabresi and Melamed (1972) argued that a property rule is superior to a liability rule whenever transaction costs are low and information imperfect. This is because property rules induce bargaining, which will presumably lead to an efficient outcome. They argue that under a liability rule, the courts might not be able to assess appropriate damages or an efficient allocation. In a wide-ranging reassessment, Kaplow and Shavell (1996) disagreed with Calabresi and Melamed, pointing out that when transaction costs are low, the parties have incentives to bargain under *both* regimes. Our own analysis adopts the same point of view. Focusing on intellectual property, Blair and Cotter (1998) analyzed how the profit is distributed under the lost-profit and unjust-enrichment doctrines in the out-of-equilibrium event of infringement and concluded that the unjust enrichment rule is superior. However, they did not analyze injunctions.

Our own analysis of liability and property rules differs from the earlier literature in that we focus on *equilibrium* profits. We assume frictionless bargaining, which leads to *efficient* use of the intellectual property, and are solely interested in the liability and property rules for their effect on the division of profit. Infringement will never occur in equilibrium, but the possibility of infringement sets the "threat points" for establishing licenses. Our focus is on equilibrium profit because that is what determines incentives to innovate.

Our perspective is that intellectual property rights are exercised as the right to collect license fees by threatening to exclude (under a property rule) or threatening to collect damages (under a liability rule). Provided the research tool owner can collect license fees, he has the incentive to encourage other firms to use the tool in developing products. Legal scholars such as Eisenberg (1989) and Heller and Eisenberg (1998) have been less optimistic about contracting than we are. Their analyses are directed at the *ex post* question of how to ensure that inventions are put to good use even when contracting fails, whereas we assume that contracting will not fail. Injunctions can foreclose the use of research tools when licensing fails, and for this reason Eisenberg argues against giving patentholders injunctive relief for research tools. Instead she proposes that courts impose damages equal to reasonable royalty payments. Merges (1996) takes a different position, arguing that to exclude injunctive relief and to rely exclusively on damage remedies would put an unmanageable burden on the courts to set damages or compulsory licensing fees in a way that serves the public interest. This problem can be avoided by permitting injunctions. We also conclude that a property rule can be superior to a liability rule for research tools, but for a different reason, namely, that damages consistent with the prevailing doctrine can be too low.

The article is organized as follows. In Section 2 we discuss the legal basis for the prevailing liability and property regimes. In Section 3 we present a stylized model in which a firm has developed a proprietary research tool that is needed to develop a commercial product.[2] We discuss how the division of profit depends on the remedies for infringement and the opportunity to seek injunctions. In Section 4 we suppose that there is an alternative technology to the proprietary research tool, but that developing the product is more costly when using the alternative tool. This possibility changes our analysis of injunctions, but not of the damage doctrines. In Section 5 we discuss the complexities that arise when multiple research tools are required for each proprietary product. Section 6 examines the case where the patentholder can compete in developing the commercial product. In Section 7 we present a more general model that subsumes research tools and other intellectual property as special cases.

2. Legal doctrines: damages and injunctions

Damage doctrines. The case law enunciates two doctrines of damages, "unjust enrichment" and "lost profit/reasonable royalty." These doctrines appear to be aimed at different objectives. The doctrine of unjust enrichment is focused on a just punishment for the infringer, who is required to disgorge all the profits from infringement. In contrast, the doctrine of lost profit seems aimed at compensating the patentholder, so as to maintain his incentives to invest in R&D (*England v. Deere & Co.*, 221 F. Supp. 319, 1963). Before 1946, when the current statutory rules on damages took form, the courts appear to have given greater weight to unjust enrichment. In the postwar period the courts have relied exclusively on the lost-profit/reasonable-royalty doctrine. In that doctrine, the sole basis for recovery is the patentee's damages and not the infringer's profits, though the latter may be relevant evidence for computing the patentee's actual damages or a reasonable royalty (e.g., *Zegers v. Zegers, Inc.*, 458 F.2d 726, 1972).

Unjust enrichment. Under this doctrine, the patent owner is entitled to recover profits realized by the infringer on the theory that the infringer should not profit from his wrongdoing. The infringer is viewed as holding these profits "in constructive trust" for the infringed party. This doctrine was prominent in the late part of the 19th century and was used as late as World War II (*Littlefield v. Perry*, N.Y. 1875, 188 U.S. 205; *Amusement Corp. of America v. Mattson*, C.C.A. Fla. 1943, 138 F.2d 693). In most case law, the measure of unjust enrichment was the profits realized by the

2 The model has the cumulative features of Scotchmer (1991), and Green and Scotchmer (1995), who implicitly assumed a property rule and discussed how patent breadth (the probability of infringement) affect the terms of licensing. Their models extend to research tools, but they do not discuss liability rules.

infringer (e.g., *Leman v. Krentler-Anzold Hinge Last Co.*, 284 U.S. 448, 1932). However, a number of cases enunciated the subtler principle that the measure of unjust enrichment should be the advantage gained by using the infringed invention instead of other available, nonproprietary alternatives.[3]

Lost profit and reasonable royalty. This doctrine shifts the focus from the infringer's profits to the patentee's loss (*Yale Lock Mfg. Co. v. Sargent*, 117 U.S. 536, 1886). The doctrine as currently applied was enunciated in *Panduit Corp. v. Stahlin Bros Fibre Works* (575 F.2d 1152, 1978). The court stated that the patentee is entitled to recover "actual damages" (also referred to as "lost profit") or, when these cannot be proved, not less than a "reasonable royalty." The principle is to restore the patentee to the position "but for" the infringement. Whether lost profit is lost sales or lost licensing revenues depends on whether the owner would have developed the application himself or would have licensed to another firm. From an evidentiary point of view, this distinction would be hard for courts to assess.[4]

Not surprisingly, despite judicial efforts to identify the relevant considerations in setting a reasonable royalty (e.g., *Georgia-Pacific Corp. v. United States Plywood Corp.*, 38 F. Supp. 1116, 1970), the doctrine has proved difficult to implement in a consistent and predictable manner (Conley, 1987). In this article we will make a stronger criticism: when the source of profit is licensing revenue, the doctrine involves a circularity, with the consequence that a whole range of damage measures may be logically consistent with it. To emphasize this circularity, we shall refer to "lost royalty" instead of "reasonable royalty."

Injunctions. Under a property rule, the patentholder can sue to enjoin an infringing use of the proprietary research tool. In the model below, we assume that the injunction precipitates a settlement. If the research tool is the sole means to develop the enabled product, the settlement will be more favorable to the patentholder if costs have already been sunk by the infringer. Thus the patentholder will have an incentive to delay the injunction. But if there is a substitute for the research tool (for example, a research tool that is less efficient), we argue that the patentholder's incentive to delay is reversed or muted.

Delay is constrained by the *doctrine of laches*. The right to enjoin can be forfeited if it is not exercised in a timely manner, and if the

---

3 For example, *Mowry v. Whitney*, 81 U.S. 620, 1872; *Horvath v. McCord Radiator and Mfg. Co.*, 100 F.2d 326, 1938; *Gordon Form Lathe Co. v. Ford Motor Co.*, C.C.A. Mich., 133 F.2d 487, 1943.

4 *Panduit* addressed the evidentiary problem by requiring the patent owner to establish four things in order to recover the profit on lost sales: a demand for the patented product, that there were no acceptable noninfringing substitutes, a manufacturing and marketing capability to supply the market, and the profit that would have been made on lost sales.

patentee's unreasonable delay caused the injury to the infringer (*Columbia Broadcasting System, Inc. v. Zenith Radio Corp.*, 391 F. Supp. 780, 1975). A defense of laches is more likely to be granted to an infringer if he made significant investments during the period of delay.[5] Once sufficient investments have been made, the infringer can sometimes force the issue by asking for a declaratory judgment. The goal of such a suit is a ruling of patent invalidity or non-infringement. A declaratory judgment suit is unlikely if the infringement can be hidden, or if there are many targets for an infringement suit. But it is plausible when there is a single, visible infringer – or after the infringement is discovered by the patentholder. In fact, the courts have held in a series of recent cases that a delay of six years triggers a rebuttable *presumption* of laches and shifts the burden of proof to the patentee to show that the defense of laches does not apply.[6]

In addition to laches, an infringer may invoke the related defense of estoppel. Estoppel can be invoked if the patent owner made representations by statements or conduct that implied the patent would not be enforced, and if the defendant relied upon them and suffered injury as a result.[7] Unlike laches, a defense of estoppel does not require unreasonable delay by the patent owner, and it can be invoked at any time.

According to interviews we conducted with patent counsel in biotechnology firms, the owner of a research tool typically learns about infringement when the infringer conducts field trials, which usually begin about halfway in the development process and, presumably, after some of the development costs have been sunk. Thus it is reasonable to assume that there is a lower bound to the proportion of the infringer's costs that must be sunk before the patentholder can seek an injunction.

We know of no cases establishing whether a product developed with a proprietary research tool infringes the patent. For process patents, the law is clear: a product that is manufactured with an unlicensed, proprietary process constitutes an infringement. The patentholder on the process can sue for damages or enjoin the production and selling of the product. However, we know of no cases establishing rules for research tools, where the patent would be infringed during *development* of the commercial product rather than during manufacture. In the analysis that follows, we suppose that the patentholder can seek an injunction and *ex post* settlement if he

---

5 *Rome Grader & Machinery Corp. v. J.D. Adams Mfg. Co.*, 135 F.2d 617, 1947; *Whitman v. Walt Disney Productions, Inc.*, 148 F. Supp. 37, 1957; *Siemens Aktiengesellschaft v. Beltone Electronics Corp.*, 381 F. Supp. 57, 1974.

6 *Jensen v. Western Irr. and Mfg., Inc.*, C.A Or. 1980, 650 F.2d 165; *Lemelson v. Carolina Enterprises, Inc.*, D.C.N.Y. 1982, 541 F.Supp. 645; *Advanced Cardiovascular Systems, Inc. v. Scimed Life Systems, Inc.*, C.A.Fed. (Minn.) 1993, 988 F.2d 1157.

7 *See Studiengesellschaft Kohle mbH v. Eastman Kodak Co.*, C.A. Tex. 1980, 616 F.2d 1315. For more extensive references to the case law on laches and estoppel, see USCA (1984), sections 282 and 286.

detects infringement during development, but not afterward. Even if there were a right to enjoin or collect damages afterward, there is a serious evidentiary problem of establishing that the research tool was used.[8]

3. Licensing a research tool

In this section we suppose that there is one research tool and a nonanonymous user with whom the tool owner will bargain. (In a later section we suppose that there are several research tools.) The research tool is owned by a patentholder, firm 1, and the tool is needed by a second firm (a potential infringer, firm 2) to develop a commercial product. The product will have commercial value v and can be developed by the potential infringer at cost c. We say that investment is *efficient* if $v - c \geq 0$, and in this section we restrict attention to projects in which investment is efficient. For the moment we assume that the patentholder specializes in research tools and does not have the expertise to use the tool in developing the commercial product. Thus the patentholder's only prospect for profit is through licensing.

We assume that the parties will achieve *ex post* efficiency. Once intellectual property is invented, the patentholder can profit by using it efficiently. The owner will license on terms that the users will accept, since it is better to license at a low price than not to license at all. Thus, with frictionless contracting, the patent does not jeopardize development of second-generation products. However, there is no guarantee that the patentholder's costs will be covered, and that is why it is desirable to maximize his profit, subject to the self-imposed constraint that second-generation products are not jeopardized.

Unauthorized development of the product by firm 2 is an infringement of the research tool. If no license agreement is reached, then under the liability regime, firm 2 must either forgo his product or develop it without authorization and pay damages afterward, say d. If he infringes under the property rule, he will be enjoined after investing some portion of costs, and the firms will reach a settlement. Neither firm can make a take-it-or-leave-it offer in any negotiation. Rather, they bargain for a license agreement in the shadow of what would happen if no bargain is struck, which determines their "threat points." The bargaining surplus is always shared according to $(\lambda, 1 - \lambda)$, $0 < \lambda < 1$.

We first discuss the liability regime. If the damages were high enough to deter infringement, then the threat points for the licensing negotiation would be $(0, 0)$, and the bargaining surplus would be the social surplus $v - c$. The license would lead to profits of $(\lambda(v - c), (1 - \lambda)(v - c))$ for the

---

8 This evidentiary problem is not unique to research tools, however. It applies to all process patents. In some countries burden of proof is switched to the defendant in infringement cases involving process patents in order to deal with this problem. It may be advisable to adopt such a rule for research tools.

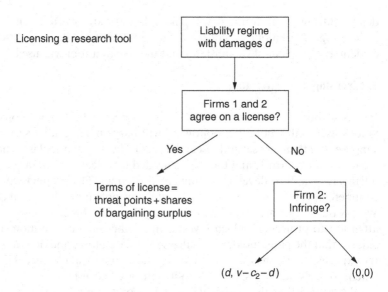

Figure 1 Licensing a Research Tool

two firms respectively.[9] This would be relevant, for example, under the doctrine of unjust enrichment, if infringement would be deterred. If damages were not high enough to deter infringement, the threat points for the licensing negotiation would be $(c, v - c - d)$, where d represents the damages awarded. See Figure 1.

If a license is achieved, the license fee is L. The license fee establishes how the surplus $v - c$ is shared by the two firms and, in particular, whether the patentholder collects the full profit surplus, which is $L = v - c$. Licensing will always occur in equilibrium, but the equilibrium license fee L will depend on the doctrine of damages through the threat points, which reflect the prospective damages d. We propose that the following hypothesis is a good assessment of how the damages rules would be interpreted for research tools:

Hypothesis 1. Damages d are consistent with the lost royalty doctrine if $d \in [0, v - c]$ and equilibrium license fees satisfy $L = d$. Damages d are consistent with the unjust enrichment doctrine if $d = v - c$.

The argument behind the hypothesis is as follows. Regarding lost royalty, suppose that the anticipated damages satisfy $d \in [0, v - c]$. Then the patentholder has no incentive to license at $L < d$, and at any higher fee,

---

9 If there were several potential developers, the patentholder might auction the right to use the patent. But due to the patentability of the commercial product, the patentholder can still not collect all profit (Scotchmer, 1996). One can think of λ as a parameter that reflects the maximum he can collect.

firm 2 would decline to license and pay damages *ex post*. Hence the license fee must satisfy $L = d$. Symmetrically, if the license fee would satisfy $L \in [0, v - c]$, and firm 2 infringes the patent, then lost royalty is L, which becomes the damages, $d = L$. But this argument is self-referential. For any $d \in [0, v - c]$ there is an equilibrium with a license at price $L = d$. No other measure of damages is consistent with the lost-royalty doctrine. If $d > v - c$, then d cannot be interpreted as lost royalty. Firm 2 would never agree to such a royalty, since it would then earn negative profit. The argument for the hypothesis on unjust enrichment is that if firm 2 infringes successfully, then he illicitly earns $v - c$ and must disgorge it.

We use π^{LP} and π^{UR} to designate the patentholder's equilibrium profit under the lost-profit and unjust-enrichment doctrines. For research tools, the patentholder's profit is exactly his license revenue. (For other proprietary products, the profit includes both license fees and market revenues, as in Section 7 below.) The following lemma follows immediately from the hypothesis and bargaining assumption.

Lemma 1 (liability regime). Suppose that a single research tool is required to develop a proprietary commercial product, and that damages are measured as in Hypothesis 1. Any equilibrium profit $\pi^{LP} \in [0, v - c]$ is consistent with the lost-profit doctrine of damages. The patentholder's profit under the unjust-enrichment doctrine is $\pi^{UR} = \lambda(v - c)$ if infringement would be deterred under that doctrine, and $\pi^{UR} = (v - c)$ if infringement would not be deterred.

Thus, the unjust-enrichment doctrine does a better job of protecting the patentholder if infringement would not be deterred, but otherwise the two doctrines cannot be ranked. The lost-profit doctrine is unreliable in that there are multiple equilibria, with different damages and distributions of profit.

We now turn to how and whether the possibility of injunctions can improve on either of the liability rules. Under a property regime, we assume that the patentholder can enjoin an infringing research program before the commercial product is complete. Without a settlement, the infringer is permanently barred from completing or marketing the commercial product. But it will be rational for the firms to reach a settlement, since otherwise neither will profit from the new product. We assume that they will bargain over the surplus remaining at the time of injunction, and that they settle according to bargaining shares $(\lambda, 1 - \lambda)$. The bargaining surplus at settlement depends on how much of the infringer's cost has been sunk.

We do not model the strategic behavior surrounding injunctions, but we interpret the relevant aspects of the law to mean that there is some proportion of cost, say f, $0 \leq f \leq 1$, that must be sunk before the injunction issues. The interpretation is that if less than f is sunk, the

infringer cannot seek a declaratory judgment to force an earlier injunction and settlement. If more than f is sunk, the doctrine of laches will
bite. The bargaining surplus at settlement is $v - (1 - f)c$, which is
positive, since $v - c$ is positive. The firms' threat points for the bargain
are $(0, - fc)$, so their profits including settlement are $(\lambda[v - (1- f)c]$,
$(1 - \lambda)[v - (1 - f)c] - fc)$. If $f = 0$, then the equilibrium profits are the
same as if infringement were deterred altogether, namely $(\lambda(v - c), (1 - \lambda)$
$(v - c))$.

We first consider how the firms would like to affect f after the infringing
research program has begun, and then we consider whether firm 2 would
embark on the infringing research program, knowing how it would turn
out. Finally we show how the patentholder's equilibrium profit depends
on f. The second part of the lemma says that the patentholder's profit is
not monotonic in f.

Let

$$f^* = \min \left\{ \frac{(v - c)}{c} \frac{(1 - \lambda)}{\lambda}, 1 \right\}. \tag{1}$$

Lemma 2 (injunctions). Suppose that a single research tool is required to
develop a proprietary commercial product, and that a property regime is
in effect. Then

(i) once infringement has begun, the patentholder prefers to delay injunction and settlement until all the infringer's costs have been sunk ($f = 1$),
while the infringer prefers that injunction and settlement occur as early
as possible ($f = 0$).

(ii) for $f = 0$ and $f > f^*$, the patentholder's equilibrium profit is $\lambda(v - c)$.
For $f \in (0, f^*]$, the patentholder's equilibrium profit is $\lambda(v - (1 - f)c)$.

Proof. (i) follows because equilibrium profits are

$$((\lambda(v - (1 - f)c), (1 - \lambda)(v - (1 - f)c) - fc)).$$

(ii) follows because the patentholder's profit is increasing in f. But if $f > f^*$,
then the infringer would end up with negative profit. Anticipating this,
he would not begin the infringing research project, and a license
agreement would have to be made at the beginning, just as if $f = 0$.
In that case, the profit of the patentholder is $\lambda(v - c)$.

Q.E.D.

The patentholder's equilibrium profit is larger when $0 < f < f^*$ than
when $f = 0$ or $f \geq f^*$. Thus, despite Lemma 2(i), the patentholder is better
off if the doctrine of laches actually constrains him so that he cannot delay
the injunction indefinitely. Without the constraint, the patentee will delay

until the end. The prospect of indefinite delay would force an *ex ante* agreement, which the patentholder prefers to avoid.

These lemmas allow us to reach the following conclusion. The statement that the patentholder "typically prefers" one regime to another means that profits might be equal under the two regimes, but in "most" equilibria, profits are greater under the preferred regime.

Proposition 1 (research tools: liability versus injunctions). Suppose that a single research tool is required to develop a proprietary commercial product, and that damages are measured as in Hypothesis 1.

(i) Suppose that infringement would not be deterred under the unjust-enrichment doctrine. Then the patentholder typically prefers the unjust-enrichment doctrine to either the lost-royalty doctrine or to a property rule.

(ii) Suppose that infringement would be deterred under the unjust-enrichment doctrine. Then the patentholder typically prefers the property rule to the unjust-enrichment doctrine. The lost-profit doctrine leads to multiple equilibria, some with greater profit than under the unjust-enrichment doctrine or property rule, and some with less.

The effectiveness of the property rule in transferring the surplus depends on when the doctrine of laches takes effect, as modelled in the parameter f. Like the lost-royalty rule, the property rule is an unreliable vehicle for enforcement unless the laches parameter is interpreted efficiently at f^*.

When $f^* < 1$ it has an interesting interpretation: f^* is proportional to the rate of return on investment, $(v - c)/c$, where the factor of proportionality $(1 - \lambda)/\lambda$ decreases with the patentholder's bargaining power λ. This interpretation provides some guidance to courts as to how to enforce the doctrine of laches in different contexts. For example, if the relative bargaining power $(1 - \lambda)/\lambda$ is proportional to relative firm size (or perhaps cash flow), then the doctrine of laches should take effect sooner in cases where the patentholder is larger (or cash rich) and when the product being developed with the research tool is less valuable.

Remark 1. To achieve maximum profit for the patentholder, the doctrine of laches should take effect sooner when products are less valuable or when the patentholder has greater bargaining power.

We have assumed that either the property regime or the liability regime applies, but not both. In practice, patentholders often seek injunctions and damages at the same time. Damages are usually calculated with regard to market sales before the injunction. With research tools, nothing is bought and sold before the injunction, so that issue does not arise (assuming that the injunction occurs before production begins). If injunctions were appended to a liability regime in our model, the injunction could no longer force a settlement. Instead of bargaining over the remaining surplus, $v - (1 - f)c$, as we have assumed, damages would be paid. One party or the other would prefer damage payments to negotiation, so the threat of injunction would not change what would happen under the liability rule.

4. Licensing in the presence of substitutes

Our analysis so far has assumed that the research tool is indispensable. For some research tools, such as a genetic sequence required to develop a medical therapy, this is so. For others, such as methods for inserting foreign genetic material into cells, there may be substitutes. The threat points for *ex ante* licensing are then established by the costliness of avoiding the proprietary tool. We shall now assume that without the tool, development of the commercial product costs σ instead of c, where $\sigma > c$. The size of σ can be influenced by the breadth of the patent on the research tool, since a broader patent makes it more difficult to develop a close substitute. The *profit surplus* in this situation is $\sigma - c$ rather than $v - c$ (provided $v > \sigma$), and $\sigma - c$ is the most that the patentholder would hope to receive. A modified hypothesis on damages is

Hypothesis 2. Damages d are consistent with the lost-royalty doctrine if $d \in [0, \sigma - c]$ and equilibrium license fees satisfy $L = d$. Damages d are consistent with the unjust-enrichment doctrine if $d = \sigma - c$.

As we point out in the proposition below, the liability doctrines operate very much as above, except that the bargaining surplus is $(\sigma - c)$ rather than $(v - c)$. However, there is an interesting difference in how the property rule operates. In the previous section, as time passed without injunction and settlement, the bargaining surplus kept increasing because the infringer continued to sink costs in the commercial product. Thus delay was profitable to the patentholder. When a substitute tool is available, delay may either increase or decrease the bargaining surplus, depending on the cost of switching between tools. If there is no switching cost, our previous conclusion is overturned: Delay decreases the bargaining surplus, and the patentholder wants to avoid delay. More generally, the bargaining surplus consists of two parts: the cost that can be saved by using the proprietary tool rather than the substitute, which decreases with time, and the holdup value due to the switching costs, which increases with time.

Formally, let α be the fraction of development costs that must be incurred again if firm 2 switches to the alternative tool, and let f be the fraction of development that has already occurred when the infringement is enjoined. After injunction, firm 2 could continue development with the inferior technology, bearing costs $(1 - f)\sigma$, which is wasteful in amount $(1 - f)(\sigma - c)$. In addition he would bear a switching cost $\alpha f c$.

A settlement will allow the firms to avoid both costs. The bargaining surplus at the time of the injunction is thus $(1 - f)(\sigma - c) + \alpha f c$. The patentholder's profit at *ex post* settlement is his share of the bargaining surplus, since his threat point is zero. The patentholder's profit is thus $\lambda[(1 - f)(\sigma - c) + \alpha f c]$.

Proposition 2 (research tools with substitutes: liability and injunctions). Suppose that a commercial product can be developed either with a proprietary research tool at cost c, or with a noninfringing substitute at greater cost σ, and that damages are measured as in Hypothesis 2.

  (i) Suppose that infringement would not be deterred under the doctrine of unjust enrichment. Then the patentholder prefers that doctrine to a property rule, and typically prefers it to the lost-royalty rule.
 (ii) Suppose that infringement would be deterred under the unjust-enrichment doctrine. Then the patentholder typically prefers that doctrine to a property rule. There are multiple equilibria under the lost-profit rule, some of which provide more profit to the patentholder than the unjust-enrichment rule or property rule, and some less.

Proof. The patentholder's profit under the property rule is no greater than $\lambda(\sigma - c)$. Whether the patentholder's profit increases or decreases with delay depends on α. The patentholder's profit is increasing or decreasing in f according to whether α is larger or smaller than $(\sigma - c)/c$. Thus, if $\alpha \geq (\sigma - c)/c$, the patentholder's profit is no greater than $\lambda \alpha c$ (which is the profit at settlement, $\lambda[(1 - f)(\sigma - c) + \alpha f c]$, evaluated at $f = 1$), which is no greater than $\lambda(\sigma - c)$. If $\alpha < (\sigma - c)/c$, profit is no greater than $\lambda(\sigma - c)$ (which is the profit at settlement, $\lambda[(1 - f)(\sigma - c) + \alpha f c]$, evaluated at $f = 0$).

Reasoning as in Proposition 1, the patentholder earns profit anywhere in the interval $[0, \sigma - c)$ under the lost-royalty doctrine, whereas under the unjust-enrichment doctrine, he earns either $\lambda(\sigma - c)$ or $\sigma - c$ according to whether infringement would or would not be deterred. Part (i) follows because the patentholder earns $(\sigma - c)$ under the unjust-enrichment doctrine; profit is bounded above by $\lambda(\sigma - c)$ under the property rule; and profit can be anything in the interval $[0, \sigma - c]$ under the lost-royalty doctrine. Part (ii) follows because the patentholder earns either $\lambda(\sigma - c)$ under the unjust-enrichment doctrine; can earn any profit in the interval $[0, \sigma - c]$ under the lost profit doctrine; and earns no more than $\lambda(\sigma - c)$ under a property rule.

                                                                    Q.E.D.

5. Licensing several tools

We now briefly examine how the ideas of Section 3 apply when many research tools are required for the commercial product, rather than only one. We first maintain our hypothesis that the market for licenses is "nonanonymous," so that the user negotiates with each tool owner. We then consider the case of anonymous licensing.

Nonanonymous licensing. Suppose that there are N tools, indexed $i = 1, \ldots N$, all of which are required to develop a commercial product of value v. In the case of bioengineering, the tools might be a sequence needed for gene expression, a sequence that codes for a protein, and a method of gene insertion. The natural hypothesis on damages, analogous to the one above, is

Hypothesis 3. Suppose $\{L_j\}_{j=1}^N$ are equilibrium license fees for a particular user. Then damages $\{d_j\}_{j=1}^N$ are consistent with the lost-royalties doctrine if $d_j = L_j$ for $j = 1,\ldots,N$, and $(v - c) - \Sigma_{j=1}^N L_j \geq 0$. Damages $\{d_j\}_{j=1}^N$ are consistent with the unjust-enrichment doctrine if $d_j = (v - c) - \sum_{1 \neq j} L_i$.

The hypothesis on the lost-royalty doctrine reflects the same circularity discussed above. No licensor could license at a price higher than prospective damages, since the licensee would infringe rather than take the license. And the licensor has no incentive to agree to a lower license fee, hence $d_j = L_j$. The license fees are indeterminate as regards the division of profit not only between licensors and licensees, but also among tool owners. As before, license fees that more than exhaust the value of the application could not arise in equilibrium, and could not be "lost royalty."

We now work out the consequences of the hypothesis for unjust enrichment. For the case that infringement would be deterred under the unjust-enrichment doctrine, we assume that the bargaining shares are $\{\lambda_j\}_{j=0}^N$ where λ_0 is the bargaining share of the user. Then if infringement would be deterred, absent a complete set of licenses, and if the user gets a positive bargaining share $\lambda_0 > 0$, the equilibrium license fees will not exhaust the profit surplus in equilibrium. Damages and license fees must simultaneously satisfy $d_i = (v - c) - \sum_{j \neq i}^N L_i$ and $L_j = \lambda_j(v - c)$ for $i, j = 1,\ldots,N$. These conditions imply that each tool owner's potential damages are equal to the unpaid license fee plus the profit surplus that the user receives in equilibrium:

$$d_i = \left(1 - \sum_{j \neq 0, i}^N \lambda_j\right)(v - c) = (\lambda_i + \lambda_0)(v - c)$$

Thus the potential damages exhaust more than the profit (but damages are not paid in equilibrium), while license fees exhaust less than the profit (the user gets a bargaining share).

If infringement would not be deterred, then damages take away all the infringer's profit, and $L_j = d_j$ would hold for each tool j. If the license fee were higher than prospective damages, the licensee would prefer to pay damages rather than license. If the license fee were lower than prospective damages, then the tool owner would withhold the license and collect damages instead. Thus

$$(v - c) - \sum_{j=1}^{N} L_j = (v - c) - \sum_{j=1}^{N} d_j = 0.$$

We summarize these conclusions as

Lemma 3 (liability regime). Suppose that several proprietary research tools are required to develop a commercial product. Suppose that the market for research tools is non-anonymous, so that tool owners and licensees bargain for user-specific license fees, and that damages are measured as in Hypothesis 2. Then

(i) Under the lost-profit doctrine of damages, there are multiple equilibria with different license fees, and the tool owners will not necessarily collect all the profit surplus.
(ii) Under the unjust-enrichment doctrine of damages, tool owners will collect all the profit surplus if infringement is not deterred under that doctrine, but not otherwise.

Now we investigate injunctions. When a single tool owner enjoins an infringer from developing a product, the infringer and all the other tool owners are potentially deprived of profit. We again use the bargaining shares $\{\lambda_j\}_{j=0}^{N}$ where $\lambda_0 > 0$ is the bargaining share of the user. Any one of the tool owners can withhold a license, leading to injunction and settlement, and this is known to all of them. We assume that the threat point for every tool owner's license is what would happen if no licenses were issued and infringement went forward to injunction and settlement.

The definition of f^{**} below, and Lemma 4 that follows, are similar to those in Section 3, except that we must substitute "the tool owners" for "the patentholder," and the tool owners' joint profit, $(v - c)\Sigma_{j=1}^{N}\lambda_j$, for the patentholder's profit. With infringement, injunction, and settlement, the tool owners' joint profit at settlement would be $(\Sigma_{j=1}^{N}\lambda_j)\left(v - (1-f)c\right)$, and the infringer's profit, accounting for his bargaining share at settlement and his sunk costs, would be $(1 - \Sigma_{j=1}^{N}\lambda_j)\left(v - (1-f)c\right) - fc$.

Let

$$f^{**} = \min\left\{ \frac{(v - c)}{c} \frac{\left(1 - \sum_{j=1}^{N}\lambda_j\right)}{\sum_{j=1}^{N}\lambda_j}, 1 \right\} \qquad (2)$$

No infringement will occur if $f > f^{**}$ because the infringer's profit would be negative. With no infringement $(f > f^{*})$, each tool owner's "threat point" for a licensing negotiation is zero, and equilibrium profits are $\lambda_j(v-c), j = 1, \ldots, N$. The tool owners' joint profit is $\left(\sum_{j=1}^{N} \lambda_j\right)(v-c)$, which is less than $(v-c)$ since $\sum_{j=1}^{N} \lambda_j = 1 - \lambda_0$. That is, if f is too large (injunction occurs too late), then infringement would be deterred. Deterrence leads to an upfront settlement in which the user gets a positive profit share.

Lemma 4 (injunctions). Suppose that several research tools are required to develop a proprietary commercial product, and that a property regime is in effect. Then

(i) Once infringement has begun, the tool owners prefer to delay injunction and settlement until all the infringer's costs have been sunk $(f = 1)$, whereas the infringer prefers that injunction and settlement occur as early as possible $(f = 0)$.
(ii) For $(f = 0)$ and $f > f^{**}$, the tool owners' joint equilibrium profit is $\left(\sum_{j=1}^{N} \lambda_j\right)(v-c)$. For $f \in (0, f^{**}]$, the tool owners' joint equilibrium profit is $\left(\sum_{j=1}^{N} \lambda_j\right)(v-(1-f)c)$.

This argument, together with the preceding lemma, leads us to the following proposition.

Proposition 3 (nonanonymous licensing of several tools). Suppose that several proprietary research tools are required to develop a commercial product. Suppose that the market for research tools is nonanonymous, so that tool owners and licensees bargain for user-specific license fees, and that damages are measured as in Hypothesis 3. Then

(i) if infringement would not be deterred under the unjust-enrichment doctrine, the tool owners as a group typically earn more profit under the unjust-enrichment doctrine than under the lost-profit doctrine or a property rule.
(ii) if infringement would be deterred under the unjust-enrichment doctrine, the tool owners as a group typically earn less profit under the unjust-enrichment doctrine than under the property rule. The lost-profit doctrine leads to multiple equilibria, some with greater profit for the tool owners than under the unjust-enrichment doctrine or property rule, and some with less.

Anonymous licensing. The difference between anonymous and nonanonymous licensing is that with anonymity there is a market by which to evaluate lost royalties. By anonymous licensing we mean that each licensor faces a demand curve for his licenses, as when there are many potential applications. He sets a common fee for all users. Anonymity can be reflected in the notion of damages under the lost-profit doctrine, but it vanishes with the unjust-enrichment doctrine. Unjust enrichment of necessity refers to the infringer's specific circumstances, in particular $(v - c)$.

We make the following hypothesis on damages under the lost-profit doctrine when tools are licensed anonymously in markets with common prices.

Hypothesis 4. Suppose $\{L_j\}_{j=1}^N$ are anonymous equilibrium license fees. Any nonnegative damages $\{d_j\}_{j=1}^N$ are consistent with the lost-profit doctrine if $d_j = L_j, j = 1, \ldots, N$. Damages $\{dj\}_{j=1}^N$ are consistent with the unjust-enrichment doctrine if $d_j = (v - c) - \Sigma_{i \neq j} L_i$.

Hypothesis 4 differs from Hypothesis 3 in that it does not impose for any particular user that $(v - c) - \sum_{j=1}^N L_{jj} \geq 0$. If an infringer has a project with low net value, $v - c$, he might be dissuaded from investing if the license fees are too high. This is because the court could reasonably assess lost royalty by looking at the fees charged to other firms, rather than by considering what license terms the two firms "would have" reached, absent the infringement. This is the only case we consider where investment might not be efficient. The inefficiency arises from anonymous pricing.

The analyses of injunctions and the unjust-enrichment doctrine are exactly as for nonanonymous licensing. We thus have the following proposition:

Proposition 4 (anonymous licensing of several tools). Suppose that several proprietary research tools are required to develop a commercial product. Suppose that the market for research tools is anonymous, and that damages are measured as in Hypothesis 4. Then under the lost-profit (lost-royalty) doctrine, a commercial application might not be developed even though it provides positive surplus. Profits for the tool owners can be compared under the different enforcement regimes exactly as in Proposition 3, parts (i) and (ii).

As already mentioned, the reason that investment is always efficient with nonanonymous bargaining is that the court has more latitude in assessing "lost royalty" *ex post* than with anonymous licensing. The court will never assess higher lost royalties than the potential licensee could have paid, as that would contradict the notion that the potential licensee "could have" licensed at that price.

An advantage of the unjust-enrichment doctrine is that it undermines anonymity and implicitly encourages licensors and the potential infringer to agree on terms that would allow every efficient investment to be made. The unjust-enrichment doctrine permits the licensors to discriminate in their license fees according to the value of the applications. (Of course we are ignoring the bargaining complexities that arise from an inability of the potential infringer to communicate his net value $(v - c)$ credibly in this negotiation.)

6. Competition from the patentholder

We now suppose that both the patentholder and the potential infringer are capable of developing the commercial product, although one may be more efficient (have lower costs) than the other. Infringement might lead to a race between the patentholder and a potential infringer.

Suppose that the patentholder and potential infringer have respective costs c_1 and c_2. The *profit surplus* is now max $\{v - c_1, v - c_2\}$. Efficiency has two aspects: the commercial product should be developed whenever the profit surplus is positive, but in addition, it should be developed by the lower-cost firm, which might or might not be the patentholder.

We will assume that if the infringer and patentholder race for the commercial product, the patentholder wins with probability p. This probability might depend on the relative costs, but we suppress this dependence to avoid notation. In equilibrium the patentholder's profit π^{LP} will either be licensing fees or the net value of the commercial product if the patentholder develops it himself, and it might involve elements of both.

Our hypothesis on damages is now given in Hypothesis 5.

Hypothesis 5. Under the unjust-enrichment doctrine and lost-profit (royalty) doctrine, respectively, damages are measured as

$$d^{UR} = v - c_2 \tag{3}$$

$$d^{LP} = \pi^{LP}. \tag{4}$$

The damages will be paid only if the infringer actually achieves the commercial product. If the patentholder races against the infringer and wins, then we assume that no damage suit is brought and no damages are paid. See Figure 2. Thus infringement does not always result in damages, and the profits in the proofs below should reflect this.

Lemma 5 (lost-profit doctrine: research tools with competition). Suppose that the patentholder and potential infringer are both capable of developing the commercial product at respective costs c_1, c_2. Suppose that damages are given by (4). Then under the lost-profit doctrine the patentholder's equilibrium profit can be any $\pi^{LP} \in [v - (c_1/p), v - c_2]$ if the infringer has lower costs, and it is $\pi^{LP} = v - c_1$, if the patentholder has lower costs.

Proof. First we argue that the patentholder would not race against an infringer. If he raced, he would receive damages with probability $(1 - p)$, and his expected profit in the race would be $pv - c_1 + (1 - p)d^{LP} = pv - c_1 + (1 - p)\pi^{LP}$. This would be the threat point for achieving a license to avoid the infringement. The efficiency surplus available by licensing is cost avoidance, namely, max $\{c_1, c_2\}$. Our bargaining rule is that the firms

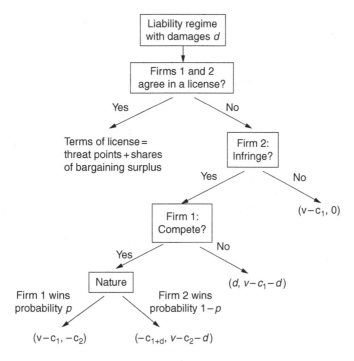

Figure 2 Licensing to avoid a Race

divide the efficiency surplus in shares $\{\lambda, 1 - \lambda\}$. Thus the patentholder's equilibrium profit must satisfy

$$\pi^{LP} = pv - c_1 + (1 - p)\pi^{LP} + \lambda \max\{c_1, c_2\}. \tag{5}$$

Solving for π^{LP} on the assumption that the patentholder will race against the infringer, the equilibrium profit and damages satisfy

$$\pi^{LP} = \frac{1}{p}[pv - c_1 + \lambda \max\{c_1, c_2\}] \tag{6}$$

$$d^{LP} = \frac{1}{p}[pv - c_1 + \lambda \max(c_1, c_2)]. \tag{7}$$

Now test the premise: Does the patentholder want to race against the infringer? If the patentholder stays out of the race and collects d^{LP} with probability 1 rather than with probability p, also giving up the possibility that he wins the race, he earns greater expected profit: $d^{LP} > pv - c_1 + (1-p)d^{LP}$, where the inequality follows from (7). Thus the patentholder will not race against an infringer under the measure of damages in (4).

Suppose then that the patentholder would not race against the infringer. The patentholder's equilibrium profit with licensing is his "threat point" d^{LP}

plus his bargaining share of any efficiency surplus. Thus his equilibrium profit satisfies $\pi^{LP} = d^{LP}$ if $c_2 < c_1$, and $\pi^{LP} = d^{LP} + \lambda (c_2 - c_1)$ if $c_1 \leq c_2$.

If the potential infringer is the more efficient firm ($c_2 < c_1$), there is no efficiency surplus to share in a licensing bargain. Any level of damages $d^{LP} = \pi^{LP}$ is consistent with equilibrium, provided the premises hold: Infringement is not deterred ($v - c_2 - d^{LP} \geq 0$) and the patentholder prefers not to race ($pv - c_1 + (1 - p)d^{LP} \leq d^{LP}$). Thus, for the case that the infringer is the more efficient firm, any $d^{LP}, \pi^{LP} \in [v - (c_1/p), v - c_2]$ are consistent with equilibrium. The equilibrium profit π^{LP} is collected as a license fee.

On the other hand, if the patentholder is the more efficient firm ($c_1 \leq c_2$), and if infringement would occur, absent a license, then the patentholder's equilibrium profit would have to satisfy $\pi^{LP} = d^{LP} + \lambda(c_2 - c_1)$. But this is inconsistent with (4), so damages cannot lead to infringement, absent a license. The only possibility is that $d^{LP} = \pi^{LP} = v - c_1$, and infringement would be deterred.

$Q.E.D.$

The content of Lemma 5 is that if the patentholder is more efficient at working his patent, then he will earn the same profit as if no potential infringer were present. If the potential infringer is more efficient, license fees are indeterminate (as in Section 3), but the license fees cannot be too low because the patentholder would then develop the product himself, even in the face of infringement.

We now turn to the doctrine of unjust enrichment. The following lemma says that there are two rather disjoint circumstances in which the patentholder can collect the full surplus: if he is the more efficient firm and infringement is deterred, and if he is the less efficient firm but infringement is not deterred. Otherwise the potential infringer gets part of the cost savings that are available by licensing.

Lemma 6 (unjust enrichment doctrine: research tools with competition). Suppose that the patentholder and potential infringer are capable of developing the commercial product at respective costs c_1, c_2. Suppose that damages are given by (3).

    (i) Under the unjust-enrichment doctrine, the patentholder collects the full surplus, $\max\{v - c_1, v - c_2\}$, in two circumstances: if he is the more efficient firm and infringement is deterred, and if he is the less efficient firm but infringement is not deterred.

   (ii) If $c_1 \leq c_2$ and infringement is not deterred, absent a license, the patentholder collects $\pi^{UR} = (v - c_2) + \lambda(c_2 - c_1)$ (less than the full surplus) in equilibrium.

  (iii) If $c_1 > c_2$, and infringement is deterred, absent a license, the patentholder collects $\pi^{UR} = (v - c_1) + \lambda(c_1 - c_2)$ (less than the full surplus) in equilibrium.

Proof. Suppose first that infringement would be deterred. Then if the patentholder is the more efficient (lower-cost) firm, deterrence leaves him free to pursue the invention on his own, and he collects the full surplus $\pi^{UR} = v - c_1 = \max\{v - c_1, v - c_2\}$. If the potential infringer is the more efficient firm, deterrence gives him a holdup right over the cost reduction he can provide. The bargaining surplus is $(c_1 - c_2)$, and the patentholder's profit is $\pi^{UR} = (v - c_1) + \lambda(c_1 - c_2) < v - c_2 = \max\{v - c_1, v - c_2\}$.

Suppose that infringement would not be deterred. If the infringer is the more efficient firm, infringement is a good thing for the patentholder, because he can collect the full surplus $\pi^{UR} = d^{UR} = \max\{v - c_1, v - c_2\}$ $= v - c_2$ as damages. If the patentholder is the more efficient firm, the damage collected *ex post* is $v - c_2 < \max\{v - c_1, v - c_2\}$ (less than the full surplus). The licensing agreement that avoids this outcome has the odd feature that the patentholder pays the infringer not to infringe. He shares with the infringer the cost reduction that the patentholder himself can provide, namely, $c_2 - c_1$. Thus the patentholder receives π^{UR} $= (v - c_2) + \lambda(c_2 - c_1)$.

Q.E.D.

Proposition 5 (research tools: liability in the context of patent races). Suppose that damages are measured as in Hypothesis 5.

(i) If the patentholder is more efficient than the potential infringer, then he may collect less profit under the unjust-enrichment doctrine than under the lost-profit doctrine, and never collects more.

(ii) If the patentholder is less efficient than the potential infringer, and if infringement would not be deterred, absent a license, under the unjust-enrichment doctrine, then the patentholder typically prefers that doctrine to the lost-profit doctrine.

(iii) If the patentholder is less efficient than the potential infringer, and if infringement would be deterred, absent a license, under the unjust-enrichment doctrine, then the patentholder may earn more profit or less profit under that doctrine than under the lost-profit doctrine.

Proof. Parts (i) and (ii) follow from Lemmas 5 and 6. Using the same two lemmas, part (iii) follows because profit under the unjust-enrichment doctrine is $\pi^{UR} = (v - c_1) + \lambda(c_1 - c_2)$, and $v - (c_1/p) < (v - c_1) + \lambda(c_1 - c_2) < v - c_2$.

Q.E.D.

7. A more general model

We now investigate whether the above conclusions apply in other contexts where licensing is the natural use of intellectual property, or whether our conclusions are specific to research tools. To do this we consider a more general model that subsumes research tools and proprietary products as special cases. We again assume that the patentholder and a potential infringer will bargain for a license. If no license is agreed upon, then infringement might occur, followed by a damage award. Whether there will be infringement depends on the prospective damages, and this prospect sets the threat points for licensing, as before.

Suppose that without licensing, the patentholder's monopoly profit is π^M. If an infringer enters the market, the two firms will compete in ways that will be specific to the context. Let π_I^P, π_I^C be the profits earned by the patentholder and infringer with such competition, where the subscript on π denotes (I)nfringement and the superscripts denote (P)atentholder and (C)ompetitor (infringer). In Figure 1, the threat-point payoffs at the bottom of the tree with infringement would be either $\left(\pi_I^P + d, \pi_I^C - d\right)$ or $(\pi^M, 0)$.

If licensing entails an efficiency gain, e.g., productive efficiency, the joint profit with licensing will be greater than π^M. Let π^J be the maximum joint profit that the two firms can earn jointly if they produce efficiently and maximize joint profit, e.g., by agreeing to high royalties. We assume that $\pi_I^P + \pi_I^C \leq \pi^J$ and $\pi^M \leq \pi^J$. If $\pi^M < \pi^J$, licensing should occur in equilibrium, since it allows an efficiency gain that increases joint profit. The joint profit can be shared with complete flexibility through a lump-sum transfer.

Damages under the unjust-enrichment doctrine would naturally be measured as $d = \pi_I^C$. However, damages under the lost-profit doctrine are more difficult to assess. The notion of lost profit could have two parts: the amount by which the patentholder's profit on his own activities is diminished by the infringement and the lost revenue that he should have received through licensing. We shall again assume that infringement is an out-of-equilibrium act, and that lost profit (royalty) is assessed with reference to equilibrium. Admittedly, this notion of lost profit would be difficult for the court to assess, but assessing it seems to be the challenge posed by the doctrine itself. This is why we emphasize that we have an equilibrium theory of damages. Without equilibrium as a reference point, it is unclear what lost profit means.

We let $\left(d^{LP}, \pi^{LP}\right)$ and $\left(d^{UR}, \pi^{UR}\right)$ represent the damages and equilibrium profits of the patentholder that are consistent with the lost-profit and unjust-enrichment doctrines, respectively. It is important to notice that $\left(\pi_I^P, \pi_I^C, \pi^J, \pi^M\right)$ are parameters of the economic environment, whereas whereas π^{LP} and π^{UR} are equilibrium values. Since the firms will always license in a way that leads to maximal joint profits π^J, the licensee will earn equilibrium profit $\pi^J - \pi^{LP}$ or $\pi^J - \pi^{UR}$ under the two rules respectively. We again assume that if there is a bargaining surplus to share, the shares are $(\lambda, 1 - \lambda)$.

With this notation, we do not need to include licensing explicitly in our measure of damages, as licensing revenues are incorporated in the equilibrium profit π^{LP}. Our hypothesis on damages, in accordance with the view articulated above, is

Hypothesis 6. Under the unjust-enrichment doctrine and lost-profit (royalty) doctrine, respectively, damages are measured as

$$d^{UR} = \pi_I^C \tag{8}$$

$$d^{LP} = \pi^{LP} - \pi_I^p. \tag{9}$$

We can now characterize the equilibrium profits π^{LP} and π^{UR}. The unjust-enrichment doctrine is the easier one to analyze. The following lemma points out that under the unjust-enrichment doctrine, the patentholder's profit depends on whether infringement would be deterred, absent a license. The patentholder's profit can be higher without deterrence in the circumstance that $\pi_I^C + \pi_I^P > \pi^M$, as could occur with a research tool that cannot be worked by the patentholder. If the research tool cannot be worked by the patentholder, $\pi^M + \pi_I^P = 0$, and $\pi_I^C = \pi^J$.

Lemma 7. Suppose that the measure of damages is given by (8). If infringement would not be deterred under the unjust-enrichment doctrine, the patentholder's equilibrium profit is $\pi^{UR} = (1 - \lambda)(\pi_I^C + \pi_I^P) + \lambda\pi^J$. If infringement would be deterred, the patentholder's equilibrium profit is $\pi^{UR} = (1 - \lambda)\pi^M + \lambda\pi^J$.

Proof. Without deterrence, since the threat points for the licensing agreement are $(d^{UR} + \pi_I^P, 0) = (\pi_I^C + \pi_I^P, 0)$ and the bargaining surplus is $\pi^J - (\pi_I^C + \pi_I^P)$, the patentholder's equilibrium profit is as stated. The argument with deterrence is analogous.

$$Q.E.D.$$

When the patent is on a proprietary product or cost-reducing process, it will generally hold that $\pi^J > \pi_I^C + \pi_I^P$. That is because competition will dissipate some of the joint profit that would be available under a licensing agreement. π^M is the monopoly profit earned by the patentholder without licensing, and π_I^C, π_I^P are the oligopoly profits of the two firms when both use the patentholder's technology and compete in the market. Generally it will be the case that $\pi_I^C + \pi_I^P < \pi^M < \pi^J$.

Proposition 6 (liability doctrines: proprietary products). Suppose that damages are measured as in Hypothesis 6, and that $\pi_I^P + \pi_I^C < \pi^M < \pi^J$. Then, provided infringement would not be deterred under the unjust-enrichment doctrine, the patentholder claims more profit under the lost-profit doctrine than under the unjust-enrichment doctrine. If infringement would be deterred under the unjust-enrichment doctrine, the patentholder earns the same profit under the two doctrines.

Proof. The patentholder's equilibrium profit is equal to the threat point plus λ times the bargaining surplus. Thus the following must hold under the lost-profit doctrine:

$$\pi^{LP} = \pi_I^P + d^{LP} + \lambda(\pi^J - \pi_I^P - \pi_I^C) \quad \text{if } \pi_I^C - d^{LP} \geq 0 \tag{10}$$

$$\pi^{LP} = \pi^M + \lambda(\pi^J - \pi^M) \quad\quad\quad \text{if } \pi_I^C - d^{LP} < 0 \tag{11}$$

However, (10) is inconsistent with (9), so damages cannot satisfy $\pi_I^C - d^{LP} \geq 0$. Thus the patentholder's equilibrium profit satisfies (11). Equations (9) and (11) imply that $d^{LP} = \pi^M + \lambda(\pi^J - \pi^M) - \pi_I^P$. Since $\pi_I^C - d^{LP} < 0$, infringement is deterred. The patentholder's equilibrium profit is $\pi^{LP} = (1 - \lambda)\pi^M + \lambda\pi^J$, from which the result follows, using Lemma 7.

$$Q.E.D.$$

However, the conclusions are different under the assumptions that naturally apply to research tools, namely, $\pi_I^P = \pi^M = 0$ and $\pi_I^C = \pi^J$ (In the notation of Section 3, $\pi_I^C = v - c$). This is the situation in which the patentholder is (counterintuitively) better off if infringement is not deterred (see Lemma 7). If infringement is not deterred under the unjust-enrichment doctrine, then the patentholder unambiguously prefers it to the lost-profit doctrine. But if infringement would be deterred, then the two doctrines cannot be ranked. Some of the equilibria under the lost-profit doctrine are more profitable than under the unjust-enrichment doctrine. The next proposition replicates the results of Proposition 1 in this more general model.

Proposition 7 (liability doctrines: research tools). Suppose that the measures of damages are given by Hypothesis 6 and that $\pi_I^P = \pi^M = 0$, $\pi_I^C = \pi^J$. Equilibrium is not unique under the lost-profit doctrine, and the patentholder's equilibrium profit can be any $\pi^{LP} \in [0, \pi^J]$. In all equilibria except the most profitable one, the patentholder earns less profit under the lost-profit doctrine than under the unjust-enrichment doctrine, assuming that infringement would not be deterred under the unjust-enrichment doctrine. If infringement would be deterred under the unjust-enrichment doctrine, the patentholder's profit is unique under that doctrine, and it may be greater or lesser than his profit under the lost-profit doctrine.

Proof. The patentholder's equilibrium profit is equal to the threat point plus λ times the bargaining surplus. Thus the following must hold:

$$\pi^{LP} = \pi_I^P + d^{LP} + \lambda(\pi^J - \pi_I^P - \pi_I^C) = d^{LP} \quad \text{if } \pi_I^C - d^{LP} \geq 0 \tag{12}$$

$$\pi^{LP} = \pi^M + \lambda(\pi^J - \pi^M) = \lambda\pi^J \quad\quad \text{if } \pi_I^C - d^{LP} < 0 \tag{13}$$

Equation (12) is the same as (9), so (unlike the previous lemma) damages can satisfy $\pi_I^C - d^{LP} \geq 0$. On the other hand, damages cannot satisfy $\pi_I^C - d^{LP} < 0$ because (13) is inconsistent with (9) under the hypotheses. Since $\pi_I^C - d^{LP} \geq 0$, infringement is not deterred in equilibrium, absent a license. The only restrictions imposed by equilibrium are $\pi^{LP} = d^{LP}$ and $\pi_I^C - d^{LP} = \pi_I^C - \pi^{LP} \geq 0$. Thus damages d^{LP} are consistent in equilibrium with the lost-profits doctrine if and only if $d^{LP} \in [0, \pi^J]$. Using Lemma 7, the result follows.

Q.E.D.

8. Concluding remarks

Our main observation is that infringement of patents on research tools is a real possibility under both doctrines of damages and might also be a credible threat under a property rule, depending on how the doctrine of laches is applied. But, counterintuitively, a credible threat of infringement can increase the patentholder's profit rather than decrease it. Under the unjust-enrichment doctrine, all the profit would be transferred to the patentholder *ex post*. This puts the patentholder in the best possible position. The lost-profit doctrine could also lead to infringement, due to the circularity discussed above. However, it is an unreliable way to measure damages, in that many damage measures are consistent with the doctrine, and most of them are less profitable to the patentholder than the damages consistent with unjust enrichment. Infringement under the property rule is profitable because the patentholder will end up settling.

The efficacy of a property rule depends on the earliest date that the infringement will be enjoined. Both parties have legal rights in determining this date, as discussed above. In cases where the research tool is indispensable, delay increases the bargaining surplus. If the infringement is enjoined very early, then the infringer has sunk only a small part of his costs, and the infringer has a holdup power over the market opportunity, just as if infringement were deterred entirely. On the other hand, if the patentholder can delay substantially before enjoining infringement, he will wait until the infringer has sunk a large portion of his costs, and this improves his bargaining position. Consequently, the efficacy of the property rule depends critically on how the legal doctrines of laches and declaratory judgment are applied. The situation can be reversed when there is an alternative to the research tool. In that case, delay reduces the bargaining surplus (the remaining cost advantage from the research tool). Consequently, the patentholder has an incentive to enjoin as early as possible and the doctrine of laches is no longer a binding constraint.

Our arguments lead us to the conclusion that the best liability rule depends both on the context (the best rule for owners of research tools can be different from the best rule for owners of other proprietary products), and on whether infringement would be deterred under the doctrine of unjust enrichment. We do not wish to sidestep the latter issue, but rather to emphasize it as one of our main conclusions. Every scholar who contemplates damages will confront the same realization.

We have compared existing liability and property rules, rather than deriving an optimal enforcement scheme. However, the analysis provides lessons for both optimal damage awards and for the property rule. First and most important, for research tools, optimal damages should be just low enough not to deter infringement in the absence of a license, and high enough to transfer most of the infringer's profit to the patentholder. Under our assumptions of complete information and frictionless bargaining, such a transfer increases the incentives to develop research tools without impeding their efficient use. The second lesson, for an optimal property rule, involves the timing of injunctions. The doctrines of laches and declaratory judgment strongly affect the division of profit, and they should be treated as policy instruments.

There are three important extensions to this line of research. The first is to introduce imperfect bargaining into the analysis. We have focused on how different liability and property rules affect the *ex ante* incentives to develop research tools, assuming that efficient bargaining takes place. Most of the earlier literature focuses on the consequences of bargaining failures. Future work will need to bridge this gap, at the same time recognizing that the extent of bargaining failure itself is endogenous and may be affected by the liability or property rules. The second extension, as suggested in Section 5, is to find reasonable hypotheses on bargaining when each application requires the use of many tools. The third extension is to introduce moral hazard on the part of the user of the research tool. In our analysis, the cost of developing the second stage product is fixed and known. If the quality of the commercial product (or its completion date) is a function of the effort by the research tool user, then it will be efficient to have a division of the (endogenous) rents between the research tool owner and user.[10] Even with efficient *ex ante* bargaining, this could change the relative merits of the different liability and property regimes.

References

BLAIR, R. D. AND COTTER, T. E. "An Economic Analysis of Damages Rules in Intellectual Property Law." *William and Mary Law Review*, Vol. 39 (1998), pp. 1585–1694.

---

10 For an analysis of patent protection in a model of cumulative innovation with moral hazard, see Denicolò (2000). He does not analyze infringement or bargaining in the shadow of liability and property rules.

CALABRESI. G. AND MELAMED, A. D. "Property Rules, Liability Rules, and Inalienability: One View of the Cathedral." *Harvard Law Review*, Vol. 85 (1972), pp. 1089–1126.

CONLEY, N.L "An Economic Approach to Patent Damages." *American Intellectual Property Law Assn. Quarterly Journal*, Vol. 15 (1987), pp. 354–390.

DENICOLÒ, V. "Two-Stage Patent Races and Patent Policy." *RAND Journal of Economics*, Vol. 31 (2000), pp. 488–501.

EISENBERG, R. S. "Patents and the Progress of Science: Exclusive Rights and Experimental Use." *University of Chicago Law Review*, Vol. 56 (1989), pp. 1017–1055.

GREEN, J. R. AND SCOTCHMER, S. "On the Division of Profit in Sequential Innovation." *RAND Journal of Economics*, Vol. 26 (1995), pp. 20–33.

HELLER, M. A. AND EISENBERG, R. S., "Can Patents Deter Innovation? The Anticommons in Biomedical Research." *Science*, Vol. 280 (1998), pp. 698–701.

KAPLOW, L. AND SHAVEL, S. "Property Rules Versus Liability Rules: An Economic Analysis." *Harvard Law Review*, Vol. 109 (1996), pp. 713–790.

LEITZEL, J. "Reliance and Contract Breach." *Law and Contemporary Problems*, Vol. 52 (1989), pp. 87–106.

MERGES, R P. "Contracting into Liability Rules Intellectual Property Rights and Collective Rights Organizations." *California Law Review*, Vol. 94 (1996), pp. 1293–1393.

SCOTCHMER, S. "Standing on the Shoulders of Giants: Cumulative Research and the Patent Law." *Journal of Economic Perspectives*, Vol. 5 (1991), pp. 29–41.

——."Protecting Early Innovators: Should Second-Generation Products be Patentable?" *RAND Journal of Economics*, Vol. 27 (1996), pp. 322–331.

United States Code Annotated, (USCA). *Title 35: Patents*. (USCA). St. Paul. Minn.: West Publishing Co., 1984 (updated 1998).

CHAPTER 21

Pamela Samuelson and Suzanne Scotchmer, "The Law and Economics of Reverse Engineering" (2002)

INTRODUCTION   PAMELA SAMUELSON

When I think of the body of work that I have produced over the past 35 years – which includes almost 90 law review articles and more than 100 columns in computing journals – I believe the article with the best chance of having some lasting influence is one that I coauthored with Suzanne Scotchmer on the law and economics of reverse engineering. I realize now that I should have been thinking harder and sooner about producing writings that would have significance over time. Fifty or one hundred years from now, perhaps no one will want to read articles about the Google Book Search litigations and proposed settlement, the Digital Millennium Copyright Act, the Supreme Court's *MGM* v. *Grokster* decision, or the Federal Circuit's *Oracle* v. *Google* ruling, so all the virtual ink I spent writing about those legal developments was arguably not a good investment. Still, those and other papers addressed issues of the day and I enjoyed writing them. So they were, in the end, not a total waste of my time and hopefully performed some service.

The article which follows began when Prof. Scotchmer and I co-taught a seminar on the law and economics of intellectual property. For millennia, humans have made complex artifacts that other humans have taken apart to examine their component parts and analyze how they were made and of what, and then used what they learned to make new ones. Reverse engineering is a fundamental human practice. Intellectual property laws have had to adopt rules about reverse engineering, not all of which are the same. Teaching the seminar encouraged us to puzzle out the differences in legal rules and question whether those differences were justifiable. Trade secrecy law treats reverse engineering as a fair means of competition. Patent law allows reverse engineering for purposes of repair, but not reconstruction. Copyright law regards reverse engineering of computer programs as lawful when done for purposes of extracting unprotectable elements of the software, but not otherwise.

Anti-circumvention rules outlaw reverse engineering of technical protection measures used by copyright owners to protect access to their works as well as tools with which to engage in such reverse engineering. Our article on the law and economics of reverse engineering grew organically out of those conversations about whether the legal rules made economic sense.

My initial inclination was to write our nascent article by focusing on each of the relevant legal doctrines and working through the economics of the rules within each legal category. Prof. Scotchmer had a better idea, which was to focus on the industrial contexts within which the legal rules had arisen and were typically applied and work out the economics in each specific industrial context.

The first major section of the article focused on conventional manufacturing industries. This was the context in which trade secrecy and patent rules had originally developed. Here, reverse engineering typically involved taking apart an artifact that the engineer had purchased in the marketplace. This practice is so time-consuming, intellectually challenging, and costly that it is unlikely to erode the lead time that the trade secret claimant could expect to enjoy for a product embodying a secret that contributed to the product's value. And if trade secrecy law outlawed reverse engineering of manufactured products, this would, in effect, confer a longer and stronger exclusive right in the secret innovation than if the claimant had gotten a patent.

Economic considerations, then, generally supported the trade secrecy rule on reverse engineering. However, not all reverse engineering of manufactured products was justifiable economically. The article recognized that plug-molding processes – that is, using an existing artifact, such as a boat hull, as a "plug" for a molding process that could produce a mold from which identical copies of the artifact could be made – was too cheap, easy, and inexpensive to enable the manufacturer of the original product to recoup expenses in creating that artifact. The article supported a limit on this form of reverse engineering.

A second section of the article discussed reverse engineering in the semiconductor industry. In the 1970s and early 1980s, American chip makers, principally Intel Corp., became very upset that foreign and domestic competitors were copying the layout of circuits in innovative chips after purchasing some in the marketplace. The copyists would photograph each layer of the chip's layout of circuits and then prepare masks with which to manufacture identical chips to sell in competition with the innovator's chips. Although innovators often had patents on particular components of their chips, most patents were cross-licensed to other firms, and in any event, no one could expect to get a patent that would cover the layout of an entire chip. Intel brought a copyright infringement lawsuit against one such competitor, claiming that its chips were protectable derivative works of the copyrighted drawings that Intel used in the design process. Intel also led the fight in Congress to outlaw this form of copying, pointing out that to develop an innovative chip design, it had to spend millions of dollars while copyists could produce identical products for $50,000 and undermine Intel's ability to recoup its investments in chip innovation.

Prof. Scotchmer and I perceived similarities between plug-molding and chip-copying as market-destructive types of reverse engineering. We supported as economically sound legislation that outlawed it. The Semiconductor Chip Protection Act (SCPA) did not outlaw all forms of reverse engineering. Indeed, Intel and other chip makers strongly supported including a reverse engineering privilege in the law so long as it did not result in identical or near-identical products. Everyone in the semiconductor industry engaged in reverse engineering and thought that learning from other products was important to ongoing competition and innovation in the field. But each chip manufacturer was, after enactment of SCPA, under a legal obligation to make chips with different circuitry layouts. We concluded that the SCPA legislation was economically sound.

A third section of our article addressed challenging issues posed by reverse engineering of computer programs, in particular, when done for the purpose of getting access to information that the reverse engineer needed to develop a program capable of interoperating with another firm's software. Sega Enterprises and Nintendo both sued software developers who made copies of Sega and Nintendo code in the course of reverse engineering to get access to interface information. Because computer programs are protected by copyright law and copyright owners have an exclusive right to control the reproduction of their works in copies, the *Sega* and *Nintendo* lawsuits were plausible infringement cases. Yet, the courts in both cases decided that this kind of reverse engineering copying was a fair and non-infringing use of the Sega and Nintendo programs under US copyright law. Prof. Scotchmer accepted my assertion that permitting such reverse engineering was a reasonable interpretation of copyright law, but was it economically sound?

We struggled over this question for several weeks and ultimately reached consensus that this legal rule was, on balance, economically sound. As with reverse engineering of manufactured products, reverse engineering of program code is time-consuming, intellectually challenging, and costly, and the reverse engineer must also work hard to reimplement interfaces in independently written non-infringing code. Consequently, reverse engineering of software to achieve compatibility was unlikely to have market-destructive consequences.

The economics of software reverse engineering were, for us, more complicated than in other industrial contexts. Sega and Nintendo (as well as Microsoft and Apple) had made substantial investments in creating a popular platform, as well as applications to run on the platform, recoupment of which might be undermined by unlicensed developers. The work of Augustin Cournot suggested that allowing a single firm to control the sale of complementary products forming a whole would lead to lower prices than if the complements were sold by different firms. Platform developers such as Sega and Nintendo, moreover, typically sold their platforms at a loss and relied on revenues from their own video games and from licensed developers to recoup these investments. Competition among platforms was another factor to weigh in the calculus. The success of one platform might induce another firm to invest in developing a more innovative platform and draw away customers from the first platform developer. The role of reverse engineering in platform software markets was far from simple. Yet, Prof. Scotchmer concluded, and I concurred, that allowing reverse engineering of software was, on balance, economically justifiable.

A fourth section of the article examined the economics of rules that outlaw reverse engineering (that is, circumvention) of technical protection measures (TPMs) that prevent unauthorized access to and copying of copyrighted works, such as motion pictures, as well as the making and distribution of tools with which to engage in this reverse engineering. Prior to working with Prof. Scotchmer on this article, I had been a staunch critic of the anti-circumvention rules because I regarded reverse engineering and tool-making as freedoms that should generally be respected and legally protected. Prof. Scotchmer, however, was convinced that the anti-circumvention rules were economically justifiable insofar as they protected against copyright infringements. Although I lost my quest to persuade her on the general point, I persuaded her to recognize that copyright owners might be tempted to use TPMs to limit competition and ongoing innovation, and it was important that there be meaningful limits on the scope of these rights.

A few years after our article was published, the maker of a garage door opener brought an anti-circumvention lawsuit against the maker of a competing garage door opener because the latter bypassed the digital handshake that the former had embedded in the software of its device. This was the kind of anti-competitive assertion of anti-circumvention rules that we predicted and warned against in the article. Prof. Scotchmer and

I were pleased that an appellate court rejected the plaintiff's interpretation of the anti-circumvention rules.

What gives "The Law and Economics of Reverse Engineering" its timeless character may partly be due to the careful analysis that we did of the economics of reverse engineering in these various industrial contexts. These parts of the article may be helpful when courts and legislators are asked to regulate reverse engineering in a new context. What makes the article more timeless, however, is the section that offers insights about reverse engineering as one of the policy levers that policymakers can use to adjust intellectual property rules. Of course, the law can be set "on" or "off" with this policy lever (that is, allow in all instances or disallow). But it can also be set in other ways as well.

The article identifies five other strategies for setting the reverse engineering policy lever. The law can, for instance, ban a particular type of reverse engineering, as anti-plug-mold rules do. It can impose a breadth requirement, as SCPA does, requiring reverse engineers to add something new to their design and not just copy that of another firm. The law can permit reverse engineering for some purposes, but not all, as the software copyright rules do. The law can also regulate tools, as the anti-circumvention rules do. Finally, the law can restrict what information a reverse engineer can disseminate to others, as the European software copyright directive does. These five strategies may not exhaust all possible ways that the law can address reverse engineering, but they are options that our article offers as possibly useful lessons for the future.

Neither Prof. Scotchmer nor I could have written an article like this one by ourselves. She did not know the legal rules and how they had evolved and been applied over the years in the depth I did. And I did not comprehend the economics of intellectual property rules in the deep way she did. The result of this collaboration was, consequently, more than the sum of its parts. Working on the issues was a great learning process because we were both willing to invest in learning from the other person and in working together to develop a satisfying analysis. Some timeless articles have certainly been written by sole authors, but a collaboration such as ours is more likely to yield an intellectual product that offers future readers some insights worth keeping in the literature.

Suzanne Scotchmer's writings have a timeless quality. The problems that deeply interested her were ones that humans have struggled with over long spans of time, and her insights about how to think through the economics underlying them have relevance beyond the years of the articles' publication. Under what circumstances will grants of intellectual property rights promote investments in innovation? How should patent length and breadth be optimized? How should the rewards flowing from cumulative innovation be shared amongst first generation and subsequent generation creators? These questions have preoccupied scholars and policymakers for many decades, indeed, centuries. Suzanne Scotchmer contributed significantly to the ongoing scholarly dialogue on these questions.

Yale Law Journal
Vol. 111 (May, 2002): 1575–1663

The Law and Economics of Reverse Engineering

Pamela Samuelson[*] and Suzanne Scotchmer[**]

I. Introduction

Reverse engineering has a long history as an accepted practice. What it means, broadly speaking, is the process of extracting know-how or knowledge from a human-made artifact. Lawyers and economists have endorsed reverse engineering as an appropriate way to obtain such information, even if the intention is to make a product that will draw customers away from the maker of the reverse-engineered product. Given this acceptance, it may be surprising that reverse engineering has been under siege in the past few decades ...

We start in Part II with a discussion of the well-established legal right to reverse-engineer manufactured goods. In our view, the legal rule favoring reverse engineering in the traditional manufacturing economy has been economically sound because reverse engineering is generally costly, time-consuming, or both. Either costliness or delay can protect the first comer enough to recoup his initial research and development (R&D) expenditures. If reverse engineering (and importantly, the consequent

[*] Professor of Law and Information Management, University of California at Berkeley.
[**] Professor of Economics and Public Policy, University of California at Berkeley.

Research support for this Article was provided by NSF Grants Nos. 98 18689 and 99 79852. We wish to thank Kirsten Roe, Eddan Katz, and Christine Duh for their excellent research assistance in connection with this Article. We are also grateful for insightful comments on earlier drafts by Rochelle Cooper Dreyfuss, Joseph Farrell, Neil Gandal, Robert J. Glushko, Wendy J. Gordon, Mark A. Lemley, Ejan MacKaay, Stephen Maurer, David McGowan, Michael Moradzadeh, Maureen O'Rourke, Eva Ogliveska, Jerry Reichman, Dan Rubinfeld, Hal Varian, Fred von Lohmann, and participants in the Boston University Intellectual Property Workshop Series, the University of Washington Law School's Innovation Workshop, and the Yale Legal Theory Workshop.

reimplementation) of manufactured goods becomes too cheap or easy, as with plug-molding of boat hulls, it may be economically sound to restrict this activity to some degree.

In Parts III, IV, and V, we consider the law and economics of reverse engineering in three information-based industries: the semiconductor chip industry, the computer software industry, and the emerging market in technically protected entertainment products, such as DVD movies. In all three contexts, rules restricting reverse engineering have been adopted or proposed. We think it is no coincidence that proposals to restrict reverse engineering have been so common in information-based industries. Products of the information economy differ from traditional manufactured products in the cost and time imposed on a reverse engineer. With manufactured goods, much of the know-how required to make the goods remains within the factory when the products go to market, so that reverse engineering can capture only some of the know-how required to make the product. The information-rich products of the digital economy, in contrast, bear a higher quantum of applied know-how within the product distributed in the market ... The challenge is to design legal rules that protect information-rich products against market-destructive cloning while providing enough breathing room for reverse engineering to enable new entrants to compete and innovate in a competitively healthy way ...

Part III focuses on the semiconductor chip industry. When the competitive reverse engineering and copying of semiconductor chip designs became too easy and too rapid to enable innovators to recoup their R&D costs, Congress responded by enacting the Semiconductor Chip Protection Act of 1984 (SCPA) to protect chip makers from market-destructive cloning while affirming a limited right to reverse-engineer chips. The SCPA allows reverse engineers to copy circuit design to study it as well as to reuse information learned thereby in a new chip, but it imposes a forward engineering requirement that inevitably increases a second comer's development time and increases its costs. In the context of the chip industry, we think this restriction on reverse engineering is economically sound.

Part IV focuses on the software industry. Reverse engineering is undertaken in the software industry for reasons different from those in other industrial contexts. The most economically significant reason to reverse-engineer software, as reflected in the case law, is to learn information necessary to make a compatible program. The legal controversy over whether copies made of a program during the decompilation process infringe copyrights has been resolved in favor of reverse engineers. But as Part IV explains, the economics of interoperability are more complex than legal commentators have acknowledged. On balance, however, we think that a legal rule in favor of reverse-engineering computer programs for purposes of interoperability is economically sound.

Part V discusses the emerging market for technically protected digital content. Because technical protection measures may be defeated by countermeasures, copyright industry groups persuaded Congress to enact the Digital Millennium Copyright Act (DMCA), which creates new legal rules reinforcing technical measures used by copyright owners to protect their works ... In our view, these new rules overly restrict reverse engineering, although the core idea of regulating trafficking in circumvention technologies may be justifiable.

Part VI steps back from particular industrial contexts and considers reverse engineering as one of the important policy levers of intellectual property law, along with rules governing the term and scope of protection. The most obvious settings for the reverse engineering policy lever are "on" (reverse engineering is permissible) and "off" (reverse engineering is impermissible). However, our study reveals five additional strategies for regulating reverse engineering in the four industrial contexts studied: regulating a particular means of reverse engineering, adopting a "breadth" requirement for subsequent products, permitting reverse engineering for some purposes but not others, regulating tools used for reverse engineering, and restricting the dissemination of information discerned from reverse engineering. In this discussion, we distinguish between regulations affecting the act of reverse engineering and those affecting what the reverse engineer can do with the resulting information. Some restrictions on reverse engineering and on post-reverse-engineering activities may be economically sound, although we caution against overuse of restrictions on reverse engineering because such restrictions implicate competition and innovation in important ways. Part VI also considers policy responses when innovators seek to thwart reverse engineering rights by contract or by technical obfuscation ...

II. Reverse Engineering in Traditional Manufacturing Industries

Reverse engineering is generally a lawful way to acquire know-how about manufactured products. Reverse engineering may be undertaken for many purposes. We concentrate in this Part on reverse engineering undertaken for the purpose of making a competing product because this is the most common and most economically significant reason to reverse-engineer in this industrial context. We argue that legal rules favoring the reverse engineering of manufactured products have been economically sound because an innovator is nevertheless protected in two ways: by the costliness of reverse engineering and by lead time due to difficulties of reverse engineering. If technological advances transform reverse engineering so that it becomes a very cheap and rapid way to make a competing product, innovators may not be able to recoup their R&D expenses, and hence some regulation may be justified. An example discussed below is the plug-molding of boat hulls.

B. An Economic Perspective on Reverse Engineering

The economic effects of reverse engineering depend on a number of factors, including the purpose for which it is undertaken, the industrial context within which it occurs, how much it costs, how long it takes, whether licensing is a viable alternative, and how the reverse engineer uses information learned in the reverse engineering process. In this Section, we concentrate on the economics of reverse engineering undertaken for the purpose of developing a competing product.

We argue that a legal right to reverse-engineer does not typically threaten an innovative manufacturer because the manufacturer generally has two forms of protection against competitors who reverse-engineer: lead time before reverse engineers can enter and costliness of reverse engineering. Lead time serves the same function as a short-lived intellectual property right. Costliness may prevent reverse engineering entirely, especially if the innovator licenses others as a strategy for preventing unlicensed entry. Provided that the cost of reverse engineering is high enough, such licensing will be on terms that permit the innovator to recoup its R&D expenses, while at the same time constraining the exercise of market power in order to dissuade other potential entrants.

Our economic assessment of reverse engineering recognizes that this activity is only one step in what is typically a four-stage development process. The first stage of a second comer's development process is an awareness stage. This involves a firm's recognition that another firm has introduced a product into the market that is potentially worth the time, expense, and effort of reverse engineering ...

Second is the reverse engineering stage. This begins when a second comer obtains the innovator's product and starts to disassemble and analyze it to discern of what and how it was made ...

Third is the implementation stage. After reverse-engineering the innovator's product, a second comer must take the know-how obtained during the reverse engineering process and put it to work in designing and developing a product to compete in the same market ...

The fourth stage in the second comer's development process is the introduction of its product to the market. How quickly the new product will erode the innovator's market share and force the innovator to reduce prices to be competitive with the new entrant will depend on various market factors.

In the chart and discussion below, we use four criteria to assess the social welfare effects of the law's recognition of a right to reverse-engineer. The criteria are the effects on the following: incentives to innovate, incentives to engage in follow-on innovation, prices, and socially wasteful expenditures of resources. At first glance, these considerations seem to cut in opposite directions in the manufacturing industry context. On the negative side, the right to reverse-engineer seems to decrease incentives for first comers to introduce new products and to encourage wasteful expenditures on reverse engineering. On the positive side, a right to reverse-engineer can increase competition in the market-place, lead to lower prices, and spur follow-on innovations by second comers.

However, the argument against reverse engineering based on wasted costs is misleading because the cost of reverse engineering can be avoided by licensing. Licensing should be in the interest of both the innovator and potential reverse engineers as they can share the saved costs.

The key question, however, is how the threat of reverse engineering affects incentives to innovate. If reverse engineering actually occurs, it will erode market power and reduce the innovator's profit to an extent determined by the costliness and time required for reverse engineering. With licensing, the threat of reverse engineering will reduce the innovator's profit to a similar extent. In order to avoid reverse engineering by unlicensed entrants, the licensor must make sure that reverse engineering by unlicensed entrants is unprofitable. He can do this by allowing some measure of competition from licensees (e.g., by licensing with low royalties).[1] How much competition he authorizes will depend on the costs that unlicensed entrants would have to bear in reverse engineering and how long it would take them. The profit earned by the innovator will depend on the relative costs of the innovator and potential reverse engineers, and on the time required for reverse engineering, but not very much on whether reverse engineering is avoidable by licensing.

Table 1 illustrates the social welfare effects of two possible reverse engineering rules in the context of traditional manufacturing industries: one allowing it and one disallowing it. As to each criterion, the effects of permitting reverse engineering are compared with the effects of forbidding it.

On balance, we conclude that a legal rule favoring reverse engineering of traditional manufactured products is economically sound.

---

1 [footnote 57 in original] This argument follows an argument in Stephen M. Maurer and Suzanne Scotchmer, "The Independent Invention Defence in Intellectual Property," 69:535 *Economica* (2002). That article considers the consequences of allowing entry by independent inventors in markets with patented products. The authors argue that the threat to a rightsholder's market depends on the cost of entry by rivals, in particular the cost of independent invention or inventing around a patent. Reverse engineering is just another costly way to enter the market. Reverse engineering differs from independent invention or inventing around a patent in that the product is typically not patented, and reverse engineering may be less costly than inventing around. Nevertheless, the effect of entry depends only on cost, and the same argument applies in all three contexts...

Table 1. Social Calculus of Reverse Engineering in the Manufacturing Sector

Social Welfare Criterion	Reverse Engineering Legal	Reverse Engineering Illegal
Incentives to innovate	Worse (but generally adequate)	Better (but may be excessive)
Incentives for follow-on innovation	Better	Worse
Prices	Lower	Higher
Wasted costs	Worse (but avoidable by licensing)	Better

A prohibition on reverse engineering would, in effect, give firms perpetual exclusive rights in unpatented innovations. Given that the costs and time required for reverse engineering already protect most innovators, a ban on reverse engineering is unnecessary. On the positive side, a right to reverse-engineer has a salutary effect on price competition and on the dissemination of know-how that can lead to new and improved products.

C. Anti-Plug-Mold Laws: An Exception to Reverse Engineering Rules?

In the late 1970s through the 1980s, twelve states adopted laws to prohibit plug-molding of manufactured products. These laws typically forbade use of a manufactured item, such as a boat hull, as a "plug" for a direct molding process that yielded a mold that could then be used to manufacture identical products in direct competition with the plugged product. Florida's legislature had apparently been convinced that plug-molding of boat hulls was undermining incentives to invest in innovative boat designs, thereby harming a significant Florida industry. California passed a more general anti-plug-mold law ...

From an economic perspective, anti-plug-mold laws illustrate that even in the context of traditional manufacturing industries, a form of reverse engineering and reimplementation that produces cheap, rapid, identical copies has the potential to have market-destructive consequences. "[Q]uick imitation robs innovation of value." Insofar as market-destructive effects can be demonstrated, it may be economically sound for the law to restrict a market-destructive means of reverse engineering and reimplementation for a period of time sufficient to enable the innovator to recoup its R&D expenses. Plug-molding is only one example of technological advances that have changed the economic calculus of reverse engineering rules, as subsequent Parts show.

III. Reverse Engineering in the Semiconductor Industry

The semiconductor industry is in many respects a traditional manufacturing industry. However, we give it separate treatment here for two reasons. First, semiconductors are information technology products that bear a high quantum of the know-how required to make them on their face. This made them vulnerable to rapid, cheap, competitive cloning that industry leaders asserted undermined their ability to recoup the very high costs of R&D necessary to produce new chips. Second, Congress responded to these industry concerns about "chip piracy" by creating a new form of intellectual property protection for semiconductor chip designs ...

C. An Economic Rationale for the SCPA Rules

Part II argued that reverse engineering does not unduly undermine incentives to invest in innovation as long as it is costly, time-consuming, or both. During the time that the SCPA and predecessor bills were pending in Congress, reverse engineering of chips could be done very cheaply and quickly by peeling away layers of a purchased chip, one at a time, photographing each layer, making a mask from these photographs, and then using these masks to manufacture identical chips. The SCPA rules made this cheap and rapid route to competitive entry illegal and required reverse engineers to design original chips in order to avert infringement liability. The forward engineering requirement lengthened second comers' development time and increased their costs, thereby giving the innovator more lead time to recoup its R&D expenses and more protection against clone-based pricing. The forward engineering requirement also increased the likelihood that second comers would advance the state of the art in semiconductor design. As long as second comers had to make their chips different, they might as well make them better.

Table 2 uses the same social welfare criteria as Table 1 to illustrate our assessment of the economic effects of pre-SCPA rules as compared with post-SCPA rules.

Incentives to invest in innovative chip designs were too low before enactment of the SCPA because cloners rapidly eroded lead time advantages for innovators. In the short run, this may have brought low prices and few wasted costs, but prices were too low to allow innovators to recoup R&D expenses as long as cloning was legal. Incentives to innovate were restored once cloning was no longer an option. Incentives to invest in follow-on innovation were also very low in the pre-SCPA era because firms capable of investing in improved chips chose instead to

Table 2. Social Calculus of Reverse Engineering in the Chip Industry Pre- and Post-SCPA

Social Welfare Criterion	Pre-SCPA	Post-SCPA
Incentives to innovate	Worse (too little)	Better
Incentives to improve	Worse (too little)	Better
Prices	Lower (but too low)	Higher
Wasted costs	Better	Worse (but avoidable by licensing)

clone while it was still legal. When chip cloning became illegal, firms had strong incentives to invest in improvements. Although consumers may have initially benefited from lower prices in the pre-SCPA era, prices were so low that innovators could not recoup their costs. The SCPA may result in more socially wasteful costs because some second comers may spend resources making chip circuitry different to satisfy the originality requirements. However, some of these wasted costs are avoidable by licensing.

From an economic standpoint, the anticloning rules of the SCPA are designed to achieve much the same result as the anti-plug-mold rules discussed in Part II, although they do so by a different technique. Chip cloners were no more engaged in innovation-enhancing discovery of applied industrial know-how than were plug-molders. The SCPA rule inducing second comers to join the ranks of innovation-enhancing firms is similar to the anti-plug-mold rule that induced second comers to engage in more conventional forms of reverse engineering likely to advance the state of the art of boat-hull design. The SCPA achieves this result by establishing a kind of "breadth" requirement for subsequent products in contrast to the anti-plug-mold laws that instead outlawed a particular means for making a competing product ...

IV. Reverse Engineering in the Computer Software Industry

Reverse engineering is as standard an industry practice in the computer software industry as it is in the traditional manufacturing and semiconductor industries. For much of the past two decades, however, the legality of two common forms of software reverse engineering, namely, decompilation and disassembly of object code, has been challenged on trade secret, copyright, patent, and contract law theories ...

A. Reverse Engineering of Software and Copyright Law

Commercial developers of computer programs generally distribute software in object code form. They do so for two principal reasons: First, because users mainly want the functionality that object code forms of programs provide and do not want to read the program's text; and second, because the developers want to maintain source code forms of their products and other human-readable documentation as trade secrets. Decompilation or disassembly of object code provides a way for reverse engineers to "work[] backwards from object code to produce a simulacrum of the original source code." From this approximation of source code, reverse engineers can discern or deduce internal design details of the program, such as information necessary to develop a program that will interoperate with the decompiled or disassembled program. Lawyers for some major software producers argue that decompilation and disassembly should be illegal as a matter of copyright and trade secrecy law. They argue that the unauthorized copies of programs made in the process of decompiling or disassembling them infringe the program copyright, and this infringement makes the decompilation or disassembly an improper means of obtaining program trade secrets.

The principal decision testing this legal theory was *Sega Enterprises Ltd. v. Accolade, Inc.* Accolade, a small U.S. computer game company, disassembled Sega game programs in order to get information necessary to make its games compatible with the Sega Genesis console. Accolade then sold its independently developed games in competition with those made by Sega and third-party developers licensed by Sega. Accolade raised a fair use defense to Sega's claims that the disassembly copies were infringing. The Ninth Circuit gave little weight to the commercial purpose of Accolade's copying because it regarded the copying as having been done "solely in order to discover the functional requirements for compatibility with the Genesis console – aspects of Sega's programs that are not protected by copyright." Reverse engineering was, moreover, the only way that Accolade could gain access to this information. Although Accolade had copied the whole of Sega's programs in the course of its reverse analysis, the court discounted this conduct because it occurred in an intermediate stage of Accolade's software development process. Although the court recognized that Accolade's games affected the market for Sega games, they did not do so in a way about which copyright law is concerned. Accolade's decompilation "led to an increase in the number of independently designed video game programs offered for use with the Genesis console. It is precisely this growth in creative expression ... that the Copyright Act was intended to promote." An important policy consideration was the court's recognition that if it ruled that disassembling computer programs was unlawful, this would confer on Sega "a *de facto* monopoly over [the unprotected] ideas and functional concepts [in the program]." To get a monopoly on such ideas and functional concepts, a creator needs to seek patent protection.

Still, the court did not give a green light to all reverse engineering of program code, but only to that undertaken for a "legitimate reason," such as to gain access to the functional specifications necessary to make a compatible program, and then only if it "provides the only means of access to those elements of the code that are not protected by copyright." ...

Sega v. Accolade has been followed in virtually all subsequent cases. It has been widely praised by legal commentators. It is also consistent with the rules of other nations. Those who argued that decompilation was and should be illegal predicted grievous harm to the software industry if this form of reverse engineering was deemed lawful. These predictions have not been borne out. The American software industry has done well since 1992 when the *Sega v. Accolade* decision came down ...

B. The Economics of Interoperability and Software Reverse Engineering

Sega v. Accolade and its progeny show that reverse engineering is undertaken in the software industry for reasons different from those in other industrial contexts studied thus far ... However, reverse engineering of object code is generally so difficult, time-consuming, and resource-intensive that it is not an efficient way to develop competing but nonidentical programs ...

1. Incentives for Interoperable or Noninteroperable Strategies

Before considering the role that reverse engineering plays in the interoperability debate, we discuss the incentives for firms to design their systems to be interoperable or noninteroperable ... The developer of a new platform might decide to publish its interfaces or make them available under open license terms – an act that makes reverse engineering unnecessary – in order to make it easy for application developers to adapt existing applications or make new applications for the platform. An important reason to open interfaces is to drive demand for the new platform ...

Publishing or broadly licensing interfaces can, however, be risky for platform developers, even if beneficial for consumers and competitors ... IBM [for example] lost market share in part because the openness of its PC architecture enabled the PC to be "commoditized" or cloned.

Alternatively, firms may choose to keep their interfaces closed, not only as a defensive measure against the platform being commoditized, but as an offensive measure to capture the market ... But just as publishing interfaces can be risky, so can the strategy of keeping them closed. If application developers and consumers are not attracted to the system, losses can be considerable. Even if initially successful, a noninteroperable system may lose out over time if other firms develop new systems to wrest away the incumbent's market share ...

Into this strategic environment we now introduce reverse engineering. Platform developers typically copyright operating system programs, and they may also patent some components of their systems, but APIs are typically maintained as trade secrets. If reverse engineering is unlawful or if the platform is otherwise immune from reverse engineering (e.g., because the interfaces are too complicated or change rapidly), trade secrets can be a very effective form of intellectual property protection for platform APIs.[2] If reverse engineering is both lawful and feasible, trade secrecy protection for platform APIs is at risk. Reverse engineering clearly threatens to upset a platform developer's noninteroperability strategy, whether unlicensed entry occurs at the applications level or at the platform level. From the standpoint of an unlicensed application developer, reverse engineering offers a means of achieving compatibility between its products and the large installed base of a successful system. Although it would have been easier and quicker to license the Sega Genesis interface, Accolade would have had to stop writing for other platforms, due to Sega's insistence on exclusivity. Reverse engineering gave Accolade an alternative way to access the Sega interfaces and enter the market with competing applications.

2. Welfare Effects of Reverse Engineering To Achieve Interoperability

Table 3 compares the principal economic effects of allowing or disallowing reverse engineering to achieve interoperability in the software industry. Although we use criteria similar to those for the traditional manufacturing

---

2 [footnote 214 in original] Economists Joseph Farrell and Michael Katz assume that intellectual property law determines the extent of network externalities between rival networks. They do not distinguish platforms from applications, but argue that intellectual property rights in the interface increase the incentive for quality improvements in a system as a whole. Joseph Farrell & Michael L. Katz, "The Effects of Antitrust and Intellectual Property Law on Compatibility and Innovation," 43 *Antitrust Bull.* 609 (1998). We caution, however, that intellectual property rights in the interface may be unnecessary if platforms and applications are themselves protected. With intellectual property rights in platforms and applications, intellectual property rights in the interfaces may serve no beneficial purpose and may only allow developers to leverage market power in a way that was unintended as a matter of intellectual property law.

Table 3. Social Calculus of Reverse Engineering of Software for Purposes of Interoperability

Social Welfare Criterion	Reverse Engineering Legal	Reverse Engineering Illegal
Incentives to develop platforms	Worse (Adequate?)	Better (Too high?)
Incentives to develop applications	Good (Better?)	Good
System prices • Short-run • Long-run	Ambiguous Lower	Ambiguous Higher
Wasted costs	Better?	Worse?

and semiconductor chip industries, the welfare effects of reverse engineering rules in the software industry are more complicated and ambiguous. We explain the reasons for this below.

The conclusion about which we have the greatest confidence is that incentives to invest in platform development will be lower if reverse engineering is lawful. If third parties can legally reverse-engineer program interfaces, this erodes the market power of a noninteroperable platform developer. In this respect, reverse engineering has the same effect in the software industry as in traditional manufacturing industries: It erodes market power by facilitating unlicensed entry or by inducing licensing on terms more favorable to the licensee than if reverse engineering were prohibited. Of course, this does not necessarily mean that reverse engineering should be made illegal in order to protect platform developers. That would depend on the cost and time required for reverse engineering. Because decompilation and disassembly are time-consuming and resource-intensive, these forms of reverse engineering do not, we believe, significantly undermine incentives to invest in platforms.

As for applications, there are strong incentives to develop them whether interfaces are open or closed. If interfaces can lawfully be reverse-engineered and hence are potentially open, any software developer will be able to develop applications for the platform, not just the developers licensed by the platform developer. Accolade, for example, adapted its Mike Ditka football game program to run on the Sega Genesis system, increasing the number of applications available for that platform. As this example shows, open interfaces facilitate not only third-party development of applications, but also the adaptation of applications to multiple platforms, which saves software development costs.

There are also strong incentives, however, to develop applications when interfaces are proprietary and cannot be reverse-engineered. The developer of a noninteroperable platform wants a large installed base of customers. It can attract customers by providing a large number of attractive applications, especially those that are exclusive to that platform. Independent software developers may easily be drawn to developing applications if they think the platform will emerge as the dominant one. If the platform is struggling to gain a toehold, its creator may have an even larger incentive to develop applications, perhaps doing so in-house or subsidizing independent developers who might otherwise be reluctant.

Incentives to develop platforms and applications are naturally tied up with equilibrium prices. Two key market ingredients that affect pricing are, first, whether systems are compatible or incompatible, and, second, whether platform owners supply their own applications. We refer to the latter as "integrated" systems, in contrast to "unintegrated" systems in which independent firms supply applications for separately owned platforms. We think the most natural stylization of the pricing problem is that closed interfaces lead to incompatible and integrated systems, while open interfaces lead to compatible and unintegrated systems.

We have not found an economic model with which to compare prices or incentives to develop platforms and applications in these two market structures. The economics literature has mainly compared two types of integrated ownership, namely, ownership with interoperable applications and ownership with noninteroperable applications. That literature yields inconclusive results. In any case, it seems that integrated ownership of compatible systems would likely be unstable. With open interfaces, achieved by reverse engineering or otherwise, independent application developers will enter with compatible applications, and platform providers will enter with compatible platforms. Both undermine the integrated market structure.

It is difficult to compare prices between the two market structures. In an integrated system, platforms and applications may be sold as a unit, but they may also be sold separately with cross-subsidies between system components. In an unintegrated system, platforms and applications are priced and sold separately, at prices that are governed by the degree of competition in both markets, and possibly by intellectual property law. Our entries in Table 3 are inconclusive about pricing, but they indicate that when reverse engineering is illegal, so that systems may be integrated and incompatible, prices may be higher in the long run than in the short run due to the threat of tipping.

"Tipping" means that a single interface succeeds in becoming the standard in the market, creating a monopoly. Such tipping may be detrimental to consumers, but it is beneficial to the winning platform owner. By buying up talented independent application developers, entering into exclusive licensing agreements with them, or simply attracting them with its large installed base, a platform owner may create sufficient network externalities to drive out rivals and remain the sole platform provider.

A right to reverse-engineer may neutralize this threat of tipping. If the interface becomes open through reverse engineering or otherwise, other firms can develop platforms to compete with the proprietary platform and thereby undermine the latter's monopoly pricing strategy. Insofar as this interface becomes a standard, consumers will benefit because more applications will be available for the platform and application developers will be in a better position to negotiate with firms competing in the platform market for better access to interface information.

Minimizing wasted costs is the fourth social welfare criterion. It too yields somewhat mixed policy prescriptions. Duplicated or wasted costs may arise in the software industry from at least three activities: the act of reverse engineering itself (costs wasted by the reverse engineer); the process of devising ways (e.g., technical protection measures) to make interfaces difficult or impossible to reverse-engineer (costs wasted by the platform developer); and the development of different applications for different interfaces rather than the same applications for all interfaces (costs wasted by application developers generally). A prohibition on reverse engineering would avoid the first two but may well encourage the third. A platform provider can, of course, avoid the first cost by licensing, and as in other industrial contexts, a legal rule in favor of reverse engineering may provide powerful incentives for firms to license to avoid having their products reverse-engineered.

It is difficult to integrate these disparate welfare effects into an unassailable view as to whether reverse engineering for interoperability purposes should be legal. On balance, we believe that consumers benefit from interoperability because it encourages the development of a larger variety of software applications from a wider array of software developers with fewer wasted application development costs. Incentives to develop platforms are generally adequate owing to the high costs and difficulties of reverse-engineering software. Furthermore, interoperability lessens the potential for tipping into monopoly. Reverse engineering to achieve interoperability may also lessen a monopoly platform provider's market power by providing application developers with an alternative means of entry if the monopolist's licensing terms are unacceptable . . .

V. Reverse Engineering of Technically Protected Digital Content

The market for copyrighted works seems to be in a transitional period. For many years, copyright industries have derived the bulk of their revenues from the sale of physical products, such as books and videocassettes, in the mass market. Advances in digital technology have opened up the possibility of a future in which a substantial portion of copyright industry revenues may come from mass-marketing of technically protected digital content . . .

C. An Economic Analysis of the DMCA Rules

Broadly speaking, the anticircumvention rules have consequences for protection of, access to, and uses of digital content, and competition in creating and marketing technical protection systems. Protection of digital works was, of course, the principal motivation for the DMCA anticircumvention rules. We argue, however, that the anticircumvention rules go further than necessary to accomplish the goal of protecting digital content, causing collateral harm that could be avoided. In particular, the rules may unduly impinge on fair and other noninfringing uses of digital content, on competition within the content industry, on competition in the market for technical measures, and on encryption and computer security research.

From an economic standpoint, we believe that it would be desirable to maintain the DMCA's prohibition on public distribution of tools designed to circumvent technical protection measures that protect against copyright infringement. We recommend, however, exempting individual acts of circumvention and private tool-making incidental to such circumventions. Hence, we propose narrowing the DMCA rules in accord with our economic arguments. This is consistent with the [Clinton Administration's] original [1995] White Paper proposal, which did not recommend legislation to outlaw acts of circumvention, but only to outlaw the manufacture and distribution of circumvention tools. While our proposed anti-tool rule is narrower than the White Paper's proposal, it nevertheless focuses on the same risk for copyright owners. As reflected in Table 4, the essence of our argument is that the narrower rule would achieve the intended benefits for copyright owners while reducing harms to fair uses and improving incentives to develop, improve, and use technical protection measures.

1. Protecting Copyrighted Works

As is apparent from the legislative history, Congress's concern in enacting the DMCA was to protect copyrights in digital content. Without technical protections, digital content is vulnerable to uncontrolled copying. Technical protections generally do not prevent copying, but only make the digital content uninterpretable without authorized use of a key or detection of a watermark. An alternative to authorized use of a key is unauthorized decryption or circumvention, which involves reverse engineering. Decryption and circumvention are costly and difficult, and this is a significant check on the threat to copyright owners.

Most users have neither the inclination nor the ability to circumvent a technical protection measure. A potential infringer will only infringe rather than buy a legitimate copy if the cost of circumventing the technical measure is less than the price of the copy. Content providers will take account of the potential for circumvention in setting their prices. As compared to the DMCA, content providers have an incentive to moderate

Table 4. Social Calculus of Reverse Engineering of Technically Protected Content

Social Welfare Criterion	Pre-DMCA	DMCA	Narrower Rule (i.e., Ban on Tool Distribution)
Incentives to develop content	Worse	Better	Good
Opportunity for fair use of content	Better	Worse	Good
Incentives to develop and improve technical protection measures	Good	Worse	Better
Price of content	Low	High	Moderate
Expenditures on technical protection measures by content providers	Worse	Better	Good
Wasted costs	Worse	Better	Good

their prices under the narrower rule and also to employ effective technical measures.

The DMCA gives no incentive for the content providers to moderate their prices, and it gives little incentive to employ effective technical measures. The DMCA allows criminal penalties in cases of individual acts of willful circumvention and infringement. A circumventor would seem to be in jeopardy of criminal penalties even if the circumvention is trivial. Fear of such penalties is more likely than technical measures to deter infringement. Under the DMCA, any trivial technical measure may suffice because circumventing a technical measure raises the specter of criminal prosecution. Thus, the stringent penalties under the DMCA for individual acts of circumvention could have the odd consequence of reducing reliance on technical protection measures, as compared to the situation before the DMCA was enacted and as compared to the narrower rule we propose. By reducing the market for effective technical measures, the DMCA also reduces the incentive to develop them and improve them, as we discuss below.

Table 4 reflects these arguments. The price of copyrighted content susceptible to technical protection is likely to be highest under the DMCA and lowest without any such legislation. The narrower anti-tool rule helps enforce copyrights, but the price of content under this narrower rule is constrained by the threat of circumvention and infringement in a way that can be modified by the copyright holder in his choice of technical measure.

Table 4 also shows that content providers' expenditures on technical measures will be higher under the narrower rule than under the DMCA and probably highest with no legislation at all. Under a pre-DMCA regime of no prohibitions on circumvention, costs will likely be wasted on a measures-and-countermeasures war. Anticircumvention rules may curb this war, but as explained above, the DMCA goes too far. It protects content owners without encouraging them to use really effective technical measures. A narrower anti-tool rule could both curb the measures-and-countermeasures war and also encourage content providers to use effective technical measures for protection. There is, of course, a sense in which all expenditures on technical measures are "wasted," at least by comparison to an idealized world in which intellectual property is automatically respected. But in Table 4, we have separated "expenditures on technical measures" from "wasted costs." The latter reflect the cost of a measures-and-countermeasures war that can be avoided by appropriate circumvention rules.

Content providers would likely spend more on technical measures under the narrower rule than under the DMCA, but we do not view this as a reason to prefer the DMCA. As we have explained, the DMCA protects rightsholders by increasing the penalties for copyright infringement, not by encouraging the use of technical measures. We contend that if Congress wants to strengthen criminal penalties for copyright infringement, then it should do it straightforwardly, rather than through the back door of the DMCA. While the narrower rule we propose is likely to increase the sums that content providers spend on technical measures, it avoids unnecessary criminalization of copyright infringement.

Our proposal for a narrower rule still maintains that the *public distribution* of circumvention tools should be prohibited. Otherwise, a single reverse engineer could induce widespread infringement by distributing the tool.[3] As Bruce Schneier puts it, "Automation allows attacks to flow backwards from the more skilled to the less skilled." In our view, that is

---

3 [footnote 311 in original] The premise of this argument is that, although *creating* a circumvention tool is time-consuming and costly, the *use* of the tool is not. We notice, however, that notwithstanding the widespread availability of DeCSS, a program capable of bypassing the Content Scrambling System that protects DVD movies, sales of DVD movies remain very strong and the motion picture plaintiffs in *Universal City Studios, Inc. v. Reimerdes*, 111 F.Supp.2d 294 (S.D.N.Y. 2000), were unable to identify a single act of infringement of their movies attributable to the use of DeCSS. Ibid. at 314. Thus, at least in the short run, and possibly in the long run, there may be impediments to using circumvention tools. Such impediments would also protect content owners and thus render the extensive DMCA prohibitions unnecessary.

the real threat that undermines the efficacy of technical measures, and it should be kept in check. It is also worth noting that a rule against distribution would be easier to enforce than a rule against individual circumvention because distribution is easier to detect.

2. Casualties of the DMCA: Fair Use and Competition

The main premise underlying the DMCA act-of-circumvention rule is that circumvention will overwhelmingly be undertaken for purposes of infringement. We dispute that premise. As the nine exceptions to this rule demonstrate, there are many reasons to circumvent technical protections that have nothing to do with copyright infringement. We note that three of the nine exceptions – those permitting reverse engineering to achieve interoperability among programs, encryption research, and computer security testing – are principally aimed at promoting follow-on innovation, either by permitting development of new products or by improving products that already exist. The other six recognize that reverse engineering of technically protected digital content, such as reverse analysis of filtering software to discern what sites it blocks and decryption incidental to law enforcement and national security activities, may be reasonable and do not undermine copyright protection.

There are, however, many other reasons for reverse analysis of technical protections that promote follow-on innovation. These include: locating, assessing, and fixing bugs in software; analyzing software to understand how to add additional features; understanding the internal design of a technical protection measure for research purposes; understanding its internal design to develop a competing product; understanding its internal design in order to make a compatible product, such as an alternative nonsoftware platform; analyzing a technical measure to enable interoperability with data; and enabling critical commentary on a technically protected movie by taking fair use clips from it ...

A narrower anti-tool rule might also prevent anticompetitive uses of the DMCA by content providers. In the past three years, plaintiffs have asserted violations of the DMCA rules in order to exclude competitors from the marketplace, to control the market for complementary products, and to facilitate their preferred market allocation and pricing strategies.

Joint ownership of a proprietary technical protection system by major content providers may conceivably allow them to leverage their market power as to content into the market for equipment. For example, the motion picture industry controls the DVD player industry by its joint ownership of patent rights necessary to make DVD players; one of the conditions of this license is installation of the Content Scrambling System. More recently, the recording industry has sought to leverage its market power over digital music into the market for players, through the Secure Digital Music Initiative (SDMI). The goal of the SDMI is to develop standard digital watermarks for digital music. The watermark must be detected by software in the player before the music can be heard. In both examples, players and content become a "system" much like the operating systems and applications software discussed in Part IV. In the digital entertainment systems, entry into the player market is foreclosed, in part because of the DMCA rules, which essentially make the interface proprietary.[4] In the absence of legislation mandating installation of technical controls, the market power that is implicitly facilitated may be the only way to ensure that highly protected products will enjoy success in the marketplace.

3. Competition in the Market for Technical Protection Measures

The incentive to develop and improve technical measures depends on the market for them, which in turn depends on whether copyright owners need them to enforce copyrights. We argue that our proposed narrower anticircumvention rule will increase the demand for effective technical measures, which will increase the incentive to develop and improve them.

The super-strong protection of the DMCA not only erodes incentives to use technical measures, it also erects barriers to entering the market to supply them. The DMCA creates an extremely strong form of trade-secret-like protection for technical protection measures, far beyond that provided by any other law. Ordinarily, an unpatented product such as a technical measure would be subject to reverse engineering and competition. As in the traditional manufacturing context, the vulnerability of unpatented products to reverse engineering limits market power in a competitively healthy way. The DMCA rules effectively insulate makers of technical protection measures from competitive reverse analysis. This result could be avoided by the narrower rule we propose.

The narrower anti-tool rule would also enhance the ability of researchers to learn from each other. The DMCA inhibits research and hence follow-on innovation in technical measures because it limits the ability of researchers to learn from their predecessors. A reverse engineer who discovers a problem with another firm's technical measure and offers suggestions about how to improve it is at risk of getting indicted on criminal DMCA charges, rather than being offered a commercial or academic opportunity to improve the product.

Reverse engineering lies at the very heart of encryption and computer security research ... Encryption and computer security may be crippled if

---

4 [footnote 326 in original] In the software context, the market power constrained by reverse engineering lies in the platform provider because of its control over APIs. In the digital entertainment context, the market power is chiefly wielded by those who are rightsholders in the applications market. The economics of interoperability are the same, although the DMCA rules change the legal analysis significantly at least when firms want to develop alternative platforms to interoperate with digital data. ...

researchers are at risk of liability under the DMCA in the ordinary course of their research. As we argued in the case of the SCPA, reverse engineering can facilitate competition for improvements. The right balance between facilitating improvements and protecting earlier innovators can be achieved by granting a kind of "leading breadth" to each innovation, but not by prohibiting researchers from access to knowledge, as the DMCA does.

VI. Reverse Engineering as a Policy Lever

All intellectual property rights regimes – utility patent, plant variety protection, copyright, and the SCPA – have certain policy levers in common, wielded to a greater or lesser extent. All establish, for example, a length of protection, a breadth of protection (sometimes legislated and sometimes evolving through case law interpretations), and some fair use or policy-based limitations on the scope of protection. By wielding the available policy levers appropriately, legal regimes can be made sensitive to the technological and industrial contexts they regulate so as to avoid either over-rewarding or under-rewarding innovators.

We conceive of the legal status of reverse engineering as one such policy lever. This policy lever is set differently in different legal contexts. Trade secrecy law, for example, exposes innovators to reverse engineering whereas patent law limits it to some degree. A rationale for this difference lies in the disclosure obligations that patent law imposes on innovators that trade secret owners avoid. For the traditional subject matters of copyright law, namely, artistic and literary works, reverse engineering has not been an issue because viewers and readers do not need to reverse-engineer these works to understand them. Yet as copyright's subject matter expanded to include computer software, reverse engineering became a significant policy issue in copyright law as well.

The optimal setting for any given policy lever depends in part on how the other levers are deployed. Consider, for example, the interaction of reverse engineering rules and the length of protection. Outlawing decompilation of computer programs is inadvisable in part because of the long duration of protection that copyright provides to programs. If decompilation and disassembly were illegal, programs would be immune from an important source of competition for almost a century, which would likely impede innovation in the software industry. Such a rule would provide far more protection than necessary to protect innovative software firms against market-destructive appropriations.

Our study of reverse engineering in various industrial contexts leads us to two general conclusions. The first is that reverse engineering has generally been a competitively healthy way for second comers to get access to and discern the know-how embedded in an innovator's product. If reverse engineering is costly and takes time, as is usually the case, innovators will generally be protected long enough to recoup R&D expenses. More affirmatively, the threat of reverse engineering promotes competition in developing new products, constrains market power, and induces licensing that enables innovators to recoup R&D costs.

Second, we have found it useful to distinguish between the act of reverse engineering, which is generally performed to obtain know-how about another's product, and what a reverse engineer does with the know-how thereby obtained (e.g., designing a competing or complementary product). The act of reverse engineering rarely, if ever, has market-destructive effects and has the benefit of transferring knowledge. Harmful effects are far more likely to result from post-reverse-engineering activities (e.g., making a competing product with know-how from an innovator's product). Because of this, it may be more sensible to regulate post-reverse-engineering activities than to regulate reverse engineering as such. This view is reinforced by difficulties of enforcement. Acts of reverse engineering typically take place in private and are more difficult to detect than post-reverse-engineering activities (such as introducing competing or complementary products to the market). They are, as a consequence, less susceptible to effective regulation. In the discussion below, we distinguish between regulatory strategies aimed at acts of reverse engineering and those aimed at post-reverse-engineering activities.

The bluntest way to deploy the reverse engineering lever is to switch it "on" (making it legal) or "off" (making it illegal). Our study has revealed five more nuanced ways to deploy this lever: regulating a particular means of reverse engineering, establishing a breadth requirement for subsequent products, using purpose- and necessity-based requirements for judging the legitimacy of reverse engineering, regulating reverse engineering tools, and restricting publication of information discovered by a reverse engineer.

We review these options in Section VI.A for two reasons. First, they have been adopted in some industrial contexts and should be assessed for their economic reasonableness. Second, proposals for additional restrictions on reverse engineering may be made in the future. Legal decisionmakers may be better equipped to respond to such proposals if they understand how reverse engineering has been regulated in the past and under what conditions restrictions on reverse engineering are justifiable.

In Section VI.B, we observe that a legal right to reverse-engineer may be so threatening to some innovators that they will endeavor to render the legal right moot through one of two strategies: by requiring customers to agree not to reverse-engineer their products, or by configuring their products to make reverse engineering extremely difficult or impossible. Legal decisionmakers have the option of responding to such efforts by deciding not to enforce such contractual restrictions or by forcing disclosure of product know-how.

A. Ways To Regulate Reverse Engineering

1. Regulating a Market-Destructive Means of Reverse Engineering

When a particular means of reverse engineering makes competitive copying too cheap, easy, or rapid, innovators may be unable to recoup R&D expenses. If so, it may be reasonable to regulate that means. Anti-plug-mold laws, discussed in Section II.C, are an example. Using a competitor's product as a "plug" to make a mold from which to make competing products permits competitive copying that is so cheap and fast that it undermines the incentives to invest in designing an innovative product. Restrictions on plug-molding may restore adequate incentives to make such investments. Notwithstanding the Supreme Court's characterization of plug-molding as an efficient means of reverse engineering, we suggest that plug-molding is better understood as an efficient means of reimplementing the original innovation. Plug-molding has the potential to undermine an innovator's incentives without any offsetting social benefit of follow-on innovation because a plug-molder does not aim to learn anything that might lead to further innovation. Thus, one of the key benefits of reverse engineering will be lost if plug-molding is used to make competing products.

Another controversial act of reverse engineering was decompilation and disassembly of computer programs, discussed in Part IV. Some industry participants feared that reverse engineering would allow second comers to appropriate valuable internal design elements of programs. Decompilation and disassembly were eventually accepted as legal, in part because they require so much time, money, and energy that the original developer is not significantly threatened. If reverse engineering actually occurs in the face of these costs, it may enable the development of interoperable products and erode the market power of industry leaders in a competitively healthy way.

Our advice to policymakers is this: Before banning a means of reverse engineering, require convincing evidence that this means has market-destructive consequences. Realize that existing market participants may want a ban mainly because they wish to protect themselves against competitive entry. Any restriction on reverse engineering should be tailored so that it does not reach more than parasitic activities. For example, it may be sensible to make the restriction prospective rather than retroactive, to require that innovations embody some minimal creativity, or to limit the duration of the ban. Another possibility is to outlaw market-destructive reimplementations of innovations, rather than banning reverse engineering as such. Alternatively, reverse engineers could be required to compensate rightsholders for research uses of the innovation aimed at development of follow-on innovation.

2. A Breadth Requirement for Products of Reverse Engineering

Another policy option is to establish a breadth requirement for products developed after reverse engineering. If second comers must invest in some forward engineering and not simply free-ride on the previous innovation by copying it exactly, the second comer's efforts are more likely to advance the state of technology and to take time so that the earlier innovator is still protected. The Semiconductor Chip Protection Act was our principal example. The SCPA permits intermediate copying of chip circuitry for purposes of study and analysis; it also permits reuse of some know-how discerned in the reverse engineering process. This is a useful boost to competitors designing integrated circuits. The SCPA, however, requires reverse engineers to design an "original" chip rather than simply making a clone or near-clone of the integrated circuit that was reverse-engineered.

Since the SCPA rules allow later innovators to learn from earlier ones while still allowing chip designers to recoup expenses, we think it is competitively healthy. More generally, we find merit in the idea of establishing a breadth requirement to ensure that reverse engineering leads to further advances while still preserving enough market power so that the innovator recoups costs in markets where cloning of the innovator's product would be market-destructive. Again, policymakers should be wary of undocumented claims that reverse engineering is per se destructive. Establishing breadth requirements may be unnecessary to protect the lead time of innovators in many industries because the costliness and difficulties of reverse engineering and reimplementation may provide adequate protection. The SCPA rules responded to specific perturbations in the semiconductor chip market that undermined lead time.

While most legal regimes do not link the legitimacy of reverse engineering with technical advance, the software copyright case law may do so implicitly. In *Sega v. Accolade*, for example, the court's perception that Accolade's reverse engineering was legitimate rested in no small part on the defendant's having developed a new, noninfringing program that promoted the very kind of progress that copyright law was intended to bring about. Nevertheless, a linkage between the legitimacy of reverse engineering and a breadth requirement in the software industry may be unnecessary for two reasons: First, decompilation and disassembly of programs are so difficult and time-consuming that second comers generally do not find it profitable to develop market-destructive clones in this way. Second, reverse engineering of software does not generally lead to the development of a competing product, but rather to the development of interoperable programs or to the fixing of software bugs. Breadth requirements seem most appropriate when the goal is development of a competing product.

3. Purpose- and Necessity-Based Criteria for Determining the Legitimacy of Reverse Engineering

A third way to deploy the reverse engineering policy lever is to judge its legitimacy based on its purpose or necessity. As with regulation of particular means, this approach focuses on the act of reverse engineering itself. Purpose-based rules assume that reverse engineering is sometimes socially beneficial and sometimes harmful, and at a deeper level, that society will benefit from a reverse engineer's acquisition of some types of know-how embedded in commercially distributed products but not others. Necessity-based rules assume that societal resources should not be expended on reverse engineering if the information being sought is already available. It is worth noting that the legitimacy of reverse engineering has traditionally not depended on its purpose or necessity. For traditional manufactured items, the right to reverse-engineer has been almost absolute.

Two examples of purpose- and necessity-based privileges from this study are *Sega v. Accolade* and its progeny, which permit reverse engineering of computer software for the purpose of achieving interoperability, and the DMCA anticircumvention rules that permit reverse engineering of access controls for some purposes, including achieving interoperability.

We have mixed reactions to purpose- and necessity-based criteria for regulating reverse engineering. Of course it is true that the economic effects of reverse engineering depend on the reverse engineer's purpose, and purpose-based reasoning is common in intellectual property law. A second comer's purpose often determines whether he or she qualifies for an exception to or limitation on intellectual property rights. Copyright's fair use doctrine, for example, gives considerable weight to the purpose of a fair use claimant's activities.

One positive consequence of purpose-based rules is to induce knowledge-sharing through licensing or voluntary disclosure. European policymakers legalized decompilation of computer programs for purposes of achieving interoperability in order to make the threat of reverse engineering credible enough so that software developers would disclose interface information voluntarily or license it on reasonable terms. This ensured that European software developers could enter software markets with interoperable products. European policymakers did not wish to encourage licensing of other program know-how, but rather sought to encourage second comers to do their own independent design work, and hence, they restricted the privilege to decompilation for interoperability.

A downside of purpose-based regulations is that if reverse engineering is not averted by licensing, wasteful litigation may be the only way to determine the reverse engineer's purposes. Antitrust law faces similar difficulties, as when a court must decide whether a certain defendant (say, Microsoft) engaged in certain acts for good purposes (e.g., integrating its browser into its operating system to benefit consumers) or bad purposes (e.g., trying to put Netscape out of business). Moreover, reverse engineers may have multiple purposes, only some of which may be privileged by purpose-based rules.

We believe that purpose-based rules are better than necessity-based rules as a strategy for limiting reverse engineering. Necessity-based rules may be a trap for the unwary. For example, if a software developer offers to license interface information on terms a second comer deems unreasonable, reverse engineering may seem necessary to the second comer, but not to the prospective licensor. Similarly, a software developer may be willing to license a minimal amount of interface information, but not enough to make the program fully interoperable. Once again, whether reverse engineering is necessary is disputable. A further problem arises if the information is available in an obscure place unknown to the reverse engineer who, in ignorance, exposes himself to liability by going ahead with reverse engineering he believed to be necessary. Necessity-based rules would also seem to be largely unnecessary given that rational second comers would almost always prefer to avoid the expenses of reverse engineering if the desired information was available without it.

Finally, we observe that enumerating exceptions to a general prohibition has different consequences than enumerating exceptions to a general privilege. The DMCA has a general prohibition of reverse engineering of access controls that is subject to various purpose-based exceptions. This approach implies that reverse engineering of access controls for every other purpose is illegal. Given that the principal objective of the DMCA rule is to prevent copyright infringements, a more straightforward approach would have been to establish a general privilege in favor of reverse engineering, but to disallow it for the purpose of enabling infringement of copyrighted work. Because the DMCA adopts the more restrictive approach, a host of reasonable circumventions must be presumed illegal. Those who reverse-engineer for unenumerated but benign purposes can only hope that their activities will escape the notice of the copyright industries and federal prosecutors.

4. Regulating Reverse Engineering Tools

The DMCA anticircumvention rules are unique among the legal regimes we studied in regulating the development and distribution of tools for reverse engineering. This strategy does not regulate the act of reverse engineering or post-reverse-engineering activities so much as preparatory activities necessary to engage in reverse engineering. For reasons given in Part V, we think the DMCA's anti-tool rules are overbroad. We recognize, however, that the anti-tool rules cannot be judged by the same considerations used in other industrial contexts. Our general assumption about reverse engineering has been that once the proper boundaries of intellectual property are established, the property right will be enforced. The anti-tool rules, in contrast, are directed at the problem of enforcement.

The enforcement problem arises because digital content is very cheap and easy to copy. To overcome this, the entertainment industry is increasingly using technical measures to protect its content from unauthorized access and use. Circumvention undermines this strategy. Since circumvention tools are essential to reverse-engineer these technical measures, the entertainment industry persuaded Congress to outlaw circumvention tools. We agree that there are some good economic arguments for regulating trafficking in circumvention technologies. Without ready access to circumvention tools, both large-and small-scale infringements may be prevented. It is, moreover, easier to detect and police a public market in circumvention technologies than to control private acts of circumvention and copying. Nevertheless, we have argued that the anti-tool rules of the DMCA are defective because they reach many activities that have little value for enforcement purposes. Overbroad anti-tool rules are also harmful because they have provided copyright owners with a potent weapon for excluding competitive or complementary products from the market. They also facilitate the ability of copyright owners to leverage their market power in content into the equipment market.

5. Restricting Publication of Information Discovered by a Reverse Engineer

A fifth policy option is to allow reverse engineering but to forbid publication or other disclosures of information obtained thereby. For the most part, the law has not had to address this issue because reverse engineers have generally had little incentive to publish or otherwise disclose information they learn from reverse engineering. Reverse engineers have typically kept the resulting know-how secret for competitive advantage.

Publishing information learned through lawful reverse engineering has long been legal in the United States. In *Chicago Lock Co. v. Fanberg,* for example, the Ninth Circuit overturned an injunction against publication of a book containing compilations of key codes for tubular locks whose manufacturer claimed the codes as trade secrets. Because the author of the book, himself a locksmith, had gathered the information from fellow locksmiths who had lawfully reverse-engineered the information in the course of helping their customers, there was no misappropriation of Chicago Lock's trade secrets.

In recent years, restrictions on publication and other disclosures of reverse-engineered information have begun to appear. In the early 1990s, for example, the European Union adopted a directive on the legal protection of computer software that forbade publication or licensing of information obtained in the course of lawful decompilation of programs to achieve interoperability. In 1998, the U.S. Congress adopted the DMCA anticircumvention rules, which impose numerous restrictions on information learned in the course of privileged acts of reverse engineering. A reverse engineer can, for example, bypass technical protections when necessary to achieve program-to-program interoperability, but cannot disclose information learned therefrom unless the sole purpose of the disclosure is to accomplish interoperability ...

B. Policy Options When Innovators Try To Prevent Reverse Engineering

The very reasons that reverse engineering is socially beneficial – for example, that it erodes a first comer's market power and promotes follow-on innovation – may be why some innovators desire to prevent reverse engineering altogether or render it moot. When reverse engineering is lawful, firms may seek to thwart it in one of two ways: by requiring customers to agree not to reverse-engineer the product or by designing the product to make it very difficult or impossible to reverse-engineer. This Section addresses the policy responses available to deal with attempts to circumvent legal rules permitting reverse engineering.

1. Avoiding the Threat of Reverse Engineering by Contract

Software licenses often prohibit reverse engineering, even when (or especially when) reverse engineering is allowed by law. Whether such contracts should be enforceable as a general matter is an unsettled question of law . . .

We believe that in markets for products heavily dependent on intellectual property rights, such as computer software, there is reason to worry about contractual restrictions of reverse engineering. Some market power is inevitable in such markets, or else the intellectual property right has no purpose. The policy levers that define the intellectual property right are devices that both grant market power and limit its boundaries. If the intellectual property regime is well designed in the first place, we see no intrinsic reason why contracting should be allowed to circumvent it, especially in markets with strong network effects. Hence, it may be reasonable not to enforce contract terms purporting to override reverse engineering privileges in intellectual-property-dependent markets such as software, as the European Union has done by nullifying license terms forbidding decompilation of computer programs.

2. Avoiding the Threat of Reverse Engineering by Technical Obfuscation

Firms sometimes design their products so that it will be difficult or impossible to reverse-engineer them. Such expenditures would be unnecessary if reverse engineering were unlawful. In the economic calculus of reverse engineering, we must count expenditures to thwart reverse engineering as socially wasteful. Efforts to prevent reverse engineering may, however, be unsuccessful or only partially successful. Determined second comers may figure out enough through reverse engineering to make a competitive product, albeit one missing some of the innovator's "secret sauce." Sometimes, however, efforts to circumvent reverse engineering may be successful. In addition, even when firms do not intentionally design their products to make reverse engineering impossible, products may, as a practical matter, be immune from reverse engineering because of the sheer complexity of the product or because details of the product design change so rapidly that by the time a reverse engineer finished his work, the next version of the product would be in the marketplace.

One policy option for dealing with such a situation is to force the innovator to disclose certain information about her product. For example, if arguments in favor of open interfaces have merit and interfaces cannot be effectively discerned by reverse engineering, then it may sometimes make sense to require interfaces to be made public. This is essentially what happened some years ago in Europe when antitrust authorities brought suit against IBM for abuse of its dominant position because it had been altering the interfaces to its mainframe computers frequently, thereby disadvantaging European makers of peripheral products. The dispute was eventually resolved by IBM's agreement to announce changes to its interfaces in advance so that peripheral manufacturers could adjust their products accordingly. Some have suggested a similar remedy in *United States v. Microsoft*. Microsoft has maintained its monopoly position in the operating systems market in part through control over the APIs to the Windows platform. Reverse engineering of the Windows APIs is far more difficult than, say, reverse engineering interfaces of game platforms, and it may be impracticable. Forcing Microsoft to publish its APIs would certainly erode its market power, but this raises a host of other difficulties.

VII. Conclusion

Reverse engineering is fundamentally directed to discovery and learning. Engineers learn the state of the art not just by reading printed publications, going to technical conferences, and working on projects for their firms, but also by reverse engineering the products of others. Learning what has been done before often leads to new products and advances in know-how. Reverse engineering may be a slower and more expensive means for information to percolate through a technical community than patenting or publication, but it is nonetheless an effective source of information. Reverse engineering leads to dependent creations, but this does not taint them, for in truth, all innovators stand on the shoulders of both giants and midgets. Progress in science and the useful arts is advanced by dissemination of know-how, whether by publication, patenting, or reverse engineering.

We think it is no coincidence that in the past two decades most of the proposals to restrict reverse engineering have arisen in the context of information-based products, such as semiconductors and software. The high quantum of know-how that such products bear on or near their face makes these products more vulnerable than traditional manufactured goods to market-destructive appropriations. This is especially true when the information is in digital form. Copying and distribution of digital products is essentially costless and almost instantaneous in the digital network environment. The vulnerability of information products to market-destructive appropriations may justify some limitations on reverse engineering or post-reverse-engineering activities, but reverse engineering is important to innovation and competition in all of the industrial contexts we studied.

Adapting intellectual property law so that it provides adequate, but not excessive, protection to innovations is a challenging task. In considering future proposals to limit reverse engineering, policymakers should find it helpful to consider the economic effects of mechanisms that have been employed in the past. Restrictions on reverse engineering ought to be imposed only if justified in terms of the specific characteristics of the industry, a specific threat to that industry, and the economic effects of the restriction.

We worry that the recent DMCA restrictions on reverse engineering may propagate backward and erode longstanding rules permitting reverse engineering in other legal regimes. As Professors Dreyfuss and Kwall have observed, "the distinction between, say, breaking into a factory (improper) and breaking into the product (proper) may seem artificial." It is, however, a distinction that has been a foundational principle of intellectual property and unfair competition law, at least until enactment of the DMCA. It is, moreover, a distinction whose abandonment could have detrimental consequences for innovation and competition.

CHAPTER 22

S. M. Maurer and S. Scotchmer, "Profit Neutrality in Licensing: The Boundary Between Antitrust Law and Patent Law" (2006)

INTRODUCTION   STEPHEN M. MAURER

Prof. Scotchmer and I finished the working paper version of "Profit Neutrality" (National Bureau of Economic Research Working Paper No. 10546 [June 2004]) as *Innovation and Incentives* (2004) was going to press. This was a pivotal time for her research agenda. On the one hand, the book provided a capstone account of her decade-long inquiry into how the law divides reward across multiple inventors. From that standpoint, "Profit Neutrality" used the familiar tools to analyze yet another licensing problem. But, at a deeper level, it was far more ambitious, not least in deliberately setting out to attack a notorious doctrinal puzzle that had defied judges' best efforts for nearly a century.

This approach required extreme interdisciplinarity. In particular, no formal economics or legal reasoning tool was off the table. Instead, "Profit Neutrality"'s theorist and lawyer voices alternate so that section 3, for example, deploys mathematical economics while section 5 presents a quintessentially legal argument for rationalizing conflicting case law. This structure was itself a borrowing from legal briefs, which classically divide "facts," "law," and "argument" in distinct sections, each of which tends to use its own distinct toolkit of conventions, emphasis, and argument styles. It is worth pointing out that the various sections absolutely did *not* reflect authorship. For example, Prof. Scotchmer drafted the first version of the article's proposed per se rules (section 5) and shared equally in the revisions that followed. Readers familiar with her writing style will have no difficulty spotting her imprint throughout the various "legal" sections.

The article opens with a standard legal analysis showing how doctrine finds itself stuck in a logical cul-de-sac (section 1) and proceeds to identify three principles that courts have said any solution must satisfy (section 2). Here the only concession to economic theory – hardly a stretch – lies in phrasing the legal principles carefully enough for use in formal models. The middle part of the paper turns to economics. Section 3 addresses the common case where the patent owner uses her IP *both* to manufacture new inventions that do not infringe any previous patent *and* to extract a royalty from rivals. Section 4 extends this analysis to the cumulative innovation case where the rivals hold so-called blocking patents on the underlying invention so that neither side can act without the other's permission. The final sections of the article return to the paper's legal scholarship voice by proposing a carefully worded rule that encodes the paper's economic theory insights (section 5), explains why legal scholars should be skeptical of alternative approaches that depend on courts' discretion (section 6), and recapitulates the main arguments for reform (section 7).

Choosing the Problem. I do not know how Prof. Scotchmer came to this doctrinal problem. However, her cumulative innovation research had fostered a strong interest in blocking patents which would have quickly led her to the Supreme Court's well-known *Line Material Co.* decision (US Supreme Court, 1948). Reading that opinion, in turn, would have led her back to the Court's earlier and still more controversial *General Electric* decision (US Supreme Court, 1926).

What I do know is that, from the very beginning, she explained her reasons for writing the paper as an attempt to solve "The *General Electric* problem." This lawyer-like phrase is revealing. As every IP law professor can tell you, this part of antitrust doctrine was famously incoherent. The difficulties had begun in 1926, when the Supreme Court had controversially announced that IP owners could write price-fixing terms into their licenses. The trouble was that the rule had existed in a kind of limbo ever since. On the one hand the Supreme Court had upheld the rule – albeit by just one vote – in 1947 and again in 1964. But on the other, lower courts always found reasons to avoid enforcing it. The result was that IP lawyers no longer wrote price-fixing terms at all. This might have been fine if the original 1924 case was wrong, but of course the Supreme Court had not said that. In the meantime, the chaotic state of the law had suppressed thousands of business deals that might or might not be good for society. It also led to a kind of vicious circle in which lawyers' aversion to writing such contracts suppressed the issue, so that judges no longer had occasion to think about and perhaps reform the doctrine.

The Three Principles. The article starts by proposing three *legal* principles that any licensing rule should respect. Significantly, each had appeared repeatedly in the case law so that judges would be prepared to accept it. The novelty, of course, consisted in stating them more precisely in a way that rigorous economic models could address:

Derived Reward. Prof. Scotchmer often emphasized that any deadweight loss attributable to IP was bounded by consumers' willingness to buy goods that benefited from the protected knowledge. This implied the still deeper rule that the IP reward should derive exclusively from the invention itself. So long as this was done, an inventor who exploited her patent monopoly in-house was entitled to this "derived reward." If scholars thought that this reward was too large or too small, it was up to Congress, not judges, to change the law.

Profit Neutrality. By itself, the derived reward benchmark is incomplete. Legal scholars (Furth, 1958) and economists (Arrow, 1962) had long noted that the reward could change depending, for example, on whether the inventor owned factories or had access to capital. It followed that courts should approve licenses that extracted the same profits that the owner would have earned but for such accidents of birth. Formal economic models were by far the most natural way to show this equivalence.

Minimalism. Antitrust judges sometimes worry that firms will organize illicit cartels around terms smuggled into nominally lawful "sham contracts." In the *General Electric/Line Material* context this meant asking whether profit neutrality could be achieved without price fixing, output restrictions, nonlinear royalties, and similar terms. Sections 3, 4, and 6 use formal models to specify when these additional terms are and are not required.

For lawyers, the paper's main novelty lay in using these principles to unite two bodies of law – "patents" and "antitrust" – that are almost always analyzed separately. This was a reminder, following "Giants," that IP reward depends on both. This meant, among other things, that both IP and antitrust had to have the same objective function. This already presented an implicit challenge to the common claim that antitrust law is exclusively focused on maximizing consumer welfare (see, e.g., Kirkwood and Lande, 2008) while patent incentives are meant to reward inventors. Lawyers should probably take this as a broad hint that the usual formulations are inconsistent and need to be rethought. For economists, on the other hand, the paper was unusual mainly because it spent so much energy trying to understand and, if possible, reform real legal doctrines. This was far harder than the usual strategy of proposing and then analyzing simple hypothetical rules.

Economics Insights. One might have thought that analyzing case law was a poor way to learn economics. However, working lawyers know that new cases have a way of surfacing previously overlooked issues. At least in retrospect, it was not surprising that Prof. Scotchmer's analysis of *General*

Electric would reveal a new phenomenon. Previous IP licensing papers had found that owners can extract maximal profit through a combination of (a) per-unit royalties that force licensees to charge the monopoly price, and (b) fixed fees that extract the monopoly reward. Now, Prof. Scotchmer showed that this statement is *not* true when the licensor also manufactures the product. (The reason is that he receives *all* of the revenue from expanded production but can still shift half of the resulting lost sales onto licensees.) Knowing this, licensees will always demand lower royalties unless and until the licensor commits to limit his own production. This makes some version of output restrictions, price fixing, nonlinear royalties, or the like unavoidable.

A New Kind of Paper. Prof. Scotchmer spent much of her remaining years working on papers that refined this same basic technique of merging legal and economic reasoning in a way that paid attention to actual doctrine. In practice, this meant learning how practicing lawyers read precedents for legal guidance. For them – unlike the average law and economics paper – arguing that the judge misunderstood the purpose of the law, or should have found some other facts from the evidence presented, is not very helpful. The whole point of precedent is that such matters are settled and should not ordinarily be reopened. But that still left economic reasoning, for which judges invariably relied on analogies and verbal arguments. Every economist understood just how quickly that sort of logic could slip into error. This was precisely the point at which formal models were valuable.

For lawyers, on the other hand, the approach represented a bet that stalled doctrines could be revived by revisiting the court's economic reasoning with rigorous mathematical analyses. The "Profit Neutrality" paper makes this point repeatedly, arguing that courts had "stumbled over the economics" despite an otherwise "sound" approach to licensing. This was much less speculative than it seemed: if clever lawyers had tried to fix a doctrine for years, all the obvious logical flaws would have been found already. At that point, it only made sense to deploy the theorist's powerful toolkit to ask whether the court had overlooked some subtle feature in the economics. The approach also examined these tools critically to see when judges should take them seriously. Here, Prof. Scotchmer invoked the characteristic lawyer insight that courts are only allowed to pay attention to models supported by specific evidence.[*] The "Profit Neutrality" article picks up this theme when it remarks that its central economic argument that the manufacturer/licensor has an incentive to cheat is more robust than any single model. Litigants seeking loopholes would therefore "have to produce (a) a model where the effect vanishes, and (b) evidence that the model is more

---

[*] This means, for example, that litigants who want to invoke Cournot models must persuade the Court that firms really do behave like price-takers (US District Court, 2003).

appropriate to the facts than the very standard model discussed in this paper." More complicated models should similarly "produce the evidence or models to justify them, and say how they implement the three principles."

Surprisingly, the approach also offered benefits for economic theory. The reason, as most common law lawyers know, is that litigation has a way of surfacing subtleties that previous judges have overlooked. This meant that the economic issues raised by stalled legal doctrines would often be interesting in their own right. And of course, the legal literature is full of stalled doctrines.

The question is whether this style of paper has a future. After all, hardly any economists have Prof. Scotchmer's facility in law. Still, that is only a matter of making the investment, and the papers she did write show how large the research payoffs can be. I like to think that, even now, some shrewd young theorist is busy learning the law.

American Law and Economics Review,
Vol. 8 No. 3 (2006): 476–522

Profit Neutrality in Licensing: The Boundary Between Antitrust Law and Patent Law

Stephen M. Maurer and Suzanne Scotchmer, University of California[1]

Abstract

We address the patent/antitrust conflict in licensing and develop three guiding principles for deciding acceptable terms of license. Profit neutrality holds that patent rewards should not depend on the rightholder's ability to work the patent himself. Derived reward

1 This article profited from comments received from participants at the Antitrust, Patent and Copyright Conference held at Ecole des Mines de Paris (CERNA), jointly sponsored by Boalt School of Law, on January 15 – 16, 2004, from participants at Harvard Law School, March 23, 2004, and from participants at the annual meeting of the American Law and Economics Association, May 2004. We especially thank Louis Kaplow, Marty Adelman, Susan DeSanti, Carl Shapiro, Guofu Tan, Jean Tirole, and Mark Lemley for helpful comments. We thank the Toulouse Network on Information Technology for financial support.

Send correspondence to: Stephen Maurer, 2607 Hearst Avenue, University of California, Berkeley, CA 94720–7320; Fax: 1–510–643–9657; E-mail: smaurer@berkeley.edu or scotch@berkeley.edu.

holds that the patentholder's profits should be earned, if at all, from the social value created by the invention. Minimalism *holds that licenses should not be more restrictive than necessary to achieve neutrality. We argue that these principles are economically sound and rationalize some key decisions of the twentieth century such as* General Electric *and* Line Material.

1. Introduction

Patent law and antitrust concerns were born side by side. On the one hand, the Statute of Monopolies (1623) announced a general ban on monopolies "for the sole Buying, Selling, Making, Working, or Using of any Thing within this Realm. . ." On the other hand, it created new monopolies as an incentive for inventions. The decision to treat the same legal concept – monopoly – as a crime in one case and a reward in the other presents unique problems for judges. "[B]ecause the patentee's authority is an island of permission in a sea of prohibition, there is no area at the edge of permission toward which the law is indifferent: what is not authorized is forbidden" (Baxter, 1966). Expanded antitrust enforcement during the twentieth century has made this problem increasingly acute.

Over the twentieth century, courts and commentators explored many different proposals for defining the boundary between intellectual property and antitrust law. The simplest approach, "inherency," resolves the issue by allowing one body of law to dominate the other in any conflict (Adelman and Juenger, 1975). Early in the twentieth century, patent law dominated so that restrictive licenses were generally upheld. As argued by Kaplow (1984), commentators during the 1960s urged a different version of inherency that would have made antitrust dominant. Although generally disfavored, inherency arguments are still being made (Gifford, 2002; Patterson, 2000).

The alternative to inherency is balancing. However, if antitrust and patent law have different objectives, it is not obvious how to strike a balance. For this reason, most commentators have advocated balancing according to a single, agreed-upon objective such as "wealth maximization" or "consumer welfare" (Bork, 1965, 1978; Bowman, 1973). But even with a single objective, there is no obvious calculation that courts should use to balance *ex ante* incentives against *ex post* deadweight loss. Almost all cases and commentators argue that courts should infer the correct balance from Congress's intent as codified in the patent laws.

There are many different ways to divine intent. Twentieth-century judges and scholars have offered a bewildering variety of schemes for balancing. In general, there are two schools. The earliest, which dates from the 1920s, seeks to develop clear per se rules that can be applied more or less mechanically. Courts following this tradition have approved restrictions on licensees' prices (*General Electric*, 1926), on choice of customers (*General Talking Pictures*, 1938; Schlicher, 2002), and on licensees' geographic markets (Hovenkamp, Janis, and Lemley, 2004). Over time, the Supreme Court seems to have lost confidence in the per se agenda. In fact, the Court came within one vote of overruling *General Electric* in 1948 and again in 1965. Lower courts have also adopted exceptions,[2] to the point where many commentators argue that *General Electric* is a "vestige" that prudent practitioners should not rely on (Weinschel, 2000). Nevertheless, it remains the law of the land.

The second school, dominant since the 1940s, argues for a more flexible "rule-of-reason" standard.[3] Courts currently use rule of reason for a wide variety of license restrictions (Weinschel, 2000, section 2, p. 90). However, this program has yet to develop widely recognized principles or rules. At its worst, "rule of reason" can be little more than a label disguising "amorphous" and "freewheeling" standards (Adelman and Juenger, 1975). Since the 1980s, however, scholars have thought hard about the questions that any principled rule of reason must resolve.

Most commentators agree that current law is unsatisfactory. In the words of Chisum (2003), "[f]rom the decisions, it is clear that the courts lack a clear and general theory for resolving that inquiry. Thus, individual problems are resolved in a piecemeal fashion, and it is difficult to harmonize decisions in one area (such as price restrictions) with another (such as field of use restrictions)." This doctrinal confusion has practical consequences. Blue ribbon panels have complained since the 1950s that legal uncertainty deters patentees from licensing their inventions (*Hensley*, 1967).

In this article, we take a fresh look at these issues, motivated mainly by *General Electric* and price restrictions, but also addressing the issues in

---

2 For example, *General Electric* may not apply to the unpatented product of a patented machine (Hovenkamp, Janis, and Lemley, 2004; Weinschel, 2000), to patentholders with multiple licensees (Hovenkamp, Janis, and Lemley, 2004; Weinschel, 2000), to patentholders who do not manufacture the patented item (Hovenkamp, Janis, and Lemley, 2004; *Royal Industries*, 1969; Schlicher, 2002), to licenses that are said to "predominantly benefit" licensees rather than the patentholder (*Ethyl*, 1940; Weinschel, 2000), to licenses where the patent does not "completely cover" the product (Hovenkamp, Janis, and Lemley, 2004; Schlicher, 2002), to patentholders who acquire their rights by purchase rather than internal R&D (Hovenkamp, Janis, and Lemley, 2004), or to intellectual property rights other than patents (Hovenkamp, Janis, and Lemley, 2004; *Interstate Circuit*, 1939).

3 Although we find it convenient to speak of per se and rule-of-reason approaches as completely distinct, the truth is considerably more complicated. The Supreme Court has warned that "there is often no bright line separating per se from Rule of Reason analysis" (*California Dental Assn.*, 1999). Judges who apply rule of reason must be guided by our general knowledge of economic theory (Areeda and Hovenkamp, 2003), and judges must be prepared to change per se rules, however reluctantly, as knowledge and experience accumulate (Areeda and Hovenkamp, 2003).

Line Material. We start by stating three principles suggested – or at least consistent with – the case law and commentary that have developed over the past half century. As many courts have implicitly followed them, we think the principles have merit from a doctrinal point of view. Perhaps more importantly, we argue that they have merit from a welfare point of view, in addressing the patent/antitrust conflict. Needless to say, the motivating problem of price fixing does not exhaust the list of situations where antitrust and patent laws collide,[4] and our three principles may not be determinative in every instance. However, we show that they also apply to the leading cases that involve improvement patents.

Section 2 explains the three principles, gives their normative foundation, and says how they relate to case law and commentary. In section 3, we analyze the licensing of a product patent, as in *General Electric*, showing why price restrictions might be consistent with profit neutrality and minimalism. In section 4, we consider product enhancements or additives as in *Ethyl Gasoline* and *Line Material*. In section 5, we list three possible per se rules and analyze their strengths and weaknesses. In section 6, we compare rule of reason's strengths and weaknesses with a revived per se approach. Section 7 is a short conclusion.

To the extent that this article focuses on the conflict between efficient use of intellectual property, which provides market power, and the goal of competition, it raises many of the same issues as in the economics of vertical relationships (Rey and Tirole, 2006). What is added in this context is that market power is a proper consequence of intellectual property, and this must be added into the balance.

2. The Three Principles

By the 1920s, the Supreme Court had abandoned the inherency view that a patentholder could impose whatever license restrictions he desired. When the Court concluded that at least one license restriction (tying) violated the antitrust laws, they opened the door to questioning others. Which restrictions should be legal and which not? The *General Electric* opinion announced a new standard: to be lawful, license restrictions would have to be "reasonably adapted to secure pecuniary reward for the patentee's monopoly" (*General Electric*, 1926). As Kaplow (1984) remarks, most courts and commentators seem to believe that this phrase entitles the patentee to a "specific level of aggregate reward." In our view, however, a better and more plausible interpretation is that courts should ask

---

4 Prominent examples include tying, field of use and geographic restrictions, package licensing, post-expiration royalties, grant-back provisions, the first sale doctrine, restrictions on users' right to repair patented machines, settlement agreements, and agreements that extend rights beyond the scope of the antitrust laws.

whether the patentee's methods are reasonable while remaining agnostic about whether the amount of the reward is reasonable.

We argue that much of twentieth-century jurisprudence about licensing can be summarized in three principles and that these principles make sense from a normative point of view. They are *profit neutrality*, *derived reward*, and *minimalism*. Their normative merits, discussed below, take as given that intellectual property law is well designed to start with, but if not, the antitrust treatment of licensing is not a remedy.

Profit neutrality is our label for the principle that a patentholder's reward should not depend on whether he has the ability to work the patent efficiently himself. Profit neutrality codifies the principle that if an R&D idea is worth pursuing – if its benefits outweigh the R&D costs – then the decision to invest should not depend on extraneous accidents of history such as whether the potential inventor owns manufacturing facilities, is liquid, or has access to financing. Profit neutrality is particularly important in a research environment where "ideas are scarce" (Scotchmer, 2004), so that an innovator's inability to exploit his invention fully may cause the idea to be lost.

Courts implicitly embrace profit neutrality when they proclaim that "[a] patentee is generally entitled to determine how it wishes to commercialize its invention in order to optimize its economic benefit from the patent grant" (*Carborundum*, 1995). Commentators agree. Furth (1958) suggests the same principle when he argues that "price-fixing clauses should not enable the patentee and his licensees to acquire a greater total return or a greater power over the market than the patentee, assuming ability to exploit the patent fully himself could otherwise command." See also Baxter (1966).[5] Still other commentators have stressed that licensing lets small independent inventors and businesses exploit their patents, discourages inefficient integration, and puts production in the hands of the most efficient manufacturer (Bowman, 1973; Landes and Posner, 2003).

Of course, to evaluate whether a given license term is required for profit neutrality, the court needs to assess the market consequences with and without the disputed term of license. This is a fallible process. The economic reasoning in *General Electric* was clearly inadequate. The Court paraphrased the rightholder's goals as, "Yes, you may make and sell articles under my patent, but not so as to destroy the profit that I wish

5 "[I]t could be said, the economic value of the invention is best measured by the extent of restriction and profits that would attend direct patentee exploitation; and to prevent the patentee from capturing a part of these incremental profits by splitting them with licensees on whom he has conferred sheltered positions is to deprive the patentee of part of that value." Baxter ultimately rejects this argument on the ground that companies that held strong patents always prefer in-house production to licensing – that is, that profit neutrality cannot be achieved in practice through licensing. Although we do not dispute that there may be obstacles to perfect licensing, we nevertheless argue that profit neutrality is a legitimate goal and demonstrate terms of license that may be necessary to achieve it.

to obtain by making them and selling them myself." As Bowman (1973) has remarked, "surely it is net receipts that should interest General Electric rather than the sheer accounting joy of attributing profits to its own manufacturing operations." Whether profit neutrality was in the Court's mind, the justices certainly lacked the economics modeling tools to implement it.

Derived reward is our label for the principle that the profit reward of the patent must be derived from the social value of the invention and that, if licensing increases the social value of the innovation, the patentholder is justified in profiting from the increase. In medieval times, sovereigns sometimes rewarded favorites by conferring monopolies in goods they did not invent. The danger of such a practice is that the reward can be much larger than the value created, causing investors to make inefficient investments. The Statute of Monopolies (1623) introduced a limitation: the state can only grant a monopoly in what was actually invented. The genius of this restriction is that the rightholder can never earn more than consumers are willing to pay for the patented invention. Our derived reward principle formalizes the principle that courts should look to the source of the reward (the social value of the invention) rather than size per se.

The derived-reward principle is also in keeping with United States (U.S.) law and legal scholarship. For example, we claim that the U.S. Supreme Court implicitly recognized derived reward when it held that a license cannot be used to create a monopoly on any product other than the invention itself (Schlicher, 2002) and that the patent monopoly should exclude "all that is not embraced in the invention" (*Morton Salt*, 1942). Indeed, the derived-reward principle is woven into the U.S. Constitution. Constitutionally, neither the Congress nor the courts has the power to give a patentee "more than the rewards of his discovery" (*Hensley*, 1967; see also *Line Material*, 1948 [Douglas concurring]). Commentators since the 1960s have uniformly argued that the patent reward should measure "the patented product's competitive superiority over substitutes" (Adelman and Juenger, 1975; Baxter, 1966; Bowman, 1973; Patterson, 2000). The derived-reward principle does this automatically. It also describes why any attempt to impose a reward on products not part of the patented invention – sham licensing – should be condemned.

Finally, *minimalism* is our label for the principle that licenses should contain no more restrictions than are necessary to achieve profit neutrality and derived reward. If it is possible to strike down license restrictions and still satisfy those two principles, courts should do so. Minimalism is rooted in the practicalities of antitrust enforcement and recognizes that superfluous restrictions are inherently dangerous.

However, despite the minimalism principle, we believe that judicial suspicion of contracts can be taken too far. We show in the next section how licensing can increase profit legitimately by increasing the efficiency of production. We therefore disagree with commentators who have argued that licensing can never improve efficiency over in-house production. The inevitable corollary to that point of view is that the real purpose of licenses must be to camouflage an illegal cartel, and licenses are therefore suspect (Neal Report, 1969). We know of no evidence for that view.

Of course, some licenses can still be shams. Even commentators who approve of licensing admit that it "substantially increase[s]" the danger that the parties will organize illegal cartels (Bowman, 1973). The *General Electric* rule, which offers immunity for price fixing, would be a particularly handy way for conspirators to implement collusion disguised as legitimate licensing (*Ethyl*, 1940).

Courts and commentators have implicitly invoked minimalism to strike down license restrictions that seem superfluous. For example, *Shapiro* (1979) argues that the rightholder's power to restrict the sale of patented products should expire the first time a product is sold because "(t)he patentee can obtain the full reward of the patent in the first sale; a right to restrict the goods in more remote channels of trade is not a traditional part of the patent grant *nor is it needed in order for the patentee to fully enjoy the monopoly of the patent*" (emphasis supplied).

We do not, however, claim that our version of minimalism completely determines which terms of license should be allowed. Profit neutrality can be implemented by alternative contract terms, for example, output restrictions, price restrictions, and nonlinear royalties. To choose among them, courts will have to invoke principles beyond our model to say which restriction is truly minimal. The traditional suspicion of certain restrictions like price fixing will presumably bulk large in such an analysis.

In the next section, we investigate the problem of licensing a product patent, when the patentholder competes with a licensee. This is the case that the Supreme Court faced in *General Electric*, and also in *Line Material*, in a slightly different circumstance. Fixed fees and per-unit royalties cannot achieve efficient production or profit neutrality when the licensor and licensee compete and when marginal cost is increasing. Perhaps surprisingly, it is the licensor's output that must additionally be constrained, not the licensee's.

3. Licensing the Production of New Products

We start by considering product inventions, such as in *General Electric*. Using the notion of derived reward, we derive the natural meaning of benchmark profits for the purpose of defining profit neutrality and then discuss the terms of license that achieve the benchmark profit. In particular, we show that the price-setting clause in *General Electric* can be justified by profit neutrality, although other terms of license would also serve that purpose.

Since the invention opened a product market that otherwise would not exist, the value of the invention is the social value of the new product, out of which the reward must be derived. Furthermore, the product must be produced efficiently to derive the full value. However, there are many reasons why the patentholder may not be situated to serve the whole market, such as being unable to raise the money for production or distribution facilities. Profit neutrality implies that licensing should mimic efficient in-house production.

We will let $\Gamma(q)$ represent the cost of producing q units of the product in a single plant. We assume that

$$\Gamma(q) = C + \int_0^q \gamma(\hat{q})\mathrm{d}\hat{q}$$

and that the marginal cost of production, γ, is given by a convex, positive, increasing function γ. We assume that, because of the setup cost C for each plant, efficient production requires a finite number of plants. For simplicity, we assume two. Our focus is on how production is distributed between the plants.

We suppose that the inverse demand curve (the willingness to pay for the marginal unit at quantity q) is defined by $p(q) = a - q$, where q is the total supply of all firms.[6] When two plants supply the market with quantities q_1, q_2, the market price will therefore be $p(q_1 + q_2) = a - (q_1 + q_2)$. The total available profit as a function of total output is

$$p(q)q - 2\Gamma\left(\frac{q}{2}\right). \tag{1}$$

The profit-maximizing total supply q^* and resulting price satisfy

$$q^* = \frac{1}{2}\left[a - \gamma\left(\frac{q^*}{2}\right)\right] \tag{2}$$

$$p(q^*) = \frac{1}{2}\left[a + \gamma\left(\frac{q^*}{2}\right)\right], \tag{3}$$

and the resulting benchmark profit is $p(q^*)q^* - 2\Gamma(q^*/2)$.

The benchmark profit can also be achieved by licensing all production to two licensees, using fixed fees and fixed per-unit royalties. (Courts routinely approve fixed fees and royalties.) An explicit derivation of the

---

6 The easiest interpretation is that each agent buys a fixed amount of the good in each period, which we shall understand as one unit. The potential buyers are indexed by their willingness to pay $\theta \in (0, 1)$. If agent θ buys the good at price p, her utility is $\theta - p$. If θ is uniformly distributed on the interval $(0, 1)$, the number of agents for whom $\theta - p > 0$ is $1 - p$. If q units of the good are supplied, the market-clearing price is $1 - q$, as that is the price that provides nonnegative utility to the q buyers with $\theta > 1 - q$ but negative utility to the others.

required license terms can be found in our (2004) working paper, but the argument is easy to see from symmetry. If both firms are charged the same royalty, they face the same "marginal cost" and will produce the same output in equilibrium. The patentholder can control the price by controlling the royalty and can collect profits through the fixed fee. By wielding these two instruments, he can replicate the profit and production that is available if he controls the two production plants himself.[7]

However, we now argue that, if the patentholder operates one production facility and a licensee operates another under license, fixed per-unit royalties and fixed fees cannot achieve the benchmark level of profit. The patentholder will need additional license terms to achieve the benchmark profits.

In licensing the other supplier, the patentholder will need to use a positive per-unit royalty to keep the price up. But that makes the licensee's "effective" marginal cost (the resource cost y plus the royalty) higher than that of the patentholder. Facing higher costs, the licensee will produce less. Hence, the marginal resource cost of the last unit produced by the licensee is less than the marginal cost of the last unit produced by the licensor, and production is inefficient. Resource costs could be saved by decreasing the licensor's production and increasing the licensee's production. Because the arrangement does not achieve productive efficiency, it cannot achieve the benchmark level of profits for the patentholder. This conclusion depends only on the hypothesis that, in equilibrium, the firm with higher "effective" marginal cost produces less. We formalize this argument in Proposition 1 in the Appendix [omitted – ed.], assuming that the patentholder and licensee are Cournot competitors.

The same problem can be stated in strategic terms. Suppose the patentholder and licensee are each producing $q^*/2$ units, as is efficient. Once the license agreement is in place, the patentholder can "exploit" the licensee by unilaterally increasing output. Such an increase reduces the market price and total profit but does not change the royalties and fixed fees paid by the licensee to the licensor. Much of the loss falls on the licensee. Licensors themselves will profit through increased sales and continued royalties, which outweigh their own loss in the market because of price erosion, provided the increase in supply is not too large.

The prospect of such *ex post* opportunism undermines the licensor's *ex ante* profit. The licensee will rationally predict that, after the license is signed, the licensor will supply more than $q^*/2$ units, and the market price will be lower than the profit-maximizing price. The terms that the licensee will accept at the outset will reflect this prediction. As a consequence, licensors cannot charge the fixed fees that they could charge if they could commit to producing only half the monopoly output, $q^*/2$. This is a subtle

---

7 A nuance is that the fixed fees might have to be negative, depending on the size of the setup costs.

point that courts and commentators seem to have overlooked. For example, Bowman (1973) remarks that it "strains credulity" to think that General Electric would adopt a scheme "to restrain its own trade in patented lamps...." In fact, this is exactly what General Electric must do to ensure profit neutrality.

The lesson here is that, to ensure efficient production, the licensor must find a way to restrict his own output rather than that of the licensee. He must find a way to commit against the opportunism described in the previous paragraphs. We now describe three ways to do this:

- Output restrictions: restrict the licensor's output.
- Price setting (as in *General Electric*).
- Nonlinear royalties: allow the royalty rate to decrease with the licensor's supply.

It is also worth noticing what will not work. It will not suffice for licensors to set a fixed price for the licensee without constraining their own price at the same time. We develop this point in Proposition 2 in the Appendix [omitted – ed.].

3.1. Output Restrictions

The easiest way for the licensor to commit against an opportunistic increase in supply is to cap his own output at $q^*/2$, as part of the license. Such a commitment improves the terms of license that the licensee will agree to, as the licensee is then guaranteed that the market price will be the monopoly price. Since the resulting license would be profit neutral with respect to the benchmark, we see nothing wrong with such a commitment. Courts have held that restricting the licensee's output does not pose an antitrust problem (Hovenkamp, Janis, and Lemley, 2004; Weinschel, 2000), but we are unaware of any case where restricting the licensor's output has been challenged.

3.2. Price Setting

The *General Electric* price-fixing exception allows the licensor to state a price for both the licensor and the licensee. The Supreme Court opinion says "the license in effect provided that the Westinghouse Company would follow prices and terms of sales from time to time fixed by the Electric Company and observed by it, and that the Westinghouse Company would, with regard to lamps manufactured by it under the license, adopt and maintain the same conditions of sale as observed by the Electric Company in the distribution of lamps manufactured by it." We therefore assume that the firms make their supply decisions after the royalty and fixed fees have been set, and after the licensor has stated the price.

We argue that the licensor can ensure the monopoly outcome by stating the monopoly price $p(q^*)$ and setting the royalty to be the difference between the monopoly price and the cost of the marginal unit when both firms are producing optimally:

$$\rho = p(q^*) - \gamma\left(\frac{q^*}{2}\right). \tag{4}$$

The fixed fee must be set so that the licensee's profit is zero if both firms produce $q^*/2$. If we can show that neither firm wants to deviate from $q^*/2$, then the licensor gets all the profit and production is efficient.

Consider first the licensee. The licensee cannot benefit by reducing supply below $q^*/2$. Since each of the inframarginal units provides him with revenue (price) higher than the royalty plus marginal cost, reducing supply will cause him to lose net revenue. (Notice that if the price could increase, the licensee would typically want to reduce supply. A reduction would cause the price to increase on all the inframarginal units, whereas the loss on the marginal unit would be zero.) The licensee also cannot benefit by increasing supply above $q^*/2$. If the licensee increases supply, the market will have an excess supply at price $p(q^*)$. If the licensee does not manage to sell his marginal units, then he has wasted the cost of producing them. If he does sell them, he cannot cover costs, since the price is not higher than the royalty plus marginal cost of the incremental units. That is, $p(q^*) - [\rho + \gamma(q)] < p(q^*) - [\rho + \gamma(q^*/2)] = 0$ for $q > (q^*/2)$.

The licensor will also be content to supply $q^*/2$. Keeping the contractual price fixed at $p(q^*)$, reducing supply reduces profit, as $p(q^*) - \gamma(q) > 0$ for $q < (q^*/2)$. Suppose instead that he increases supply above $q^*/2$. As the price is fixed at $p(q^*)$, either the marginal unit crowds out a unit that would otherwise be sold by the licensee or the marginal unit is not sold at all. If not sold, it wastes the costs of production. If it crowds out a unit sold by the licensee, then the licensor loses the royalty ρ on that unit. But using equation (4) and the fact that $\gamma(\cdot)$ is increasing, it follows that $\rho > p(q^*) - \gamma(q)$ for $q > (q^*/2)$; hence, the licensor would rather collect the royalty from the licensee than to crowd out that unit and produce it himself.

This shows that with a royalty that satisfies equation (4) and price fixed at $p(q^*)$, there is an equilibrium with efficient production, even though the licensor competes with the licensee. The licensor can collect all the profit through fixed fees and royalties.

This analysis differs from that of Landes and Posner (2003) who argue that price fixing only serves "to increase the total costs of manufacture, to the detriment of the patentee qua patentee" or Baxter (1966) who argues that price and output restraints are counterproductive because they allow licensees to share in oligopoly profit. Licensors can recover profits by charging fixed fees as well as royalties.

3.3. Nonlinear Royalties

Suppose that, instead of imposing a fixed royalty, the licensor imposes a royalty rate ρ that falls with his own output, in particular, according to equation (5).

$$\rho(q_2) = p(q^*) - \gamma\left(\frac{q^*}{2}\right) - \left(q_2 - \frac{q^*}{2}\right). \tag{5}$$

Then $\rho(q^*/2)$ is the same as the royalty (4), but $\rho'(q_2) = -1$. It is intuitive that the licensor will restrict his output to avoid the fall in the royalty rate, and it is easy to verify that (5) represents the rate of decrease that sustains supply $q_2 = (q^*/2)$.

Of course, this scheme requires that the licensor send a royalty bill to the licensee based on the licensor's own output, which might create an enforcement nightmare for the licensee. The licensor will always want to argue that his supply was lower than it was, and the licensee will want to argue that it was higher.

Nonlinear royalties based on the licensee's supply are common, and at least two courts have said that such agreements do not violate the antitrust laws (*du Pont*, 1953; *Stockham Valves*, 1966). However, in the model presented here, royalties that increase or decrease with the licensee's supply will not lead to profit neutrality because they do not punish the licensor for trying to exploit the licensee once the terms of license are fixed. To punish the licensor for increasing supply beyond that to which he would like to commit, the royalty must vary with the licensor's supply, not the licensee's supply. Baxter (1966) has previously analyzed the role that sliding scale royalties play in partitioning the market between two licensees but did not consider the case where a patentholder/manufacturer is substituted for one of the licensees.

This is a good place to return to our inquiry about minimalism. The point of stipulating royalties that decline with the licensor's output is to soften the competition that the licensor provides to the licensee. It is even more direct to write license terms that restrict the licensor's supply. Many commentators believe, on somewhat slender case law, that U.S. law permits patentholders to impose minimum output levels on their licensees (Hovenkamp, Janis, and Lemley, 2004; Weinschel, 2000), but we know of no cases in which a licensor's commitment to self-restraint has been at issue.

The point we want to emphasize, however, is that the *General Electric* rule satisfies our three principles just as well as output restrictions and nonlinear royalties do. Nevertheless, a court could overrule *General Electric* while retaining profit neutrality and derived reward, by arguing that one type of restriction – say, nonlinear royalties – was somehow more "minimal" than the other two. This extended version of minimalism would go beyond our analysis and presumably be based on a judgment that some restrictions facilitate illegal cartelization more readily than others. To implement it, a court might have to strike some *actual* contract restriction in favor of some *hypothetical* restriction.

4. Licensing the Production of Improved Products

The Supreme Court has also considered cases where the rightholder owns a technology for enhancing a preexisting product. We explore three cases. First, the underlying product may rely on public domain technology, in which case we will assume that it is competitively supplied. The Court considered such a case in *Ethyl Gasoline*, where the rightholder attempted to control the price of high-performance gasoline made with its patented additive. The Court struck down this license, arguing that the patentholder's right to control the additive's price did not extend to products made from it. Second, the enhancement may improve an underlying patented technology without infringing it. This may happen, for example, because a new entrant successfully invents around the original invention. Finally, the patented enhancement may infringe the underlying patented technology so that neither rightholder can practice the enhancement without the other's permission. The Court considered such "blocking patents" in *Line Material*, in which patents on the unimproved product (an electrical fuse) and its improvement prevented each firm from marketing the improved fuse without a license from the other. Once again, the Court struck down a price-fixing license, arguing that the *General Electric* rule should be limited to new products and not extend to enhancements to existing ones.

We will assume in what follows that each consumer's willingness to pay for the improved product is larger than for the original product by amount Δ. As before, we will suppose that the demand for the underlying good, say, unimproved gasoline, is given by $1 - p$, where p is the price, and that the inverse demand curve is therefore given by $p(q) = 1 - q$. We assume that the demand for improved gasoline at price p is $1 + \Delta - p$, and the inverse demand curve becomes $p(q; \Delta) = 1 + \Delta - q$. To be as clear as possible, we will assume that the production costs for the two products are the same.

Profit neutrality holds that innovators should not be penalized for not being able to work the patent efficiently themselves. Just as for the case of product patents, the patentholder should be able to license for efficient production. However, where the new product enters as an improvement to an existing, patented product, the question arises whether licensing can be to the original patentholder. Licensing to the rival raises the specter of collusion.

Below we show that collusion is less a threat than it seems. We also use our principles to explain why licensing of blocking patents should be more permissive than licensing of noninfringing patents.

4.1. Patented Improvements to Unpatented Goods

If a patentholder is not liquidity constrained, he can supply the whole market with the improved product. Because of potential competition with the unimproved product, the patentee's price cannot exceed the (potential or actual) price of the unimproved product by more than Δ. However, if the potential competitors already own production plants, it is more efficient to license production to the potential competitors. Under the profit-neutrality principle, the patentholder should be able to license at a per-unit royalty of no more than Δ, and in fact, this outcome will be disciplined by the market. Minimalism holds that price fixing should not be permitted if this profit opportunity can be exploited with royalties alone. In *Ethyl Gasoline*, the Court struck down additional terms, because they believed the additional terms supported a sham license and therefore violated the derived-reward principle.

We now argue that a constant per-unit royalty is, in fact, sufficient to achieve the patentholder's proper, profit-neutral reward.

We assume that the underlying good is competitively supplied, that the resource cost of producing the enhancement is zero, and that the minimum average cost of producing the improved or unimproved product (which is equal to the marginal cost at the efficient scale of production) is $c < 1$. In a competitive market, the cost of the improved product will then be $p = c + \rho$ if ρ is the royalty. Assuming that the licensor charges the entire value as royalty, $\rho = \Delta$, the price of the product will go up by Δ, so that sales of the improved product are the same as without the improvement. During the life of the patent, it is the patentholder rather than the user who collects the social value. This is consistent with the derived-reward and profit-neutrality principles.

If the improvement is large, $\Delta > 1 - c$, and the improver charges the monopoly price for the improved product, then competitive suppliers of the unimproved product will drop out of the market. Despite the monopoly price, consumers are better off than without the innovation. The price charged by the monopolist improver is nevertheless smaller than the value Δ created for them, and the outcome is therefore consistent with the derived-reward and profit-neutrality principles.[8] For small improvements, $\Delta < 1 - c$, the proprietor will have to license the competitive suppliers because they will not disappear. The licensor's best option is to charge a royalty equal to the full value of the additive, $\rho = \Delta$. No distributor would pay a larger royalty for the additive, and a smaller royalty yields less profit for the patentholder.

---

8 The monopoly price of the improved product is larger than the competitive price of the unimproved product by $(1/2)(1 + \Delta + c) - c$, which is smaller than Δ when $\Delta > 1 - c$. Consumers prefer the improved product at the monopoly price to the unimproved product at the competitive price.

We conclude that in the case of patented enhancements to competitively supplied goods, and also in the case of cost reductions, which can be analyzed in the same way as product enhancements, royalties are a rich enough licensing instrument to collect profit from the value created. As long as the competitive suppliers are free to sell unimproved gasoline, the royalty will only be the value of the enhancement, Δ, and the price of improved product cannot be larger than $c + \Delta$.[9]

4.2. Noninfringing Improvements to Patented Goods

We now assume that both goods are patented, but that the improved good does not infringe the prior patent. Because the products are noninfringing, two firms have the right to be in the market. We would expect, and Congress apparently intended, that there would be rivalry between the two firms. Assuming that both firms operate without liquidity constraints and can build as many plants as necessary, this is the profit-neutral benchmark. Even if the improver ends up supplying the whole market efficiently in two or more plants, potential competition from the prior patentholders will constrain his supply.

However, the total social surplus is greater if both firms produce the improved product, and especially if they do so efficiently. Licensing can increase the total social surplus available, and by the derived-reward principle, the improver should be allowed to collect part of the increase as profit. The question is whether this social improvement can be achieved through licensing without creating a collusive situation in which the licensor collects more than the social surplus contributed by the invention. The essence of the discussion below is that, provided the original patentholder cannot commit against supplying the unimproved product, potential competition will limit the price of the improved product and also limit the improver's reward. However, there is also a limit to this good news. By allowing some productive inefficiency, the firms can reduce the attractiveness of the licensee introducing the unimproved product, and can thus support a higher price.

We begin by considering what happens in the profit-neutral benchmark where the firms compete without a license. Let p^u be the price of the unimproved good, and let p^e be the price of the improved good. If both

---

9 Of course the patentholder may try to support a cartel with "sham licensing" that uses hidden understandings to achieve a result beyond the plain text of the license. This could be done, for example, by combining a license that sets royalties higher than Δ with an unwritten understanding that the parties will not produce unimproved gasoline. Historically, courts have shown no hesitancy in finding that facially acceptable licenses were shams designed to cloak such a cartel. In any case, such an arrangement is difficult to sustain if there is free entry in the market for unimproved gasoline.

goods are supplied, the equilibrium price of the inferior good must be smaller by the value of the improvement Δ, that is,

$$p^u = p^e - \Delta. \tag{6}$$

Thus, if both goods are supplied, it will hold that

$$p^e = (1 + \Delta) - (q_1 + q_2) \tag{7}$$

$$p^u = 1 - (q_1 + q_2), \tag{8}$$

where q_1 is firm 1's supply of the unimproved good, and q_2 is firm 2's supply of the improved good. Using these prices, the profit functions of firms 1 and 2 without licensing are given by

$$q_1[1 - (q_1 + q_2)] - \Gamma(q_1) \tag{9}$$

$$q_2[(1 + \Delta) - (q_1 + q_2)] - \Gamma(q_2). \tag{10}$$

To characterize this equilibrium, let $q^D(\Delta)$ be the duopoly supply when both firms supply the improved good (defined for each Δ). Then, in equilibrium, firm 1's supply will be greater than $q^D(0)$, and firm 2's supply will be less than $q^D(\Delta)$.[10]

This outcome is inefficient in two senses that could be remedied by licensing. It is inefficient in the sense that some consumers buy the unimproved good, and it is also productively inefficient when marginal cost is increasing, since $q_1 < q_2$.

Consider first a license that specifies a constant royalty ρ and perhaps fixed fees. The royalty must satisfy $\rho = \Delta$. Firm 1 would not accept a greater royalty (it would supply the unimproved good instead), and firm 2 would not offer a smaller royalty, as a smaller royalty would result in a lower market price and less total profit. (We assume here that the license is designed to maximize joint profit, as the profit can be divided by fixed fees.[11]) It is because the royalty is constrained to satisfy $\rho \leq \Delta$ that licensing cannot cartelize the market.

With licensing, the licensee's profit function is given by (11), and q_1 represents a supply of improved product:

$$q_1[(1 + \Delta) - (q_1 + q_2) - \rho] - \Gamma(q_1). \tag{11}$$

---

10 We are implicitly assuming here that only one plant produces each good. More plants would introduce more fixed costs, and we are implicitly assuming it is not worth it. The duopoly supply of firm 2 satisfies $q_2 = (1/2)[1 + \Delta - q_1 - \gamma(q_2)]$, and the duopoly supply of firm 1 satisfies $q_1 = (1/2)[1 - q_2 - \gamma(q_1)]$. If both firms supplied the improved good, the duopoly supply would be $q^D(\Delta) = (1/3)[1 + \Delta - \gamma[q^D(\Delta)]]$ for each Δ including $\Delta = 0$.

11 As we want to focus on whether the royalty can be used for collusion, we ignore the subtlety that there may be a constraint on fixed fees, namely, to be positive. Embedded in the assumption that the licensor cares only about total profit is the notion that fixed fees can be positive or negative, as necessary to divide the profit to reflect bargaining positions.

Because equations (9) and (11) coincide when $\rho = \Delta$, both firms have the same profit functions with and without licensing, and hence the same equilibrium supplies (q_1, q_2). With licensing, q_1 represents the improved good, which eliminates the inefficient consumption of the unimproved good, but does not eliminate productive inefficiency, as the royalty elevates the licensee's "effective" marginal cost (including the royalty) above that of the licensor.

We now ask whether price or quantity restrictions can solve the problem of productive inefficiency. Are there licensing instruments that allow the firms to take advantage of the original patentholder's production facility while ensuring that all consumers are served with the better product and also preserving rivalry and productive efficiency?

The instruments we have previously considered are price-fixing and quantity restrictions. Although these seem like natural instruments for collusion, we argue in Propositions 3 and 4 in the Appendix [omitted – ed.] that, for relatively small improvements, potential competition will limit the price of the improved product, regardless of the licensing terms. For large improvements, the improved product drives out the unimproved product, even with monopoly pricing and no licensing.

When the improvement is relatively small, the profit-neutral benchmark involves productive inefficiency. One might have imagined that *General Electric* style price fixing could once again be used to support efficient production. However, Proposition 3 tells us that price fixing cannot lead to smaller supply than the duopoly output and thus cannot improve on a license that only has fixed fees. This is because the fixed-price license fixes the price of the licensor as well as the licensee and thus encourages the licensee to undermine the price by also supplying the unimproved product. As that type of price-fixing clause will not accomplish the desired goal, the Court is justified in striking it down on the basis of minimalism.

Quantity constraints may be a better option, but for small improvements, Proposition 4 tells us that the price is still kept in check by the threat of entry. If the quantities supported by the license are efficient (equal), they cannot be lower than those supplied by a duopoly where both firms supply the unimproved product. But, in any case, the profit-maximizing license will not support efficient production. Proposition 5 says that, starting from a situation of efficient production, total profit can be increased by reducing the licensor's own output and increasing that of the licensee, so that the licensee has less incentive to supply the unimproved product in parallel.

We have focused on licenses that fix both the licensee's and licensor's price because that is the type of license considered in *General Electric*. However, in Proposition 6 and Example 1 in the Appendix, [omitted – ed.] we consider licenses that fix only the price of the licensee. Such a license can only support efficient production for relatively large improvements and with total supply that is bounded below, again, by duopoly supply.

However, the firms can again increase profit by introducing an inefficiency of a different kind. Namely, they can implement a kind of price discrimination by forcing the licensee to sell at a high price, whereas the licensor sells at a low price.[12]

The thrust of these arguments is that when the patented products are noninfringing, and where one product clearly dominates its predecessor, it is difficult to mediate the conflict between ensuring rivalry and supporting efficiency. To ensure rivalry, the patents should not be consolidated in the hands of one owner with exclusive licensing, and the owner of the original patent should not be allowed to renounce his right to produce the original product. To ensure efficiency, both firms should produce the better product, which requires licensing. But then the firms have an incentive to favor the owner of the original patent in the licensing agreement (assuming that they can divide total profit by fixed fees), to reduce his temptation to introduce the unimproved product in parallel. This may lead to productive inefficiency.

4.3. Blocking Patents

We continue with the same model, but now assume that the improved product infringes the patent on the original product so that the patent-holders have blocking patents. Unlike the cases discussed above, licensing cannot be avoided if the improved product is to come to market. With or without liquidity constraints, the improver's market outcome without licensing is to earn zero profit. In light of this apparent mandate for licensing, courts have struggled for the past sixty years to set bounds on what types of licenses are allowable. In general, the question is whether the parties should share a full monopoly reward.

In *Line Material* (1948), the U.S. Supreme Court resisted such a solution, in particular, holding that price fixing should not be extended from the circumstances of *General Electric* to blocking patents, because that would reduce "[t]he stimulus to seek competitive [i.e., noninfringing] inventions." Although the Court's discussion is elliptical, the Court seems to assume that inventors have a choice between creating an infringing or noninfringing improvement; that noninfringing improvements are to be encouraged because they lead to duopoly competition; and that patent law ought not to reward an innovator for making a strategic choice to create an infringing improvement when a noninfringing improvement is possible. However, the Court's assumption that the inventor faces a strategic choice

---

12 When the firms sell at different prices, the outcome in the market depends on which consumers end up in the favored position of buying at the lower price. The results about price fixing depend on a "rationing rule" that describes our assumption about this. Different rationing rules would give different outcomes in the market, and none is entirely defensible.

whether to infringe is unrealistic if the underlying patent is broad. If broad, infringement is inevitable.

In our discussion of noninfringing improvements above, we only considered one-way royalties because there is no justification under the derived-reward principle for letting the first innovator profit from the incremental value of the improvement. We showed that one-way royalties, and one-way licenses more generally, will not lead to monopoly pricing of the improved product, because of the first patentholder's ability to supply the unimproved product in parallel.

In contrast, bringing an infringing improvement to market requires two-way licensing, which introduces the possibility of supporting the monopoly price. Suppose, for example, that the cross license on the improved good provides for cross royalties (ρ_1, ρ_2), with firm 2 paying a royalty ρ_2 and firm 1 paying a royalty ρ_1, each to the other firm. Higher royalties will lead to a higher market price for the improved good. In fact, we show in Proposition 7 that if the marginal cost function can be written $\gamma(q) = bq$, the total market supply depends only on the sum of the royalties, $\rho_1 + \rho_2$, and is an increasing function of $\rho_1 + \rho_2$. If the royalties can satisfy equation (12) without also calling forth a supply of the improved product, the cross license will support the monopoly price

$$\rho_1 + \rho_2 = \frac{2}{4+b}(1+\Delta). \tag{12}$$

Thus, cross licensing with cross royalties can undermine the Line Material agenda of preserving competition.

However, the royalties must also satisfy (13), as otherwise the first patentholder would supply the unimproved product instead.

$$\rho_1 \leq \Delta. \tag{13}$$

But Proposition 7 shows that if $\rho_1 < \rho_2$, firm 1 will choose a larger supply than firm 2, and production will be inefficient. If it is impossible to satisfy equations (12) and (13) together with $\rho_1 = \rho_2$, there is a conflict between productive efficiency and supporting the monopoly price. Licensing to mitigate the productive inefficiency will lead to lower royalties and a lower price than the monopoly price. Thus, the constraint (13) creates price benefits for users that are similar to those created by direct competition between the firms, even though the constraint is due to *potential* competition from the unimproved product. Moreover, the downward pressure on price is present even if the firms use quantity constraints or price fixing, provided they do not use a covenant against the manufacture and sale of the unimproved good. Without such a covenant, two-way price fixing will not improve the firms' joint profit, by Proposition 3. According to our minimalism principle, the *Line Material* Court was therefore justified in striking it down. It serves no legitimate purpose that is unattainable by other means, and might disguise a sham.

In *Line Material*, the Court does not address the possibility that it is impossible for an improver to invent around the underlying patent, for example, because the underlying patent is very broad. In that case, infringement is inevitable rather than strategic. We adopt the conceit that, as a matter of patent law, the prior patent is that broad (infringement is inevitable) only if there is no alternative path to the improved product. The value of the improvement should then be counted as part of the social value provided by the first innovator (Scotchmer, 1991). Because he created the option on the improved product, the first inventor is as responsible for the improved product as the improver. Using the derived-reward principle, the first inventor should be allowed to collect any fraction of the social value embodied in the combined innovations, and the improver should be allowed to collect any fraction of the incremental social value of the improvement. Monopoly pricing of the improved product is no more offensive to competition policy than if a single inventor had developed the enhanced product in the first instance without any intermediate step.

The problem then becomes how to support the monopoly price. Because neither firm can market the improved product without a license, the problem should be easier than when the products are noninfringing. However, providing for efficient production is harder than one might think. Suppose, for example, that one patentholder sells his patent to the other patentholder. (This would be presumably be prohibited by the *Line Material* Court, under their assumption that infringement is strategic rather than inevitable.) The owner of both patents is then a monopolist, and the improved product has a market position similar to the patented product analyzed in section 3. We uncovered three methods to ensure productive efficiency: by fixing the price of both firms, by using quantity constraints, or by imposing a nonlinear royalty.

These methods only work, however, if the unimproved product can be kept off the market. Propositions 3 and 4 show that it is difficult to support the monopoly price if one of the parties has the option to revert to the unimproved product.[13] To avoid that, the license could prohibit sales of the unimproved good explicitly. Such a provision would be offensive to competition policy in the case of noninfringing patents, but is less offensive here, because of our argument that licensing should support the monopoly profit. Nevertheless, it would be better to achieve the result (monoply pricing and efficient production) with more traditional instruments. The problem, as we have seen, is that cross licensing with cross royalties can only support the monopoly price at the cost of productive efficiency.

---

13 To make this story even more complicated, if users have different willingness to pay for the quality improvement, as in the case considered by O'Donoghue, Scotchmer, and Thisse (1998), then the monopolist might want to supply both products as a means of price discrimination.

5. Possible *Per Se* Rules

Antitrust law, famously, requires courts to analyze some practices de novo ("rule of reason") while allowing courts to condemn others using short-hand rules of thumb ("per se rules"). Deciding which rules should govern in any particular situation is subtle. With perfect judicial reasoning, rule of reason would always be preferable to per se rules. The great advantage of per se rules is that they save courts the trouble of re-capitulating economic analysis for each case. Over the past seventy-five years, courts and commentators have reached an impressive degree of unanimity on many questions – but only at the cost of innumerable missteps and misconceptions along the way. Codifying this learning in clear, per se rules, allows judges and lawyers who are new to the subject – always the great majority – to avoid old errors and misunderstandings.

The dichotomy between rule of reason and per se rules is both real and useful. However, it is easily overstated. As Judge Bork remarked almost forty years ago, "The current shibboleth of per se illegality in existing law conveys a sense of certainty, even of automaticity, which is delusive ... Alongside cases announcing a sweeping per se formulation of the law there has always existed a line of cases refusing to apply it" (Bork, 1965).[14] Commentators attempting to disentangle patent and antitrust law have traditionally recognized this flexibility by simultaneously proposing per se rules and recognizing the evidentiary showing that would be needed to rebut them (Adelman and Juenger, 1975; Baxter, 1966; Landes and Posner, 2003). We adopt this strategy in what follows.

This section suggests several possible per se rules that follow from the three principles, discusses some of their advantages and disadvantages, and points out which ones are firmly established in law and practice. Where the presumption in favor of these rules can be rebutted, we think the rules that replace them should use the three principles as a guide.

1. Patent licenses based on a combination of fixed fees and constant per-unit royalties should be presumed lawful.
2. In a market where the patentholder does not compete with potential licensees, licenses that (a) fix product prices for the licensee and licensor, (b) require the licensee or licensor to observe quantity limits, or (c) reduce the licensee's per-unit royalties as licensor output increases should be presumed lawful.
3. In a market with noninfringing patents, combining ownership of the patents, or writing a covenant to prohibit the sale of one of the patented products, should be presumed unlawful.

---

14 The point remains equally valid today: "In fact, the per se rule is not so tightly prohibitive and the rule of reason not so hospitable to a claim as is often thought" (Areeda and Hovencamp, 2003).

4. In a market with a patented product where noninfringing entry with another patented product is possible, a covenant to restrict the sale of either product should be deemed unlawful.
5. In a market with a patented product where noninfringing entry is impossible, a covenant to restrict sale of the patented product should be deemed lawful.

Rule 2, following the analysis in section 3, endorses three equivalent tools for achieving the patentholder's profit-neutral reward. Rule 2(a) (price fixing) is the *General Electric* rule. Rules 4 and 5 address the case where an improver enters the market, resulting in blocking patents, as otherwise there is little reason to restrict sale of the patented product. Rule 4 says that the firms with blocking patents should not be allowed to avoid potential competition when it would have been possible to invent around the first patent. This implements the *Line Material* Court's suggestion that inventors not receive a greater reward for creating inventions that infringe than for creating ones that do not infringe. Rule 5 says that, where inventing around is impossible, it is consistent with our principles to let the firms avoid potential competition to achieve the monopoly outcome. Rule 5 limits *Line Material* to the case where inventing around is possible.

These rules would reduce but not eliminate uncertainty for licensors. First, they establish presumptions, as do most per se rules created by courts (Areeda and Hovenkamp, 2003) and commentators (Adelman and Juenger, 1975; Baxter, 1966; Kaplow, 1984), but presumptions can be challenged. Judicial suspiciousness of licensing has, in fact, fluctuated. In an earlier era, when licensing was seen as an inferior way to exploit a patent, judges were always on the lookout for sham licensing (Adelman and Juenger, 1975; Baxter, 1966). The modern view, reflected here, is less suspicious and operates from a presumption that licenses are pro-competitive in the absence of evidence that royalties exceed the value of the defendant's invention or other departures from our principles that clearly point to collusion.

Second, some of our conclusions follow from a standard, but nevertheless specific, economic model about how licensors and licensees behave – they compete on quantity. However, the principles and intuition are more robust than that model. Productive inefficiency arises with one-way royalties because the licensor perceives a lower marginal cost of production than the licensee and will produce too much relative to the licensee. It is hard to see how any form of competition between the licensor and the licensee would change this conclusion as long as marginal cost is increasing. In any case, per se rules can be rebutted with new and convincing arguments. A successful rebuttal would have to include (1) a model where the effect vanishes and (2) evidence that the model is more appropriate to the facts than the very standard model discussed in this article.

Third, more complicated economic environments might call for different rules. For example, when firms cannot observe cost or demand conditions, it is difficult to use licensing for efficiency, and when courts are burdened by the same lack of information, they may find it difficult to detect shams (Adelman and Juenger, 1975; Landes and Posner, 2003). At the same time, courts' inability to find all the relevant facts is a traditional justification for having per se rules in the first place (Areeda and Hoven-kamp, 2003). These competing arguments cannot be evaluated without evidence and economic modeling, and we propose our three principles as an evaluative lens.

Fourth, our focus on productive efficiency does not exhaust the licensing landscape. Some commentators argue that licensing undermines the incentive to challenge a bad patent, as it creates collusion between otherwise competitors (Adelman and Juenger, 1975; Hovenkamp, Janis, and Lemley, 2004; Landes and Posner, 2003; Shapiro, 2003). This argument is not actually about the patent/antitrust boundary, as it goes to the proper functioning of the patent system itself. Scholars also argue that cross licensing should be permitted in cases where it is needed to save transaction costs or suppress wasteful patent races (Landes and Posner, 2003). However, the firms' private incentive to avoid a patent race does not generally accord with what is socially efficient (Scotchmer, 2004, chapter 6).

Fifth, although the minimalism principle would allow courts to strike down unnecessary restrictions in licenses, it says nothing about whether some other, completely different, bundle of restrictions would impose even fewer burdens on the economy. It is difficult for judges to compare licensing terms against alternatives not before the court (Kaplow, 1984).

6. Rule of Reason

The previous section suggested how our principles could be embodied in per se rules. The first and third rules are mostly uncontroversial. The second acknowledges that, if patentholders are liquidity constrained, they may need terms of license beyond a constant per-unit royalty to collect their just reward. The fourth extends the implicit agenda of *Line Material* by preserving some measure of competitive pressure where an infringing improver, by hypothesis, could have chosen a noninfringing improvement. The fifth embodies the idea that licensing privileges should be more liberal if the underlying patent is broad enough to be uncircumventable.

Our principles could alternatively be understood as considerations in a rule-of-reason analysis. However, rule of reason is seldom based on a complete, well-articulated principle.[15] The most ambitious attempt to

---

15 For example, the U.S. Department of Justice and Federal Trade Commission says that the benefits of allowing the licensor "to exploit its [intellectual] property as efficiently and effectively as possible" must outweigh the harm to competition (1995 *Antitrust Guidelines*). The problem with this approach is that it fails to specify how courts should balance *ex post* deadweight loss against *ex ante* incentives to innovate.

enunciate principles is due to Kaplow (1984). He argues that Congress implicitly encoded its judgment about the optimal balance of *ex ante* and *ex post* efficiency when it designed the patent statute. A licensing restriction should be acceptable to the court if it generates a profit-to-deadweight-loss ratio larger than that which Congress implicitly accepted in defining, for example, breadth or patent life. This procedure saves the court from having to decide how much reward an innovator should receive, at least directly. The optimal reward is implicitly established in the profit-to-deadweight-loss ratio.[16]

Kaplow concedes that any practical application of the ratio test is "quite complex." Given that the required information "will not generally be available," court decisions "must inevitably be speculative."[17] He concludes that "any careful attempt to resolve patent-antitrust issues will be far more complex than has previously been realized" and that fact reveals the "insufficiency of prior formulations by courts and commentators." Scholars in the past twenty years have done little to change this assessment.

Any rule-of-reason approach directed at maximizing an aggregate measure of consumer welfare will face the same practical and theoretical difficulties identified by Kaplow. Given Kaplow's pessimistic forecast as to whether the ratio test can be implemented, the more likely approach seems that implied by the 1995 *Antitrust Guidelines*, requiring judges to weigh de novo the value of rewards (*ex ante* efficiency) against the value of competition (*ex post* efficiency) in each case. But this opens up a host of inquiries. Should the court naively determine the necessary reward based on the actual costs of the patentholder? Should the factual inquiry about costs instead consider that some other inventor could have achieved the patent more cheaply and that too much reward only encourages waste? Should the inquiry consider that research is risky and that discoverers would only have invested if they expected a super-reward for success? Given that the research endeavor was eventually successful, what evidence could be adduced to show that it might not have been and with what probability?

The ways that such an inquiry can go astray are almost endless, as noted by other commentators. First, the factual inquiry is so complex as to be unavoidably speculative and may defer to ideological prejudice. Baxter (1966) argues that the weighing of proper rewards is "peculiarly

16 The ratio test has been revived by authors studying patent breadth; see chapter 4 of Scotchmer (2004) for a summary.
17 Kaplow admits that in practice it is probably impossible to estimate Congress's subjective cost/benefit judgment by analyzing the patent statutes. He therefore proposes a less ambitious use of his ratio called cost-effectiveness. This procedure asks judges to reshuffle the law by making currently permitted licenses with low ratios illegal in exchange for legalizing currently prohibited practices with high ratios. Kaplow concedes, however, that even this more modest project may not be possible given current uncertainty about the "economic effects of various restrictive practices."

appropriate" to the political branches of government.[18] Of course, one can argue that judges' opinions do not matter provided that Congress can easily correct them. In practice, most judicial attempts to weigh *ex ante* and *ex post* efficiency will never be reviewed, much less corrected.

Second, any such inquiry requires specialized knowledge and is likely to be lengthy and complex. Landes and Posner (2003) argue that the *ex ante/ ex post* tradeoff "may well be beyond the capacity of the courts." Kaplow (1984) is more optimistic, observing that the required analysis "is probably more developed at both the theoretical and empirical levels than is the analysis of a vast array of other issues that the courts regularly confront."

Third, the inquiry will almost always depend on parties and evidence not before the court. Except when the government is a party or citizens file amicus briefs, the interests of third parties will almost always be under-represented. However, there is reason to suspect that many patent agreements derive their value "precisely because [they] are injurious to third persons" (Baxter, 1966). The temptation to impose costs on third parties – who are seldom in a position to know, let alone complain – may be overwhelming.

Fourth, permitting judges to set the balance each time they decide a case will inevitably make patent rewards less certain (Adelman and Juenger, 1975; Bork, 1978). Inventors will demand a larger reward – with greater attendant deadweight loss – for any given level of inventive effort (Gifford, 2002).

Fifth, courts almost always examine controversies *ex post*, whereas legislatures and executive agencies tend to make policy *ex ante*. As the particular innovation before the court cannot be uninvented, there may be a built-in bias toward addressing antitrust issues at the expense of innovation. More broadly, judges may conclude that their judgment in a single case cannot possibly affect innovation in the broader society. Nevertheless, the aggregate effect of court decisions will likely be substantial

7. Conclusion

Subsequent case law has made the *General Electric* price-fixing exception quite narrow. Critics have therefore argued that the price-fixing exception is a discredited "vestige." We disagree. Based on the analysis above, a narrow price-fixing exception is consistent with the three principles of derived reward, profit neutrality, and minimalism where marginal cost of production is increasing.

---

18 Balancing innovation against *ex post* deadweight loss also requires normative judgments about intergenerational transfers. Judges have no objective standards for deciding "whether, in any given case, it would be desirable to sacrifice more or less consumer satisfaction of other wants by devoting more or fewer resources to the promotion of innovation" (Bork, 1965).

Our analysis also sheds light on *Line Material*. We interpret the *Line Material* agenda as an attempt to preserve competition between infringing patentholders when the infringement is a strategic choice, i.e., when a noninfringing alternative would have been possible. The strategic choice itself should not be rewarded. Competition can be preserved by disallowing covenants that take the unimproved product off the market. Without such a covenant, *General Electric* style price fixing is not a very attractive tool, so the Court is justified in suspecting an illegitimate purpose.

Under our derived-reward principle, it is justifiable to suppress the prior product and to avoid competition between the patentholders if the prior product is a necessary foundation for the improved product. The improvement implements an option created by the prior product, and its social value can be counted as part of the social value created by the prior patentholder. In that case, we assume that the patents are inevitably blocking. Here, we would limit *Line Material* by allowing the parties to suppress the underlying invention and to earn a full monopoly reward on the improved product. Price fixing can then be justified in the same way as in *General Electric*, namely, to support productive efficiency. Nonlinear royalties and quantity constraints would be acceptable for the same purpose.

Our analysis based on the three principles is more favorable to per se rules than is currently the fashion. The alternative, rule of reason, must be applied with some well-articulated objective in mind. One problem is that there is no consensus on the right objective, and another is that the main proposals are hard to implement on the basis of facts likely to be before a court. Consequently, rule of reason gives scope for unpredictability in outcomes, which creates uncertainty for patentholders and reduces Congress's control over patent incentives. Uncertainty can chill patentholders' willingness to write creative license terms, even when justified, and consequently can chill their ability to exploit patented knowledge. On the positive side, rule of reason lets judges tailor rewards to individual circumstances. However, the required inquiry is so inherently speculative that flexibility may not lead to any net improvement.

We do not suggest that our three principles will give guidance in every licensing situation. But where they apply, such as in the core patent/ antitrust cases of the twentieth century that we have discussed, they bound the inquiry by economic considerations of efficiency. Courts may occasionally have stumbled over the economics, but their approach to licensing, which we interpret to be based on our three principles, seems sound.

References

Adelman, Martin J., and Friedrich K. Juenger. 1975. "Patent-Antitrust: Patent Dynamics and Field-of-Use Licensing," 50 *New York University Law Review* 273–308.

American Bar Association Section of Antitrust Law. 2002. *The Federal Antitrust Guidelines for the Licensing of Intellectual Property: Origins and Applications*, 2nd ed. Chicago: ABA Publishing.

Areeda, Phillip E., and Herbert Hovenkamp. 2003. *Antitrust Law: An Analysis of Antitrust Principles and Their Application*. New York: Aspen Publishers.

Baxter, William. 1966. "Legal Restrictions on Exploitation of the Patent Monopoly: An Economic Analysis," 76 *Yale Law Journal* 267–370.

Bork, Robert H. 1965. "The Rule of Reason and the Per Se Concept: Price Fixing and Market Division," 74 *Yale Law Journal* 775–847.

———. 1978. *The Antitrust Paradox: A Policy at War With Itself*. New York: Basic Books.

Bowman, William S. 1973. *Patent and Antitrust Law: A Legal and Economic Appraisal*. Chicago: University of Chicago Press.

Chisum, Donald S. 2003. *Chisum on Patents: A Treatise on the Law of Patentability, Validity and Infringement*. Newark, NJ, and San Francisco: Matthew Bender & Co.

Furth, Helmut F. 1958. "Price-Restrictive Patent Licenses Under the Sherman Act," 71 *Harvard Law Review* 814–842.

Gifford, Daniel J. 2002. "The Antitrust/Intellectual Property Interface: An Emerging Solution to an Intractable Problem," 31 *Hofstra Law Review* 398–418.

Hovenkamp, Herbert, Mark D. Janis, and Mark A. Lemley. 2004. *IP and Antitrust: An Analysis of Antitrust Principles Applied to Intellectual Property Law*. New York: Aspen Publishers.

Kaplow, Lewis. 1984. "The Patent-Antitrust Intersection: A Reappraisal," 97 *Harvard Law Review* 1813–912.

Landes, William M., and Richard A. Posner. 2003. *The Economic Structure of Intellectual Property Law*. Cambridge, MA: Belknap Press of Harvard University Press.

O'Donoghue, Ted, Suzanne Scotchmer, and Jacques Thisse. 1998. "Patent Breadth, Patent Life and the Pace of Technological Progress," 7 *Journal of Economics and Management Strategy* 1–32.

Patterson, Mark R. 2002. "When is Property Intellectual: The Leveraging Problem," 73 *Southern California Law Review* 1133–60.

Rey, Patrick, and Jean Tirole. 2006. "A Primer on Foreclosure." In M. Armstrong and R. Porter, eds., *Handbook of Industrial Organization* III. Amsterdam: Elsevier (forthcoming).

Schlicher, John W. 2000. *Patent Law: Legal and Economic Principles*. Eagan, MN: Thomson/West.

Scotchmer, Suzanne. 1991. "Standing on the Shoulders of Giants: Cumulative Research and the Patent Law," 5 *Journal of Economic Perspectives* 29–41.

———. 2004. *Innovation and Incentives*. Cambridge, MA: MIT Press.

Shapiro, Carl. 2003. "Antitrust Limits to Patent Settlements," 34 *RAND Journal of Economics* 391–411.
Weinschel, Alan J. 2000. *Antitrust-Intellectual Property Handbook*. Little Falls, NJ: Glasser LegalWorks.

Case and Statutory References

Arthur J. Schmitt Foundation v. Stockham Valves and Fittings, Inc., 292 F. Supp. 893 (N.D. Ala. 1966).
California Dental Assn. v. FTC, 526 U.S. 756 (1999).
Carborundum Co. v. Molten Metal Equip. Innovations, Inc., 72 F.3d 872 (Fed. Cir. 1995).
Ethyl Gasoline Corp. v. U.S., 309 U.S. 436 (1940).
General Talking Pictures Corp. v. Western Electric Co., 305 U.S. 124 (1938).
Hensley Equip. Co., Inc. v. Esco Corp., 383 F.2d 252 (5th Cir. 1967).
Interstate Circuit v. U.S., 306 U.S. 208 (1939).
Morton Salt v. G.S. Suppiger Co., 314 U.S. 488 (1942).
Neal Report (White House Task Force Report on Antitrust Policy), *Antitrust & Trade Regulation Reports* 411 (Pt. 2) (1969).
Royal Industries v. St. Regis Paper Co., 420 F.2d 449 (9th Cir. 1969).
Shapiro v. General Motors Corp., 472 F. Supp. 636 (D. Md. 1979).
Statute of Monopolies, 21 Jam. I, c.3 (1623)(Eng.).
U.S. v. E.I. du Pont De Nemours & Co., 118 F. Supp. 41 (D. Del. 1953).
U.S. v. General Electric Co., 272 U.S. 476 (1926).
U.S. v. Line Material Co., 333 US 287 (1948).

PART IV

CLUB THEORY

CHAPTER 23

Joseph Farrell and Suzanne Scotchmer,
"Partnerships" (1988)
and
Bryan Ellickson, Birgit Grodal, Suzanne
Scotchmer, and William R. Zame, "Clubs
and the Market" (1999)

INTRODUCTION   ROBERT M. ANDERSON
AND CHRIS SHANNON

What determines the features of organizations in an economy, and what
role does competition play in shaping incentives and institutional design?
These broad questions were central themes throughout Suzanne Scotchmer's work. The power and scope of her work on these questions comes
from the wide interpretation of "organization" it encompasses, including
firms, contracts, mechanisms, partnerships, local public goods, and games.

Much of Scotchmer's work on this theme fits under the rubric of club
theory, and constitutes major advances in this field. In this essay we give
an overview of some of the ideas and challenges in this theory, and
illustrate how Scotchmer's work, particularly in the papers that follow,
engages these themes and has overcome some of these major challenges.
We do not attempt a survey of the club's literature, which is vast. We focus
instead on highlighting some of Scotchmer's work in this area, and provide
some context for the papers that follow. For more background on the
literature, see Scotchmer (2002, 2008) and references therein.

In club theory, "club" stands for a group of agents engaged in a joint activity
and who might care about each other's characteristics. As Scotchmer (2008)
notes, the term "club" is perhaps unfortunate, with its frivolous connota-
tions of golf clubs or book clubs, much like "games" is for game theory. The
term club originates in the foundational work of Buchanan (1965), who
introduced the idea in the context of a small group of agents sharing a public
good. Buchanan's insight was to identify goods that are non-excludable but

at least partially rivalrous, for example due to congestion effects, and thus mix aspects of public and private goods. He used clubs to model such goods, called local public goods, like public parks or swimming pools.

Many scholars then picked up on this idea of clubs as small groups, and used this concept much more generally to encompass ideas like local public goods, firm formation, matching, or partnerships. A central conjecture in the large literature that followed was that competition should lead to optimal group formation. This conjecture echoed earlier ideas of Tiebout (1956), who argued that local public good provision would be optimal if agents could choose their jurisdictions, and these jurisdictions were sufficiently small and varied. As a necessary precursor to progress on this conjecture, a large body of work developed to provide competitive models of group formation, and to explore the competitive foundations of market models of group formation, such as connections between the core in coalition formation games and equilibria in markets for groups.

Formalizing and proving such results at the same level of generality and abstraction as classical competitive equilibrium theory proved quite difficult. In classical competitive equilibrium, trade is organized solely through the institution of anonymous prices that equilibrate supply and demand. Agents do not interact directly, and care only about their own consumption. Goods are private and infinitely divisible, and the commodity space is independent of the set of agents. Powerful results hold under mild assumptions, in particular the Pareto efficiency of equilibria.

This competitive equilibrium concept has strong connections with more primitive definitions of perfect competition, notably through group trading notions such as the core. In the core, trade is institution-free, and imagined to occur through direct exchange between agents. A group or coalition of agents blocks an allocation if they can do better by seceding from the whole and trading only among themselves. Blocking thus refines the set of allocations. This leads to the equilibrium notion of the core, which consists of all allocations not blocked by some coalition. Although the possibility of coalitions disciplines the set of allocations, no coalitions actually form. Thus while the notion of the core is motivated by the idea of trading in smaller groups, it does not actually involve such group formation in the end.

Some of the most important results in classical general equilibrium theory establish the tight connection between the core and the set of competitive equilibria. In particular, in a large exchange economy, every core allocation is an approximate competitive equilibrium. This result hinges on the absence of market power, and in particular on some version of the requirement that no agent is a monopolist in supplying any goods. Although the core makes no mention of prices, prices emerge from the approximate convexifying effects of the large economy, via the Shapley Folkman Theorem, and the

Separating Hyperplane Theorem. This provides a very successful theory of consumption, once production decisions have been made. But this does not lead to a very successful theory of production decisions within firms, or of firm formation or other small group interactions.

Work in club theory long sought a model at the level of generality and flexibility of classical general equilibrium models that would integrate small group interactions with competitive markets. Reaching this ideal would require a model that provides an artful mix of features from classical general equilibrium theory, public goods economies, and game theory. Like classical general equilibrium theory, this model would require that the commodity space be defined independently of agents, that all commodities be priced and priced anonymously, that agents take prices as given and choose optimally within their budget sets, and that equilibrium be determined by market clearing conditions for all goods.

Earlier work on competitive models of group formation typically had limitations regarding some of these features. In some models, for example, the commodity space depended on the set of agents. In others, agents were limited to choosing at most one group membership, either because the model had only a single type of group or by exogenous assumption. Such models cannot incorporate applications in which different types of groups and multiple memberships are important, such as investments in education important for job choice that link school choice to firm formation. In contrast, many subtleties arise in formulating models with multiple group memberships. Other models restricted attention to a single private good, often with transferable utility. While providing valuable simplifications that allow focus on other aspects of group formation, such restrictions rule out important applications in which groups are firms in a production economy.

Models like these, while employing assumptions more specific than a competitive market ideal, can instead provide richer and more nuanced predictions for particular types of group formation problems by virtue of their additional structure. The first paper in this section, "Partnerships" (1988), is an archetypal example. In this paper, Farrell and Scotchmer focus on "partnerships," which they define as coalitions that work together to benefit from cooperation, and divide output equally. While coalitions can be of any size, and variations in coalition size emerge endogenously as a feature of equilibrium, a key assumption is the fixed equal sharing rule. Two focal examples that motivate their model are law partnerships and information sharing in commercial salmon fishing in the Pacific Northwest. They argue that in both cases, as in a number of other settings, strong forces support the norm of equal division and the absence of other explicit side payments even though more flexible sharing rules or side payments might be natural in other joint ventures.

Many coalition formation games without side payments lack equilibria or else have multiple equilibria. In contrast, the partnership game Farrell and Scotchmer develop always has equilibria, and equilibrium is generically unique. Their proof that equilibria exist is actually constructive, and thus demonstrates precisely when multiple equilibria might arise.

The resulting partnerships need not be efficient, however. The fixed equal sharing rule and absence of side payments creates a force for inefficiently small coalitions. For example, with economies of scale, larger coalitions would always be more valuable. But if players are ranked by ability, then players with higher ability might prefer to inefficiently limit the size of their groups in order to limit the subsidies they provide to less able players through equal sharing. Farrell and Scotchmer show that if economies of scale are bounded, however, then efficiency can be recovered in the limit as the distribution of abilities is replicated through the formation of many small homogeneous coalitions. This final result on the power of a large population to restore efficiency in group formation foreshadows some of Scotchmer's later work, including some of the main findings from the second paper included here.

In a series of papers, Scotchmer then turned to addressing the challenge of building a competitive theory of group formation that would meet the ideal of the classical model (see Ellickson, Grodal, Scotchmer, and Zame, 1999, 2001, 2005; Scotchmer and Shannon, 2015). The second paper in this section, "Clubs and the Market," lays out the heart of this model. Like a standard general equilibrium model of consumption, the model starts with an arbitrary finite set of private goods. The central new addition of the model is a finite set of club types. Each club type consists of a finite set of members, defined by characteristics rather than by agents' names, and an output production function which depends on members' inputs and characteristics. These characteristics can either be fixed as in Ellickson, Grodal, Scotchmer and Zame (1999) or chosen by the agents (Ellickson, Grodal, Scotchmer, and Zame, 2005; Zame, 2007; Scotchmer and Shannon, 2015). This allows the model to be extended to cover a range of important applications in which agents might invest in education or other characteristics to qualify to take certain positions (Ellickson, Grodal, Scotchmer, and Zame, 2005), or in which hidden information or hidden actions affect club outcomes (Zame, 2007; Scotchmer and Shannon, 2015). Related but different models connecting clubs with firms and private information can also be found in Cole and Prescott (1997) and Prescott and Townsend (2006). Agents can join more than one club, which allows the model to include applications such as educational choices that qualify workers for different jobs.

Agents' preferences depend jointly on private goods and on club memberships, including the characteristics of other members of the clubs they join.

Thus the model allows externalities from small group interactions both directly, through preferences, and indirectly, through group outputs shared among members. The model allows for increasing, but bounded, returns to scale as no clubs are large enough to exert market power. Club memberships are priced and traded in markets along with private goods. Membership prices can be positive, so people pay to join, or negative, reflecting wages or some share of club profits. Clubs break even by assumption, so membership prices must sum to zero and any profit or loss is fully distributed to members.

The clubs that actually form arise endogenously in equilibrium along with membership prices, and these are determined in conjunction with private goods allocations and prices. As in standard general equilibrium theory, demand and supply are derived from agents' optimal choices as a function of prices and budgets, and equilibrium occurs at prices equating demand and supply. Market clearing conditions must be extended to memberships, along with private goods, to formalize such an equilibrium. Unlike private goods, however, memberships do not come in fixed exogenous supply.

The central subtlety in the model lies in formulating an appropriate notion of market clearing for club memberships. This is done by way of a consistency condition which says that demand for each membership (expressed as the mass of agents choosing each membership) is the same within each club type. Consistency guarantees that all agents choosing a membership in a given club type can be matched with agents choosing complementary memberships in that club type, and thus that their demand will be met. Importantly, consistency allows that this demand can vary across club types, and in particular that some clubs do not form in equilibrium while others do. Despite the many subtleties in formulating the model, the paper shows that club equilibria exist with a continuum of agents under mild conditions.

The core has a natural analog in this model, and is naturally linked with small group interactions in clubs. An assignment of club memberships and goods to agents is in the core if there is no coalition that could block it by proposing different clubs, involving only coalition members, and a different allocation of goods, feasible for the coalition, that would make every coalition member better off. In the core of a club economy, coalitions do form, through clubs, in contrast to the standard exchange economy. The core again provides a test of the notion of competition embedded in club equilibrium. One of the paper's central results is to show that club equilibrium is indeed competitive in this sense. In their model with a continuum of agents, core equivalence holds: the set of club equilibrium allocations and membership assignments coincides with the core.

A companion paper explores analogs of all of their results for large finite economies (Ellickson, Grodal, Scotchmer, and Zame, 2001). Given the indivisibilities inherent in club memberships, it is not surprising that the core might be empty and that equilibria might fail to exist for an arbitrary finite set of agents. Indeed, the core seems particularly problematic in a finite economy, since a few people left out of clubs might entice others to leave their assigned clubs, and cause the whole structure of clubs in the economy to unravel. Remarkably, this unraveling problem can be solved by passing to an appropriate approximate notion of the core. Using this approximate core notion, they then show that a version of core convergence holds: every approximate core allocation is also an approximate equilibrium.

Scotchmer's work in club theory has opened up rich and important new research avenues in understanding both group formation and markets. Interpreting clubs as firms, for example, as emphasized in Ellickson, Grodal, Scotchmer and Zame (2005), her work provides the foundation for a general theory of firm formation in competitive markets, including what firms form in equilibrium, what they produce, and how workers, managers, and shareholders are compensated. By building a competitive theory of group formation that meets the ideals of classical general equilibrium theory, she has left us a powerful and deep framework for understanding the interplay between competition and a wide array of organizations including firms, contracts, mechanisms, and games.

Quarterly Journal of Economics,
Vol. 103 No. 2 (May, 1988): 279–296

Partnerships*

Joseph Farrell and Suzanne Scotchmer

A partnership is a coalition that divides its output equally. We show that when partnerships can form freely, a stable or "core" partition into partnerships always exists and is generically unique. When people differ in ability, the equal-sharing constraint inefficiently limits the size of partnerships. We give conditions under which partnerships containing abler people will be larger, and show that if

* We thank Mary Curran, Drew Fudenberg, Roger Guesnerie, Andreu Mas-Colell, Mordecai Kurz, Ed Lazear, Eric Maskin, James Mirrlees, Todd Sandler, Tom Schelling, Hal Varian, Michael Whinston, and Ulrich Zachau for useful comments and information. We thank Michael Whinston for pointing out an error. We also thank our spouses, without whom this paper would not have been written. NSF Grants IRI 87 12238 and SES 86 10021 supported this research.

the population is replicated, partnerships may become more or less homogeneous, depending on an elasticity condition. We also examine when the equal-sharing inefficiency vanishes in the limit.

I. Introduction

A central feature of economic life is that people form groups to exploit gains from cooperation. Many economists have analyzed such cooperation when these gains can be flexibly divided among participants. But such flexible allocation systems are not universal: often, the rewards from joint effort are shared according to rather rigid rules. In particular, *equal sharing* is common, even when the participants contribute unequal amounts. We call a group that divides its output equally among its members a *partnership*.

For instance, as we discuss below, law partners often share profits equally. Salmon fishermen in the Pacific Northwest tell each other where the fish are, thus sharing the efficiency gains from better information; and although they know who is good at finding the schools of salmon, they refrain from side payments. Marriage is an equal sharing, and we avoid making spouses' payoffs depend on their outside opportunities. In economics (though not in the physical sciences), scholars share equally in the credit for joint work, even if one contributes considerably more than another.

In most of these examples, some subtle side payments or differences in treatment may exist, but there are clearly strong forces toward equal division. We therefore ask in this paper, what would happen if groups were obliged to divide output equally?[1] We analyze a coalition-formation game in which people who differ in ability can get together to exploit economies of scale, but must share their output equally within groups.[2]

---

1 A complementary problem is why groups that could share unequally often ignore obvious differences in contribution or opportunity costs, and share equally instead. One possible answer is pure social convention: people often simply think equal division is appropriate. A second, related reason is to satisfy a concept of justice. Various authors (see for instance Thomson and Varian [1985]) have discussed symmetry or equality as a social choice criterion. A third, and efficiency-based, reason is the inefficient rent-seeking that might arise if a group opens up the question of how to divide its output among the members.

2 Selten [1972] defines an "equal-division core" in which blocking coalitions must divide output equally, but equilibrium coalitions need not. As Greenberg [1986] convincingly argues, it seems sensible to impose the same requirements on equilibrium coalitions and on blocking coalitions, and this is what we do. Guesnerie and Oddou [1981] study a model of the provision of local public goods when agents' wealth levels vary and the only means available to finance public goods is a linear wealth tax. In their model, as in ours, the inability to choose individualized taxes makes groups too small and reduces efficiency. A similar inefficiency arises in Greenberg and Weber [1986], for a similar reason. Spulber [1986] defines a restricted notion of core designed to show how price stability may arise in decreasing cost industries. Prices in a blocking coalition are anonymous and linear, and hence the core is "second-best." A similar problem was studied by Sorenson, Tschirhart, and Whinston [1978a,b], who find that with nonlinear prices the first-best can be sustained.

Many coalition-formation games without side payments have no equilibrium, or have multiple equilibria.[3] Section II below shows that in our equal-division game, equilibrium always exists and is generically unique. Indeed, our proof shows exactly how to construct the equilibrium and shows when it is nonunique. Unlike core allocations in games with side payments, equilibrium is typically not efficient. When players can be ranked by ability, the equal-sharing rule makes the ablest people reluctant to admit the less able to their group: while they would always like a big group so as to exploit economies of scale, they do not want to go too far down the distribution of abilities, since they then subsidize less able members.

In Section III we characterize equilibrium when players can be ranked by ability, and there are economies of scale. The main qualitative feature, which follows directly from our constructive proof of existence, is that equilibrium groups are "consecutive": each consists of all people in some interval of abilities. If ability is uniformly distributed, then the groups with the highest abilities are the largest. Section III also contains an example showing how the inefficiency due to too small groups varies with the importance of economies of scale.

Equal sharing is inefficient because people cannot exploit economies of scale except by sharing with less able people: they cannot achieve size without heterogeneity. This might suggest that equal sharing would be efficient in the limit if we replicate the distribution of abilities, since in the limiting economy, groups can be infinitely large while still being homogeneous. In Section IV we show that efficiency in the limit depends on the limiting value, as group size becomes large, of the elasticity of average productivity with respect to group size. If it converges to zero, then replication of the economy ensures that the grand coalition forms in the limit, and we have efficiency. Efficiency also occurs in the limit (with many coalitions) if (as is plausible) economies of scale are bounded. Otherwise, inefficiency persists.

In Sections III and IV we focus on the inefficiency of groups being too small. But if people have complementary skills, so that there is no well-defined "ability," equal sharing causes another inefficiency: groups may be too homogeneous. Efficiency may require heterogeneous groups, and then the homogeneity caused by equal sharing is inefficient quite apart from any effect on group size. We hint at these issues in Section V by giving an example in which group size is not at issue, but in which equilibrium has inefficiently homogeneous groups.

Section VI describes in more detail two examples – information sharing in salmon fishing, and law partnerships – which particularly inspired our interest in this subject. We also point out dimensions in which equal sharing can be relaxed without changing our basic results. Section VII concludes.

---

3 Schelling [1978] discusses a number of examples.

II. Existence and Uniqueness

We prove existence and uniqueness for a slightly more general case than the model we introduce here. We give the special model first because it is the model we use in Sections III and IV. In Sections V and VI we shall discuss extensions for which the more general existence argument is required.

We suppose that each individual has an ability e^i. The productivity, or total payoff, to a group S is $t(|S|)$ times the sum of abilities in the group, $t(|S|)\sum_S e^i$, where $|S|$ is the size of the group. To let $t(|S|)$ represent economies of scale, we assume that $t'(|S|) > 0$. Since an individual's payoff is the average product of the group, it is also useful to define $a(|S|) = t(|S|)/|S|$, so that the average payoff is $a(|S|)\sum_S e^i$. We assume that $a'(|S|)\sum_S e^i < 0$ for large enough $|S|$: otherwise all members want to expand the group, irrespective of heterogeneity, and equilibrium yields one large efficient group.

The important restriction in this model is that complementarities are "anonymous": The enhancement of a member's productivity, $t(|S|)$, depends on the group's size, but not on its composition. This model is designed to study the social loss that results from inefficiently small equilibrium groups, but does not address inefficiencies that result from nonoptimal blending of skills (see Section V).[4]

The proof that follows applies to equal sharing, irrespective of whether we have the special structure just described, and therefore applies to models of the type discussed in Section V. It also applies to the extensions discussed in Section VI.

We assume that there is a function $u(S)$ that describes every agent's ranking of coalitions S that contain him or her. In the case described above, $u(S)$ is the average profit $a(|S|)\sum_S e^i$. The actual utility achieved by a person can be any individualized monotone transformation of $u(S)$, as discussed in Section VI. Since the payoff to a group is one-dimensional, groups can be ranked by their average payoff that each member achieves. The core allocation then has a very intuitive description: first, the "best" group forms (the group that gives the highest average payoff); then the "best" group from those remaining, and so on. This description makes it easy to characterize equilibrium in the next section.

Theorem. Let N be a finite set of agents. Suppose that there is a function $u(S)$ that describes every agent's ranking of coalitions that contain him or her. Then (i) there is a partition of the players into coalitions such that no new coalition could form and make all its members strictly better off; (ii) that partition is generically unique.

---

4 In the fishing example discussed below, the assumption means that, while fishermen may differ in their ability to find fish, their abilities to harvest fish from the school are the same. In law, the economy of scale may arise from specialization or the ability to smooth the work load when business comes in lumps.

Proof of the Theorem. We construct an equilibrium. First, form a coalition S_1^* that maximizes $u(\cdot)$, which we shall call a "best coalition." From the remaining agents, $(N - S_1^*)$, choose a "second-best coalition," S_2^*, and so on. Eventually, all the remaining agents will unanimously want to join together.[5]

We claim that $\{S_i^*\}$ is a core partition. To see this, simply observe that no blocking coalition could contain any member of S_1^*, the best coalition, for it is impossible to give any member of S_1^* more than he or she is currently getting. But, by the same argument, given that no member of the best coalition would join the defectors, they could not attract any member of the second-best coalition S_2^* either; and so on.

What if this construction yields two possible "best" coalitions (or "second-best" coalitions, etc.)? If those two coalitions contain some of the same individuals, they cannot both be in the same core partition (since no individual may belong to two different coalitions). There is a core partition containing one of the coalitions, and another core partition containing the other: The core partition is not unique. However, this kind of coincidence is unlikely or nongeneric in the following sense. If people's abilities are perturbed slightly so that each coalition's product is perturbed,[6] there will no longer be two coalitions with the same payoffs.

Aside from this nongeneric possibility, equilibrium is unique: if S_1^* is unique, then it must appear in any equilibrium (else it blocks); and so on. Thus, the core is generically unique.

                                                                    Q.E.D.

Two qualifying remarks about this equilibrium are in order. First, Zachau [1987] has pointed out that if blocking coalitions need only make a weak improvement, rather than strictly increase the payoff to every member, equilibrium may fail to exist when two possible coalitions with some of the same members give the same average payoff.[7]

---

5 This last coalition is made up from the leftovers, those who were not previously invited to join a coalition. Typically they will wish their coalition were larger. In many coalition-formation models (e.g., Pauly [1970]) such leftover groups cause existence problems, sometimes called "integer problems." No such problems arise here because the leftovers cannot bribe others to join them. They have no power to disrupt the coalitions with higher payoffs.

6 When the payoff to members is generated by splitting a real-valued output, perturbation of abilities causes outputs of different coalitions to change slightly.

7 A version of the example is this: suppose that there are three players, 1, 2, and 3. Coalitions {1,2} and {2,3} give average payoff one, while any agent alone gets zero. Then whether equilibrium exists depends on the blocking requirement. If a blocking coalition must make every agent strictly better off, then the two configurations [{1,2},3] and [{2,3},1] are equilibria. Equilibrium fails to exist with the weaker blocking condition that a coalition need only make some members strictly better off. The failure of existence is nongeneric in the sense that typically two coalitions will not yield the same average payoff.

Second, small departures from equal sharing may cause equilibrium not to exist.[8] Since most market games that come to mind do not satisfy equal sharing exactly, this is disturbing. However, the examples of nonexistence we have constructed begin from nongeneric cases in which several coalitions give the same average payoff.

III. Characterization of Equilibrium

Because our existence proof was constructive, one can say easily what partnerships will form. Characterizing equilibrium is easiest with a continuum of individuals,[9] with the distribution of abilities, e, described by a distribution function $F(e)$ on support $[0,M]$. The payoff to each member of a group consisting of everyone in a set of abilities S is then $a(|S|)\int_S edF(e)$.

If an individual's productivity were affected differently by different groups – that is, if individuals were more complementary with some people than with others as in Section V below – then "ability" would have no clear meaning. Since "ability" is well defined in our case, we would expect equilibrium payoffs to reflect the individual's intrinsic ability e.

Proposition 1. Every individual gets at least as much utility in equilibrium as a lower ability individual.

Proof of Proposition 1.[10] Suppose otherwise. Either the lower ability individual with more utility is in a group alone, or his group has other members. If he is alone, then the higher ability individual can improve her utility by defecting and being alone. If the lower ability individual is in a group with others, then that group can increase its payoff by eliminating the lower ability individual and substituting the higher ability individual. This will increase the payoff of previous members, since they have the same size group but more total ability, and will therefore also increase the payoff of the higher ability individual they adopted.

Q.E.D.

8 Suppose that there are three players: 1, 2, and 3. Agents alone or in a group of three get payoff zero. The average payoff in each coalition of two players is 1. Then any two players together, with the other player alone, is an equilibrium. Now suppose we perturb the profit sharing so that coalitions share profit as follows: {1,2} get {1 + ε, 1 − ε}. {2,3} get |1 + ε, 1 − ε}. {1,3} get {1 − ε, 1 + ε}. Then there is no function $u(S)$ that simultaneously describes the players' rankings of coalitions, and no equilibrium exists. This example is essentially due to Michael Whinston.
9 If a blocking coalition must strictly improve the utility of each member, the core is also nonempty in this case. If only weak improvements are required, the core will be nonempty if blocking coalitions must differ from equilibrium coalitions by a set of positive measure. Otherwise, the core would be empty, because the most able coalition could always expand by one lower ability individual (who has measure zero) without reducing the group's average ability, but increasing that individual's payoff.
10 Since this proof refers to "individuals," it applies to the case of finitely many players. For the continuous case, we need to refer to sets of agents of positive measure.

The next feature of equilibrium in this model is that groups are "consecutive" – they contain all the agents with abilities in some interval.[11]

Proposition 2. *Equilibrium groups have the "consecutive" property that all individuals between the lowest and highest ability in the group are also in the group.*

Proof of Proposition 2. This follows from our construction of equilibrium. The equilibrium group S_1^* is the coalition that maximizes per capita payoff. This group is composed of the most able individuals, down to some cutoff. The next equilibrium group maximizes per capita payoff among coalitions of people not in the most able group. This group again includes the ablest individuals in the remainder, down to some cutoff. Thus, each group is composed of the individuals whose abilities lie in some interval.

Q.E.D.

Since each equilibrium group is consecutive, groups can unambiguously be ordered by ability. We show next that the size of equilibrium partnerships increases with ability, at least when the distribution of abilities is uniform. To understand this, consider the incentive for the more able members to form a new partnership excluding the least able member. This increases the average ability in the group. When the distribution of abilities is uniform, eliminating the least able member increases average ability by the same absolute amount for every size-n group. In contrast, the loss to eliminating the marginal member differs for groups with different abilities, when those groups are the same size. The contribution of the least able member is higher in a high-ability group, and this provides the incentive for abler groups to expand. Another way to see this is to note that, in the uniform case, while the absolute difference in ability between the group's mean and its least able member is independent of its mean (among same-sized groups), this difference becomes *proportionally* less important as the mean ability grows.

Proposition 3. *When ability is uniformly distributed, the sizes of equilibrium groups increase with ability: if one equilibrium group contains abler individuals than another group contains, it will be larger.*

11 "Consecutive" groups are discussed by Greenberg and Weber [1986].Their model, which examines jurisdiction formation and production of local public goods, has a prespecified division of taxes, but utility is not shared in a prespecified way, since preferences depend differently on the amount of local public goods provided. That their equilibrium is fundamentally different from ours is evident in the fact that no individual in their equilibrium would want to move, irrespective of whether the other coalition wants to accept him. In our model, every individual would like to join the best partnership.

Before proving Proposition 3, we introduce some notation. Let $n(l, m)$ be the number of people between abilities l and m; that is, $n(l, m) = F(m) - F(l)$. By Proposition 2, the group with top ability m that maximizes average payoff is an interval $[l(m), m]$ of abilities, containing $n[l(m), m]$ people. Proposition 3 says that $n[l(m), m]$ increases with m if F is uniform.

Proof of Proposition 3. $l(m)$ maximizes $a[n(l, m)] \int_l^m e \, dF(e)$, which is the product of average payoff per unit ability and total ability in the group. Taking logarithms before differentiating, and multiplying by $n(l, m)/f$, where f is the density, we can write the first-order condition[12] as

$$\gamma[n(l, m)] - l/[\mu(l, m)] = 0, \tag{1}$$

where $\mu(l, m)$ is the mean ability in the interval and $\gamma(n)$ is the elasticity of average product:

$$\mu(l, m) \equiv \frac{1}{n(l, m)} \int_l^m e \, dF(e) \quad \text{and} \quad \gamma(n) \equiv -\frac{n a'(n)}{a(n)}.$$

Suppose that, when m increases, l were to increase just enough to maintain n. Then the first term in (1) would be unchanged; and the second term l/μ would increase, given that F is uniform.[13] So (1) would now be negative, and it would pay to reduce l a little, increasing n.

Q.E.D.

It is of interest to ask how "robust" this conclusion is to the distribution of abilities. The basic insight is that partnerships will be larger if groups can be expanded without introducing too much heterogeneity. An equilibrium with equal-size partnerships (that is, $n[l(m), m]$ constant) would require that high ability groups have a large difference, $\mu - l$, which discourages expansion. The density of abilities would have to be declining. This is exactly correct. The distribution of abilities that generates partnerships of equal size has density k/e, where k is a constant, as can easily be verified.

Distributions of ability that have flatter slope than k/e will generate equilibria in which the more able partnerships are larger than the less able, and vice versa for distributions that are more steeply sloped (more skewed) than k/e. For instance, the right-hand tail of the normal distribution is more skewed than k/e, so the most able people will work in small groups if ability is normally distributed.

---

12 The logarithm of the objective function is concave, provided that $\gamma(n)$ is not decreasing too fast.

13 $\mu = 1/2(l + m)$, so $l/\mu = 2/(1 + m/l)$. If one adds the same amount to l and m, so as to hold n fixed, then $1/\mu$ rises.

We now solve a simple example to illustrate the social loss in output due to the abler people's unwillingness to be partners with the less able.

Example.

Suppose that $a(n)$ has constant elasticity γ. Ability is uniformly distributed on $[0, M]$. The per capita payoff in a coalition S is $|S|^{-\gamma} \int_S e\, de$. Provided that $\gamma > 0$, total output is maximized by having one grand partnership, but that is not an equilibrium. Instead, the unique core partition is given by

$$S_1^* = (m_1, m_0]$$
$$S_2^* = (m_2, m_1], \text{ etc.}$$

where $m_0 = M$ and $m_i = [\gamma/(2 - \gamma)]^i M$. Thus, the population $[0, M]$ splits into infinitely many partnerships, the higher ability ones being also larger (as in Proposition 3). Calculation shows that total output is

$$\sum_{i=0}^{\infty} (m_i - m_{i+1})^{-\gamma} \int_{m_{i+1}}^{m_i} e\, de = M^{3-\gamma} \left[\frac{2(1-\gamma)}{2-\gamma} \right]^{2-\gamma} \frac{1}{2-\gamma} \frac{1}{1 - [\frac{\gamma}{2} - \gamma]^{3-\gamma}}$$

as compared with the maximum possible output, which is

$$M^{1-\gamma} \int_0^M e\, de = \frac{1}{2} M^{3-\gamma}.$$

It is easy to check that at $\gamma = 1$, when there is neither social nor private gain to cooperation (that is, $t(n)$ is constant), the equilibrium outcome is efficient. At $\gamma = 0$ (that is, $a(n)$ is constant), we again find efficiency, because equilibrium will have one group. The proportional loss is greatest at about $\gamma = 0.7$, when almost 25 percent of total possible output is lost as a result of the inability to keep the whole group together.

IV. (In)Efficiency in the Limit

In this section we ask how heterogeneity of equilibrium groups depends on population size. We study this by replicating the set of agents. Intuitively, such replication allows partnerships to expand without having to increase heterogeneity, or to reduce heterogeneity without having to shrink. Size and homogeneity are "goods" for a partnership, and replication expands the feasible set. As in the ordinary theory of demand, agents may exploit their improved opportunities by taking more of both goods (size and homogeneity) or by taking more of only one. We find that replication may cause the top group to become either more or less homogeneous, depending on the elasticity of a $(\cdot)$.

We multiply the original distribution function by a parameter $v > 1$, so that the replicated population has abilities distributed according to $vF(e)$

and the population size is v. Let $l(m, v)$ denote the bottom ability cutoff of the equilibrium group that would form if m were the top ability. Then we can describe how l changes as v increases, in terms of the elasticity of average payoff (per capita) with respect to group size, $\gamma(n) = -na'(n)/a(n)$.

Proposition 4. *As the population is replicated, groups become more or less homogeneous according as* $\gamma(n)$ *is increasing or decreasing. More precisely:*

(i) If $\gamma(n)$ is decreasing, then $l(m, v)$ is decreasing in v (for any m). Therefore, as v grows, partnerships become less homogeneous and grow faster than v.

(ii) If $\gamma(n)$ is constant, then $l(mv)$ is independent of v (for any m). As v grows, each partnership grows in proportion, but its composition does not change.

(iii) If $\gamma(n)$ is increasing, then $l(m, v)$ is increasing in v. As v grows, equilibrium partnerships become more homogeneous.

Proof of Proposition 4. A group with top ability m has size $n(l, m, v) = v[F(m) - F(l)]$. The equilibrium choice $l(m, v)$ maximizes

$$\pi(l, m, v) \equiv a[n(l, m, v)] \int_l^m v e \, dF(e)$$

and therefore also maximizes its logarithm. The first-order condition, multiplied by $n(l, m, v)/f(l)$, is[14]

$$0 = \gamma[n(l, m, v)] - \frac{l}{\mu(l, m)} \equiv \frac{\partial \log(\pi)}{\partial l} \frac{n(l, m, v)}{f(l)}. \tag{2}$$

To see how the equilibrium choice of lower cutoff, $l(m, v)$, varies with v, we must sign the cross-derivative $\partial^2 \log[\pi(\cdot)]/\partial v \partial l$ at the optimum. From (2) we see that this is simply $\gamma'[n(l, m, v)\partial n(l, m, v)/\partial v]$, evaluated at $l = l(m, v)$. But clearly $\partial n(l, m, v)/\partial v > 0$, so $\partial l(m, v)/\partial v$ has the same sign as $\gamma'[n(l, m, v)]$. This establishes Proposition 4.

The inefficiency described above results from the fact that economies of scale are underexploited because of able agents' intolerance of heterogeneity. As we replicate the economy, scale economies can be exploited with less heterogeneity. One might therefore hope that, at least on a per capita basis, these inefficiencies would vanish in the limit. In general, however, they do not. Although equilibrium groups become large in the limit as $v \to \infty$, we cannot generally argue that in the limit, all economies of scale are exhausted in equilibrium groups. The fact that a representative

---

14 The average ability in the interval $[l, m], \mu(l, m)$, is independent of v.

group-size $n[l(m, v), m, v]$ is unbounded as v gets large does not imply that the limit of $t[n(l(m, v), m, v)]/t(v)$ is one. The problem is that $n[l(m, v), m, v]$ may grow too slowly, and the function $t(\cdot)$ may be such that that matters in the limit.

In Proposition 5, we show that if $t(n)$ is bounded above (and thus approaches a finite limit) as n grows large, then we *do* have efficiency in the limit, even though the number of groups becomes large.[15] This is the likely case, because otherwise economies of scale are unbounded in the sense that feasible per capita payoffs are unbounded in the limit.

Proposition 5. *If $t(n)$ approaches a finite limit as n grows large, then groups in the limiting equilibrium as v becomes large will become homogeneous and the social loss per capita will approach zero.*

Proof of Proposition 5. First, we show that if $t(n)$ is bounded and thus converges to a finite limit as $n \to \infty$, then $\gamma(n)$ converges to 1. Since $\gamma(n) = 1 - nt'(n)/t(n)$, it is enough to show that $nt'(n) \to 0$. (It is obvious that $t'(n) \to 0$, but not that $nt'(n) \to , 0$.) Suppose that there exists $\varepsilon > 0$ and $N > 0$ such that $nt'(n) \geq \varepsilon$ for all $n > N$. Then for such n,

$$t(n) - t(N) = \int_N^n t'(x)dx \geq \varepsilon \int_N^n \frac{dx}{x} = \varepsilon \log \left(\frac{n}{N}\right),$$

which implies that $t(n)$ is unbounded as n grows, contrary to assumption. This proves that $nt'(n)$ must come arbitrarily close to zero infinitely often. We simply assume away oscillatory behavior and conclude that $nt'(n) \to 0$ and $\gamma(n) \to 1$.

Because $\gamma(n) \to 1$, the first-order condition (2) implies that groups become very homogeneous in the limit if they grow large (and certainly become homogeneous in the limit if they do not !). Thus, the economy becomes very finely divided $(n(v)/v \to 0)$, and, recalling that efficiency requires that everyone be in one group, one might well expect that this means inefficiency in the limit. But when $n(v) \to \infty$ and $t(n)$ is bounded above, $t(n(v))/t(v) \to 1$. It does not matter that each group grows more slowly than the economy.

Q.E.D.

If $\gamma(n)$ is constant and less than one, then a constant number of equilibrium partnerships are replicated in size when the economy is replicated. Both

---

15 The limiting equilibrium is very similar to core allocations in club economies with anonymous crowding, in which coalitions will usually be homogeneous and no side payments will occur because identical agents get equal utility in the core. It is generally assumed in club economies, however, that economies of scale are exhausted at a finite group size.

terms of (2) remain constant. We show in Proposition 6 that this is inefficient. If $\gamma(n)$ converges to any number strictly between 0 and 1, the limiting equilibrium will be inefficient. This shows that convergence of $t'(n)$ to zero is not enough to get efficiency in the limit, even though groups become large. In order to get efficiency in the limit, the economies of scale must be exhausted fast relative to how fast equilibrium partnerships become large.

Proposition 6. (Appendix [omitted – ed.].). *If the elasticity of average product, $\gamma(n)$, converges to any number strictly between 0 and 1 for large n, then the limiting equilibrium is inefficient.*

At the opposite extreme, economies of scale may persist for all n, rather than being exhausted. If average payoff per find is constant (and positive) for all n, then members will not object to enlarging the group, no matter how heterogeneous the group is, and there will be one grand coalition. If average payoff becomes constant in the limit, then there will be one grand partnership in the limit, which is efficient. Again, in the limit, equal sharing has no bite. We state this as a Proposition.

Proposition 7. *If $\gamma(n)$ approaches zero as n grows, then the limiting equilibrium, as v becomes large, has one grand partnership consisting of all individuals, and is efficient.*

Proof of Proposition 7. The top group in the limiting equilibrium becomes either infinitely large or finite and homogeneous. Suppose that $l[M,v]$ does not converge to the average ability in the group, $\mu[l(M,v),M]$, as v becomes large, so that in the limit the top group is heterogeneous and its size n is unbounded. Then in the limit the value of the derivative (2) is negative, since $\gamma(n)$ converges to zero, and it pays to expand the group, until $l[M,v]$ is the lowest ability in the support of F, zero. Likewise, if the top group is finite and homogeneous, it pays to expand, since $\gamma(n)$ can never equal one if $t(n)$ is strictly increasing, and hence the value of the derivative (2) is negative whenever n is finite and v becomes very large.

Q.E.D.

V. Social Loss Due to Composition Rather Than Size

The inefficiency discussed above is a problem of size, rather than composition. This is because we assumed complementarities are anonymous in the sense that the enhancement of each member's productivity, $t(n)$, depends on the size of the group, n, but not on who the other members are. Equilibrium groups are inefficiently small because the only way to increase homogeneity is to decrease size. More complicated forms of complementarity in a model of equal sharing will lead to social loss due to incorrect composition, as well as size. This can be seen in the following example, in which size is not at issue.

There are two types of agent, A and B, with two copies of each. Any group of size different from two gets payoff zero. The average payoffs to groups AA, AB, and BB are, respectively, 4, 3, and 1. An efficient allocation that maximizes total payoff requires groups of type AB. But type A will block that allocation, since they individually can get higher payoff by forming inefficient homogeneous groups of type AA. Equilibrium has groups of type AA and BB exclusively.

Again, the social loss occurs because equal sharing demands that high-ability members subsidize the low-ability members in the efficient heterogeneous groups. This inefficiency will not vanish in the limit as the economy becomes large, as may occur when the inefficiency is one of size. This class of models, in which equal sharing leads to nonoptimal composition of groups, is an important one to explore further.

The proof of existence above applies to all coalition formation games with equal sharing, and thus applies to cases such as this.

VI. Examples

Although we think equal division is widely used as an allocative mechanism, our interest is motivated especially by two examples discussed in this section. The first example is the Pacific salmon trolling industry. Much of the difference in skill among fishermen is not in the ability to catch fish once located, but in finding schools of fish, which involves knowing the underwater terrain and the habits of fish. The ability parameter e^i represents the expected number of schools of fish found per unit time. "Cooperation" means telling other fishermen when one has found a school of fish. There are gains to cooperation because fishermen who would otherwise be idle (or fruitlessly searching) are catching fish from the school before it disperses. Provided that the total number of fish caught from a school is an increasing function of the number of boats fishing it, efficiency requires sharing "finds" with all other fishermen.[16] If all fishermen had the same ability e, to find fish, they would all share information in equilibrium, even without side payments.[17] If a flexible system of side payments were

---

16 This analysis is not about the problem of the commons, and we thus ignore the fact that individually rational fishermen may collectively overfish. From this point of view, the reduction in total catch due to equal sharing may be socially desirable. Current regulation to prevent overfishing certainly involves policies that are not first-best efficient: fishermen are deliberately kept idle much of the season. From the point of view of the theory of the core, the problem of the commons corresponds to externalities among coalitions, which are discussed, for example, by Zachau [1987]. The profit opportunities of one coalition would depend on the total catch of other coalitions. But this is a different subject.

17 A partner could possibly fail to inform the others. But deception is difficult because fish are unloaded in public.

available, it would also be an equilibrium for all fishermen to share information, even if they differed in ability. But pride and social convention rule out such payments.

In fact, there are multiple groups of fishermen, and information is shared within groups, but not between groups.[18] The best fishermen form a group that is highly respected, and in which membership is coveted. This group, the "highliners," is often larger than the groups of less skilled fishermen. Our result that abler groups are larger, unless the distribution of abilities is highly skewed, is a possible explanation of this.

The assumption of strict equal division is stronger than we need for our conclusions. The partner who actually finds the school can fish it alone for a while before his partners arrive. It is natural to model this by specifying that the payoff to a fisherman of ability e^* who belongs to a partnership S is $a(|S|)\int_S edF(e) + e^*g$, where g is the amount he can catch before the others arrive. The last term, e^*g, will not affect which partnership he joins because it is independent of the size or composition of the group. Our results, including existence and the characterization of equilibrium, are unaffected if g is unequal to zero or differs across fishermen. By letting g be negative, we can allow for costs of finding (or searching for) opportunities, but only when such costs never deter effort: we do not deal with free-rider and related moral hazard problems, which themselves have implications for group size. (See, for instance, Holmstrom [1982].)

Our second example is that of law firms. Lawyers obviously differ in many dimensions of ability, but a particularly important ability for partners is bringing in business. The ability parameter e^i represents the number of clients brought in per unit of time. As with fishing, the inhibition on forming very large groups when no side payments are allowed is that skillful attorneys do not want their high ability diluted by less able attorneys. It seems that well-connected, experienced (hence, productive) attorneys tend to agglomerate in large firms, while there are many smaller firms composed of less experienced, less well-connected, and perhaps less skilled, attorneys.[19] Like the similar observation in the fishing industry, this is consistent with our theory.

There are three basic systems by which profit is divided among law partners, but there are essentially no data on how many firms use each

---

18 Since communication takes place on public air frequencies, fishermen have elaborate codes in which information is passed during the course of conversation. The groups are called "coding partnerships"; one says "Alan codes with Tony" or "Alan is Tony's coding partner."

19 This is obviously difficult to verify by observing attorneys' abilities, but it is consistent with the fact that average earnings of partners increase with firm size. Flood [1985, p. 48] reports that in 1981 partners in firms of two to four lawyers averaged $49,500, partners in firms with five to nine lawyers averaged $76,300, and partners in firms with ten or more lawyers averaged $89,400. In the few hundred law firms with more than fifty partners, earnings in six figures are common.

system (since partnerships have no reason to make public their compensation schemes). The first and most straightforward system is that all members with the same seniority receive the same profit share. Since junior partners eventually become senior partners, such a system would be equal division if the firm's profitability were constant over time. Such a sharing scheme corresponds quite closely to our assumption, and is probably used by most two-or three-person law firms, which account for about 2/3 of all firms (although less than half the lawyers).[20] A second division system is that the firm's founders or dominant partners have authority to decide compensation, presumably constrained by their desire not to lose partners. This system works well until the founders retire. If there are no obvious heirs, the system breaks down, and may be replaced by the third system, under which the partners elect a finance committee to make compensation decisions. Many such committees use formulas that compensate according to time billed, business brought in, and (sometimes) public stature. The latter two compensation schemes are designed for the needs of large firms. But firms with more than twenty partners comprise less than 3 percent of law firms, and less than one quarter of lawyers.

There are two useful benchmarks in studying the equilibrium partition of lawyers into partnerships. First, if side payments (compensation rules) are unrestricted, then, as in any game of coalition formation, the partition would be efficient. But, while the compensation schemes described above are more flexible than strict equal-sharing, they are not unrestricted. One possible approach to studying the formation of partnerships would be to start from the benchmark of unrestricted side payments and try to characterize the bias introduced to group formation by the disallowance of some particular forms of compensation. Our approach addresses the other extreme: equal division of profit within the partnership.

A generalization similar to the one we gave for fishermen is also possible in the law-partnership example. Here, it is not reasonable to suppose that the profitability of a client depends on which partner brings him in, as is required above if g differs among fishermen. However, our characterization applies if all partnerships pay the same bonus to the partner who brings in the business, and this bonus may even depend on the size of the partnership, although not additionally on the identity or on the talents of the lawyer.[21]

---

20 The data reported here are taken from the Lawyer Statistical Report, 1980, and from Flood [1985].

21 The profitability of a client brought into a size-n firm is $t(n)$. The part which is split among the partners would then be $[t(n) - g(n)]$. Thus, unlike in the generalization just given for fishing, the equilibrium does depend on $g(\cdot)$, but our existence and characterization proofs still apply.

VII. Conclusion

When cooperation is organized through equal-division partnership, equilibrium partnerships are more homogeneous than in the social optimum. For the case studied here, that economies of scale are "anonymous," the inclination toward homogeneous groups causes groups to be inefficiently small. Equilibrium groups are consecutive, and if the distribution of abilities is uniform or not too skewed, then size of group will increase with ability.

When the economy becomes large, groups can grow without introducing more heterogeneity. The social loss due to group size may (or may not) vanish as the economy becomes large. Inefficiencies of composition, rather than size, will typically not vanish as the economy becomes large. Inefficiencies can often be blamed on the fact that social marginal product does not guide agents' actions. In the problem of the commons, for example, the entering sheepherder is enticed by average product rather than marginal product. The social loss of overgrazing occurs because the previous members cannot keep the new member out. Just the opposite occurs in our model: every agent's marginal and average product is highest in the most able group (at least when the most able group is the largest group), and the social loss occurs because the previous members can keep new members out.

References

Flood, John, *The Legal Profession in the United States* (Chicago, IL: The American Bar Foundation, 1985).

Greenberg, Joseph, "Stable Standards of Behavior: A Unifying Approach to Solution Concepts," IMSSS Technical Report No. 484, Stanford University, Dept. of Economics, March 1986.

—— , and Shlomo Weber, "Strong Tiebout Equilibrium under Restricted Preferences Domain," *Journal of Economic Theory*, XXXVIII [1986], 101–17.

Guesnerie, Roger, and Claude Oddou, "Second Best Taxation as a Game," *Journal of Economic Theory*, XXV [1981], 67–91.

Holmstrom, Bengt, "Moral Hazard in Teams," *Bell Journal of Economics*, XIII [1982], 324–40.

Pauly, Mark, "Cores and Clubs," *Public Choice*, IX [1970], 53 65.

Schelling, Thomas, *Micromotives and Macrobehavior* (New York, NY: Norton, 1978).

Selten, Reinhard, "Equal Share Analysis of Characteristic Function Experiments," Tubingen, *Contributions to Experimental Economics*, III [1972].

Sorenson, J., J. Tschirhart, and W. Whinston, "A Theory of Pricing under Decreasing Costs," *American Economic Review*, LXVIII [1978a], 614–24.

—— "Private Good Clubs and the Core," *Journal of Public Economics* 10 [1978b], 77–95.

Spulber, Daniel, "Second-best Pricing and Cooperation," *RAND Journal of Economics*, XVII [1986], 239–50.

Thomson, William, and Hal Varian, "Theories of Justice Based on Symmetry," in *Social Goals and Social Organizations: Essays in Memory of Elisha Pazner*, L. Hurwicz, D. Schmeidler, and H. Sonnenschein, eds. (Cambridge: Cambridge University Press, 1985), Chapter 4.

Zachau, Ulrich, "Who Cooperates with Whom?" mimeograph, Nuffield College, Oxford, 1987.

Econometrica,
Vol. 67 No. 5 (September, 1999): 1185–1218

Clubs and the Market

By Bryan Ellickson, Birgit Grodal, Suzanne Scotchmer, and William R. Zame[1]

This paper defines a general equilibrium model with exchange and club formation. Agents trade multiple private goods widely in the market, can belong to several clubs, and care about the characteristics of the other members of their clubs. The space of agents is a continuum, but clubs are finite. It is shown that (i) competitive equilibria exist, and (ii) the core coincides with the set of equilibrium states. The central subtlety is in modeling club memberships and expressing the notion that membership choices are consistent across the population.

KEYWORDS: *Clubs, continuum models, public goods, core, club equilibrium.*

1 We thank Robert Anderson for tutelage and Kenneth Arrow and Joe Ostroy for helpful arguments. We thank seminar audiences at CalTech, the Conference on City Formation at Washington University in St. Louis, the Midwest Mathematical Economics Meetings (Fall 1996), the Public Choice Society Meetings, the Santa Fe Institute, the Stanford Institute for Theoretical Economics (Summer 1996), UC Berkeley, UC Santa Cruz and UCLA, and the University of Copenhagen (especially Mike Akemann, Larry Blume, Sara Castellanos, John Conley, David Cooper, Mike Ryall, Karl Vind, and Federico Weinschelbaum), three referees and the editor for many comments that improved both the content and the exposition. We thank the UCLA and UC Berkeley Academic Senate Committees on Research, the National Science Foundation and the Fulbright Foundation for financial support and the UCLA and UC Berkeley Departments of Economics and the Institute of Economics of the University of Copenhagen for gracious hospitality to Grodal, to Zame, and to Scotchmer and Zame, respectively during preparation of this paper.

1. Introduction

CONSUMPTION IS TYPICALLY A SOCIAL ACTIVITY. The company we keep affects our demand for private goods, and our consumption of private goods affects the company we seek. General equilibrium theory focuses on the interactions of consumers with the market, largely ignoring the social aspect of consumption. Club theory focuses on the social activity of consumption, largely ignoring the interactions of individuals with the market. This paper integrates club theory and general equilibrium theory, building a framework in which both markets and relationships matter.

We build here a competitive model of clubs, and thus follow a long tradition initiated by Buchanan (1965). (See Cornes and Sandler (1996) and Kurz (1997) for overviews of the literature.) Marriages, gyms, academic departments, golfing foursomes, and restaurant clienteles are the sorts of clubs we have in mind (but not large organizations like political jurisdictions in the sense of Tiebout (1956)). In addressing competition in club economies, the existing literature has treated economies with a finite number of agents, but such an assumption does not lead to an entirely satisfactory model of clubs or of competition. Club choice is intrinsically indivisible (one joins a club or one does not); as a consequence, the core of a club economy with a finite number of agents may well be empty. Moreover, in a finite economy individuals will generally have market power, so there is no reason to view such economies as perfectly competitive (even when the core is not empty). The clubs literature for the most part has concentrated on special circumstances or approximate notions of core and competition.[2] Our approach is quite different: following Aumann (1964), we build a general equilibrium model with a *continuum* of agents. In this framework, we define a decentralized notion of price-taking equilibrium parallel to the usual notion in exchange economies, show that (exact) equilibrium always exists, that equilibrium allocations are Pareto optimal and belong to the core (so that the core is always nonempty), and that club economies pass a standard test of perfect competition, the coincidence of the core with the set of equilibrium allocations.[3, 4]

Because the theory proposed here is intended as a competitive theory of clubs, we require that clubs be small relative to society as a whole. In our

---

2 See Ellickson (1973, 1979), Scotchmer and Wooders (1987), Conley and Wooders (1995), Gilles and Scotchmer (1997), and Scotchmer (1997) for instance.

3 Cole and Prescott (1997). provide a continuum model in a spirit similar to the present paper, but the objects of choice in that paper are lotteries over bundles of private goods and club memberships. Lotteries overcome the indivisibility problem by making choices divisible. Because we view the indivisibility as fundamental, we prefer to address it head-on. Closer to the present work is the unpublished paper of Makowski (1978), who interprets clubs as organizations formed by entrepreneurs.

4 Our companion paper, Ellickson, Grodal, Scotchmer, and Zame (1997b), treats approximate equilibrium and approximate decentralization in large finite economies.

continuum framework, the expression of this requirement is that clubs are finite; clubs are therefore comparable in size to individuals but infinitesimal relative to society. Because our description of a club includes the number of members in the club and their characteristics, however, it is meaningful to ask about the size and composition of clubs that form at equilibrium. Similarly, it is meaningful to ask about the relative numbers of clubs of different types that form at equilibrium (although the absolute number will always be zero or infinite).

We describe a club type by the number and the characteristics of its members and the activity in which the club is engaged. We allow formation of many possible types of clubs and trading of many private goods. The latter is especially important, because agents trade with the market and not just within clubs; if there is a single private good, there will be no trading with the market (only transfers within clubs). We allow each agent to belong to many clubs simultaneously.

Our model is competitive, despite the presence of externalities, because clubs are small and external effects are encapsulated within clubs. We assume that the number of external characteristics of individuals (the characteristics that matter to others) and the number of potential types of club are finite, and that the maximum number of clubs an individual can choose is finite. These assumptions guarantee that our choice space is finite dimensional, greatly simplifying the model and the proofs – but they are not required for competition. Useful extensions would allow an infinite number of differentiated private goods, an infinite number of differentiated external characteristics, and an infinite number of club types, and allow agents to choose an infinite number of club memberships – but such extensions will require an infinite dimensional choice space, and both the model and the proofs will necessarily be much more complicated.[5]

A key to our approach is that we define a club membership as an opening in a specific type of club, available to agents with a specified characteristic, and treat club memberships and private goods in parallel fashion as objects of choice. As in classical general equilibrium theory, where the description of a private good includes all the relevant aspects, so here the description of a club membership includes all the relevant aspects: number of other members, relevant characteristics of the other members, relevant characteristics of the member in question, purpose of the club, resources necessary to carry out that purpose, and institutional arrangements within the club. Just as a small chocolate bar, a large chocolate bar, and a large chocolate bar with almonds are different goods and may have different prices, so membership in a swimming pool club with 20 members,

---

5 See Mas-Colell (1975) and Ostroy and Zame (1994) for competitive models of exchange economies with infinitely many differentiated commodities.

a swimming pool club with 40 members, and a tennis club with 40 members are different memberships and may have different prices. Indeed, if gender matters, then admission for a female in a coeducational school is different from admission for a male in the same school, and may be priced differently.

Despite the parallel treatment of club memberships and private goods, there are important differences. First, and most importantly, the feasibility condition for trading of club memberships is different from the feasibility condition for trading of private goods. For private goods, feasibility means that demand be equal to supply. For club memberships, feasibility means that choices must be consistent across the population. For example, if a third of the population are women married to men, then a third of the population must be men married to women. This consistency condition must hold simultaneously for all types of clubs. Second, the prices of club memberships can be positive, negative, or zero (whereas prices of private goods must be positive). This is because club membership prices have two components: a (non-negative) share of the resource to form the club, and a transfer to other members of the club, which may be of any sign. These transfers internalize the externalities of club membership; in equilibrium, the value placed on these externalities will depend on tastes and on the relative supply of various characteristics. Third, club membership is inherently indivisible, with the consequence that consumption sets and preferred sets are not convex. Our continuum framework handles this difference very smoothly.[6]

Our proofs follow lines that are typical of general equilibrium theory, but with many subtleties. The central subtlety is in accommodating the club consistency condition, which has no analog in the general equilibrium literature. Another subtlety arises in the proof of core equivalence, where the separation theorem produces the decentralizing price vector; this price vector has both private good and club membership components, and we must be sure that the private good components are not identically zero. A third subtlety arises in the proof of existence of equilibrium, because the nature of club membership prices (which may be positive, negative, or zero) means that there is no obvious compact space of prices in which to apply a fixed point argument.

Following this Introduction, Section 2 provides motivating examples. The formal model is described in Section 3. Section 4 discusses welfare theorems and the core. Section 5 addresses the equivalence of the core and the set of equilibrium states, and Section 6 addresses the existence of equilibrium. The text outlines the proofs; details are in Section 7.

6 The convexifying effect of the continuum was first noted by Aumann (1964); see Mas-Colell (1977) for a model with indivisible private goods.

2. Examples

This section presents three examples illustrating various aspects of our framework. The first example uses a simple setting similar to Buchanan (1965) to highlight three important features of our approach: (i) clubs are infinitesimal in comparison to society as a whole but, because size is part of the description of a club type, it is meaningful to talk about the optimal size of a club; (ii) clubs of any particular type can be replicated with constant returns to scale (i.e. to form two clubs of a particular type requires just twice as many individuals and twice the inputs of commodities as to form a single club); (iii) congestion or a finite bound on club size is crucial: without such assumptions, equilibrium may fail to exist.

Example 2.1

(Crowding): Consider an economy with a continuum of consumers uniformly distributed on [0, 10]. There is a single private good; the endowment of consumer k is $e_k = k$. In addition to the private good, consumers have the option of constructing and using a swimming pool, either alone or in a club. Building a pool requires 6 units of the private good. A consumer who consumes x units of the private good derives utility $u(x; 0) = x$ if using no pool and $u(x; n) = 4x/n$ if belonging to a swimming pool club with n members. No one belongs to more than one club.

Normalize the price of the private good to 1, so consumer k has wealth k. Because only the size of clubs (and not their composition) matters to consumers, pool costs will be shared equally within each club, so the price of a membership in a club of size n is an equal share of the cost of production: $q_n = 6/n$. Choosing no pool will yield consumer k the utility k; sharing a pool in a club with n members will yield utility

$$u(k - q_n; n) = \frac{4}{n}\left(k - \frac{6}{n}\right).$$

In equilibrium, consumers stratify by wealth: the wealthiest consumers, those with wealth in (9, 10], have a pool of their own; consumers with wealth in (6, 9] share a pool with one other consumer; the poorest consumers, with wealth in [0, 6], consume the private good but do not enjoy the use of a pool. Clubs of size greater than 2 do not form in equilibrium.

Note how aversion to crowding provides an effective limit on club size; in the absence of any aversion to crowding, larger and larger clubs might be desirable and equilibrium might not exist. Suppose, for instance, that the utility derived from membership in a club of size n were $u(x; n) = 4x$ (rather than $u(x; n) = 4x/n$) and clubs could be of any size. Swimming pools would then be pure public goods, no equilibrium would exist, and a competitive theory of their provision would be inappropriate.

Our second example illustrates the importance of viewing and pricing club memberships for individuals with different characteristics as different commodities. The example is motivated by Arrow's (1972) commentary on Becker's (1957) discussion of market prices and segregation. The example affirms Arrow's insight that, in the absence of price discrimination, profit maximization leads to segregation, but it suggests another possibility as well: integration with price discrimination.

Example 2.2

(Segregation): Consider an economy with a continuum of consumers uniformly distributed on $[0, 1]$. Consumers in $[0, .3)$ are blue, consumers in $[.3, 1]$ are green. There is a single private good; each consumer has endowment 2. In addition to the private good, consumers have the option of constructing and using a duplex apartment. Building a duplex requires 2 units of the private good. An individual who consumes x units of the private good and no housing derives utility

$$u_B(x; 0) = u_G(x; 0) = x$$

while an individual who consumes x units of the private good and a duplex apartment derives utility according to his own characteristic and that of the occupant of the other half of the duplex:

$$u_B(x; BB) = 4x, \quad u_B(x; BG) = 6x,$$
$$u_G(x; GG) = 6x, \quad u_G(x; BG) = 4x,$$

using the obvious notation. (We omit some profiles because a consumer of type B cannot occupy a GG duplex, and so forth.)

Write $q_\omega(BB)$, $q_\omega(BG)$, $q_\omega(GG)$ for the prices paid by a consumer of type $\omega = B, G$ for the various kinds of housing. At equilibrium housing prices for each type of duplex must sum to the production cost of 2; in particular $q_B(BB) = q_G(GG) = 1$. At these prices, blue consumers can obtain utility 2 by choosing no housing, utility 4 by choosing a segregated duplex, and utility $6(2 - q_B(BG))$ by choosing an integrated duplex. Green consumers can obtain utility 2 by choosing no housing, utility 6 by choosing a segregated duplex, and utility $4(2 - q_G(BG))$ by choosing an integrated duplex. If any integrated housing is chosen at equilibrium, optimization by blue consumers entails that $6(2 - q_B(BG)) \geq 4$ and optimization by green consumers entails that $4(2 - q_G(BG)) \geq 6$. Equivalently, $q_B(BG) \leq 4/3$ and $q_G(BG) \leq 1/2$. Hence $q_B(BG) + q_G(BG) \leq 11/6$. This contradicts the fact that housing prices sum to the cost of production. At the unique equilibrium, therefore, all consumers live in segregated housing. Prices for segregated housing $q_B(BB) = q_G(GG) = 1$; prices for (undemanded) integrated housing are indeterminate, constrained only by the requirements

$$q_B(BG) \geq \frac{4}{3}, \quad q_G(BG) \geq \frac{1}{2}, \quad q_B(BG) + q_G(BG) \geq 2$$

However, segregation is not a necessary conclusion. Suppose that u_B $(x; B_G) = 10x$, with all else remaining the same. If no integrated housing is chosen at equilibrium, optimization by blue consumers entails that $10(2 - q_B (BG)) \leq 4$ and optimization by green consumers entails that $4(2 - q_G(BG)) \leq 6$. These inequalities are inconsistent with the fact that housing prices sum to the cost of production, so we conclude some blue consumers and some green consumers live in integrated housing. Because there are more green consumers than blue consumers, some green consumers must live in segregated housing; equating utilities for all green consumers we conclude that housing prices are $q_B (BB) = q_G (GG) = 1$, $q_B (BG) = 3/2$, $q_G (BG) = 1/2$. At these prices, green consumers are indifferent between integrated housing and segregated housing, but blue consumers strictly prefer integrated housing. At equilibrium, 3/7 of all green consumers live in integrated housing and the remainder live in segregated housing; blue consumers pay a premium to live in integrated housing.

Our third example shows why allowing for more than one private good matters: Because agents trade with the market, there is an interaction between the demand for club memberships and the demand for private goods; as a result, clubs can be priced out of existence. This phenomenon cannot occur when there is only one private good.

Example 2.3

(Marriage and the Market): Consider an economy with a continuum of consumers uniformly distributed on $[0, 1]$. Consumers in $[0, \beta)$ are male, and consumers in $[\beta, 1]$ are female, where $0 < \beta < 1$. There are 2 private goods; each consumer has endowment $[10, 10]$. Utility functions are (s means single and m means married):

$$u_M(x_1, x_2; s) = x_1, \quad u_F(x_1, x_2; s) = x_2$$
$$u_M(x_1, x_2; m) = u_F(x_1, x_2; m) = \frac{5}{2}\sqrt{x_1 x_2}.$$

We solve for equilibrium as a function of β, the proportion of males. Consider first the case $\beta < 1/2$. Write q_m, q_F for the gender-specific marriage prices. Because marriage is costless, $q_m + q_F = 0$ so marriage prices represent pure transfers: one sex subsidizes the other. To solve for the equilibrium, we hypothesize that marriage is an equilibrium outcome and work backwards to find prices. Normalize private good prices to sum to 1, so that everyone has wealth 10. Unmarried females (males) buy only good 2 (good 1). Married males and females spend q_m, q_F (respectively) and divide their remaining income between the two private goods. Assume that the "number" of married males is $\bar{m}$; $0 \leq \bar{m} \leq \beta$. Because utilities within marriage are Cobb-Douglas, market clearing for private goods yields:

$$(\beta - \overline{m})\frac{10}{p_1} + \overline{m}\left[\frac{10 - q_M}{2p_1} + \frac{10 - q_F}{2p_1}\right] = 10,$$

$$(1 - \beta - \overline{m})\frac{10}{p_2} + \overline{m}\left[\frac{10 - q_M}{2p_2} + \frac{10 - q_F}{2p_2}\right] = 10.$$

This uniquely determines private good prices, which are independent of the "number" of marriages: $p_1 = \beta$, $p_2 = 1 - \beta$. Suppose that some males are married. Because there are more females than males, some females necessarily remain single. Married consumers must receive at least as much utility as if single, and females must be indifferent between the two states (because some females are single at equilibrium). Thus

$$\frac{10}{1-\beta} = \frac{5}{2}\sqrt{\left(\frac{10 - q_F}{2\beta}\right)\left(\frac{10 - q_F}{2(1-\beta)}\right)},$$

$$\frac{10}{\beta} \leq \frac{5}{2}\sqrt{\left(\frac{10 - q_M}{2\beta}\right)\left(\frac{10 - q_{FM}}{2(1-\beta)}\right)}.$$

Hence we can solve for marriage prices:

$$q_F = 10 - 8\sqrt{\frac{\beta}{1-\beta}} \quad \text{and} \quad q_M \leq 10 - 8\sqrt{\frac{1-\beta}{\beta}}.$$

Because $q_M + q_F = 0$ these equations entail that $\beta \geq 1/5$. In the range $1/5 \leq \beta \leq 1/2$ we can solve uniquely for marriage prices, obtaining $q_F = 10 - 8\sqrt{\beta/(1-\beta)}$, $q_M = -q_F$. If $\beta = 1/5$ the number of married males is indeterminate; if $1/5 < \beta < 1/2$ all males are married. If $0 < \beta < 0$, the hypothesis that some males are married leads to a contradiction, so at equilibrium there are no marriages – but there are equilibria with no marriages.

For $\beta > 1/2$, the analysis is symmetrical, with the roles of men and women reversed. Finally, when $\beta = 1/2$ all males and females are married, but marriage prices are indeterminate.

We summarize the equilibrium correspondence by describing the "number" $\overline{m}$ of married males and the price q_F females pay to enter marriage. Note that m is indeterminate for $\beta = 1/5$, 4/5 and q_F is indeterminate for $0 < \beta < 1/5$, $\beta = 1/2$, and $4/5 < \beta < 1$:

$$0 < \beta < \frac{1}{5}: \quad \overline{m} = 0, \quad q_F \in \left[+10 - 8\sqrt{\frac{\beta}{1-\beta}}, -10 + \sqrt{\frac{1-\beta}{\beta}}\right],$$

$$\beta = \frac{1}{5}: \quad \overline{m} \in [0, \beta], \quad q_F = +10 - 8\sqrt{\frac{\beta}{1-\beta}},$$

$$\frac{1}{5} < \beta < \frac{1}{2}: \quad \overline{m} = \beta, \quad q_F = +10 - 8\sqrt{\frac{\beta}{1-\beta}},$$

$$\beta = \frac{1}{2}: \quad \overline{m} = \beta, \quad q_F \in [-2, +2],$$

$$\frac{1}{2} < \beta < \frac{4}{5}: \quad \overline{m} = 1 - \beta, \quad q_F = -10 + 8\sqrt{\frac{1-\beta}{\beta}},$$

$$\beta = \frac{4}{5}: \quad \overline{m} \in [0, 1-\beta], \quad q_F = -10 + 8\sqrt{\frac{1-\beta}{\beta}},$$

$$\frac{4}{5} < \beta < 1: \quad \overline{m} = 0, \quad q_F \in \left[+10 - 8\sqrt{\frac{\beta}{1-\beta}}, -10 + 8\sqrt{\frac{1-\beta}{\beta}}\right].$$

When the sex ratio is not extreme, the sex that is in short supply is subsidized to enter marriage. When the sex ratio is extreme, the subsidy that would be required is so large that the more populous sex prefers to remain single; marriage is priced out of existence.

For an example illustrating how easily our approach handles the possibility that individuals choose to belong to more than one club, see our working paper, Ellickson, Grodal, Scotchmer, and Zame (1997a).

3. Club Economies

3.1. Private Goods

Throughout, there are $N \geq 1$ perfectly divisible, publicly traded private goods; thus the space of private goods is $\mathbb{R}^N$. For $x, x \in \mathbb{R}^N$, we write $x > x'$ to mean $x_i > x_i'$ for each i, $x > x'$ to mean that $x \geq x'$ but $x \neq x'$, and $x \gg x'$ to mean that $x_i > x_i'$ for each i. We write $|x| = \sum_{n=1}^{N} |x_n|$.

3.2. Clubs

We will describe a *club type* by the number and characteristics of its members and the activity in which the club is engaged.

Let Ω be a finite set of *external characteristics* of potential members of a club. An element $\omega \in \Omega$ is a complete description of the characteristics of an individual that are relevant for the *other* members of a club. We call these characteristics "external" because they are the aspects of agents that create "externalities" within clubs, and because they are observable. Such characteristics might include sex, intelligence, appearance – even tastes and endowments, to the extent that such characteristics can be observed.

A *profile* (of a club) is a function $\pi : \Omega \to \mathbb{Z}_+ = \{0, 1, \ldots\}$ describing the external characteristics in a club. For $\omega \in \Omega$, $\pi(\omega)$ represents the number of members of the club having external characteristic ω. For π a profile, write $|\pi| = \sum_{\omega \in \Omega} \pi(\omega)$ for the total number of members.

There is a finite set Γ of *activities* available to a profile of agents. (Γ is simply an abstract set). We interpret activities as public projects in the sense of Ellickson (1979) and Mas-Colell (1980). An activity may incorporate a shared facility, a code of behavior or a publicly professed ideology. Agents may rank activities differently, and an individual's ranking may depend on his/her consumption of private goods. Activities are not traded.

A *club type* is a pair $c = (\pi, \gamma)$ consisting of a profile and an activity $\gamma \in \Gamma$. We take as given a finite set of possible club types, $Clubs = \{(\pi, \gamma)\}$. (In particular, there is a bound on club size.) Formation of the club (π, γ) requires a total input of private goods equal to $inp\,(\pi, \gamma) \in \mathcal{R}_+^N$.

A *club membership* is an opening in a particular club type for an agent of a particular external characteristic; i.e., a triple $m = (\omega, \pi, \gamma)$ such that $(\pi, \gamma) \in Clubs$ and $\pi(\omega) \geq 1$. (An agent can belong to a club only if the description of that club type includes one or more members with his/her external characteristics). Write $\mathcal{M}$ for the set of club memberships.

Each agent may choose to belong to many clubs or to none. A *list* is a function $\ell : \mathcal{M} \to \{0, 1, \ldots\}$, where $\ell(\omega, \pi, \gamma)$ specifies the number of memberships of type (ω, π, γ). Write:

$$Lists = \{\ell : \ell \text{ is a list}\}$$

for the set of lists. *Lists* is a set of functions from $\mathcal{M}$ to $\{0, 1, \ldots\}$, but we frequently view it as a subset of $\mathbb{R}^{\mathcal{M}}$, which is the set of functions from $\mathcal{M}$ to $\mathcal{R}$. We also assume throughout that there is an exogenously given upper bound M on the number of memberships an individual may choose.

3.3. Agents

The set of agents is a nonatomic finite measure space $(A, \mathfrak{F}, \lambda)$. That is, A is a set, $\mathfrak{F}$ is a σ-algebra of subsets of A, and λ is a nonatomic measure on $\mathfrak{F}$ with $\lambda(A) < \infty$.

A complete description of an agent $a \in A$ consists of his/her external characteristics, choice set, endowment of private goods, and utility function.[7] An external characteristic is an element $\omega \in \Omega$ The choice set X_a specifies the feasible bundles of private goods and club memberships, so $X_a \subset \mathbb{R}^N \times Lists$. For simplicity, we assume the only restriction on private good consumption is that it be nonnegative, so $X_a \subset \mathbb{R}_+^N \times Lists_a$ for some

7 We find it convenient to use utility functions rather than preferences.

subset $Lists_a \subset Lists.$[8] We assume that an individual can only belong to a club type offering memberships with his/her external characteristic; formally, $\ell(\omega, \pi, \gamma) = 0$ if $\ell \in Lists_a$, $(\omega, \pi, \gamma) \in \mathcal{M}$ and $\omega \neq \omega_a$. By assumption, the number of memberships an individual may choose is bounded by M, so $\ell \leq |\mathrm{M}|$ for each $\ell \in Lists_a$. The endowment is $e_a \in \mathbb{R}_+^N$. The utility function is defined over private goods consumptions and club memberships and is thus a mapping $u_a : X_a \to \mathbb{R}$. We assume throughout that utility functions $u_a(\cdot, \ell)$ are continuous and strictly monotone in private goods.

3.4. Club Economies

A *club economy* $\mathcal{E}$ is a mapping $a \to (\omega_a, X_a, e_a, u_a)$ for which:

- the external characteristic mapping $a \to \omega_a$ is a measurable function;
- the consumption set correspondence $a \to X_a$ is a measurable correspondence;
- the endowment mapping $a \to e_a$ is an integrable function;
- the utility mapping $(a, x, \ell) \to u_a(x, \ell)$ is a (jointly) measurable function (of all its arguments).[9]

We assume that the aggregate endowment $\bar{e} = \int_A e_a d\lambda(a)$ is strictly positive, so all private goods are represented in the aggregate.

3.5. States

A state of a club economy is a measurable mapping

$$(x, \mu) : A \to \mathbb{R}^N \times \mathbb{R}^{\mathcal{M}}$$

A state describes choices for each individual agent, ignoring feasibility at the level of the individual and at the level of society. *Individual feasibility* means $(x_a, \mu_a) \in X_a$. *Social feasibility* entails market clearing for private goods and consistent matching of agents.

We say that a membership vector $\bar{\mu} \in \mathbb{R}^{\mathcal{M}}$ is *consistent* if for every club type $(\pi, \gamma) \in Clubs$ there is a real number $\alpha(\pi, \gamma)$ such that

$$\bar{\mu}(\omega, \pi, \gamma) = \alpha(\pi, \gamma)\pi(\omega)$$

for each $\omega \in \Omega$ (The coefficient $\alpha(\pi, \gamma)$ may be interpreted as the "number" of clubs of type (π, γ) accounted for in $\bar{\mu}$.) A choice function $\mu : B \to Lists$ is consistent for B if the corresponding aggregate membership vector

---

8 Thus we incorporate into consumption sets various kinds of restrictions on club memberships. For instance, we may forbid some consumers to enter some club types.

9 This measurability requirement is equivalent to the usual requirement on measurability of preferences.

$\bar{\mu} = \int_B \mu_a d\lambda(a) \in \mathbb{R}^{\mathcal{M}}$ is consistent. (The aggregate membership vector $\bar{\mu}$ counts the "number" of memberships in each club type chosen by individuals in B of each characteristic. Consistency is the requirement that these numbers are in the same proportion as in the club types themselves). Write

$$Cons = \{ \bar{\mu} \in \mathbb{R}^{\mathcal{M}} : \bar{\mu} \text{ is consistent} \}.$$

Cons is a subspace of $\mathbb{R}^{\mathcal{M}}$. Because individuals choose nonnegative numbers of club memberships, feasible club choices induce aggregate membership vectors in the positive part $Cons_+ \subset Cons$.

The state (x, μ) is *feasible for* the measurable subset $B \subset A$ if it satisfies the following requirements:

(i) *Individual Feasibility*: $(x_a, \mu_a) \in X_a$ for each $a \in B$.

(ii) *Material Balance*:

$$\int_B x_a d\lambda(a) + \int_B \sum_{(\omega, \pi, \gamma) \in \mathcal{M}} \frac{1}{|\pi|} inp(\pi, \gamma)\mu_a(\omega, \pi, \gamma) d\lambda(a) = \int_B e_a d\lambda(a).$$

(iii) *Consistency*: $\int_B e_a d\lambda(a)$ is consistent.

The state (x, μ) is *feasible* if it is feasible for the set A itself.

A state of the economy will generally have "many" clubs of each club type. Because members of a club care only about the external characteristics of other members, and not about their identities, it is not necessary to distinguish different clubs of the same club type.

3.6. Pareto Optimality and the Core

We distinguish "weak" and "strong" notions of Pareto optimality and the core, and give a condition under which they coincide.

We say a feasible state (x, μ) is *weakly Pareto optimal* if there is no feasible state (x', μ') such that $u_a(x'_a, \mu_a) > u_a(x'_a, \mu_a)$ for almost all $a \in A$; we say (x, μ) is *strongly Pareto optimal* if there is no feasible state (x', μ') such that $u_a(x'_a, \mu'_a) \geq u_a(x_a, \mu_a)$ for all a' in some subset $A' \subset A$ having positive measure. We say (x, μ) is in the *weak core* if there is no subset $B \subset A$ of positive measure and state (x', μ') that is feasible for B such that $u_b(x'_b, \mu'_b) > u_b(x_b, \mu_b)$ for almost every $b \in B$; we say (x, μ) is in the *strong core* if there is no subset $B \subset A$ of positive measure and state (x', μ') that is feasible for B such that $u_b(x'_b, \mu'_b) \geq u_b(x_b, \mu_b)$ for every $b \in B$ and $u_{b'}(x'_{b'}, \mu'_{b'}) > u_{b'}(x_{b'}, \mu_{b'})$ for all b' in some subset $B' \subset B$ having positive measure. The strong Pareto set is a subset of the weak Pareto set, and the strong core is a subset of the weak core. The following assumption, adapted from Gilles and Scotchmer (1997), guarantees that the strong and weak Pareto sets coincide and that the strong and weak cores coincide.

We say that *endowments are desirable* if for every agent a and every list $\ell \in Lists(a)$, $U_a(e_a, 0) > u_a(0, \ell)$. That is, each agent would prefer to remain single and consume his endowment rather than to belong to any feasible set of clubs and consume no private goods.[10]

Proposition 3.1: *If endowments are desirable, then the weak and strong Pareto sets coincide and the weak and strong cores coincide.*

For the proof, see our working paper, Ellickson, Grodal, Scotchmer, and Zame (1997a). When endowments are desirable, we omit modifiers and refer unambiguously to Pareto optimality and the core.

3.7. Equilibrium

Competitive prices will be $(p, q) \in \mathbb{R}_+^N \times \mathbb{R}^{\mathcal{M}}$; p is a vector of prices for private goods and q is a vector of prices for club memberships. Because utility functions are assumed monotone in private goods, the prices of private goods will be nonnegative, but prices of club memberships may be positive, negative, or zero.

A *club equilibrium* consists of a feasible state (x, μ) and prices $(p, q) \in \mathbb{R}_+^N \times \mathbb{R}^{\mathcal{M}}, p \neq 0$, such that:

1) *Budget Feasibility for Individuals*: For almost all $a \in A$,

$$(p, q) \cdot (x_a, \mu_a) = p \cdot x_a + q \cdot \mu_a \leq p \cdot e_a.$$

2) *Optimization*: For almost all $a \in A$,

$$\left(x'_a, \mu'_a\right) \in X_a \quad \text{and}$$
$$u_a(x'_a, \mu'_a) > u_a(x_a, \mu_a) \Rightarrow p \cdot x'_a + q \cdot \mu'_a > p \cdot e_a.$$

3) *Budget Balance for Club Types*: For each $(\pi, \gamma) \in Clubs$,

$$\sum_{\omega \in \Omega} \pi(\omega) q(\omega, \pi, \gamma) = p \cdot inp(\pi, \gamma).$$

Thus, at an equilibrium, individuals optimize subject to their budget constraints and the sum of membership prices in a given club type is just enough to pay for the inputs to clubs of that type.

A *club quasi-equilibrium* satisfies (1), (3), and (2') instead of (2):

2') *Quasi-Optimization*: For almost all $a \in A$,

---

10 Desirability of endowments is weaker than the *indispensability assumption* of Mas-Colell (1980), which in our framework would be $u_a(0, \ell) = \min_{(x^*, \ell^*) \in x_a} u_a(x^*, \ell^*)$ for every $\ell \in Lists(a)$.

$$\left(x'_a, \mu'_a\right) \in X_a \quad \text{and}$$

$$u_a\left(x'_a, \mu'_a\right) > u_a(x_a, \mu_a) \Rightarrow p \cdot x'_a + q \cdot \mu'_a \geq p \cdot e_a$$

That is, nothing that is feasible and strictly preferred can cost strictly less than agent a's wealth. An equilibrium is necessarily a quasi-equilibrium.

In the exchange case, the possibility that quasi-equilibrium is not an equilibrium is frequently viewed as a mere technical problem, and can be ruled out by various simple assumptions (such as strictly monotone preferences and strictly positive aggregate endowments.) In the presence of indivisibilities (such as club memberships), however, the issue is more subtle. The following example illustrates the problems that may arise when private goods are used as inputs to club activities. (See Gilles and Scotchmer (1997) for an example illustrating the problems that may arise when endowments are not desirable.)

Example 3.2:

There are two private goods, a single external characteristic ω, and a single club type $c = (2, \gamma)$ consisting of two people, and requiring inputs $inp(c) = (2, 0)$. Agents can choose at most one club membership. All agents are identical, with endowment $(1, 1)$, and utility function:

$$u(x, 0) = 1 - e^{-x_1 - x_2},$$

$$u\left(x, \delta_{(\omega, c)}\right) = \sqrt{x_1} + \sqrt{x_2},$$

where $\delta_{(\omega, c)}$ is the list with unique membership (ω, c). Because endowments are desirable, the weak and strong cores coincide. In a core state, all agents belong to clubs and consume $x = (0, 1)$, so the entire supply of good 1 is used as input to the club activity. However, this state is not an equilibrium because the marginal rate of substitution of good 1 for good 2 is infinite, so the price ratio p_1/p_2 would have to be infinite also. On the other hand, the state is a quasi-equilibrium with prices $p = (1, 0)$, $q(\omega, c) = 1$. This is not an equilibrium, because good 2 is free and every agent desires more of it.)

In the familiar exchange setting, a quasi-equilibrium may fail to be an equilibrium if some agents are in the "minimum expenditure situation": consumptions require expenditures exactly equal to wealth, and slightly smaller expenditures are not possible. As the example above illustrates, this situation can arise easily in club economies because private goods are used as inputs to club activities, and club choices are indivisible. The following assumption (cf. Mas-Colell (1985)) is one of several that will guarantee that a quasi-equilibrium is an equilibrium.

Let $\mathcal{E}$ be a club economy and let (x, μ) be a feasible state. Write δ_j for the consumption bundle consisting of one unit of good j and nothing else. Say that (x, μ) is *club linked* if whenever $I \cup J = \{1, \ldots, N\}$ is a partition of the set of private goods and $x_{ai} = 0$ for all $i \in I$ and almost all $a \in A$, then for almost all $a \in A$ there exist $r \in \mathbb{R}_+, j \in J$ such that

$$u_a(e_a + r\delta_j, 0) > u_a(x_a, \mu_a).$$

That is, if, as in Example 3.2, the entire social endowment of the private goods in I is used to produce club activities, then for almost all agents a, there is some good $j \notin I$ and some sufficiently large level of consumption of good j such that agent a would prefer consuming his endowment together with this large level of good j, and belong to no clubs, rather than consume the bundle x_a in the club memberships μ_a. Say that $\mathcal{E}$ is *club irreducible* if every feasible allocation is club linked.

Proposition 3.3: *Let $\mathcal{E}$ be a club economy for which endowments are desirable. If (x, μ), (p, q) is a club quasi-equilibrium and (x, μ) is club linked, then $p \gg 0$ and (x, μ), (p, q) is a club equilibrium.*

Proof: We show first that all private good prices are strictly positive. If not, let I be the set of indices for which $p_i > 0$, and let $J \neq \oslash$ be the complementary set of indices. Fix $i \in I$. If $x_{ai} \neq 0$ some set of consumers having positive measure, then some of these consumers could sell a small amount of their consumption of x_i and buy an unlimited quantity of x_j (for any $j \in J$) and be strictly better off with a lower expenditure. This would contradict the quasi-equilibrium conditions. We conclude that, for each $i \in I, x_{ai} = 0$ for almost all $a \in A$. Club linkedness guarantees that all consumers would prefer to consume their endowments plus a large quantity of some commodity $j \in J$ rather than their quasi-equilibrium consumption. Since aggregate endowments of private goods are strictly positive, the endowments of a nonnull set of consumers have a strictly positive value and, by continuity of preferences, those consumers would prefer to consume a very large fraction of their endowment plus a large quantity of commodity x_j rather than their quasi-equilibrium consumption. Again, this would contradict the quasi-equilibrium conditions, so we conclude that all private good prices are strictly positive.

If (x, μ), (p, q) is not an equilibrium, then there is a nonnull set of agents who are quasi-optimizing, but not optimizing. For each such a there is a choice $(x', \mu') \in X_a$ that is strictly preferred to agent a's quasi-equilibrium choice and costs no more than his endowment. Desirability of endowments entails that $x' \neq 0$, so $p \cdot x' > 0$. Continuity of preferences entails that there is a bundle x'' such that $p \cdot x'' < p \cdot x'$, $(x'', \mu') \in X_a$ and (x'', μ') is strictly preferred to agent a's quasi-equilibrium choice, but costs strictly less than his endowment. This is a contradiction, so the proof is complete.

Q.E.D.

3.8. Pure Transfers

Equilibrium requires that the sum of membership prices in each club type exactly pays for the required inputs. An equivalent notion will be more convenient in proofs. Say that $q \in \mathbb{R}^{\mathcal{M}}$ is a *pure transfer* if $q \in Trans$, defined as

$$Trans = \{q \in \mathbb{R}^{\mathcal{M}} : q \cdot \mu = 0 \text{ for each } \mu \in Cons\}.$$

Thus for each club type (π, γ) and $q \in Trans$, $\sum_{\omega \in \Omega} \pi(\omega) q(\omega, \pi, \gamma) = 0$.
A *pure transfer equilibrium* is a feasible state (x, μ) and prices $(p, q) \in \mathbb{R}^n_+ \setminus \{0\} \times \mathbb{R}^{\mathcal{M}}$ such that :

1) *Budget Feasibility*: For almost all $a \in A$,

$$p \cdot x_a + q \cdot \mu_a + \sum_{(\omega, \pi, \gamma)} p \cdot \frac{1}{|\pi|} inp(\pi, \gamma) \mu_a(\omega, \pi, \gamma) \leq p \cdot e_a.$$

2) *Optimization*: For almost all $a \in A$,
   if $(x'_a, \mu'_a) \in X_a$ and $(x'_a, \mu'_a) > (x_a, \mu_a)$,
   then $p \cdot x'_a + q \cdot \mu'_a + \sum_{(\omega, \pi, \gamma)} p \cdot \frac{1}{|\pi|} inp(\pi, \gamma) \mu'_a(\omega, \pi, \gamma) > p \cdot e_a.$

3) *Pure Transfers*: $q \in Trans$.

We define a pure transfer quasi-equilibrium in the obvious way.

The following lemma tells us that equilibrium (respectively quasi-equilibrium) and pure transfer equilibrium (respectively pure transfer quasi-equilibrium) are equivalent notions; we leave the simple proof to the reader.

Lemma 3.4: *Let $\mathcal{E}$ be a club economy and let $q, q^* \in \mathbb{R}^{\mathcal{M}}$ be such that*

$$q^*(\omega, \pi, \gamma) = q(\omega, \pi, \gamma) + p \cdot \frac{1}{|\pi|} inp(\pi, \gamma).$$

Then: $(x, \mu), (p, q)$ is a pure transfer equilibrium (respectively, pure transfer quasi-equilibrium) if and only if quasi-equilibrium $(x, \mu), (p, q^*)$ is a club equilibrium (respectively, club quasi-equilibrium).

4. The Welfare Theorems and the Core

For exchange economies, the first welfare theorem asserts that equilibrium states are Pareto optimal. The corresponding result is easily established for club economies.

Theorem 4.1: *Every club equilibrium state of a club economy belongs to the weak core and, in particular, is weakly Pareto optimal. If endowments are* *desirable, every club equilibrium state belongs to the strong core and, in particular, is strongly Pareto optimal.*

Proof: Let $\mathcal{E}$ be a club economy and let (x_a, μ_a) be an equilibrium state, supported by the prices $p \in \mathbb{R}_+^N \setminus \{0\}, q \in \mathbb{R}^M$. If (x, μ) is not in the weak core, there is a subset $B \subset A$ of positive measure and a state (y, v) that is feasible for B and preferred to (x, μ) by every member of B. Feasibility of (y, v) for the coalition B entails the material balance condition,

$$\int_B y_a d\lambda(a) + \int_{B_{(\omega,\pi,\gamma)\in M}} \sum \frac{1}{|\pi|} inp(\pi, \gamma) v_a(\omega, \pi, \gamma) d\lambda(a) = \int_B e_a d\lambda(a),$$

and the budget balance condition for each club type (π, γ),

$$\sum_{\omega \in \Omega} \pi(\omega) q(\omega, \pi, \gamma) = p \cdot inp(\pi, \gamma).$$

Combining these with the consistency condition, we conclude that

$$\int_B (p, q) \cdot (y_a, v_a) d\lambda(a) = \int_B p \cdot e_a d\lambda(a).$$

Hence there is a set $B' \subset B$ having positive measure for which

$$(p, q) \cdot (y_b, v_b) \leq p \cdot e_b$$

for every $b \in B'$. Since (y, v) is unanimously preferred to (x, μ) by members of B, this contradicts the equilibrium nature of (x, μ). We conclude that (x, μ) is in the weak core, as desired. That (x, μ) is weakly Pareto optimal follows immediately by taking $B = A$ in the argument above. If endowments are desirable, the weak and strong cores coincide and the sets of weak and strong Pareto sets coincide, so the proof is complete.

Q. E. D.

For exchange economies, the second welfare theorem asserts that every Pareto optimal allocation can be supported as an equilibrium conditional on a suitable reallocation of endowments. Surprisingly, the second welfare theorem fails in club economies; for examples we refer the reader to our working paper.[11]

---

11 For exchange economies with a finite number of agents, the second welfare theorem depends on convexity of consumption sets and preferences – requirements that fail in club economies because club memberships are indivisible. However, for exchange economies with a continuum of agents, the second welfare theorem does not require convexity of consumption sets or preferences.

5. Core/Equilibrium Equivalence

In this section we establish that nonatomic club economies pass a familiar test of perfect competition: The core coincides with equilibrium states.

Theorem 5.1: Let $\mathcal{E}$ be a nonatomic club economy in which endowments are desirable and uniformly bounded above. Then every core state can be supported as a club quasi-equilibrium and every core state that is club linked can be supported as a club equilibrium. In particular, if $\mathcal{E}$ is club irreducible, then the core coincides with the set of club equilibrium states.

The proof in Section 7 parallels the Vind (1964) and Schmeidler (1969) proofs of Aumann's core equivalence theorem for exchange economies: Construct a preferred net trade correspondence and an aggregated net preferred set, and apply the Lyapunov convexity theorem to show that the aggregate net preferred set is convex. Use the core property to show that the aggregate net preferred set is disjoint from a cone that represents feasible net trades for all coalitions. Find a price that separates the aggregate net preferred set from this cone and show that this is a quasi-equilibrium price. Use club linkedness to conclude that the quasi-equilibrium is an equilibrium.

The argument contains two surprises that are not present in the exchange case. The first is that we require endowments to be bounded. As the following example demonstrates, this is not merely an artifact of the proof. If endowments are unbounded, the core may not coincide with the set of equilibrium states and equilibrium may not exist.

Example 5.2:

There is a single consumption good, two external characteristics M, F (male, female), and a single club type c consisting of one agent of each characteristic (i.e., monogamous marriage) and requiring no inputs. Agents can choose at most one membership. Agents in the intervals [0, 1/2) and [1/2, 1] are respectively males and females. Males love marriage and females hate it:

$$u_a(x,0) = x, \qquad \text{for all } a \in [0, 1],$$
$$u_a\big(x,\delta_{(M,c)}\big) = 2x, \qquad \text{for all } a \in [0, 1/2) \text{ (males)},$$
$$u_a\big(x,\delta_{(F,c)}\big) = 1 - e^{-x}, \qquad \text{for all } a \in [1/2, 1] \text{ (females)},$$

where $\delta_{(\omega,c)}$ is a list with a single membership (ω, c). Endowments are $1/\sqrt{a}$. It is easily checked that the initial state is the unique element of the core but is not an equilibrium: There is no upper bound on the amount men would pay to enter a marriage, because males are willing to give up half their endowment to enter a marriage, and male endowments are unbounded. But no female is willing to enter a marriage at any price.

The other surprise is that it will not be good enough to find prices (p, q) that separate the aggregated net preferred set from the cone representing feasible net trades; we must also be sure that $p \neq 0$. To achieve this we will separate the aggregate net preferred set from a cone that is larger than the cone representing feasible net trades. To show that the aggregate net preferred set is disjoint from this cone, we will need to show that if (y, v) is a state, $B \subset A$ is a coalition, and v is "nearly" consistent for B, then there is a large subset $B' \subset B$ such that v is (exactly) consistent for B'. This idea is formalized in Lemma 7.1.

6. Existence of Equilibrium

Theorem 6.1: *Let $\mathcal{E}$ be a nonatomic club economy. If endowments are desirable and uniformly bounded above, then a club quasi-equilibrium exists. If in addition $\mathcal{E}$ is club irreducible, then a club equilibrium exists.*

The structure of the argument will be familiar: construct an excess demand correspondence, use a fixed point theorem to find a zero, and show that this zero is an equilibrium. However, there are many subtleties:

- The balance condition for private goods is that the excess demand for private goods is 0, but the balance condition for club memberships is that the demand for club memberships is in *Cons.*
- In equilibrium, prices for private goods must be positive, but prices for club membership may be positive, negative, or 0. Hence the relevant space of all prices is not a proper cone, and the usual forms of the excess demand lemma will not apply.
- Private good prices can be normalized to sum to 1, but club membership prices admit no obvious normalization or bound.
- We assume that all private goods are present in the aggregate, but not that all external characteristics are present. Further, some club types might not be chosen at equilibrium. In effect, we must construct reservation prices for club memberships that are not available or are not chosen.

As the following example illustrates, club membership prices may be indeterminate and unbounded.

Example 6.2:

There is a single consumption good, and two external characteristics, $\Omega = \{M, F\}$. There are two club types c_1, c_2 each consisting of one male (M) and one female (F), and requiring no inputs. Agents can choose at most 2 memberships. Agents in $[0, 1/2)$ are male; agents in $[1/2, 1]$ are female. Each agent's endowment is 1. Utility functions are:

$$u_a(x, 0) = x,$$
$$u_a\left(x, \delta_{(\omega,c_1)}\right) = u_a\left(x, \delta_{(\omega,c_2)}\right) = 1 - e^{-x},$$
$$u_a\left(x, 2\delta_{(\omega,c_1)}\right) = u_a\left(x, 2\delta_{(\omega,c_2)}\right) = 1 - e^{-x},$$
$$u_a\left(x, \delta_{(\omega,c_1)} + \delta_{(\omega,c_2)}\right) = 2x,$$

where $\omega = M, F$ according to whether agent a is male or female, $2\delta_{(\omega,c)}$ is the list consisting of 2 memberships of type (ω, c) and $\delta_{(\omega,c_1)} + \delta_{(\omega,c_2)}$ is the list consisting of one membership of type (ω, c_1) and one membership of type (ω, c_2). Thus, both males and females hate belonging to a single club or two clubs of the same type, but love belonging to two clubs of different types. The core consists of a single point: all agents choose one club of each type and consume their endowments. This state is supported as an equilibrium by any private good prices and club membership prices such that $p > 0$ and

$$q(M, c_1) + q(F, c_1) = 0,$$
$$q(M, c_2) + q(F, c_2) = 0,$$
$$q(M, c_1) + q(M, c_2) = 0,$$
$$q(F, c_1) + q(F, c_2) = 0,$$

The proof circumvents the indeterminacy and unboundedness of club membership prices by focusing on list prices, which can be bounded in the following way. Normalize private good prices to sum to 1. By assumption, individual endowments are uniformly bounded, so individual incomes are uniformly bounded. Hence if $q \in \mathbb{R}^M$ is a vector of membership prices, $\ell \in Lists$ is a list, and if the list price $q \cdot \ell$ exceeds the bound on individual incomes, then the demand for ℓ will be 0. Thus the upper bound on individual incomes provides an upper bound for list prices. To construct a lower bound for list prices (keeping in mind that list prices might be negative), we show that, for lists chosen at equilibrium, if some individuals are paying large negative list prices, then others are paying large positive list prices. The construction we use is formalized in Lemma 7.2.

The existence proof in Section 7 has 8 steps:

1. For each positive integer k, construct a perturbed economy $\mathcal{E}^k$ by adjoining a few agents of each external characteristic, with utility functions linear in private good consumption.
2. For the perturbed economy $\mathcal{E}^k$, use the adjoined agents to identify a compact set of prices in which to find an equilibrium.
3–6. Construct an excess demand correspondence for $\mathcal{E}^k$, and find a fixed point that maximizes the value of excess demand. Show that this is an equilibrium for the perturbed economy: excess demand for private goods equals 0 and demand for club memberships is consistent.

7–8. The previous steps give an equilibrium for each $\mathcal{E}^k$, with associated prices (p^k, q^k). Now show that there is a sequence of such equilibrium prices that satisfy a uniform bound independent of k. Take limits of these uniformly bounded equilibrium prices as $k \to \infty$ and apply Fatou's lemma to construct an equilibrium for $\mathcal{E}$.

PROOFS: [omitted – ed.]

References

ARROW, K. (1972). "Models of Job Discrimination," in *Racial Discrimination in Economic Life*, ed. by A. H. Pascal. Lexington, MA: D. C. Heath.

AUMANN, R. (1964): "Markets with a Continuum of Traders," *Econometrica*, 32, 39–50.

BECKER, G. (1957): *The Economics of Discrimination*. Chicago: University of Chicago Press.

BUCHANAN, J. (1965): "An Economic Theory of Clubs," *Economica*, 32, 1–14.

COLE, H., AND E. PRESCOTT (1997): "Valuation Equilibrium with Clubs," *Journal of Economic Theory*, 74, 19–39.

CONLEY, J. P., AND M. WOODERS (1995): "Equivalence of the Core and Competitive Equilibrium in a Tiebout Economy with Crowding Types," Department of Economics, University of Illinois, Champaign.

CORNES, R., AND T. SANDLER (1996): *The Theory of Externalities, Public Goods and Club Goods*. Cambridge: Cambridge University Press.

ELLICKSON, B. (1973): "A Generalization of the Pure Theory of Public Goods," *American Economic Review*, 63, 417–432.

—— (1979):"Competitive Equilibrium with Local Public Goods," *Journal of Economic Theory*, 21, 46–61.

ELLICKSON, B., B. GRODAL, S. SCOTCHMER, AND W. ZAME (1997a): "Clubs and the Market: Continuum Economies," UCLA Working Paper.

—— (1997b): "Clubs and the Market: Large Finite Economies," UCLA Working Paper.

GILLES, R. P., and S. SCOTCHMER (1997): "Decentralization in Replicated Club Economies with Multiple Private Goods," *Journal of Economic Theory*, 72, 363–387.

HILDENBRAND, W. (1974): *Core and Equilibria of a Large Economy*. Princeton: Princeton University Press.

KURZ, M. (1997): "Game Theory and Public Economics," in *Handbook of Game Theory, Vol. II*, ed. by R. Aumann and S. Hart. Amsterdam: Elsevier North-Holland, 1153–1192.

MAKOWSKI, L. (1978): "A Competitive Theory of Organizations," Mimeograph.

306   B. Ellickson, B. Grodal, S. Scotchmer, and W. Zame

MAS-COLELL, A. (1975): "A Model of Equilibrium with Differentiated Commodities," *Journal of Mathematical Economics*, 2, 263–295.
—— (1977): "Indivisible Commodities and General Equilibrium Theory," *Journal of Economic Theory*, 16, 433–456.
—— (1980): "Efficiency and Decentralization in the Pure Theory of Public Goods," *Quarterly Journal of Economics*, 94, 625–641.
—— (1985): *The Theory of General Equilibrium: A Differentiable Approach*. Cambridge: Cambridge University Press.
OSTROY, J., AND W. R. ZAME (1994): "Non-atomic Economies and the Boundaries of Perfect Competition," *Econometrica*, 62, 593–633.
SCHMEIDLER, D. (1969): "Competitive Equilibria in Markets with a Continuum of Traders and Incomplete Preferences," *Econometrica*, 37, 578–585.
SCOTCHMER, S. (1997): "On Price-Taking Equilibrium in Club Economies with Nonanonymous Crowding," *Journal of Public Economics*, 65, 75–88.
SCOTCHMER, S., AND M. WOODERS (1987): "Competitive Equilibrium and the Core in Club Economies with Anonymous Crowding," *Journal of Public Economics*, 34, 159–174.
TIEBOUT, C. M. (1956): "A Pure Theory of Local Public Goods," *Journal of Political Economy*, 64, 416–424.
VIND, K. (1964): "Edgeworth Allocations in an Exchange Economy with Many Traders," *International Economic Review*, 5:165–177.

PART V

EVOLUTIONARY GAME THEORY

Eddie Dekel and Suzanne Scotchmer, "On the Evolution of Attitudes Towards Risk in Winner-Take-All Games" (1999)

INTRODUCTION ARTHUR J. ROBSON

Suzanne Scotchmer (together with coauthor Eddie Dekel) made two pioneering contributions to the emerging field of the biological basis of economics (Scotchmer and Dekel, 1992, 1999). The second of these papers follows this introduction. Both papers have had an impact, but both also have the potential to inspire further work.

1. Evolution of Optimizing Behavior

Dekel and Scotchmer (1992) examines the details of how optimizing behavior might be implemented in the class of symmetric two-player games. With limits on the types of choices allowed, "irrational" choices may survive. For example, if only pure strategies can be implemented by agents, a pure strategy that is never a best reply may survive under the replicator dynamics. This happens if the associated dominating strategy involves mixing. If mixed strategies can be implemented, however, only rationalizable strategies survive.

A more subtle result of Dekel and Scotchmer (1992) obtains when some agents implement a more sophisticated rule that seems closer to full rationality: choosing a best reply to the mix of strategies in the last period's population. Other agents make pure or mixed choices as before. Now such partial optimizers need not drive out other players who make a dominated choice. Hence an incomplete improvement in the rationality of one group of players may enable "irrational" choices to survive elsewhere.

Dekel and Scotchmer (1992) was one of the first in a strand of literature that came to consider how evolution might have acted to partially devolve control to the individual in a way that is evolutionarily optimal. This strand of the literature came to apply, explicitly or implicitly, a principal–agent metaphor – that casts evolution in the role of the principal, and the individual in the role of the agent (see, e.g., Robson, 2001).

2. Preferences for Risk-Taking

Dekel and Scotchmer (1999) investigates when winner-take-all contests engender risk-preferring behavior. Such contests may approximate the mating situations once faced by males. Hence the risk-preferring behavior that is actually now observed, particularly in young males, would have an evolutionary explanation.

When analyzed carefully, the models of Dekel and Scotchmer (1999) produce results that are conditionally supportive of the advantages of risk-taking behavior. There are two models considered.

2.1 Random Matching Model

The first of these – the "random matching model" – involves an infinite population, divided into an infinite number of finite groups, each of size m. Individuals have a choice from some finite menu of gambles. Within each group, the individual with the highest realized payoff produces m offspring, and the others produce none, so that the total population remains constant.

Suppose each of the possible gambles is taken by an associated type, and the overall infinite population starts with some interior type distribution. The distribution of types within each group of size m is then multinomial. Since there are an infinite number of groups, this multinomial distribution is represented exactly in these groups. Within each group, there is a probability that any given type, l, say, wins. Again, since there are an infinite number of groups, this probability is the exact fraction of these groups in which l wins. Hence the evolution of the type distribution is described by a deterministic replicator dynamic that allows for m player interactions.

It is intuitive that this structure will select for risk-taking. But in what precise sense is this true? Dekel and Scotchmer observe that strict first-order stochastic dominance (FOSD) is sufficient, but it is not necessary – that is, a gamble F may win over another gamble G even if F does not FOSD G.

Perhaps second-order stochastic dominance (SOSD) captures the situation better? That is, if a gamble F is riskier than a gamble G in the sense of strict SOSD then perhaps F will win over G? A counterexample for $m = 2$ disproves this as a general result; however, a result along these lines is subsequently shown to be valid for large enough m.

A general criterion that is shown to generate a winning type for large enough m is that of "tail dominance." A gamble F tail dominates G, loosely speaking, if F FOSD G for all sufficiently large outcomes. It is irrelevant then how F and G are related for smaller outcomes, which distinguishes this criterion from FOSD or SOSD. (More precisely, F "tail dominates" G if there exists $\bar{x} > 0$ such that $F(\bar{x}) < G(\bar{x})$ and $F(x) < G(x)$ for all $x \geq \bar{x}$.)

Proposition 2 states that F tail dominates G if F strictly FOSD G or if G strictly SOSD F. The notions of FOSD and SOSD are defined on page 316. In particular, the definition of SOSD relates the indefinite integrals of F and G, and is equivalent to the requirement that G is preferred to F for all increasing concave utilities. This implies that FOSD implies SOSD. If G FOSD F and so G SOSD F, Proposition 2 generates a contradiction.

However, the definition of SOSD apparently intended here assumes that the means of the gambles being compared are the same. Under that requirement, F will tail dominate G if G strictly SOSD F.

The key result for the random matching model is Proposition 5 – that any distribution in the menu that tail dominates all the other distributions will be selected by the evolutionary process in the long run, if m is large enough.

2.2 Playing the Field Model

The second of these models – the "playing the field" model – involves each player being pitted against the entire population. This population is of size n, where n is now finite. The player with the highest payoff has n offspring; the others have none, so the population remains of constant size. Mutation must be introduced into this model, since otherwise it will converge to a degenerate distribution, with only one gamble remaining, in one iteration.

Tail dominance is not now sufficient for evolutionary success. However, a strengthened version of tail dominance – "strong tail dominance" – is sufficient. (One distribution, F, say, is said to "strongly tail dominate" another distribution, G, if there is an outcome level $\bar{x} > 0$ such that $G(\bar{x}) = 1$ but $F(\bar{x}) < 1$.)

2.3 A Related Paper

There is not a large literature in economics on the evolution of greater risk tolerance among males, despite the interest and importance of this issue. However, Robson (1996) is one paper with a very similar motivation to Dekel and Scotchmer (1999).

Robson (1996) considers an explicit mating scenario, where females are identical and males differ only in terms of wealth. Females choose a male based on the share of his wealth they will be able to use to enhance fertility. Prior to these choices being made, however, males may opt to take various fair gambles over wealth. This leads to gambling by the males.

If a male, for example, currently has a wealth level that would not attract any females, he has nothing to lose from gambling. If he wins, he will have enough wealth to attract at least one mate; if he loses, he is no worse off than originally. More generally, even if the male has more wealth than that, enough to attract some number of females, it may pay to take some fair bet.

If he wins, he has enough to attract one more mate; if he loses he still has enough to attract the original number.

2.4 Empirical Predictions

Dekel and Scotchmer (1999) has an illuminating final section that discusses the relevant data – especially the implication that males might well be less risk-averse than females. In this connection, a useful survey has subsequently been published by Croson and Gneezy (2009). This documents evidence of lower risk-aversion among males in economic contexts, in particular. Although Croson and Gneezy are agnostic about whether this differential is genetic or encultured, this evidence broadly supports Dekel and Scotchmer (1999) (and Robson, 1996).

2.5 The Evolution of a Concern with Relative Wealth

Both Dekel and Scotchmer (1999) and Robson (1996) derive a concern with relative standing from evolution. A basic question with respect to this approach is as follows. Participants in a winner-take-all game, for example, who maximize fitness should care about relative standing and so should take risks, as described here. But why is an embedded concern with relative standing necessary? That is, suppose an individual cares about absolute fitness, but understands how the winner-take-all game creates a need to do well relatively, and so chooses appropriately. Such an individual could then also choose appropriately in a new game where there is no induced concern for relative standing. On the other hand, an individual with an embedded concern for relative standing is likely to behave inappropriately in such a new game.

It is empirically compelling that individuals are concerned intrinsically with relative standing. It is also highly plausible that evolution is responsible for this concern. The above argument shows, however, that it is not straightforward to model this.

An analogous argument would apply in a conventional setting where a tournament induced a concern with relative standing among individuals who are fundamentally indifferent to others. Pushing the issue back into evolutionary biology simply pushes back the question as well.

The resolution of the theoretical difficulty of accounting for non-selfish behavior, despite the strong evidence that there is in favor of it, might ultimately lie in recognizing the importance of complexity and bounded rationality. That is, we have evolved a concern with relative standing since such induced concerns were appropriate in many games we faced and, furthermore, it was cognitively too demanding to separately analyze each such game in detail.

312   E. Dekel and S. Scotchmer

3. Conclusion

Suzanne Scotchmer made pioneering theoretical contributions to the evolutionary foundations of economics. Dekel and Scotchmer (1999), which follows, demonstrates that these contributions were, at the same time, motivated by important empirical issues.

I thank the Canada Research Chair Program, the Human Evolutionary Studies Program at SFU, and the Social Sciences and Humanities Research Council of Canada for financial support.

Journal of Economic Theory,
Vol. 87, No. 1,
July 1999, pp. 125–143.

On the Evolution of Attitudes Towards Risk in Winner-Take-All Games*

Eddie Dekel[†]

Departments of Economics, Northwestern University, Evanston, Illinois and Tel Aviv University, Tel Aviv, Israel

and

Suzanne Scotchmer

GSPP and Department of Economics, University of California, 2607 Hearst, Berkeley, California 94720–7320

Received March 9, 1997; revised March 14, 1999

A long-standing conjecture is that winner-take-all games such as patent races lead to the survival of risk-takers and the extinction of risk-averters. In many species a winner-take-all game determines the males' right to reproduce, and the same argument suggests that males will evolve to be risk-takers. Psychological and sociological evidence buttresses the argument that males are more risk-taking than females. Using an evolutionary model of preference-formation, we investigate to what extent evolution leads to risk-taking in winner-take-all environments.

Journal of Economic Literature Classification Numbers: C7, D8.

* We are grateful to Drew Fudenberg, Wulong Gu, Hans Hvide, Arthur Robson, Bill Zame, two referees, and the associate editor for helpful comments. We acknowledge financial support from the NSF, IBER, and Tel Aviv University.
† This work was begun while this author was at the University of California at Berkeley.

1. Introduction

Economists typically take preferences as given. This sets them apart from other social scientists, such as psychologists, who often try to explain preferences. In this paper we explore an evolutionary model where preferences, in particular attitudes toward risk, are endogenously determined.

In economics, preferences are simply rules for choosing among feasible consumption bundles. If "successful" choice rules become more prevalent in society, then the distribution of choice rules, hence preferences, is an endogenous outcome. While there are many notions of "success" and various dynamic processes that can determine how successful rules proliferate, we consider an evolutionary process. That is, success means reproductive success, and choice rules (preferences) are inherited by offspring from their parents. Preferences can be described as inherited either if children emulate their parents' choices or if preferences are genetically coded.

Of course, if preferences are endogenous, something else must be exogenous, namely the "game" in which reproductive success is determined. We investigate winner-take-all games, which are common in nature: the leading male(s) mate with (almost) all the females, and therefore only that male's genes (hence preferences) are inherited by the subsequent generation. In a winner-take-all environment it pays to take risks, so one might expect that risk-taking preferences become dominant in the population. For example, Tirole [29, pp. 396–7] explains that R&D competitions favor riskier choices in the sense of mean-preserving spreads, since patent races resemble winner-take-all games. We explore the sense in which risk taking is selected in winner-take-all environments, and discover that the evolutionary outcome is subtler than suggested.

In particular, risk taking is not selected if the winner-take-all competition is in small groups, and in large groups the selected form of risk taking can depend on whether winner-take-all games are played simultaneously in many randomly matched groups from a large population, or whether there is only one match that comprises the entire population. In Sections 2 and 3 we present these two winner-take-all environments and show what form of risk taking evolves.

To apply our theory to humans, we need to argue that humans inherit risk-taking behavior from ancestors in whom risk-taking was evolutionarily selected via winner-take-all games. The conjecture seems more plausible for males than for females, both because there is considerable evidence from biologists and sociologists that males are more risk-taking, and because one can point to rituals in the animal world where males compete in tournaments for the right to mate. The evidence we have found, which is reviewed in Section 4, is at best indirect. To build a bridge between the observation that winner-take-all games lead to (a form of) risk taking and the conclusion that human males will therefore evolve to be risk-takers, we argue that

- among species where winner-take-all games determine reproductive success, the winning behavior can be interpreted as analogous to risk taking in humans rather than something else;
- risk taking behavior in such species is genetically coded; and
- humans inherit such genes from evolutionary ancestors who played winner-take-all games.

Among economists, early proponents of the view that preferences are endogenous included Becker [4, 5], Hirschleifer [15, 16] and Rubin and Paul [26]. Their view has recently been revived. For example, Hansson and Stuart [14] and Rogers [24] give an evolutionary account of how discount rates are determined, and cite related work on the evolution of intertemporal preferences. Waldman [30] develops an explicitly sexual model, where evolution can lead to "second-best adaptation." For example, he argues that such evolution may result in males overestimating their ability and suffering disutility from effort, instead of being "efficient" by correctly estimating ability and not suffering disutility of effort. Evolution of attitudes toward risk were explored by Karni and Schmeidler [18], Cooper [10] and Robson [22], who have used different evolutionary models to show that preferences with an expected-utility representation will be selected. Robson [22] extends his model to show how preferences conforming to non-expected utility can also evolve.

Papers more closely related to this one are Rubin and Paul [26] and recent (independent) papers of Robson [23] and Wärneryd [31]. Rubin and Paul argue in a model that is not explicitly dynamic that males may be risk taking if females only select males with income above a threshold. Robson [23] shows that if males choose lotteries over wealth with the objective to maximize offspring, and are selected by females according to their (relative) wealth, they will choose very risky lotteries if they choose any at all. Wärneryd [31] studies a rent-seeking contest which is similar to the model below in that the winner is rewarded, but differs in that many preferences can survive, since the rents are dissipated among the participants. In the (unusual) case where only one kind of preference survives, it is the one closest to risk neutrality. Skaperdas [27, 28] considers how different attitudes toward risk affect outcomes in rent-seeking games.

2. A Random-Matching Model of Winner-Take-All Games

2.1. The Model

In both the random-matching model of this section, and the playing-the-field model of the next section, players are genetically coded to choose one of a finite number of lotteries, $\mathfrak{F} \equiv \{F_1, \ldots F_L\}$. The set of lotteries is held fixed throughout the analysis. Each section examines a dynamic process on the proportions of the population choosing the different lotteries in $\mathfrak{F}$. For each of the two dynamic processes discussed in this paper we say that a particular F_l

within $\mathfrak{F}$ is *selected* (or *evolves*) if the proportion of the agents choosing it converges to 1. As is standard with revealed preference, we interpret a player's (genetically encoded) choice of a lottery in $\mathfrak{F}$ as that player's most preferred element in the set. We thus characterize the evolution of a choice *rule*, which specifies for a given finite $\mathfrak{F}$ the chosen, i.e., most preferred, lottery.

Although our model concerns selection within a given finite set of lotteries, we interpret it as a selection of preferences, i.e., a selection from all "relevant" sets $\mathfrak{F}$, where a set $\mathfrak{F}$ is relevant if the agent is "likely" to face that set. The interpretation we have in mind is that Nature determines in each period the set of lotteries, $\mathfrak{F}$, from which the agents choose. For any such set that appears "often enough," evolution will select the lottery we describe. This is not entirely satisfactory if there are uncountably many sets, in which case evolutionary forces will not have the opportunity to operate on every possible subset $\mathfrak{F}$. On the other hand, one might argue that only finitely many lotteries are distinguishable by our coarse sensory capabilities, in which case there are only finitely many subsets $\mathfrak{F}$ among which agents choose.

We apply replicator dynamics to an infinite population. The precise dynamic process is specified below. Intuitively, in each period infinitely many groups of size m are matched from the population, and Nature independently determines an outcome for each player from his chosen lottery. In each group the player with the highest outcome "wins" and has m offspring, all of whom are coded to choose the same strategy as the winner. Losers have no offspring. We will describe the population in each time period by a probability vector $\sigma(t) = (\sigma^1(t), \ldots, \sigma^L(t))$, where $\sigma^\ell(t)$ is the proportion of players in the population who choose F_ℓ when faced with $\mathfrak{F}$. We call these the type-$\mathfrak{F}_\ell$ or type-ℓ players, or just $\mathfrak{F}_\ell$ players. Our objective is to characterize how the limit of $\sigma(t), t = 1, 2, \ldots$, depends on the set $\mathfrak{F}$, starting from a population with full support, $\sigma^\ell(0) > 0$ for all ℓ.

Let $\Delta^m \equiv \left\{ k : \sum_{\ell=1}^L k_\ell = m, k \geq 0 \right\}$. For $k = (k_1, \ldots, k_L) \in \Delta^m$, we will interpret k_ℓ as the number of type-$\mathfrak{F}_\ell$ players in a group of size m. If the group is drawn randomly from a population with relative frequencies $\sigma(t)$, then k is a random variable from a multinomial distribution with probabilities $\sigma(t) = (\sigma^1(t), \ldots, \sigma^L(t))$. For each k in Δm, let $f_\ell(k) \equiv k_\ell \times \int [F_\ell(x)]^{k_\ell - 1} \prod_{i \neq \ell} [F_i(x)]^{k_i} dF_\ell(x)$. Thus $f_\ell(k)$ is the probability that any of the type-F_ℓ players wins in a match with $k = (k_1, \ldots, k_L)$ players of the different types.

If m members of the population are selected randomly (with or without replacement), then the probability of k is $\binom{m}{k} \prod_i [\sigma_i(t)]^{k_i}$, where $\binom{m}{k} \equiv \binom{m}{k_1, \ldots k_L}$. We assume that the population proportions evolve according to the following dynamic process.

$$\sigma^\ell(t+1) = \sum_{k \in \Delta^m} \binom{m}{k} \prod_i [\sigma_i(t)]^{k_i} f_\ell(k)$$

This process describes replicator dynamics (e.g., Weibull [32, p. 72]), applied to groups of size m rather than groups of size 2. Following the literature, we justify this dynamic system by appeal to the law of large numbers. Thus, we assume that the proportion of matches with profile k equals the probability of drawing the profile k. We also appeal to the law of large numbers a second time, and assume that within the matches with profile k, the proportion of matches in which a type ℓ wins equals the probability of such a win, namely $f_\ell(k)$.

Justifying the dynamic process from a more fundamental story of random matching is regrettably not as natural or as straightforward an application of the law of large numbers as one would hope. If the population is a continuum, there are the well-known technical difficulties associated with selecting i.i.d. random variables. (See Feldman and Gilles [13] or McLennan and Sonnenschein [20, footnote 4], who discuss the implications in the context of random matching.) For countably large populations, there are other difficulties. (See Boylan [7, 8] for a discussion, and Propositions 2 and 5 in [7] for a matching process that embodies the strong-law-of-large-numbers intuition.)

2.2. Orderings of Lotteries

Our results characterize which lottery from $\mathfrak{F}$ is selected. We define a lottery $\mathfrak{F}_l$ as favored within $\mathfrak{F}$ if, for any $k \in \Delta^m$, the probability that any type $\mathfrak{F}_l$ player wins is more than proportional to their number, i.e., greater than k_ℓ/m. In the next subsection we show that when $\mathfrak{F}_\ell$ is favored within $\mathfrak{F}$, then $\mathfrak{F}_l$ is selected.

Definition 1. F_1 is favored within $\mathfrak{F}$ in a random-matching environment with matches of size m, if $f_1(k) > k_1/m$ for all $k \in \Delta^m$, $0 < k_1 < m$.

The condition of being favored is a partial ordering of lotteries. It is therefore of interest to investigate how it relates to standard orders, namely first- and second-order stochastic dominance. Recall that F_1 strictly FOSD F_ℓ if $F_1(x) \le F_\ell(x)$ for all x, with strict inequality for some x; and F_1 strictly SOSD F_ℓ if $\int_{-\infty}^t F_1(x)dx < F_\ell(x)dx$ for all t, with strict inequality for some t.

Proposition 1. If F_1 strictly FOSD F_ℓ for $\ell = 2, \ldots, L$ then F_1 is favored within $\mathfrak{F}$.

Proof. $f_1(k) = k_1 \cdot \int [F_1]^{k_1-1} \prod_{\ell 1} [F_\ell(x)]^{k_\ell} dF_1(x) > k_1 \int F_1(x)^{m-1} dF_1(x) = k_1/m$, where the last integral is $1/m$ because it equals the probability that one of m players, all of whom are type F_1, wins.

Example 1

(Being favored does not imply FOSD). Suppose that $m = 2$, that G places probability 1 on the outcome 1 and F places probabilities 1/3 and 2/3 respectively on 0 and 3/2. We assume that if two players have the same outcome, each wins with probability 1/2. Clearly F is favored over G, even though it does not strictly FOSD G.

The previous example might suggest that "riskier" lotteries (those that are second-order-stochastically dominated) are always favored. However, the following example shows otherwise. Thus the result in the next section that evolution selects for favored lotteries does not confirm the intuition that it should select riskier lotteries.

Example 2

(A lottery may be favored even if it SOSD (is less risky than) another). Suppose that $m = 2$, that G places probability 1 on the outcome 1 and $\hat{F}$ places probability 2/3 on 1/4 and 1/3 on 2.5. While G strictly SOSD $\hat{F}$, G is favored over $\hat{F}$.

***Remark* 1** *(Intransitivity).* Examples 1 and 2 can also be used to show that a pairwise definition of favored does not give a transitive order: F is favored over G which is favored over $\hat{F}$, and it can be checked that $\hat{F}$ is favored over F. Both examples can be generalized to any m by changing the probability from 1/3 to $1/n$ for n sufficiently large.[1]

The result that evolution selects for favored lotteries can be shown to imply that for large m evolution selects for a condition we call *tail dominance*.

***Definition* 2.** F_1 tail dominates F_ℓ if there exists $\overline{x}_\ell$ such that $F_1(x) \leq F_\ell(x)$ for all $x \geq \overline{x}_\ell$ with strict inequality for $x = \overline{x}_\ell$.

A lottery F_1 tail dominates F_ℓ if it first-order dominates F_ℓ in an interval at the top of the supports; see Fig. 1. If F_1 tail dominates F_ℓ for each F_ℓ in $\mathfrak{F}$, then we say that F_1 tail dominates $\mathfrak{F}$. For a finite set of lotteries the tail-dominance order corresponds to an expected-utility ranking where the utility of the highest outcome in the supports of the lotteries is "much" larger than the utility of the second highest outcome, which is "much" larger than the next highest outcome, and so on.[2] Proposition 2 links tail

---

1 This intransitivity is similar to Gale's roulette wheel example, see, e.g., Binmore (1992, p. 90). If $\mathfrak{F} = \{F, G, \hat{F}\}$ then there is a "mixed-strategy equilibrium," i.e., a polymorphic steady state of the dynamic process, in which 3/7 of the population is type F, 3/7 is type $\hat{F}$, and 1/7 is type G. We have not verified whether or not this steady state is locally stable.

2 How much larger depends on the probabilities that the various lotteries assign to the different outcomes. Thus, for an infinite set of lotteries on a finite set, the same can be done if the utility function is non-standard and the utility of the highest outcome is infinitely

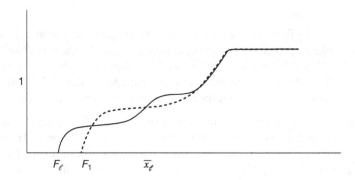

Figure 1

dominance to FOSD and SOSD, while Proposition 3 shows that for large m tail-dominating lotteries are favored.

Remark 2 (Completeness of the tail-dominance order). If we restrict attention to lotteries with finite support, tail dominance is a complete, transitive order. However, if we compare two lotteries that do not have finite support then it can happen that neither is tail dominant. Thus the order is not complete without the restriction to finite support.

It remains an open question whether some other ordering would determine the selection within a set $\mathfrak{F}$ for which no $F \in \mathfrak{F}$ tail dominates $\mathfrak{F}$.

Example 3.

A sequence $\{F^n\}$ of lotteries that tail dominate a lottery G can converge (in the weak convergence topology on lotteries) to a lottery F that is tail dominated by G. For example suppose F^n gives probabilities $\frac{1}{2}$, $(1/2 - 1/n)$, $1/n$ to the outcomes 0, 1, $1/n$ respectively. The $F^n \rightarrow F$ where F gives probabilities $\frac{1}{2}$, $\frac{1}{2}$ to the outcomes 0, 1 respectively. Suppose G gives probability 1 to the outcome 1. Then each F^n tail dominates G and G tail dominates F. Note however, that there is no finite group size m^* such that Proposition 3 below applies for all n in the sequence (i.e., such that F^n will be favored over G for all n). The minimum required group size grows with n.

Proposition 2. *If F strictly FOSD G or if G strictly SOSD F, then F tail dominates G.*

larger than that of the second highest, and so on. Otherwise the tail-dominance order need not correspond to any expected (or non-expected) utility ranking.

Proof. Obvious.

Proposition 3. *Suppose that F_1 tail dominates all other lotteries in $\mathfrak{F}$, and that the support of F_1 is an interval.[3] There exists m^* such that for $m > m^*$, $f_1(k) > k_1/m$.*

Proof. Let $\{\overline{x}_\ell\}$ be as in the definition of tail dominance. The rough idea of the proof is that, by taking m large, with high probability the winner will have value above $\overline{x}_l$ for each l, and in the region above $\overline{x}_\ell$, F_1 strictly FOSD F_ℓ so that the intuition underlying Proposition 1 can be applied.

The probability that one of the F_1 players wins is at least the probability that the winner is an F_1 player and has outcome greater than some $y(k)$, which is the probability of the winner having value at least $y(k)$ times the probability of an F_1 winning conditional on the winner being above $y(k)$.

Let

$$K \equiv \left\{ k \in \mathbb{Z}_+^L \mid k_1 > 0, \sum_{\ell=1}^{L} k_l = m \right\}$$

$$y(k) \equiv \max \{ \overline{x}_\ell \mid F_\ell \in \mathfrak{F}, k_\ell \neq 0 \} \text{ for each } k \in K$$

$$K_+ \equiv \{ k \in K \mid F_1(y(k)) > 0 \}.$$

If $F_1(y(k)) < 1$,

$$f_1(k) \geq \left(1 - \prod_{\ell=1}^{L} F_\ell(y(k))^{k_\ell} \right)$$

$$\times \frac{k_1 \int_{y(k)}^{\infty} F_1(x)^{k_1-1} \prod_{\ell=2}^{L} F_\ell(x)^{k_\ell} dF_1(x)}{1 - \prod_{l=1}^{L} F_l(y(k))^{k_l}}$$

$$= \left(1 - \prod_{\ell=1}^{L} F_\ell(y(k))^{k_\ell} \right) k_1$$

$$\times \frac{\int_{y(k)}^{\infty} F_1(x)^{k_1-1} \left[\prod_{l=2}^{L} F_l(x)^{k_l} + F_1(x)^{m-k_1} - F_1(x)^{m-k_1} \right] dF_1(x)}{1 - \prod_{l=1}^{L} F_l(y(k))^{k_l}}$$

---

3 It is straightforward to adapt this proof to the case of finite support; we present the more difficult case.

$$= \left(1 - \prod_{\ell=1}^{L} F_\ell(y(k))^{k_\ell}\right) k_1 \times \frac{\int_{y(k)}^{\infty} F_1(x)^{m-1} dF_1(x)}{1 - \prod_{\ell=1}^{L} F_\ell(y(k))^{k_\ell}}$$

$$+ k_1 \int_{y(k)}^{\infty} F_1(x)^{k_1-1} \left[\prod_{\ell=2}^{L} F_\ell(x)^{k_\ell} - F_1(x)^{m-k_1}\right] dF_1(x)$$

$$\geq \frac{k_1}{m} + k_1$$

$$\times \left\{\int_{y(k)}^{\infty} F_1(x)^{k_1-1} \left[\prod_{\ell=2}^{L} F_\ell(x)^{k_\ell} - F_1(x)^{m-k_1}\right] dF_1(x) - \frac{\prod_{\ell=1}^{L} F_\ell(y(k))^{k_\ell}}{m}\right\}.$$

So $f_1(k) > k_1/m$ if the term in large curly brackets is positive.

Choose m^*, $\delta > 0$ such that (2.2) below holds for each ℓ and each $k \in K_+$ (a finite set).

$$F_1(y(k))^{m^*-k_\ell}[F_1(y(k)+\delta) - F_1(y(k))]\left[1 - \left(\frac{F_1(y(k)+\delta)}{F_\ell(y(k))}\right)^{k_l}\right]$$

$$- \frac{1}{m^*} > 0 \text{ if } k_\ell \geq 1$$

We now demonstrate that the term in large curly brackets is positive for $m > m^*$. This is immediate for $k \in K\backslash K_+$ (i.e., k such that $F_1(y(k)) = 0$), since the integral term is positive by tail dominance, and the last term vanishes. For $k \in K_+$ the term in curly brackets above is positive if

$$F_1(y(k))^{m-k_\ell} \int_{y(k)}^{\infty} \left[F_\ell(x)^{k_\ell} - F_1(x)^{k_\ell}\right] dF_1(x)$$

$$- \frac{F_\ell(y(k))^{k_\ell}}{m} > 0 \text{ for some } \ell.$$

To verify this, first notice that $F_\ell(x)^{k_\ell} \geq F_1(x)^{k_\ell}$ for all $x \geq y(k)$ and all ℓ, using the fact that if $y(k) \leq x < \bar{x}_\ell$, then $k_\ell = 0$. Then

$$\left\{\int_{y(k)}^{\infty} F_1(x)^{k_1-1}\left[\prod_{\ell=2}^{L} F_\ell(x)^{k_\ell} - F_1(x)^{m-k_1}\right] dF_1(x) - \frac{\prod_{\ell=1}^{L} F_\ell(y(k))^{k_l}}{m}\right\}$$

$$= \left\{\int_{y(k)}^{\infty} F_1(x)^{k_1-1}\left[\prod_{\ell=2}^{L} F_\ell(x)^{k_\ell} - \prod_{\ell=2}^{L} F_1(x)^{k_\ell}\right] dF_1(x) - \frac{\prod_{\ell=1}^{L} F_\ell(y(k))^{k_l}}{m}\right\}$$

$$= \left\{\int_{y(k)}^{\infty} F_1(x)^{-1}\left[\prod_{\ell=1}^{L} F_\ell(x)^{k_\ell} - \prod_{\ell=1}^{L} F_1(x)^{k_\ell}\right] dF_1(x) - \frac{\prod_{\ell=1}^{L} F_\ell(y(k))^{k_l}}{m}\right\}$$

$$\geq \left\{ \int_{y(k)}^{\infty} \left[\prod_{\ell=1}^{L} F_\ell(x)^{k_\ell} - \prod_{\ell=1}^{L} F_1(x)^{k_\ell} \right] dF_1(x) \cdot \frac{\prod_{\ell=1}^{L} F_\ell(y(k))^{k_l}}{m} \right\}$$

$$\geq \left\{ \int_{y(k)}^{\infty} F_1(x)^{m-k_{\ell'}} \left[F_{\ell'}(x)^{k_{\ell'}} - F_1(x)^{k_{\ell'}} \right] dF_1(x) \cdot \frac{\prod_{\ell=1}^{L} F_\ell(y(k))^{k_l}}{m} \right\}$$

$$\geq F_1(y(k))^{m-k_{\ell'}} \int_{y(k)}^{\infty} \left[F_{\ell'}(x)^{k_{\ell'}} - F_1(x)^{k_{\ell'}} \right] dF_1(x) \frac{F_{\ell'}(y(k))^{k_{l'}}}{m}.$$

Since ℓ' was chosen arbitrarily, the term in curly brackets is therefore positive if (2.2) holds for some ℓ.

By considering the integral from $y(k)$ to $y(k) + \delta$, we can conclude that

$$F_1(y(k))^{m-k_\ell} \int_{y(k)}^{\infty} \left[F_\ell(x)^{k_\ell} - F_1(x)^{k_\ell} \right] dF_1(x) - \frac{F_\ell(y(k))^{k_\ell}}{m}$$
$$\geq F_1(y(k))^{m-k_\ell} [F_1(y(k) + \delta) - F_1(y(k))]$$
$$\times \left[F_\ell(y(k))^{k_\ell} - F_1(y(k) + \delta)^{k_\ell} \right] - \frac{F_\ell(y(k))^{k_\ell}}{m}$$

But the latter term is positive for $m > m^*$ by choice of δ, m^*.

2.3. Selection

We now use the orders defined above to illuminate the outcome of evolution. Our first result is that evolution selects favored lotteries.

Proposition 4. *Consider a random-matching winner-take-all environment with matches of size $m \geq 2$, and suppose that F_1 is favored within $\mathfrak{F}$. Given ψ s.t. $0 < \psi < 1$, if $\sigma^1(0) > 0$, then there exists t^* such that $\sigma^1(t) > 1 - \psi$ for $t > t^*$.*

Proof. For k such that $m > k_1 > 0$, we have $\sigma^1(t+1) = \sum_{\{k \in \Delta^m\}} \Pr(k) f_1(k) > \sum_{\{k \in \Delta^m\}} \Pr(k) k_1/m = k_1/m = \sigma^1(t)$. So $\sigma^1(t)$ increases over time and, by continuity of 2.1, it converges to a steady state, which requires $k_1 = 0$ or $k_1 = m$. The former is ruled out by assumption.

Propositions 1 and 4 imply that evolution selects for preferences that are monotonic in the sense that they respect FOSD. Proposition 4 and Example 1 imply that evolution leads to a more refined order than FOSD, but Example 2 shows that this order does not respect SOSD. Thus our intuition that evolution selects for risk-taking in winner-take-all environments is not true in general. However Proposition 5 below shows that for large m the intuition is correct, and that the appropriate notion of risk taking is tail dominance. Combined with Proposition 2, Remark 2 and Example 3, we see that for large m evolution selects for preferences that are complete and transitive, and that respect FOSD and SOSD, provided the set of feasible lotteries is finite and each has finite support. However, if the set is infinite, the order need not be continuous, and if the set includes lotteries that do not have finite support, the order may not be complete.

Proposition 5. *Consider a random-matching winner-take-all environment, where $F_1 \in \mathfrak{F}$ tail dominates all other lotteries in $\mathfrak{F}$, and the support of F_1 is an interval.[4] Given ψ s.t. $0 < \psi < 1$, if $\sigma^1(0) > 0$, then there exists m^* and t^* such that for $m > m^*$ and $t > t^*$, $\sigma^1(t) > 1 - \psi$ for all $t > t^*$.*

Proof. This follows from Propositions 4 and 3.

3. A Playing-The-Field Model of a Winner-Take-All Game

In this section we show that the preferences selected in winner-take-all games with random matching are different than those selected in winner-take-all games where each player is pitted against the entire population, which we call playing the field. Even though playing the field might correspond more immediately to the intuitive notion of a winner-take-all game, the results are (surprisingly) weaker than in random matching, and less supportive of the intuition that winner-take-all games should lead to risk taking.

In particular, we show that F can tail dominate G (as defined in the previous section) and still not be selected. However, there is a strengthening of the notion of tail dominance such that F will be selected, and it is satisfied if F is riskier than G in a particularly strong sense.

We now assume there are n players in the population who are encoded to choose between the lotteries F and G. The extension to more than two lotteries is straightforward. In each time period, each player has a random draw from his or her chosen distribution, F or G, and the player with the highest realization reproduces the next generation of n players. If there were no mutations, the dynamic process would end in the second period, since all players – and hence all future generations – would be of one type. We therefore assume that each offspring has a probability μ of mutating. (In the random matching game we did not have mutations. We argue below that the differences between playing-the-field and random-matching environments are due to whether competition is in small independent groups or in the whole group, and not due to mutations.) We will define a Markov process with three states: An "F state" means that all n players are coded to play F, a "G state" means that all players are coded to play G, and an "M state" means that the population is mixed because there was at least one mutation.

---

4 It is straightforward to adapt this proof to the case of finite support, we present the more difficult case.

There is a unique ergodic distribution of the Markov process denoted by $(\tilde{x}^F, \tilde{x}^G, \tilde{x}^M)$. (This distribution depends on n and on μ, but we suppress the notation for simplicity.) We present below an example which explains why tail-dominating lotteries, which were selected in the random-matching environment, need not be selected in the playing-the-field model. Thus, tail dominance is not a sufficiently strong notion of risk taking for selection in playing-the-field environments. However when the population n is large, and the mutation rate, μ, is small, if F "strongly" tail dominates G as defined below, then F will be selected ($\tilde{x}^F$ is close to 1).

The following example shows that two of the main results from the random-matching model do not extend to the playing-the-field environment.

- In the playing-the-field environment, first-order stochastically dominating distributions need not be selected.
- In the playing-the-field environment, tail dominating distributions need not be selected.

Thus in the playing-the-field environment, preferences will not necessarily evolve to be monotonic or risk taking.

Example 4.

Suppose that F places probabilities 1/2, 1/2 on the outcomes 1, 2 respectively, while G places probabilities 1/2, 1/2 on 0, 2. We assume that if n players have the same outcome, each wins with probability $1/n$. Clearly F tail dominates G, so F is selected in the random-matching environment of the previous section. However, F will not be selected in the playing-the-field environment. This is because for large n the probability that an F population turns into a G population is almost the same as the probability that a G population turns into an F population, hence the two populations will alternate at approximately equal intervals. If n is large, then since each player has probability 1/2 of obtaining the outcome 2, it follows that with high probability the winner in any generation (whether F or G) wins with outcome 2, and will win according to the tie-breaking rule. In order that an F population turns into a G population, there must be at least one mutation of an F player to G, and the G player must win, and similarly in reverse. Conditional on the winner having outcome 2, these are equally likely events. The probability that a G population turns into an F population is actually slightly higher than the reverse because the F's have an advantage in those outcomes where no player has outcome 2.

In the notation of the following proof, "c/d" does not converge to zero in the example as n becomes large, and therefore the proportion of the time that the population is F does not converge to 1.

Example 4 shows the contrast between playing the field and random matching. If we pit F against G in random matches, the G players will eventually disappear. In every period there are many matches and in most matches the winner will win with outcome 2 using the tie-breaking rule. The winners of tied matches will split evenly between F and G, with no aggregate effect on the population proportions. However in the other matches F will win more often than G. Therefore, in every period the proportion of F grows, albeit slowly if m is large. To highlight this, imagine that F and G both gave the outcome 2 with probability 1. Then in the random-matching environment, the population distribution between F and G would be constant: $\sigma(t) = \sigma(0)$ for all t. On the other hand, in the playing-the-field model, in every period the population would either be (almost) all Fs or (almost) all Gs.

The playing-the-field game differs from the random-matching game in three ways: It has a finite population, it has mutations, and it has competition within the whole population. We now argue that the difference in results is due to the latter. First, Example 4 can be modified to show that the difference in results is not due to population size. If there were a continuum of players, in every period after an F wins, the proportion of F types would be $1 - \mu$, and half of them would obtain the outcome 2; similarly a proportion μ would be G types, half of whom would obtain the outcome 2. The probability of shifting from an F state to a G state or conversely would then be $(\mu)/(1 - \mu)$ so that half the time would be spent in each state. In every period the winner would have outcome 2, so the difference between F and G would never be relevant.

Second, the difference in outcomes is apparently not due to the fact that mutations are permitted in playing-the-field, but not in random-matching. The intuition is that if independent mutations occur in random matches with equal probabilities for both F and G players, then if there are continuously many random matches, the mutations can have no aggregate effect.

It seems then that the difference between the outcomes of random matching and playing the field derives from the different forms of interaction, that is, competition within small random groups or within the whole group. Reasoning from the random-matching model, one might have guessed that in Example 4 above, the population should be mostly type F most of the time. This is wrong for the following reason. In almost all periods when the population switches from almost all Fs to almost all Gs, the switch has nothing to do with the outcomes other than 2, which are equally probable under the two distributions, whereas in the random-matching model there is movement in the population proportions precisely because of the outcomes other than 2.

The following definition strengthens tail dominance so as to exclude Example 3. The reason that *strong* tail dominance suffices is that if there are "many" players with the strongly tail-dominant lottery, some such player will have an outcome higher than the maximum in the support of dominated distributions, and will win.

Definition 3. F *strongly tail dominates* G *if there is an* $\bar{x}$ *such that* $F(\bar{x}) < 1$ *and* $G(\bar{x}) = 1$.

Proposition 6. *Suppose that F strongly tail dominates G. Let* $\tilde{x}^F(n, \mu_n)$ *be the stationary proportion of type-F players in a playing-the-field game of size n when the probability that each offspring mutates is* μ_n. *Then given* $\varepsilon > 0$ *there exist* n^* *and a sequence* $\mu_n \to 0$ *such that for* $n > n^*$ *we have* $\tilde{x}^F(n, \mu_n) > 1 - \varepsilon$.

Proof. We will drop the arguments (n, μ_n) to $(\tilde{x}^F, \tilde{x}^M, \tilde{x}^G)$ for simplicity. We first show that we can choose (n, μ) such that $x^M < \varepsilon/2$. In the transition matrix below, let N (for "no mutation") be either an F state or G state, and let M represent mixed generations in which at least one mutation has occurred.

	N	M
N	$(1 - \mu_n)^n$	$1 - (1 - \mu_n)^n$
M	$(1 - \mu_n)^n$	$1 - (1 - \mu_n)^n$

The probability of changing from N to M is the same whether the N generation was comprised of F players or G players. Similarly, the probability of changing from M to N does not depend on the mixture of G and F in the M generation, since the "winner" will produce n offspring, and each has the same probability of mutation irrespective of the parent's type. The probability of no mutation is $(1 - \mu_n)^n$. Recall that $\tilde{x}^N = \tilde{x}^F + \tilde{x}^G$, and the stationary probabilities are $(\tilde{x}^N, \tilde{x}^M) = ((1 - \mu_n)^n, 1 - (1 - \mu_n)^n)$. Consider a sequence $\mu_n \to 0$ such that $n\mu_n \to \varepsilon/2$. Expanding $(1 - \mu_n)^n$ as a Taylor series around $\mu_n = 0$, $(1 - \mu_n)^n$ is equal to $1 - \mu_n n$ plus a positive series. Thus, since $(1 - \mu_n)^n = \tilde{x}^N \geq 1 - \mu_n n$ and $\mu_n n \to \varepsilon/2$, $\tilde{x}^N$ is bounded below for large n by, say, $1 - \varepsilon$. That is, the population is in a mutant state at most a fraction ε of the time.

It is straightforward to adapt this proof to the case of finite support; we present the more difficult case.

We now restrict attention to the N states. Let $\tilde{x}^F$ and $\tilde{x}^G$ represent the stationary probabilities of being in the F state and G state respectively, conditional on being in one or the other: $\hat{x}^F \tilde{x}^N = \tilde{x}^F$ and $\hat{x}^G \tilde{x}^N = \tilde{x}^G$. The steady state probabilities for the Markov process described in the table below satisfy $\hat{x}^F / \hat{x}^G = d/c$. Since $\hat{x}^F + \hat{x}^G = 1$, this implies that

$\dot{x}^F = d/(c + d)$, and $\dot{x}^F = \dot{x}^N d/(c + d)$. Thus to prove the theorem it is enough to show that as n grows large, and μ_n becomes small, d is bounded above zero and c converges to zero. We complete the proof by showing these two claims.

	F	G
F	$1 - c$	c
G	d	$1 - d$

We first show that c converges to zero as n becomes large and μ_n becomes small. To get from an F state to a G state or vice versa there must be at least one mutation, and a mutant must win. We will describe a mutation state with mixed F and G players by an integer k which represents the number of type-G players it contains. The number of type-F players is therefore $n - k$. A player wins if he has the highest order statistic among the random draws of all n players. The probability that a G player wins depends on the number of G players, k. Denoting this probability by $g(k)$, the probability c of changing from the F state to the G state is

$$\sum_{k \geq 1} \binom{n}{k} \mu_n^k (1 - \mu_n)^{n-k} g(k).$$

We can calculate an upper bound on $g(k)$ as follows. The event that a G player wins is the same event as that every F player loses. Thus we want an upper bound on the event that every F player loses. Letting $q \equiv 1 - F(\bar{x})$, such a bound is $(1 - q)^{n-k}$, which is the probability that no F player has a random draw in the upper tail of F where G puts no probability. The event that no F player has a random draw in the upper tail is necessary for all the F 's to lose (if any F had a draw in the upper tail it would win), but is not sufficient. Thus the probability that all the F players lose is smaller than $(1 - q)^{n-k}$. Thus,

$$g(k) < (1 - q)^{n-k} \quad \text{and} \quad c < \sum_{k \geq 1} \binom{n}{k} \mu_n^k (1 - \mu_n)^{n-k} (1 - q)^{n-k} = [\mu_n +$$

$(1 - \mu_n)(1 - q)]^n - (1 - \mu_n)^n (1 - q)^n$.

The equality follows because the sum would be a polynomial expansion if it included the $k = 0$ term. Thus c goes to zero as n becomes large.

We turn now to the parameter d, the probability that a G state becomes an F state. We will let $f(k)$ denote the probability that one of the F players wins when there are k G 's. Thus $d = \sum_{k \geq 1} \binom{n}{k} \mu_n^{n-k} (1 - \mu_n)^k f(k)$. We want a lower bound for d, the probability that one of the F players wins. F will surely win if one of them has a random draw in the upper tail where G has no weight. The probability this does not happen is $(1 - q)^{n-k}$, and therefore $1 - (1 - q)^{n-k}$ is a lower bound for the probability that one of the F players wins.

That is, $f(k) \geq 1 - (1-q)^{n-k}$. Thus

$$
\begin{aligned}
d &\geq \sum_{k<n} \binom{n}{k} u_n^{n-k}(1-\mu_n)^k \left[1 - (1-q)^{n-k}\right] \\
&= \sum_{k<n} \binom{n}{k} u_n^{n-k}(1-\mu_n)^k - \sum_{k<n} \binom{n}{k} u_n^{n-k}(1-\mu_n)^k \;(1-q)^{n-k} \\
&= 1 - (1-\mu_n)^n - [(1-\mu_n) + \mu_n(1-q)]^n + [1-\mu_n]^n \\
&= 1 - [1 - \mu_n q]^n.
\end{aligned}
$$

Since $\mu_n q = n\mu_n q/n$ and $n\mu_n \to \varepsilon/2$, the second term converges to $e^{-\varepsilon q/2} < 1$. Thus, d is bounded above zero.

If F is riskier than G in the sense that F is created by adding strictly positive noise at every point to G, then F strongly tail dominates G. In this weak sense, risk-taking preferences are selected in the playing-the-field environment. But it is a weaker sense than the selection in the random-matching environment.

4. Biological and Behavioral Evidence about Risk-Taking

We now ask whether the ideas discussed above are relevant to the evolution of preferences in humans, and in particular, in males. Before addressing the three bullet items in the introduction, we note some of the evidence that male humans are more risk taking than females. Much of the evidence is experimental. Arch [1] summarizes it, and reports

> Research clearly supports the existence of differences between females and males in the extent of their ... risk taking. (Ellis [11]). It appears that the differences in behavior do not occur simply because males perceive the physical world as less threatening ... but because they are actually more likely to seek out and enjoy risk-ladened situations (Zuckerman [34]).

The same conclusion is corroborated by many other authors, e.g., Zinkhan and Karande [33] report a study in which "Men ... showed more risk-taking behavior than women"; Levin, Snyder and Capman [19] quote Hudgens and Fatkin [17], who concluded that "men are more inclined than women to take risks," and also describe a study in which "males responded more favorably to the hypothetical gambling options than did females." Avnery [2] comes to the same conclusion based on computer experiments with young children. Even if the evidence is confounded by environmental influences, it is nevertheless provocative.

Since our hypothesis is that risk taking among males is inherited rather than learned, we turn to the three questions identified in the introduction.

Can a meaningful concept of risk taking be distinguished from other behaviors in non-humans, so that risk taking in humans has a logical evolutionary antecedent?

Naturally it is hard to measure risk taking in nonhumans, but researchers have identified behaviors that seem observationally equivalent both to risk taking and to sensation seeking. For example, Fairbanks [12] reports variation in the willingness of vervet monkeys to enter new environments, approach new food sources and approach strangers. Possingham, Houston and McNamara [21] report that "patterns of risk-sensitive foraging in bumble bees are now well documented," where they define an animal to be risk sensitive if both the mean and the variance of the energy contributed by a reward influence their revealed preference. Battalio, Kagel and MacDonald [3] examine rats' preferences over lotteries that differ by mean preserving spreads and find evidence of risk aversion.

Do non-human males play winner-take-all games?
The reproductive games played by males are complex. An exhaustive description can be found in [9], of which one section is devoted to mammals, and in particular to deer, elephant seals, lions, vervet monkeys and baboons. While none of the examples exhibits the extreme feature of Section 3, where a single male fathers the entire next generation, they all have dominance hierarchies, which might be interpreted as winner-take-all games in small groups, as in Section 2. The behavior of elephant seals is most clear-cut: Of the sample followed by the researchers, only 8.8% of the males breeded during their lifetimes.

Is risk taking genetically coded? If so, there should be biological correlates with this behavior.
Roy, De Jong and Linniola [25] report in their abstract that "Pathological gamblers may have a disturbance of their central nervous system noradrenergic functioning," and that their "results suggest that the disturbance ... may be partly reflected in their personality." The survey in "Biology of Brain May Hold Key for Gamblers," the *New York Times* C1, Oct. 3, 1989, summarizes this study as finding that "The psychological forces that propel so many chronic gamblers ... may spring from a biological need for risk and excitement ... . The study showed that gamblers had lower levels than usual of the brain chemicals that regulate arousal, thrill and excitement."

Even if risk taking is heritable, is there any connection between different species, in particular a connection between current species and their ancestors?
The evidence here is obviously circumstantial, but nevertheless plausible. Ellis [11] reports

> Research over the past 25 years has established that androgens –
> and, to a lesser degree, other sex hormones – profoundly affect
> brain functioning, and thereby, behavior ... When one finds
> males on average behaving differently from females, therefore,
> one should suspect neuroandrogenic etiology, especially if the sex
> differences are evident in several species.

This report has demonstrated that average sex differences in several human behavior patterns have close parallels in other mammals. In addition, experiments with nonhuman mammals for many of these behavior patterns have shown that androgenic effects on brain functioning highly influence these behavior patterns. Together, these observations strongly imply that average sex differences in such behavior even among humans are at least partially the result of neuroandrogenic factors.

... at least three additional behavior patterns could be neuroandrogen influenced in light of persistent tendencies for males to display the behavior more than females, both in humans and in several other primate species. These were ... sensation seeking ....

This literature supports a biological basis for behaviors such as risk taking, and if such a basis is shared by mammals with common ancestors, then reproduction according to winner-take-all games among our ancestors, retained in other contemporary species, might explain a preference for risk taking among human males.

References

1. E. C. Arch, Risk-taking: A motivational basis for sex differences, *Psych. Rep.* **73** (1993), 3–11.
2. J. Avnery, "'Risk-Taking Behavior and Children's Achievement Motivation in Using Computer Software," Ph.D. Dissertation, School of Education, Boston University, 1992.
3. R. C. Battalio, J. H. Kagel, and D. N. MacDonald, Animals' choices over uncertain outcomes: Some initial experimental results, *Am. Econ. Rev.* **75** (1985), 597–613.
4. G. S. Becker, Crime and punishment: An economic approach, *J. Polit. Econ.* **76** (1968), 169–217.
5. G. S. Becker, Altruism, egoism, and genetic fitness, *J. Econ. Lit.* **14** (1976), 817–826.
6. K. Binmore, "'Fun and Games: A Text on Game Theory," Heath, Lexington, MA, 1992.
7. R. T. Boylan, Laws of large numbers for dynamical systems with randomly matched individuals, *J. Econ. Theory* **57** (1992), 473–504.
8. R. T. Boylan, Continuous approximation of dynamical systems with randomly matched individuals, *J. Econ. Theory* **66** (1995), 615–625.
9. T. H. Clutton-Brock, Ed., "Reproductive Success: Studies of Individual Variation in Contrasting Breeding Systems," University of Chicago Press, Chicago, 1988.
10. W. S. Cooper, Decision theory as a branch of evolutionary theory: A biological derivation of the Savage axioms, *Psych. Rev.* **94** (1987), 395–411.

11. L. Ellis, Evidence of neuroandrogenic etiology of sex roles from a combined analysis of human, nonhuman primates and nonprimate mammalian studies, *Personality Indiv. Diff.* **7** (1986), 519–552.
12. L. A. Fairbanks, Risk taking by juvenile vervet monkeys, *Behaviour* **124** (1993), 57–72.
13. M. Feldman and C. Gilles, An expository note on individual risk without aggregate uncertainty, *J. Econ. Theory* **35** (1985), 26–32.
14. I. Hansson and C. Stuart, Malthusian selection of preferences, *Amer. Econ. Rev.* **80** (1990), 529–544.
15. J. Hirshleifer, Economics from a biological viewpoint, *J. Law Econ.* **20** (1977), 1–52.
16. J. Hirshleifer, Natural economy vs. political economy, *J. Soc. Biol. Struct.* (1978), 319–337.
17. G. A. Hudgens and L. T. Fatkin, Sex differences in risk taking: Repeated sessions on a computer simulated task, *J. Psych.* **119** (1985), 197–206.
18. E. Karni and D. Schmeidler, Self-preservation as a foundation of rational behavior under risk, *J. Econ. Behavior Organ.* **7** (1986), 71–82.
19. I. P. Levin, M. A. Snyder, and D. P. Capman, The interaction of experimental and situational factors and gender in a simulated risky decision-making task, *J. Psych.* **121** (1987), 173–181.
20. A. McLennan and H. Sonnenschein, Sequential bargaining as a non-cooperative foundation for Walrasian equilibrium, *Econometrica* **59** (1991), 1395–1424.
21. H. P. Possingham, A. I. Houston, and J. M. McNamara, Risk-averse foraging in bees: A comment on the model of Harder and Real, *Ecology* **71** (1990), 1622–1624.
22. A. J. Robson, A biological basis for expected and non-expected utility, *J. Econ. Theory* **68** (1996), 397–424.
23. A. J. Robson, The evolution of attitudes towards risk: Lottery tickets and relative wealth, *Games Econ. Behavior* **14** (1996), 190–207.
24. A. R. Rogers, Evolution of time preferences by natural selection, *Amer. Econ. Rev.* **84** (1994), 460–481.
25. A. Roy, J. De Jong, and M. Linnoila, Extraversion in pathological gamblers. Correlates with indexes of noradrenergic function, *Arch. Gen. Psych.* **46** (1989), 679–681.
26. P. H. Rubin and C. W. Paul II, An evolutionary model of taste for risk, *Econ. Inquiry* **XVII** (1979), 585–596.
27. S. Skaperdas, Conflict and attitudes toward risk, *Amer. Econ. Rev.* **81** (1991), 116–120.
28. S. Skaperdas, Cooperation, conflict and power in the absence of property rights, *Amer. Econ. Rev.* **82** (1992), 720–739.
29. J. Tirole, "The Theory of Industrial Organization," MIT Press, Cambridge, MA, 1988.

30. M. Waldman, Systematic errors and the theory of natural selection, *Amer. Econ. Rev.* **84** (1994), 482–497.

31. K. Wärneryd, "Rent, risk and reputation: Political contests and preference adaption," mimeo, Department of Economics, Stockholm School of Economics, 1995.

32. J. Weibull, "Evolutionary Game Theory," MIT Press, Cambridge, MA, 1997.

33. G. M. Zinkhan and K. W. Karande, Cultural and gender differences in risk-taking behavior among American and Spanish decision makers, *J. Soc. Psych.* **131** (1992), 741–742.

34. M. Zuckerman, Sensation seeking: A biosocial dimension of personality, in "Psychological Correlates of Human Behavior" (A. Gale and A. Edwards, Eds.), Vol. 3, pp. 99–119, Academic Press, London, 1983.

Afterword: From Risk Preferences to Affirmative Action

Carol Adaire Jones

Suzanne was fascinated with the literatures from different fields suggesting that males – of both human and other species – are more risk-taking than females. This led to the paper with Eddie Dekel reprinted above, but also a second paper – somewhat further outside her main lines of inquiry – on gender discrimination and affirmative action. Here, the literature had traditionally fallen into two main categories. The first, originating with Becker (1957), assumed discriminatory intent. The second, due to Phelps (1972) and Arrow (1973), assumed that disparate impacts arise from imperfect information. Arrow's version had assumed that individual productivity starts out equal in the two worker groups but then changes endogenously due to worker investments in human capital so that employer expectations for each group become self-fulfilling. Scotchmer (2008) is closest to the Phelps variant, in which exogenous productivity differences exist across groups, and imperfect information forces employers to assign an average to each group's members. (Readers seeking additional information on the different forms of statistical discrimination and affirmative action that appear in the literature should consult Fang and Moro (2010).)

The novelty in Scotchmer (2008) is that the differences between males and females have nothing to do with productivity – which is assumed the same – but instead take place at the level of signaling behaviors. In keeping with her fondness for models that combine repeated tournaments with Bayesian updating – the most recent examples are Erkal and Scotchmer (2008) and a paper on "Picking Winners" that she was working on with Junjie Zhou at the time of her death – she focuses on promotion dynamics in a hierarchical labor market for two groups with equal productivity distributions. Formally, one group has noisy productivity signals, with higher variance than the true distribution, while the other generates accurate signals. Though her initial motivation for the noisy productivity signals is greater risk-taking by one group, which she assumes to be males, other interpretations of key gender-based factors driving promotion outcomes could lead to the opposite gender assignment, as we discuss below.

Thinking as an instrumentalist, Scotchmer asks what mechanisms best achieve a particular objective. But should the goal be process based or involve outcomes? Two natural objectives are process based – equal (gender-blind) promotion standards and equal survival rates. The third, equal average ability of survivors, is outcome based. The paper shows that different risk-taking propensities – or more fundamentally, different noisiness in signaling – creates a conflict between the process- and outcome-based goals, which are both imbedded in US antidiscrimination policy. For the first round of elimination, the model predicts that, under a gender-blind standard, more risk-takers (noisy signalers) will be promoted and have lower average ability compared to non-risk-takers. (She assumes that less than half of the group is promoted and makes plausible additional assumptions about the productivity distribution.) The risk-taking survivors have lower average ability because more are promoted and promotions are subject to mistakes of commission and omission: some high-productivity risk-takers are not promoted and some low-productivity risk-takers are promoted. An affirmative action policy to promote an equal number of non-risk-takers (accurate signalers) will apply a lower standard to non-risk-takers, but again will result in higher average productivity among non-risk-takers because of mistakes in promoting risk-takers.

The results for the first round of elimination are consistent with other models in the Phelps tradition, which feature alternative stories about the origin and function of signal variance (see, e.g., Cornell and Welch, 1996). But there is a surprise. Carrying the process forward through multiple rounds reverses the pattern at the end of the (infinite) hierarchy: risk-takers will be under-represented, and their mean ability will be higher than the mean ability of non-risk-takers. The reason for the switch is that, at every stage, the signal from each surviving risk-taker has another opportunity to fall below the promotion standard. As the hierarchy progresses, only the most able risk-takers survive. For promotions, this implies that under a gender-blind standard the proportion of non-risk-takers that survive in the limit should exceed their proportion in the original population; under an equal-abilities promotion policy, the model predicts that the ratio of surviving non-risk-takers to surviving risk-takers should be increasing with time, and should be greater in every period than in the original population.

The repeated tournament/Bayesian framework provides a powerful tool for examining the dynamics of labor market promotions for two groups with differentially noisy signals. However, it does not capture a central gender-based difference in leaky promotion pipelines. For example, the economics profession has collected extensive data on the career trajectories of Ph.D. graduates in academia. While economics Ph.D.s from 1974 to 2007 show "no worrisome drop" in the representation of women at assistant professor hiring, the data show a sizable and persistent fall in women's representation in the transition to tenured associate professor (CSWEP, 2014, p. 19).

Scotchmer (2008) suggests that we might expect this if the noisiness of signals ran in the opposite direction, for example if males were more closely observed within each promotion period than females. She also notes that differential costs of signaling can lead to different promotion rates (Bardsley and Sherstyuk, 2006). This is at least consonant with Milgrom and Oster's (1987) female "invisibility" hypothesis, a storyline further explored in Cornell and Welch (1996). Heather Sarsons, a Ph.D. student at Harvard University, provides new empirical evidence on the (low) value of women's signals for coauthored work that reinforces this hypothesis (Sarsons, 2015). Using data from economists' CVs, she finds that women incur a penalty when they coauthor that men do not experience. This is less pronounced when women coauthor with women.

Suzanne thrived on collaboration and published extensively with coauthors of both sexes. However, women were disproportionately represented among coauthors relative to their share among economic theorists (particularly if one excludes life partners). And early in her career, the preponderance of her papers were solo-authored. Was Suzanne intuitively aware of this phenomenon, or was it just a matter of taste?

One way to interpret this line of research is that Suzanne was trying to reconcile her distaste for identity politics with the equally strong instinct that the economics profession, for example, made life needlessly hard for women. At the end of the paper, Suzanne implicitly acknowledges that the explanatory power of greater male risk-taking in accounting for disparate promotions was not all that compelling. But perhaps the paper will have a second life. Even though it was originally motivated by *employee* characteristics (i.e. risk-taking), Suzanne herself pointed out that differentials in signal noise can also be due to factors on the employer side. From that standpoint, the combination of noisiness with Sarsons-style bias in updating priors hints at a more nuanced understanding that combines the most compelling features of both Becker and Phelps.

PART VI

PUBLIC POLICY

CHAPTER 25

Suzanne Scotchmer "Audit Classes and Tax Enforcement Policy" (1987)

INTRODUCTION STEPHEN M. MAURER

Prof. Scotchmer once told me that she was not interested in any research question that did not eventually lead to specific policies. I still remember thinking that this was a strange thing for a theorist to say. But I was new to the business then. Later, looking back, I noticed that almost all of her papers begin with a vividly important social goal and culminate – usually after an extended theory discussion – in some strikingly unexpected but immediately practical advice. This approach was particularly apparent in the long arc of her IP research. Remarkably, this is even true of her lifelong interest in general equilibrium theory, which began with three early papers that asked how hedonic price theory can be used to extract practical cost–benefit data (Scotchmer, 1985, 1986, 1989).

But of course, her mind was too restless to stay in any one channel. Over the years she brought her sophisticated tools to bear on whatever policy problems caught her imagination – though always in the same recognizable style.

Crime, Tax Avoidance, and Attorneys Fees. Prof. Scotchmer's first policy papers dealt with taxation, crime, and evidence. Here the unifying theme is that public policy does not consist in writing down rules. What matters is how the players react

This, of course, was a natural place to use game theory. For example, her crime papers ask whether admitting character evidence undermines deterrence in criminal cases. She finds that excluding character evidence increases crime, but that this conclusion is overturned where the jury is prejudiced or police arrest some citizens more readily than others (Schrag and Scotchmer, 1994). Similarly, limited enforcement budgets can produce high crime rates where (a) many citizens have motive and opportunity and (b) prosecutors make mistakes in the defendants they arrest and indict.

In these cases citizens may realize that they are likely to be arrested even when they are innocent, increasing incentives to commit the crime in the first place. This equilibrium is further reinforced when juries realize that arrests have a large random component and adjust their *sub rosa* standards of proof upward (Schrag and Scotchmer, 1997). Scotchmer (1998) extends these ideas to civil suits and asks how well modern evidence rules protect against the kinds of errors one might expect from Bayesian statistical reasoning.

Probably the most interesting application of these ideas was tax policy. The reprint that follows is a nice illustration of Prof. Scotchmer's approach. Conventional tax literature had traditionally assumed that tax authorities maximize revenue net of enforcement costs. But as Prof. Scotchmer pointed out, the allowable penalties are almost bounded by politics and fairness perceptions. This drives a wedge between the effective tax code and the legislated one. More specifically, one might assume that rational tax authorities would concentrate their auditing resources on returns that claim unusually low income. But in fact, audits *increase* as a function of income. This strongly suggests that the authorities are keying off additional proxies like occupational categories.

The analysis which follows is straightforward. If people who report low income are audited more often, we should also expect them to report more honestly. But in that case, nominally progressive tax policies quickly become regressive. Adding occupational data offsets this problem, but the net result is indeterminate. This might be an entirely new reason for building more progressivity into the legislated tax code. Subsequent extensions ask how equity impacts change (and can even improve) when tax authorities randomize audit penalties (Scotchmer and Slemrod, 1989), or deliberately discourage some taxpayers from hiring professional advisors to reduce uncertainty (Scotchmer, 1989). Similarly, Scotchmer and Jones (1990) explain how legislatures can reduce the social costs of one-size-fits-all regulation by requiring agencies to partially self-finance through non-compliance fines. This is true even where agencies have only imperfect information about firms' compliance costs.

Finally, Scotchmer and Rubinfeld (1993, 1998) investigated contingent fee agreements in litigation. Prior to this paper, scholars had focused on how contingent fee agreements create moral hazard by encouraging lawyers to settle claims that ought to be litigated. Scotchmer and Rubinfeld argued instead that fees provide a signaling mechanism that reduces asymmetric information concerning attorney competence on one side and client honesty on the other. This improves the deterrence effect of litigation.

R&D Procurement. Scotchmer and Gallini (2002 [this volume]) had stressed that no single R&D incentive is efficient for every problem. But this immediately raises the practical question of how to design problem-specific solutions. Suzanne liked to joke that designing incentives to promote, say, pharmaceutical discovery could not be too difficult "since even criminals know how to turn money into drugs." The problem, she stressed, was doing it cost-effectively. In practice, Washington was unsophisticated. Starting in the early 2000s, Congress and the federal agencies had announced all sorts of prizes. But if you asked why, the answers invoked naive ideological answers that government was inherently inefficient. The logical implication was that prizes should be used for every innovation challenge, but for Prof. Scotchmer, at least, that seemed lunatic.

It was only natural, then, that Prof. Scotchmer would think hard about how to put government incentives on a more rational footing. There is no question that she felt the need particularly keenly because of her decade-plus work in IP theory. But there was also a deeper reason. Politics, like nature, abhorred a vacuum. In this view, constructing rational analytical frameworks was the key to good government. Without them, programs would instead result from "hunches," "bureaucratic imperatives," and other dynamics that could only be right by accident (Quigley and Scotchmer, 1989).

Maurer and Scotchmer (2003) provides this framework by mining the economics literature to summarize the strengths and weaknesses of different incentive mechanisms. It then shows how policymakers can match these qualities against the wildly different R&D problems posed by, say, drug discovery and jet fighter procurement. For example, prizes were particularly appropriate for research problems where the best answer to a problem was known to one or two researchers whose identities were *ex ante* unknown. But they made much less sense for problems like drug discovery, where there were so many possible molecules that no chemist had ever synthesized the "best" candidate in the history of man. The paper concludes with an extended discussion of "grand challenge" technologies in which further progress requires government support. This can happen either because there is no other way to aggregate information across competing firms or because IP alone does not offer enough revenue to fund the project. While the paper explains why mixing IP and government subsidies can be a good idea, it also stresses that these circumstances are much less common than Washington likes to believe.

Database Rights. Europe adopted special IP-style protections for commercial data in the late Nineties and promptly asked the USA to follow suit. Having studied patents for over a decade, the idea of extending IP to new types of information presented a basic question that fascinated Prof. Scotchmer. Indeed, she often pointed out that the theory arguments for patenting commercial knowledge logically applied to basic insights as well. Of course, nobody really believes that subsequent researchers ought to obtain licenses each time they pay for, say, a new physics discovery. And in that case, society might quite rationally decide that non-commercial institutions like open source or universities would work better. See, e.g., Scotchmer (2010a, 2013). Even so, the decision to opt out of commercial IP incentives implied special assumptions about the nature of "basic" knowledge, the transactions costs of licensing, or both. While theory could sharpen these intuitions, the issue was ultimately empirical.

Given this indeterminacy, she turned to common-sense empirics. Here the best example was her widely read contribution to *Science* (Maurer and Scotchmer, 1999), where she pointed out that then-fashionable arguments for adopting new legal protections for commercial data could not be right since (a) US companies currently produce enormous numbers of databases, and (b) there is little or no anecdotal evidence of unfunded projects being cancelled because of piracy fears. Congress ultimately rejected the legislation.

Climate Change. Prof. Scotchmer was always passionate about the environment. So it was natural to ask how market incentives could lead to subtle and presumably unintended consequences. In one early contribution, Dekel and Scotchmer (1990) argue that spills could lead to shortages that increase oil industry profits. In that case, industry agreements to pool cleanup resources could operate as a commitment strategy for companies to take on more risk. The climate change debates of the early 2000s revived these interests in a very personal way since, as she often remarked, no one could fail to notice how much Alaska's glaciers had shrunk since her childhood. Given that she had spent years studying how different IP licenses affected output, it was especially natural to sort out the confused debate between advocates of carbon taxes and CO_2 caps.

Scotchmer (2010) presents her analysis. Under a carbon tax, electricity companies buy green technologies whenever they can save taxes. Since the royalty will normally be priced close to tax savings, however, industry cost structures (and output) barely change. Cap-and-trade schemes are more complicated. Since clean technologies let companies produce more electricity per unit carbon, they reduce costs and increase output. But the effect on R&D is subtle. If society starts out above the monopoly price p^*, increased output leads to higher revenues and, implicitly, larger innovation incentives. So far this looks better than a carbon tax. But when industry starts out below p^*, expanded output drives industry *away* from the monopoly price so that R&D incentives are suppressed. For very powerful technologies, patent-holders may even decide that it is better to ration the number of licensees in order to keep prices from falling still further. This is plainly pathological and implies that very ambitious R&D projects will never be funded at all.

Prof. Scotchmer would have been the first to say that none of this is particularly new as a matter of economic theory. But it did put that theory to work for a problem that mattered: as Suzanne liked to say, it was a chance for economists to "make themselves useful." I still remember how excited Prof. Scotchmer's Berkeley Law colleagues were to hear this work. The basic reason, I think, was that she had identified interesting and important issues that they would never have noticed on their own. It is no insult to say that very few climate scholars or policy wonks remember their freshman introduction to Cournot, let alone the perverse outcomes that start to bite above p^*. But of course, this practically guaranteed that policymakers were headed for unintended consequences. The most obvious difference for Prof. Scotchmer was that thinking about p^* was second nature, even when it came packaged within an unfamiliar cap-and-trade problem. Just as important, though, was her intuitive understanding that other disciplines would value the insight, not to mention her characteristic care in presenting it so transparently.

***

Policymakers and lawyers often assume that writing legislation is the same as making policy. But for a theorist like Prof. Scotchmer, legislation only defined the rules of the game. Whether actors will actually use their new powers, and when or how they will respond to imperfect or skewed enforcement, remained an open question. In some cases, at least, seemingly simple rules could produce unexpected and pathological results. This could reverse legislative intent entirely by, for example, turning an ostensibly progressive tax into a regressive one.

On the face of things this was a depressing possibility. But Prof. Scotchmer chose instead to see this as a chance to be useful. Economists, after all, had particularly powerful tools for analyzing such problems. No matter how sophisticated, the bottom line was delivering insights that policymakers had not noticed and could actually use.

The American Economic Review: Papers and Proceedings
Vol. 77, no.2, pp. 229–233
(May 1987)

Audit Classes and Tax Enforcement Policy

By Suzanne Scotchmer*

Compliance with the legislated tax code cannot be assured without audits and penalties on unreported income. Although compliance can most cheaply be assured with a small probability of audit (since audits are costly) and large penalties, law or social convention may prohibit stringent penalties, and the enforcement agency must then decide on an audit strategy as its sole choice variable.[1]

Without audit, the enforcement agency cannot observe true taxable income, but it may be able to observe correlates like profession, age, and gross income, as reported independently by the employer. I shall say that such information defines a taxpayer's audit class. The enforcement agency will find it lucrative to condition the probability of audit on audit class, as well as on reported income, particularly if the audit class is a good signal of income.[2]

Even when the enforcement agency undertakes its best audit strategy, allowable penalties may be so low that taxpayers underreport income in equilibrium. In that case, the effective tax code will differ from the legislated tax code, where the effective tax code reflects *actual* payments, including taxes on reported income and the expected value of fines. The proper definitions of tax equity become murky when taxpayers underreport income, especially when some taxpayers are honest. Should equal consideration be given to honest and dishonest taxpayers, as though underreporting income were a legitimate portfolio choice? Without

---

* Graduate School of Public Policy, University of California, Berkeley, CA 94720. I thank Joel Sobel and Isabel Sanchez for useful comments and discussion. This research was supported by NSF grant ES-8610021.

1 Jennifer Reinganum and Louis Wilde (1986) have studied the equilibrium audit strategy when fine rates are fixed and the enforcement agency can deviate from its announced policy once taxpayers have reported their taxable income. Reinganum-Wilde (1985), Kim Border and Joel Sobel (1986), and Dilip Mookherjeea and Ivan Png (1986) have studied the optimal choice of tax code, penalty structure and audit function when fines cannot exceed income and the enforcement agency can bind itself to an enforcement policy.

2 Carol Jones (1986) studies optimal enforcement of emission standards when the policy can depend on industry "sectors" that are signals of compliance cost. This is a very similar problem.

wishing to dismiss this question as unimportant, this paper assumes that taxpayers are amoral, and is concerned with the effective tax code when taxpayers underreport.

The optimal enforcement literature typically assumes that the object of the enforcement agency is to maximize revenue net of costs. This is a reasonable assumption in this age of budget deficits, since an enforcement agency would be replaced if it left unexploited opportunities to enhance revenue. But enforcement policies designed to maximize net revenue affect the equity properties of the effective tax code. The enforcement agency will audit tax-payers with low income reports within an audit class with higher probability than it audits high-report taxpayers, thus making it less attractive for low-income taxpayers to underreport income, and introducing a regressive bias in the effective tax code within each audit class. To see this, suppose the opposite, that the probability of audit rose with reported income. Then high-income people would have an added incentive to underreport income; namely, that underreporting reduces the probability of audit. The enforcement agency can dissuade high-income taxpayers from underreporting (thus increasing rev-enue) by making the probability of audit rise as reported income falls.[3]

This seems to defy experience, since audit probability seems to increase with reported income. But the observation that probability of audit rises with reported income pools audit classes. Taxpayers with high reported income might have high probabilities of audit because they are in audit classes that signal high income. Nevertheless, high income reports within that audit class may elicit lower probability of audit than low reports.[4] Evidence for this might be that taking more deductions increases the probability of audit.

Equity properties of the effective tax code will reflect the fact that probabilities of audit depend on audit class as well as on reported income. This may well overturn the regressive bias within audit classes, a compli-cation that has not been studied.

There are two reasons taxpayers with the same income may pay differ-ent amounts. First, since people underreport, payments differ according to whether the taxpayer is audited. A taxpayer who is caught underreporting pays tax on the true taxable income, plus a fine based on the discrepancy between true and reported income. Second, taxpayers with the same income may belong to different audit classes. Their expected payments differ both because they typically report different amounts of income and because they are audited and fined with different probabilities. This leads to variance not only in the actual payments, but also in the *expected*

---

3 See Reinganum and Wilde (1986) for a discussion of this result in the case that the agency cannot precommit, and my 1986 paper for the case that the agency can precommit.

4 My earlier paper shows that when taxpayers are risk neutral, and when the distributions of true income within audit classes differ by a scale parameter, audit classes with higher average income (but the same mass of taxpayers) will be audited more often than those with lower income.

payments (where the expectation accounts for whether or not an audit occurs) of taxpayers with the same income.

Thus, enforcement policy affects both vertical and horizontal equity. The vertical "inequity" is that expected payments do not rise with income at the legislated rate. The horizontal inequity is that taxpayers in different audit classes with the same true taxable income have different expected payments.

I present a simple model showing that the regressive bias within audit classes may be dominated by effects across audit classes. I take a linear tax code (constant marginal and average tax rates) and assume that taxpayers with high income are distributed among audit classes that signal high income. The distribution of income signals is the same for every income level, except for a shift of location. Then the average tax payment (expected tax payment, divided by true income) decreases with income within each audit class, but when one averages the expected payments of taxpayers with the same income who are in different audit classes, their average tax rates increase with true income; that is, the tax code is more progressive than stipulated.

Turning to horizontal equity, it is plausible that when the income signal becomes a better predictor of true income, the variance in expected tax payments among taxpayers with the same true income might decrease, since they might be treated more uniformly. This is unclear in the case studied below, and the effect on horizontal equity of improving the income signal is an interesting open question.

Each taxpayer has a true taxable income i. His true tax liability, as it would be assessed if he were audited, is t_i, where t is a linear tax rate. Although the enforcement agency cannot observe i without audit, it observes a signal y that is correlated with i. In addition, the taxpayer reports an amount of taxable income r. The enforcement agency must decide how often to audit taxpayers of each type; that is, it chooses a probability-of-audit function $p(r, y)$. I assume that the enforcement agency can commit to such a policy, and that the taxpayer knows the policy. A taxpayer who is audited and found underreporting must pay tax on the unreported income plus a penalty at rate f. I assume taxpayers are risk neutral and therefore that they choose their reports r to minimize expected payments:

$$\underset{r}{\text{Minimize}} \quad tr + t(1+f)\, p(r,y)(i-r). \tag{1}$$

I refer to the minimum as $\tau[i, y, p(\cdot)]$, which is achieved by the optimal report $r[i, y, p(\cdot)]$ that solves (1).

Letting the audit probability depend on the audit class is the same as choosing a different probability-of-audit function (a function of reported income) for each audit class. Since the agency can treat distinct audit classes completely separately, it is sufficient to analyze policy for one audit class. If $H(i|y)$ represents the measure of true income i in audit class y, the enforcement agency chooses $p(r, y)$ for each y to maximize

$$\int \tau[i, y, p(\cdot)]dH(i|y) - c \int p[r(\cdot), y]dH(i|y),$$ (2)

where c is the cost of an audit.

Two features of the optimal audit function are immediate. First, no audit probability will exceed $1/(1 + f)$, since unreported income then has expected value zero, and any taxpayer that faces a probability of audit this high will report truthfully. Any higher audit probability would therefore have no additional incentive effect, and would be wasteful, since audits are costly. Second, the audit function $p(r, y)$ (with y fixed) is non-increasing in r. If $r_1 < r_2$, and $p[r_1] < p[r_2]$, then expected payments (1) are greater with report r_2 than with report r_1, for every income level. Hence r_2 will never be reported, and the increasing portion of the audit function could be replaced with a constant function. Techniques developed by Roger Myerson (1981) and Eric Maskin and John Riley (1984) can be adapted to show that the optimal audit function within an audit class can be characterized as follows:[5]

LEMMA: *The optimal audit function within the audit class has the following form: For some p^y, $p(r, y) = 1/(1 + f)$ for $r < p^y$ and $p(r, y) = 0$ otherwise.*

Knowing this, one can calculate that the optimal cutoff ρ^y satisfies

$$v \equiv \frac{c}{t(1 + f)} = \frac{N^y - H(\rho^y|y)}{h(\rho^y|y)},$$ (3)

where N^y is the measure of people in the audit class.

Within each audit class, the effective tax code is regressive: low-income taxpayers report honestly and pay tax on their true income, while taxpayers with income greater than ρ^y pay tax on ρ^y. Since the dishonest high-income taxpayers never get audited, their expected payments are just $t\rho^y$.[6] The average payment schedule of high-income taxpayers is $t\rho^y/i$, which decreases with true income i.

This regressive bias is of limited importance if the most important discriminant for audit probability is the audit class, rather than reported income, as when the audit class is a very good predictor of true income.

---

5 I am grateful to Joel Sobel and Isabel Sanchez for pointing out the relevance of these papers.
6 Thus, only the honest taxpayers get audited! While the enforcement agency could save costs by refusing to audit, it has an incentive to bind itself *ex ante* to performing the audits. Otherwise the lucrative deterrence of underreporting would vanish. The enforcement agency can always do better by binding itself *ex ante* than by reserving the freedom to deviate from its announced audit policy after tax reports are in, provided taxpayers know which regime is in effect. This is because every policy that is available without precommitment is also available as a precommitment policy.

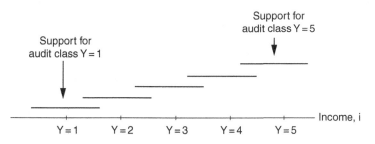

Figure 1. True incomes and audit classes.

I model this idea in the simplest possible way. True incomes i and income signals y are jointly distributed in the population according to measure $H(i, y)$. For simplicity, assume incomes in audit class y are distributed uniformly on $[y - a, y + a]$ with density $1/2a$; that is, $h(i, y) = 1/2a$ for $y - a \leq i \leq y + a$. Then the marginal distributions of i and y are uniform with marginal densities one,[7] and thus $h(i \mid y) = h(y \mid i) = h(i, y)$. Figure 1 shows supports for audit classes with increasing average incomes, y. Taxpayers with a particular income i will belong to audit classes with $i - a \leq y \leq i + a$.

The uniform density is inessential. The calculations below regarding vertical equity apply when income signals y are distributed the same for each i except for location; that is, $h(i, y)$ depends only on the difference $y - i$.

The solution to (3) is $\rho^y = y + a - v$. To calculate the effective tax code, we must calculate the average payments (across audit classes) by taxpayers with a given income, i:

$$E_y \tau[i, y, \rho^y] = \int \tau[i, y, \rho^y]\, dH(y \mid i) = t(i - k), \tag{4}$$

where k is positive.

Here I have substituted ρ^y for the probability-of-audit function in $\tau(\cdot)$ to represent the optimal audit function. $\tau(i, y, \rho^y)$ is graphed in Figure 2. The tax paid is $\tau(i, y, \rho^y) = ti$ if $i \leq y + a - v$, or $i - a + v \leq y$. That is, for large y, income i is a low income in the audit class and the taxpayer will thus report honestly. On the other hand, for small y, $y \leq i - a + v$, income i is a high income in the audit class and since the taxpayer reports the cutoff amount $y + a - v$, $\tau(i, y, \rho^y) = t[y + a - v]$ for such y. The integral can be

---

7 To ensure that we have a finite mass of taxpayers, assume that the support of $h(i, y)$ is some bounded subset of R^2. Provided that i and y are away from the boundary by at least distance a, the marginal density of i is the integral from $I - a$ to $I + a$ of $\int (1/2a)dy = 1$ and the marginal density of y is the integral from $y - a$ to $y + a$ of $\int (1/2a)di = 1$.

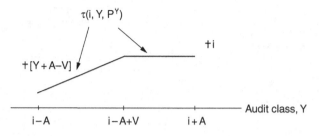

Figure 2. Expected payments of taxpayers with fixed income i.

evaluated by substituting these values for $\tau(i, y, \rho^y)$ in (4), and $(1/2a)$ for dH $(y \mid i)$ in the domain $i - a \leq y \leq i + a$.[8]

The reason expected payments are less than stipulated tax liability, ti, is simply that taxpayers in low audit classes benefit by being high-income taxpayers in low audit classes and find it advantageous to underreport income. The number of such taxpayers is the same for each income level, and thus the collective amount of unpaid tax is the same, namely tk. The consequence of this fixed underpayment is that the effective tax code is *more* progressive than the stipulated tax code, contrary to what happens *within* audit classes. The average effective tax paid, $t - tk/i$, is increasing with income i.

Turning to horizontal equity, it is clear from Figure 2 that all taxpayers with income i do not make the same payments. One might take as a measure of horizontal inequity the variance in tax payments among taxpayers with the same true income i. One might think that increasing the number of audit classes that contain income i would increase horizontal inequity. Increased variance in y might increase the variance in $\tau(i, y, \rho^y)$ for each i.

Variance in the distribution of y, conditional on i, increases with a, since, conditional on i, y is uniformly distributed on $[i - a, i + a]$. The end points in Figure 2 shift out. At the same time, the cutoff value of y separating taxpayers that report honestly from those that lie, namely $i - a + v$, shifts left. The result of increasing variance is that more type i taxpayers report honestly! For some parameter values a, the variance in tax paid by taxpayers with income i will actually decrease when they are distributed among more audit classes, y.

Many issues about equity arise, which this paper has not addressed. When profession is important in defining the audit class, it is unclear that we really want to define equity according to how much tax is paid on a year-by-year basis. Low income in one year may well be an aberration. To

---

8 If $a < v/2$, then no taxpayers will be audited. Rather, all taxpayers in audit class y will pay tax on the minimum income in the class, $y - a$.

the extent that profession is a stable indicator of *lifetime* earnings, or perhaps of "ability," it would be reasonable to base not only the probability of audit, but also the stipulated tax liability, on profession and not just on income.

During a taxpayer's career, he or she may move from being a low-income taxpayer within the audit class to a high-income taxpayer within the same audit class. The horizontal "inequity" would then vanish over a lifetime.

If there were only one audit class, as when the enforcement agency can observe nothing more about the taxpayer than reported income, then the legislature might be able to undo the regressive bias introduced by enforcement by building more progressivity into the stipulated tax code than is really desired. Such an approach will not work when the probability of audit can depend on the audit class, but the stipulated tax code cannot.

References

Border, Kim and Sobel, Joel, "Samurai Accountant: A Theory of Auditing and Plunder," Working Paper, California Institute of Technology, 1986.

Jones, Carol, "Models of Regulatory Enforcement and Compliance," mimeo., University of Michigan, 1986.

Maskin, Eric and Riley, John, "Monopoly with Incomplete Information," *RAND Journal of Economics,* Summer 1984, *15,* 171–96.

Mookherjee, Dilip and Png, Ivan, "Optimal Auditing, Insurance and Redistribution," manuscript, Graduate School of Management, UCLA, 1986.

Myerson, Roger, "Optimal Auction Design," *Mathematics of Operations Research,* February 1981, *6,* 58–73.

Reinganum, Jennifer and Wilde, Louis, "Income Tax Compliance in a Principal-Agent Framework," *Journal of Public Economics,* January 1985, *26,* 1–8.

—— **and** ——, "Equilibrium Verification and Reporting Policies in a Model of Tax Compliance," *International Economic Review,* October 1986, *27,* 739–60.

Scotchmer, Suzanne, "Equity in Tax Enforcement," Harvard Institute of Economic Research Working Paper 1233, May 1986.

PART VII

LIVING LEGACY

Modern IP economics is the work of many hands. For this reason, any account of Prof. Scotchmer's research must explore both the work that influenced her and, especially, the work that followed. Previous chapters supply much of this context. Here, we step back for a fuller assessment.

In the nature of things our estimate is tentative. This is particularly true for IP theory. More than a decade after it was written, *Innovation and Incentives* remains remarkably up to date. But it is surely not the last word. As "Giants" teaches, the value of Prof. Scotchmer's "Ideas Model" and "Cumulative Innovation" contributions includes the option value of extensions and variants that have yet to be written. We still do not know how many doors she opened.

In the meantime it is important to say what we can. Prof. Hall presents a detailed analysis of how Prof. Scotchmer's work has entered the literature so far. Beyond that, the long-term value of Prof. Scotchmer's work – like all theory papers – depends on how closely its basic premises resemble everyday life. Profs. Furman, Murray, Stern, and Williams describe the rich empirical literature that tests cumulative innovation theory's guiding assumptions.

CHAPTER 26

Suzanne Scotchmer: A Bibliographic Study[1]

Bronwyn H. Hall

Introduction. In this note I provide a brief appreciation of Suzanne Scotchmer's research via an investigation using a number of bibliographic sources. This approach allows those of us who work in one or more of her subfields to obtain a better grasp of the range of her contributions. Using citation data, I am also able to see where her work has had the greatest impact on subsequent researchers, something that seems especially appropriate given her emphasis on the cumulative nature of research.[2] In doing this, I look not only at her most highly cited papers, but also at the most highly cited papers that cite her work, which turns out to demonstrate more fully the breadth of her contributions.

The Data. The data have been collected from multiple sources, which are listed in Table 1. A starting point was Scotchmer's own University of California website, which contains a list of her papers classified by topic area.[3] This list of ninety-seven preprints and articles was crossed with the list obtained on Google Scholar after searching by her full name (which is unique, fortunately) and the Google-reported citation count obtained.[4] The two websites academic.research.microsoft.com and ideas.repec.org also yielded paper counts and citation counts. All three of these websites index both working papers and published articles; none of them is completely clean, in the sense that occasionally the same paper may appear in

---

1 My thanks go to Stephen Maurer for encouraging this project and making useful suggestions.

2 Note that this note is intended merely to give an overview of Suzanne's research and its impact. There is no comparative analysis of the numbers obtained, nor are the citation rates adjusted for differences across year and field, as they would be if a serious citation study were undertaken. The numbers are merely indicative and the emphasis is on the areas of influence that they reveal.

3 http://socrates.berkeley.edu/~scotch/publications.htm accessed April 2014 and February 2016.

4 The difference between the 97 papers listed on her site and the 85 found in Google citations is mostly because a few short notes were not on the latter site.

Table 1: Variations in measurement

Source	Comments	Total number of papers	Total number of cites
Google Scholar	Working Papers & publications; may be some duplicates	85	9979
Microsoft academic. research*	Working Papers & publications; many duplicates	143	2418
Repec.org	Working Papers & publications, but only those captured by IDEAS	61	1017
SSRN.com	Working Papers only	27	—
SSCI Web of Science	Publications only	65	2077

* Apparently not updated since 2012.

multiple forms, and the cites are not consolidated. That fact explains the variation in paper count in Table 1.[5]

The other two sources used were SSRN, which contains only working papers, and SSCI (the Web of Science), which contains only published articles. Taken together, they index eighty-seven papers, which corresponds roughly to the counts obtained elsewhere. The citation data on SSCI include only references in published articles indexed by it, which is a disadvantage in economics where publication lags are long. In what follows, I make use primarily of the Google cite data, which appear to be the most complete, as well as the most disambiguated (duplicates combined).

Discussion. Table 2 shows the range of subfields in which Scotchmer worked, and Table 3 the main journals in which she published; the classification of fields is largely based on her own classification. The mean year of publication in the difference topic areas shows that although she worked in the public finance area early in her career, her later work

---

5 The original data collection was done in April 2014. For this paper the data were recollected in January and February 2016. This accounts for any differences between the 2014 conference presentation and the tables here.

Table 2: Range of topics

Topic	Mean year	Papers	Citations	Cites per paper
Public finance	1991	13	789	61
Clubs and local public goods	1996	14	609	44
Game theory and mathematical economics	1997	20	1050	53
IP and innovation	1998	29	7187	248
Other law and economics	2000	9	344	38
Total	1998	85	9979	117

Sources: Scotchmer's own topic classification (from her website); Google Scholar cites.

Table 3: Journals

Journal	Papers published
Journal of Public Economics	7
The RAND Journal of Economics	7
Journal of Economic Theory	5
Economics Letters	4
Economic Theory	3
Journal of Mathematical Economics	2
Innovation Policy and the Economy	2
American Economic Review	2
Journal of Law, Economics, and Organizations	2

evolved towards IP and other law and economics topics. It is clear from Table 2 that her work in the IP area has had the most impact in terms of citations even though it is somewhat more recent. This may be partly accounted for by its applied nature (in comparison to game theory and mathematical economics, for example, applied economics articles do tend to garner more citations), but not entirely.

The journal list is headed by the most prestigious field journals in her areas. However, it also includes two papers in a general interest journal (on open source and collusion through insurance) as well as two in a journal targeted to policymakers. The latter two give an idea of the relevance of her research for real-world problems. One is on IP as an incentive for innovation and the other on the relative impact of cap-and-trade systems versus emission taxes in encouraging innovation in green technologies, which reaches the conclusion that taxes are better at encouraging full diffusion of energy-efficient technologies by the innovator.

The citation distribution for most well-cited researchers' papers is fairly skewed and Suzanne's is no exception, with most papers having fewer than 100 cites and four having more than 500. Table 4 lists Scotchmer's eight most highly cited papers, all of which are in the IP and innovation area, confirming the relative importance of her work there. By far the most highly cited paper is a *Journal of Economic Perspectives* paper that summarizes her work on intellectual property and cumulative innovation. The two papers that introduced this line of research (Green and Scotchmer, 1995 and Scotchmer, 1996) also appear on the list. So there is not much doubt about where she had the most impact.

As shown above, Suzanne's most highly cited paper is "Standing on the Shoulders of Giants," which emphasizes the importance of cumulative research and innovation. In this spirit, we can also look at the longer-run impacts of her research by asking which are the most highly cited of papers that cite her papers. The top ten are shown in Table 5, with the citation counts from SSCI (that is, including only published citations). Note that there will be a bias towards her older papers in these cites due to publication lags.

When we examine which of her papers are cited by these top ten citing papers (excluding the 4 self-cites), we discover two things: (1) The range is broad, with 14 cites to 12 distinct papers in several fields. (2) They fall into two groups: 7 cites are to her top-ranked papers in the IP area, and 7 to much lower-ranked papers on tax enforcement and industrial organization theory. This result both confirms her impact on the economics of IP research area and also shows that some of her less-cited theoretical work facilitated subsequent research productively.

Another way to look at the impact of Scotchmer's work is to classify the methodologies used by the highly cited papers that cite her work. Here we again see a broad range: the top ten papers include 3 empirical, 2 theoretical, 2 literature surveys, 2 papers using legal analysis, and an historical

Table 4: Most highly cited papers

Paper	Authors	Year published	Total cites	SSCI cites
"Standing on the Shoulders of Giants: Cumulative Research and the Patent Law"	Suzanne Scotchmer	1991	1585	398
Innovation and Incentives (book)	Suzanne Scotchmer	2004	1225	N/A
"On the Division of Profit in Sequential Innovation"	Jerry Green and Suzanne Scotchmer	1995	768	222
"The Law and Economics of Reverse Engineering"	Pam Samuelson and Suzanne Scotchmer	2002	528	117
"Novelty and Disclosure in Patent Law"	Jerry Green and Suzanne Scotchmer	1990	494	147
"Patent Breadth, Patent Life, and the Pace of Technological Progress"	Ted O'Donoghue, Suzanne Scotchmer, and Jacques Thisse	1998	480	110
"Intellectual Property: When Is It the Best Incentive System?"	Nancy Gallini and Suzanne Scotchmer	2002	431	N/A
"Protecting Early Innovators: Should Second-Generation Products be Patentable?"	Suzanne Scotchmer	1996	394	99

Note: N/A means that the article was not indexed in the Web of Science (SSCI).

Table 5: Most highly cited papers that cite Scotchmer

Authors	Title	Type	Journal	Year	SSCI cites	N of papers cited
Hall, Jaffe, & Trajtenberg	Market value and patent citations	empirical	RJE	2005	564	1
Hall & Ziedonis	The patent paradox revisited: an empirical study of patenting in the US semiconductor industry	empirical	RJE	2001	556	3
Weingast	The economic role of political institutions: market-preserving federalism and economic development	historical application	JLEO	1995	530	1
Merges & Nelson	On the complex economies of patent scope	law	COL. LAW REV.	1990	478	1
Andreoni, Erard, & Feinstein	Tax compliance	survey	JEL	1998	467	4
Kandel & Lazear	Peer pressure and partnerships	theory	JPE	1992	459	1

Table 5 (*cont.*)

Authors	Title	Type	Journal	Year	SSCI cites	N of papers cited
Scotchmer	Standing on the shoulders of giants: cumulative research and the patent law	survey	JEP	1991	398	4
Klemperer	Markets with consumer switching costs	theory	QJE	1987	395	1
Landes & Posner	An economic analysis of the copyright law	law	JLS	1989	384	1
Siegel, Waldman, & Link	Assessing the impact of organizational practices on the relative productivity of university technology transfer offices: an exploratory study	empirical	RP	2003	364	1

application. The next ten highly cited papers (not shown) include 3 empirical, 4 theoretical, a literature survey, and 2 applications to specific cases. Thus this sample of twenty papers citing her work suggests that it has influenced both empirical and theoretical work equally.

CONCLUSION

As most of us would have said without this data collection effort, Scotchmer's greatest impact is her work on incentives in cumulative innovation – first bringing the problem to our attention and then providing useful analytic tools for understanding the consequences of the assignment of IP rights to innovators engaged in this kind of activity. Although the cumulative nature of research had been understood for centuries (as exemplified by the famous quote[6]), connecting that to the problem of creating incentives for both the earlier and later inventors was Suzanne's contribution. This idea (and its subsequent theoretical analysis) has made a considerable contribution to our thinking about the economics of IP and optimal IP policy.

However, looking at the extended impact of her work via citation analysis produces a broader view, as it encompasses not only patents and copyright, but also topics in political economy, labor, industrial organization, technology transfer, and tax compliance. It also shows that her work has had substantial applied impact, with 11 empirical, legal, and applied papers among the top twenty papers that cite her work.

SOURCES[7]

List of papers by topic on Prof. Scotchmer's website http://socrates .berkeley.edu/~scotch/
Google Scholar http://scholar.google.com/
Microsoft with Silverlight visualization http://academic.research.microsoft .com/
repec http://ideas.repec.org/
SSRN http://www.ssrn.com/en/
SSCI Web of Science http://apps.webofknowledge.com

---

6 The phrase "standing on the shoulders of giants" is usually attributed to Isaac Newton, although there is evidence that it was in use prior to that, as early as the twelfth century.

7 Websites accessed April 2014 and February 2016.

CHAPTER 27

Standing on the Shoulders of Scotchmer: The Empirical Economics of Cumulative Innovation

Jeffrey L. Furman, Fiona E. Murray,
Scott Stern, and Heidi Williams

Over the past twenty-five years, empirical research in the economics of innovation has undergone a revolution. While empirical and historical research was always important to the field, the connection to economic theory was limited. By and large, innovation theory focused on questions that were far removed from plausible empirical settings, and much of the best work, including the pioneering use of patent citation data by Adam Jaffe, Manuel Trajtenberg, and Rebecca Henderson, was connected to theory at only a relatively limited level.

Suzanne Scotchmer's foundational papers in the 1990s developed a powerful theoretical framework that allowed for a bridge to be built between theory and empirics, resulting in a cascade of work on cumulative innovation that continues to grow each year. Indeed, as empirical researchers ourselves, it is fair to say that this bridge has been a cornerstone of our research agendas over the past fifteen years.

Two key insights lie at the heart of Suzanne's seminal papers in this area. First, while growth theorists such as Romer and Aghion were beginning to emphasize the centrality of cumulative innovation to overall economic growth, Suzanne made the role of institutions in facilitating researchers' ability to "stand on the shoulders of giants" into a central theoretical issue. She was perhaps the first to recognize – and certainly the first to make clear the importance of – the fact that, when innovation is cumulative, the incentives for innovation do not depend solely on the simple "strength" of a patent or other appropriability mechanism, but also, critically, on how that monopoly right is divided across multiple generations of innovators. Second, Scotchmer's theoretical modeling pointed out that it is not simply technical opportunity but also the interplay between the intellectual property environment and the contracting environment that determines whether appropriate incentives were in place to encourage cumulative innovation.[1]

---

1 See Scotchmer (1991) (this volume at pp. 89–102); Green and Scotchmer (1995) (this volume at pp. 102–120); and Scotchmer (1996).

These ideas inspired at least two related streams of follow-on work. On one hand, it contributed to a broad and continuously evolving literature on the relationship between intellectual property policy and innovation.[2] At the same time, Scotchmer's research inspired the development of new empirical approaches for analyzing the causal impact of innovation policies on knowledge accumulation.

It is useful to state the empirical challenge of this work. Social scientists and policy analysts find it hard to assess the extent to which any particular institution or policy influences the way in which the "knowledge stock" is created, maintained, and extended. In particular, it is difficult to separate the influence of a particular unit of knowledge from the impact of the institution or policy environment in which that knowledge is embedded, even though the two are conceptually distinct. Stated differently, for a given piece of knowledge produced or diffused within a particular institutional or policy environment, one cannot directly observe the counterfactual impact that such knowledge would have had if it had been produced in an alternative institutional or policy setting.

Linking Scotchmer's ideas to measurement thus involved addressing a number of challenges. First, measuring cumulative innovation requires tracking the rate at which knowledge progresses. The "Citation Revolution" brought on by work such as that of Jaffe, Trajtenberg, and Henderson (1993) – which was itself inspired by the seminal work of Garfield (1950), De Solla Price (1965), and Merton (1973) – demonstrated that it was possible to track knowledge flows over time and space using bibliometric measures. Second, one needs to be able to replicate the experiment in which a particular unit of knowledge is embedded in (a) the actual policy whose impact one would like to identify and (b) an alternative, baseline policy environment against which one could measure the counterfactual impact. Advances in quantitative methods in economics, sometimes referred to as the "Identification Revolution," helped point the way forward.

A cluster of papers in this area, including Furman and Stern (2006, 2011), Murray and Stern (2007), Agrawal and Goldfarb (2006, 2008), and Simcoe and Rysman (2008), addressed these challenges with a three-step approach. First, these papers each identify a set of "knowledge units" in a research area by linking them to a particular set of "core articles" or "core patents." Second, they investigate the rate at which future ideas built on that knowledge base by tracking citations to those core articles/patents. Although publications, patents, and associated citations are noisy and imperfect measures of knowledge production and accumulation, they are measures with relatively well-understood and well-characterized

---

2 See, e.g., Jaffe (2000); Sakakibara and Branstetter (2001); Gallini (2002); and Bessen and
   Maskin (2009).

limitations.[3] Third, they leverage arguably exogenous shocks to policy or institutional environments to investigate how these changes affect the rate at which follow-on research builds on the existing knowledge stock. In other words, this research employs a differences-in-differences approach to measure changes in citation patterns for a group of treatment articles/ patents affected by a shock relative to citations to a group of control articles that is expected to be unaffected and can provide a counterfactual estimate of the trajectory of knowledge accumulation absent the intervention.

Furman and Stern (2011) introduced this approach in the context of libraries for cell lines and other life science materials, known as Biological Resource Centers (BRCs). They ask whether the accession of these articles into BRCs affects the accumulation of knowledge linked to those materials. Furman and Stern take advantage of the fact that multiple sets of materials were unexpectedly moved from private collections, where they had circulated for numbers of years, into the American Type Culture Collection (ATCC), the largest BRC in the United States. For each material in these collections, Furman and Stern identify the research articles that first characterized those materials as well as a set of control articles which appear immediately before and after the BRC-linked articles in the published journal. The authors then track citation patterns both to the BRC-linked articles and to the controls in the period before and after the BRC-linked materials were moved to public collections. Since the articles are of varying ages when accessioned, it is possible to distinguish the effects of prior article quality and the impact of accession into the BRC from article cohort and year effects. Further, the impact of accession can be identified either relative to the control articles or relative to the sample of BRC-linked articles in the period before their deposit. Furman and Stern find that accession leads to a post-accession citation boost of 57–135 percent, suggesting that BRCs play a significant role in the accumulation of knowledge in life sciences research.

Murray and Stern (2007) bring the discussion closer to intellectual property "IP" institutions per se by investigating whether formal intellectual property rights limit the extent of knowledge accumulation in the context of dual-purpose ideas. They exploit the fact that some knowledge may contribute to both scientific research and useful commercial applica tions and, therefore, is disclosed both in academic papers and patents, i.e., "patent–paper pairs." The delay between paper publication and patent grant is sometimes substantial and varies across ideas. Relative to the counterfactual in which an academic paper does not end up associated with a patent, the grant of a patent constitutes a shock to the research environment in which the idea is embedded. This enables Murray and Stern

3 Hall, Griliches, and Hausman (1985); Griliches (1990, 1998); Trajtenberg (1990).

to examine whether formal patent rights lead, as the Anticommons hypothesis suggests, to a decline in academic citations (indicating a relative decline in scientific use) associated with previously published knowledge. Employing a differences-in-differences estimator for their patent-paper pairs (and including a control group consisting of other publications in the same journal for which no patent is granted), Murray and Stern find that citations to papers decline by approximately 10–20 percent after patent grant, a finding that is consistent with a modest Anticommons effect.

Murray et al. (2015) apply a similar approach to examine the relationship between openness in academic research and upstream investments in research diversity. Specifically, the authors investigate the impact of NIH regulations in the late 1990s that relaxed IP restrictions on academics' use of certain genetically engineered mice. To identify treatment and control sets, the authors identified scientific papers associated with genetically engineered mice, only some of which were affected by the NIH intervention. They then implemented the differences-in-differences approach described above to evaluate how the level and type of follow-on research using the affected mice changed using the controls to establish counterfactual evidence. The authors showed that the level of follow-on research increased on those articles associated with the mice whose IP restrictions were lifted, and also found evidence that this increase in follow-on research was associated with a substantial expansion in the number of research paths explored. Taken together, the findings provide additional evidence regarding the costs of upstream intellectual property restrictions on downstream exploration, i.e., that such restrictions inhibit both the rate and the diversity of experimentation that follows from a single idea.

Over the past several years, a range of follow-on research has used this same approach. For example, Furman, Murray, and Stern (2012) apply these techniques to the Bush Administration's controversial 2001 policy cutting off federal funding for research involving most human embryonic stem cells (hESC). Announced in August 2001, the US hESC policy constituted a plausibly exogenous shock which changed expectations regarding funding and the availability of research materials. Furman, Murray, and Stern evaluate citations to a set of fundamental papers identified by a 2001 National Institutes of Health report on the field, comparing the impact of the policy on papers with US- and non-US authors to a control group of papers in RNA interference (RNAi), a contemporaneous life sciences breakthrough that was not directly affected by the hESC intervention. Furman, Murray, and Stern find that US production of hESC research lagged 35–40 percent behind anticipated levels, although the decline was concentrated mainly in the initial years of the policy (2001–2003), ameliorated over time, and affected elite institutions and authors with international collaborators less than other scientists.

These projects accumulated an initial body of empirical evidence, but the margins of interest remained at least one step removed from the fundamental parameters in Suzanne's models. Williams (2013) takes that final step by directly addressing the role that intellectual property has on the rate and direction of innovation. In the so-called "race" to sequence the human genome, the publicly funded Human Genome Project and the private firm Celera both sought to sequence all of the genes of the human genome. The difference was that the Genome Project placed its genes in the public domain, whereas Celera attempted to patent many of its discoveries. But these patent applications were largely rejected, forcing Celera to turn to a non-patent form of intellectual property instead. Using scientific and medical datasets that track both basic research papers and the development of gene-based diagnostic tests, Williams finds evidence that Celera's non-patent form of intellectual property reduced both follow-on scientific research and follow-on commercial development by about 30 percent.

This work was not simply of academic interest. Instead, the estimates were cited in several briefs submitted to the *AMP* v. *Myriad* case, where the US Supreme Court ultimately ruled that human genes do qualify as patentable subject matter because such patents would "inhibit future innovation." In an attempt to speak more directly to patent policy, Sampat and Williams (2015) investigated how gene patents – as opposed to the non-patent form of intellectual property used by Celera – affected follow-on innovation. Building on work by Jensen and Murray (2005), Sampat and Williams link the exact DNA sequences in patent applications (both successful and unsuccessful) to the genes claimed in those applications. This lets them compare follow-on innovation across genes claimed in patent applications that were ultimately granted patents against genes in applications that were later rejected. Sampat and Williams also build on previous work by Cockburn, Kortum, and Stern (2003) to find evidence that patent examiners strongly influence whether a given patent application is granted, and develop this examiner heterogeneity into an instrumental variables framework. Taken together, Sampat and Williams's evidence suggests that gene patents per se have not reduced follow-on innovation, consistent with what would have been expected based on Suzanne's work but inconsistent with the argument which persuaded the Supreme Court in *Myriad*.

Recently, this approach has been extended to domains outside of intellectual property and openness. For example, Nagaraj (2015) examines the impact of NASA's Landsat satellite mapping project on entrepreneurship and the identification of new discoveries in the gold exploration industry. Nagaraj takes advantage of the facts that (a) topographic images generated by the Landsat mapping program proved valuable in private firms' gold exploration efforts and (b) variations in cloud cover resulted in plausibly random differences in the quality of satellite images of particular geographic regions relative to other contiguous regions. He finds evidence suggesting that gaps in mapping coverage induce substantial differences in exploration. These effects are more pronounced among smaller, more entrepreneurial firms that are less able to perform detailed research efforts, and in regions where high-quality local institutions exist which may play a complementary role in the gold exploration process. On average, the probability of finding new gold deposits doubles in areas with high-quality Landsat images relative to low-quality ones. This work highlights the role of mapping in driving economic activity and quantifies the effects of public investment (in Landsat) on private economic outcomes in one industry. By establishing a causal link between mapping the features of upstream environments and downstream economic consequences, Nagaraj's work expands the agenda inspired by Scotchmer's work.

Ultimately, the last two decades of empirical research have grappled with a question at the heart of Suzanne's agenda: does the fact that innovation is cumulative and decentralized imply that there will be a fundamental "Anticommons" problem in which too many property rights get in the way of successful commercialization, or will the ability to contract among generations of innovators allow productive investment to be made? While there are clearly individual cases where the inability to contract has hampered innovation (and this seems to be particularly salient during the early stage of a new technology), the overall body of findings highlights Suzanne's insight that institutions and the potential for contracting matter deeply in shaping innovation outcomes.

Finally, as we continue to learn from and teach Suzanne's seminal contributions to graduate students and practitioners, we have each found ourselves reflecting not just on her underlying ideas but on the unique individual that helped to shape this still emerging field. Among our many professional interactions, we were all together when she was the discussant for a paper by one of us[4] at the 2010 National Bureau of Economic Research "Rate and Direction of Inventive Activity Revisited" conference organized by another one of us.[5] As always, Suzanne's remarks were clear and fair, elucidated the key issues, and pointed out the boundaries of the work being discussed as well as potential paths for moving forward. At a meeting that included a generation of researchers such as Ken Arrow, Dick Nelson, and Paul David upon whom we have all built, Suzanne nonetheless stood out as a unique theorist. She held the distinction of not simply clarifying the logic of what is possible but also providing a framework in which to understand how to evaluate those possibilities in real-world settings and to draw out the implications for both economic theory and ultimately public policy.

---

4 F.E.M, with Joshua Gans.
5 S.S., with Josh Lerner.

PART VIII

EPILOG

CHAPTER 28

What Suzanne Would Expect of Us

Pamela Samuelson

> Lovers and thinkers, into the earth with you
> ...
> A fragment of what you felt, of what you knew,
> A formula, a phrase remains, – but the best is lost.
> ...
> Gently they go, the beautiful, the tender, the kind.
> Quietly they go, the intelligent, the witty, the brave.
> I know. But I do not approve. And I am not resigned.
>
> Edna St. Vincent Millay
> "Dirge Without Music" (1928)

I was on an airplane on the tarmac of the San Francisco Airport when I first learned that my friend and coauthor Suzanne Scotchmer had passed away suddenly from an aggressive cancer. I remember it as if it happened yesterday. I was in deep shock. Of all the people I knew, I was sure she would live longer and more lucidly than the rest of us with that hearty Alaskan constitution and the love of life and work she seemed to embody.

Readers who have come this far will know that Suzanne was a brilliant economist who wrote many important papers on intellectual property and innovation. At the time of her death she had been working on the economics of digital markets, which is one of the most challenging topics of the day. I was eagerly waiting to see her conclusions.

Suzanne's death hit me and her other friends hard. That was partly because she had not told us that she was sick. So there was no chance to say goodbye. In the years since her passing, waves of grief still come over me when I least expect them. She had even more influence on me than I knew at the time.

Struggling in my grief, I felt I needed to act. That instinct, at least, was like Suzanne herself. So I began organizing a symposium to honor her many contributions to the fields of intellectual property and innovation policy.[1] That conference brought together dozens of colleagues who had worked with and been influenced by her. We celebrated the legacy she left to us and paid tribute to her as a person as well as a scholar. I'm convinced this was the sort of event that she would have wanted. I just wish we could have done it while she was alive.

Grief can, of course, immobilize and overwhelm. But grief can also motivate. You have to choose. Suzanne's death has motivated me to think hard about what she would expect me and others to do when she was gone.

One of Suzanne's most substantial accomplishments was her book, *Innovation and Incentives*, that synthesizes the long series of insights she developed in the decade-plus research arc that followed "Giants." I have been thinking for several years about writing a book on the importance of limits in copyright law, and particularly how those limits promote the progress of knowledge, as the US Constitution envisions.

It is perhaps a strange time to think about writing a book given how disruptive digital networks have been for traditional copyright industries, such as book publishing. Academic publishers in particular are struggling to reimagine their futures (and some surely worry that they may not have one). But since Suzanne's passing, I find that my desire to write that book has crystalized. I want to do it while I still have the acuity and strength that the task requires.

Thank you, Suzanne, for your kindness, your generosity, your brilliance, your insights, and now finally for motivating me to re-set my priorities and make the most of the time I have. I know you would have wanted your friends and colleagues to continue with our work. I promise the same joyful spirit you brought to yours.

---

1 "Innovation and Intellectual Property: A Tribute to Suzanne Scotchmer's Work," Berkeley, California (May 1, 2014).

Bibliography

Publications by Suzanne Scotchmer

Readers who have come this far will know that Prof. Scotchmer had many different research interests, many of which she pursued throughout her career. A simple chronological list of publications obscures this diversity and, in particular, the progression of her ideas from one paper to the next. This section seeks to avoid the problem by dividing her work into six categories: "innovation," "game theory," "club theory," "law and economics," "public finance," and "creative writing." Inevitably, this additional structure is somewhat arbitrary. That said, it is at least convenient since it both mirrors the organization of the current volume and largely tracks the categories that Prof. Scotchmer herself used to describe her work.[1]

INNOVATION

Maurer, S. M. and S. Scotchmer. 2014. "The Lost Message of Terminal Railroad," *California Law Review: Circuit* (October 8).

Scotchmer, S. 2013. "Patents in the University: Priming the Pump and Crowding Out," *Journal of Industrial Economics* 61(3): 817–844.

Scotchmer, S. and J. Zhou. 2011. "Picking Winners in Rounds of Elimination." Available at http://socrates.berkeley.edu/~scotch/winners.pdf.

Scotchmer, S. 2010a. "Cap-and-Trade, Emissions Taxes, and Innovation," *Innovation Policy and the Economy* 11: 29–54.

Scotchmer, S. 2010b. "Openness, Open Source, and the Veil of Ignorance," *Proceedings of the American Economic Association* 100: 165–171.

Erkal, N. and S. Scotchmer. 2009. "Scarcity of Ideas and R&D Options: Use It, Lose It, or Bank It," *National Bureau of Economic Research Working Paper 09-14940*.

Menell, P. and S. Scotchmer. 2007. "Intellectual Property," in M. Polinsky and S. Shavell (eds.), *Handbook of Law and Economics*, pp. 1472–1570. Amsterdam: Elsevier.

---

1 http://socrates.berkeley.edu/~scotch/publications.htm.

Maurer, S. M. and S. Scotchmer. 2006a. "Profit Neutrality in Licensing: The Boundary Between Antitrust Law and Patent Law," *American Law and Economics Review* 8: 476–522. Reprinted in this volume at pp. 234–261.

Maurer, S. and S. Scotchmer. 2006b. "Open Source Software: The New IP Paradigm," in T. Hendershott (ed.), *Handbook of Economics and Information Systems*, pp. 285–319. Amsterdam: Elsevier.

Park, Y. and S. Scotchmer. 2005. "Digital Rights Management and the Pricing of Digital Products," *National Bureau of Economic Research Working Paper 11532*.

Schankerman, M. and S. Scotchmer. 2005. "Still Looking for Lost Profits: The Case of Horizontal Competition," *UC Berkeley Institute of Business and Economic Research Working Paper E05-344*.

Maurer, S. M. and S. Scotchmer. 2004. "Procuring Knowledge," in G. Libecap (ed.), *Intellectual Property and Entrepreneurship: Advances in the Study of Entrepreneurship, Innovation and Growth*, Vol. 15, pp. 1–31. Amsterdam: Elsevier.

Scotchmer, S. 2004a. "The Political Economy of Intellectual Property Treaties," *Journal of Law, Economics, and Organizations* 20: 415–437.

Scotchmer, S. 2004b. *Innovation and Incentives*. Cambridge MA: MIT Press.

Scotchmer, S. 2003. "Intellectual Property – When Is It the Best Incentive Mechanism for S&T Data?," in J. M. Esanu and P. F. Uhlir (eds.), *The Role of Scientific and Technical Data and Information in the Public Domain: Proceedings of a Symposium*, pp. 15–18. Washington DC: National Academies Press.

Samuelson, P. and S. Scotchmer. 2002. "The Law and Economics of Reverse Engineering," *Yale Law Journal* 111: 1575–1663. Reprinted in this volume at pp. 201–229.

Maurer, S. M. and S. Scotchmer. 2002. "The Independent-Invention Defense in Intellectual Property," *Economica* 69: 535–547.

Gallini, N. and S. Scotchmer. 2002. "Intellectual Property: When Is It the Best Incentive System?," in A. Jaffe, J. Lerner, and S. Stern (eds.), *Innovation Policy and the Economy*, Vol. 2, pp. 51–78. Cambridge MA: MIT Press. Reprinted 2007 in Fabrizio Cafaggi, Antonio Nicita, and Ugo Pagano (eds.), *Legal Orderings and Economic Institutions*. Milton Park, UK: Routledge. Reprinted in this volume at pp. 59–82.

Schankerman, M. and S. Scotchmer. 2001. "Damages and Injunctions in the Protection of Intellectual Property," *RAND Journal of Economics* 32: 199–220. Reprinted in this volume at pp. 167–195.

Maurer, S. M. and S. Scotchmer. 1999. "Database Protection: Is it Broken and Should We Fix It?," *Science* 284: 1129–1130.

Scotchmer, S. 1999a. "On the Optimality of the Patent Renewal System," *RAND Journal of Economics* 30: 181–196.

Scotchmer, S. 1999b. "Delegating Investment in a Common-Value Project," *UC Berkeley Institute of Business and Economic Research Working Paper E99–266.*

O'Donoghue, T., S. Scotchmer, and J.-F. Thisse. 1998. "Patent Breadth, Patent Life, and the Pace of Technological Improvement," *Journal of Economics and Management Strategy* 7: 1–32.

Scotchmer, S. 1998a. "Incentives to Innovate," in Peter Newman (ed.), *New Palgrave Dictionary of Economics and the Law*, pp. 273–277. London: Macmillan.

Scotchmer, S. 1998b. "R&D Joint Ventures and Other Cooperative Arrangements," in R. Anderson and N. Gallini (eds.), *Competition Policy and Intellectual Property Rights in the Knowledge-Based Economy*, pp. 203–222. Calgary: University of Calgary Press.

Scotchmer, S. 1996a. "Protecting Early Innovators: Should Second-Generation Products be Patentable?," *RAND Journal of Economics* 27: 322–331.

Scotchmer, S. 1996b. "Patents as an Incentive System," in B. Allen (ed.), *Economics in a Changing World*, Vol. 2, pp. 281–296. London and New York: Macmillan Press.

Green, J. and S. Scotchmer. 1995. "On the Division of Profit Between Sequential Innovation," *RAND Journal of Economics* 26: 20–33. Reprinted in this volume at pp. 102–120.

Gandal, N. and S. Scotchmer. 1993. "Coordinating Research through Research Joint Ventures," *Journal of Public Economics* 51: 173–193.

Scotchmer, S. 1991. "Standing on the Shoulders of Giants: Cumulative Research and the Patent Law," *Journal of Economic Perspectives* 5(1): 29–41. Reprinted in Edwin and Elizabeth Mansfield (eds.), *The Economics of Technical Change*. Cheltenham: Edward Elgar Publishing Company, 1993. Reprinted in this volume at pp. 89–102.

Green, J. and S. Scotchmer. 1990. "Novelty and Disclosure in Patent Law," *RAND Journal of Economics* 21: 131–146.

Game Theory and Mathematical Economics

Scotchmer, S. 2008. "Risk Taking and Gender in Hierarchies," *Theoretical Economics* 3: 499–524.

Scotchmer, S. 2005. "Consumption Externalities, Rental Markets and Purchase Clubs," *Economic Theory* 25: 235–253.

Ellickson, B., B. Grodal, S. Scotchmer, and W. Zame. 2005. "The Organization of Consumption, Production and Learning," in K. Vind (ed.), *The Birgit Grodal Symposium*. Berlin: Springer-Verlag.

Scotchmer, S. 2002. "The Core and Hedonic Core: Reply to Wooders (2001), with Counterexamples," *Journal of Mathematical Economics* 37(4): 341–353.

Ellickson, B., B. Grodal, S. Scotchmer, and W. Zame. 2001. "Clubs and the Market: Large Finite Economies," *Journal of Economic Theory* 101: 40–77.

Ellickson, B., B. Grodal, S. Scotchmer, and W. Zame. 2000. "A Theory of Firm Formation and Skills Acquisition," Conference paper presented at World Congress of the Econometric Society, Seattle, WA (August 11–16).

Dekel, E. and S. Scotchmer. 1999. "On the Evolution of Attitudes Towards Risk in Winner-Take-All Games," *Journal of Economic Theory* 87: 125–143. Reprinted in this volume at pp. 308–312.

Ellickson, B., B. Grodal, S. Scotchmer, and W. Zame. 1999. "Clubs and the Market," *Econometrica* 67: 1185–1218. Reprinted in this volume at pp. 285–306.

Minehart, D. and S. Scotchmer. 1999. "Ex Post Regret and the Decentralized Sharing of Information," *Games and Economic Behavior* 27(1): 114–131.

Engl, G. and S. Scotchmer. 1997. "The Law of Supply in Games, Markets and Matching Models," *Economic Theory* 9: 539–550.

Diamantaris, D., R. Gilles, and S. Scotchmer. 1996. "The Decentralization of Pareto Optima in Economies with Public Goods and Inessential Private Goods," *Economic Theory* 8: 555–564.

Engl, G. and S. Scotchmer. 1996. "The Core and the Hedonic Core: Equivalence and Comparative Statics," *Journal of Mathematical Economics* 26: 209–248.

Farrell, J. and S. Scotchmer. 1994. "Irrational Behavior in the AT&T Investment Game," *Economics Letters* 45: 471–474.

Scotchmer, S. and J.-F. Thisse. 1994. "The Implications of Space for Competition," *Studies in Regional and Urban Planning* 3: 227–246. Also printed in A. Kirman, L.-A. Gerard-Varet, and M. Ruggiero (eds.). 1995. *Space and Value in Economics in the Next Ten Years*. New York and Oxford: Oxford University Press.

Dekel, E. and S. Scotchmer. 1992. "On the Evolution of Optimizing Behavior," *Journal of Economic Theory* 57(2): 392–406.

Scotchmer, S. and J.-F. Thisse. 1992. "Space and Competition: A Puzzle," *Annals of Regional Science* 26: 269–286.

Farrell, J. and S. Scotchmer. 1988. "Partnerships," *Quarterly Journal of Economics* 103(2), 279–297. Reprinted in this volume at pp. 269–285.

Scotchmer, S. 1986. "Market Share Inertia with More than Two Firms: An Existence Problem," *Economics Letters* 21(1): 77–79.

Clubs and Local Public Goods

Scotchmer, S. and C. Shannon. 2010. "Verifiability and Group Formation in Markets." Available at http://socrates.berkeley.edu/~scotch/groups-77.pdf.

Scotchmer, S. 2008. "Clubs," in L. Blume and S. Durlauf (eds.), *New Palgrave Dictionary of Economics*, 2nd edn., Vol. 1, pp. 834–839. London: Macmillan.

Ellickson, B., B. Grodal, S. Scotchmer, and W. Zame. 2005. "The Organization of Consumption, Production and Learning," in C. Schultz and K. Vind (ed.), *The Birgit Grodal Symposium*, pp. 149–186. Berlin: Springer-Verlag.

Scotchmer, S. 2005. "Consumption Externalities, Rental Markets and Purchase Clubs," *Economic Theory* 25: 235–253.

Scotchmer, S. 2002. "Local Public Goods and Clubs," in Alan Auerbach and Martin Feldstein (eds.), *Handbook of Public Economics*, Vol. IV, pp. 1997–2042. Amsterdam: North-Holland Press.

Ellickson, B., B. Grodal, S. Scotchmer, and W. Zame. 2001. "Clubs and the Market: Large Finite Economies," *Journal of Economic Theory* 101: 40–77.

Jehiel, P. and S. Scotchmer. 2001. "Constitutional Rules of Exclusion in Jurisdiction Formation," *Review of Economic Studies* 68: 393–411.

Ellickson, B., B. Grodal, S. Scotchmer, and W. Zame. 1999. "Clubs and the Market," *Econometrica* 67: 1185–1218.

Gilles, R. and S. Scotchmer. 1998. "Decentralization in Club Economies: How Multiple Private Goods Matter," in David Pines, Ephraim Sadka, and Itzak Zilcha (eds.), *Topics in Public Economics: Theoretical and Applied Analysis*, pp. 121–138. New York: Cambridge University Press.

Gilles, R. and S. Scotchmer. 1997. "Decentralization in Replicated Club Economies," *Journal of Economic Theory* 72: 363–387.

Jehiel, P. and S. Scotchmer. 1997. "Free Mobility and the Optimal Number of Jurisdictions," *Annales d'Economie et de Statistiques* 45: 219–231.

Scotchmer, S. 1997. "On Price-Taking Equilibria in Club Economies with Nonanonymous Crowding," *Journal of Public Economics* 65(1): 75–88.

Glazer, A., E. Niskanen, and S. Scotchmer. 1997. "On the Uses of Club Theory: Preface to the Club Theory Symposium," *Journal of Public Economics* 65(1): 3–8.

Scotchmer, S. 1996. "Externality Pricing in Club Economies," *Ricerche Economiche* 50(4): 347–366

Scotchmer, S. 1994. "Concurrence et biens publics," *Annales d'Economie et de Statistique* 33: 157–186. Also published as "Public Goods and the Invisible Hand," in J. Quigley and E. Smolensky (eds.). 1994. *Modern Public Finance*, pp. 93–119. Cambridge MA: Harvard University Press.

Scotchmer, S. and M. Wooders. 1987. "Competitive Equilibrium and the Core in Club Economies with Anonymous Crowding," *Journal of Public Economics* 34: 159–173.

Scotchmer, S. 1986. "Local Public Goods in an Equilibrium: How Pecuniary Externalities Matter," *Regional Science and Urban Economics* 16: 463–481.

Scotchmer, S. 1985. "Two-Tier Pricing of Shared Facilities in a Free-Entry Equilibrium," *RAND Journal of Economics* 16(4): 456–472.

Scotchmer, S. 1985. "Profit-Maximizing Clubs," *Journal of Public Economics* 27: 25–85.

Other Law and Economics Topics

Rubinfeld, D. and S. Scotchmer. 1998. "Contingent Fees," in P. Newman (ed.), *New Palgrave Dictionary of Economics and the Law*, pp. 415–420. London: Macmillan.

Scotchmer, S. 1998. "Rules of Evidence and Statistical Reasoning in Court," in P. Newman (ed.), *New Palgrave Dictionary of Economics and the Law*, pp. 389–394. London: Macmillan.

Schrag, J. and S. Scotchmer. 1997. "On the Self-Reinforcing Nature of Crime," *International Journal of Law and Economics* 17: 325–335.

Schrag, J. and S. Scotchmer. 1994. "Crime and Prejudice: The Use of Character Evidence in Criminal Trials," *Journal of Law, Economics, and Organizations* 10(2): 319–342.

Rubinfeld, D. and S. Scotchmer. 1993. "Contingent Fees for Lawyers: An Economic Analysis," *RAND Journal of Economics* 24: 343–356.

Public Finance

Scotchmer, S. 2002. "Local Public Goods and Clubs," in Alan Auerbach and Martin Feldstein (eds.), *Handbook of Public Economics*, Vol. IV, pp. 1997–2042. Amsterdam: North-Holland Press.

Scotchmer, S. 1992. "The Regressive Bias in Taxation and Enforcement," *Public Finance* 58: 366–371.

Dekel, E. and S. Scotchmer. 1990. "Collusion Through Insurance: Sharing the Costs of Oil Spill Cleanups," *American Economic Review* 80: 249–252.

Jones, C. A. and S. Scotchmer. 1990. "The Social Cost of Uniform Regulatory Standards," *Journal of Environmental Economics and Management* 19: 61–72.

Quigley, J. and S. Scotchmer. 1989. "What Counts? Analysis Counts," *Journal of the Association for Policy Analysis* 8(3): 483–489.

Scotchmer, S. 1989a. "Who Profits from Taxpayer Confusion?," *Economics Letters* 29: 49–55.

Scotchmer, S. 1989b. "The Effect of Tax Advisors on Tax Compliance," in J. Roth and J. Scholz (eds.), *Why People Pay Taxes: A Social Science Perspective*, pp. 182–199. Philadelphia PA: University of Pennsylvania Press.

Scotchmer, S. 1989c. "Equivalent Variation with Uncertain Prices," *Economics Letters* 29: 127–128.

Scotchmer, S. and J. Slemrod. 1989. "Randomness in Tax Enforcement," *Journal of Public Economics* 38: 17–32.

Scotchmer, S. 1987. "Audit Classes and Tax Enforcement Policy," *American Economic Review: Papers and Proceedings* 77(2): 229–233. Reprinted in this volume at pp. 340–347.

Scotchmer, S. 1986."The Short Run and Long Run Benefits of Environmental Improvement," *Journal of Public Economics* 30: 61–81.

Scotchmer, S. 1985. "Hedonic Prices and Cost/Benefit Analysis," *Journal of Economic Theory* 37(1): 55–75.

CREATIVE WRITING (AS SUZANNE ANDERSEN).

"Rain," appeared in "Half-Baked Alaska," *Alaska Magazine*, March 1997. Available at http://socrates.berkeley.edu/~scotch/alaska/rain.pdf.

"Ghosts of Christmases Past" (aka "Reminders of Home"), *Alaska Magazine,* December 1996. Available at http://socrates.berkeley.edu/~scotch/alaska/ghosts.pdf.

"Devils Club Tea," *Anchorage Daily News Sunday Magazine (We Alaskans)*, October 20, 1996. Available at http://socrates.berkeley.edu/~scotch/alaska/devils.pdf.

"Smoked Fish: A Christmas Story," published in *Seattle Times Sunday Magazine (The Pacific)*, December 17, 1995 and *Anchorage Daily News Sunday Magazine (We Alaskans)*, December 17, 1995. Available at http://socrates.berkeley.edu/~scotch/alaska/smkedfsh.pdf.

VIDEO LECTURES

Duke University: Frey Lecture 2008. "Suzanne Scotchmer, A Nonobvious Discussion of Patents." Available at www.youtube.com/watch?v=MhE68 ZHYJXM.

Barcelona Graduate School of Economics: "Use It, Lose It, or Bank It," November 10, 2009. Available at www.youtube.com/watch?v=xnu8k EzRCMY.

University of California at Berkeley: Commencement Proceedings. Andrés Roemer Remembers Prof. Scotchmer (May 17, 2014). Available at https://gspp.berkeley.edu/events/webcasts/andrs-roemers-honors-professor-suzanne-scotchmer-at-2014-uc-berkeley-commen.

ADDITIONAL REFERENCES

Acemoglu, D. and U. Akcigit. 2012. "Intellectual Property Rights Policy, Competition and Innovation," *Journal of the European Economic Association* 10(1): 1–42.

Agrawal, A. and A. Goldfarb. 2008. "Restructuring Research: Communication Costs and the Democratization of University Innovation," *American Economic Review* 98(4): 1578–1590.

Agrawal, A. and A. Goldfarb. 2006. "Restructuring Research: Communication Costs and the Democratization of University Innovation," *National Bureau of Economic Research Working Paper No. 12812.*

Anon. n.d. "Edison and the Invention Factory." Available at http://edison.rutgers.edu/inventionfactory.htm.

Arrow, Kenneth J. 1973. "The Theory of Discrimination," in O. Ashenfelter and A. Rees (eds.), *Discrimination in Labor Markets*, pp. 3–33. Princeton: Princeton University Press.

Arrow, K. J. 1962. "Economic Welfare and the Allocation of Resources for Invention," in H. M. Groves (ed.), *The Rate and Direction of Inventive Activity: Economic and Social Factors*, pp. 609–626. Princeton and Oxford: Princeton University Press.

Bardsley, Peter and Katerina Sherstyuk. 2006. "Rat Races and Glass Ceilings," *Topics in Theoretical Economics* 6(1): Article 13.

Becker, Gary S. (1957, 1971, 2nd edn.). *The Economics of Discrimination.* Chicago: University of Chicago Press.

Bessen, J. and E. Maskin. 2009. "Sequential Innovation, Patents, and Imitation," *RAND Journal of Economics* 40(4): 611–635.

Bush, V. 1945. *Science, The Endless Frontier.* Washington DC: US Government Printing Office.

Cockburn, I., S. Kortum, and S. Stern. 2003. "Are All Patent Examiners Equal? Examiners, Patent Characteristics, and Litigation Outcomes," in W. Cohen and S. Merrill (eds.), *Patents in the Knowledge-Based Economy*, pp. 19–53. Washington DC: National Academies Press.

Cornelli, F. and M. Schankerman. 1999. "Patent Renewals and R&D Incentives," *RAND Journal of Economics* 30(2): 197–213.

Croson, Rachel and Uri Gneezy. 2009. "Gender Differences in Preferences," *Journal of Economic Literature* 47(2): 448–474.

CSWEP (Committee on the Status of Women in the Economics Profession). 2014. "Report: Committee on the Status of Women in the Economics Profession (CSWEP)" *American Economic Review* 104(5): 664–681.

Dasgupta, P. and J. Stiglitz. 1980. "Uncertainty, Industrial Structure, and the Speed of R&D," *Bell Journal of Economics* 11: 1–28.

De Solla Price, D. 1965. "Networks of Scientific Papers," *Science* 149. 510–515.

Fang, Hanming and Andrea Moro. 2010. "Theories of Statistical Discrimination," in Jess Benhabib, Alberto Bisin, and Matthew Jackson (eds.), *Handbook of Social Economics*, Vol. IB, pp. 133–200. Amsterdam: North-Holland Press.

Fershtman, C. and N. Gandal. 2011a. "A Brief Survey of the Economics of Open Source Software," in S. N. Durlauf and L. E. Blume (eds.), *The*

New Palgrave Dictionary of Economics. London: Palgrave Macmillan. Available at www.dictionaryof economics.com/article?id=pde2011_ O000108. doi: 10.1057/9780230226203.3855.

Fershtman, C. and N. Gandal. 2011b. "Direct and Indirect Knowledge Spillovers: The 'Social Network' of Open Source Projects," *RAND Journal of Economics* 42: 70–91.

Furman, J. L., Murray, F., and S. Stern. 2012. "The Impact of the Bush Stem Cell Policy on the Geography of Scientific Discovery," *Journal of Policy Analysis and Management* 31(3): 661–705.

Furman, J. L. and S. Stern. 2011. "Climbing Atop the Shoulders of Giants: The Impact of Institutions on Cumulative Research," *American Economic Review* 101(5): 1933–1963.

Furth, Helmut F. 1958. "Price Restrictive Patent Licenses Under the Sherman Act," *Harvard Law Review* 71: 814–842.

Galasso, A. and M. Schankerman. 2015. "Patents and Cumulative Innovation: Causal Evidence from the Courts," *Quarterly Journal of Economics* 130(1): 317–369.

Gallini, N. 2014. "Cooperating with Competitors: Patent Pooling and Choice of a New Standard," *International Journal of Industrial Organization* 36: 4–21.

Gallini, N. 2002. "The Economics of Patents: Lessons from Recent U.S. Patent Reform," *Journal of Economic Perspectives* 16(2): 131–154.

Gallini, N. 1992. "Patent Policy and Costly Imitation," *RAND Journal of Economics* 23(1): 52–63.

Gallini, N. 1984. "Deterrence by Market Sharing: A Strategic Incentive for Licensing," *American Economic Review* 74(5): 931–941.

Gallini, N. and R. Winter. 1985. "Licensing in the Theory of Innovation," *RAND Journal of Economics* 16(2): 237–252.

Garfield, E. 1955. "Citation Indexes for Science – A New Dimension in Documentation through Association of Ideas," *Science* 122: 108–111.

Geiger, Roger L. 1986. *To Advance Knowledge: The Growth of American Research Universities, 1900–1940.* New York and Oxford: Oxford University Press.

Gertner, J. 2012. *The Idea Factory: Bell Labs and the Great Age of American Innovation.* New York: Penguin.

Gilbert, R. and C. Shapiro. 1990. "Optimal Patent Length and Breadth," *RAND Journal of Economics* 21(1): 106–112.

Griliches, Z. 1998. *R&D and Productivity: The Econometric Evidence.* Chicago: University of Chicago Press.

Griliches, Z. 1990. "Patent Statistics as Economic Indicators: A Survey," *Journal of Economic Literature* 92: 630–653.

Hall, B., Z. Griliches, and J. Hausman (1986). "Patents and R and D: Is There a Lag," *International Economic Review* 27(2): 265–283.

Hall, B., C. Helmers, G. V. Graevenitz, and C. R. Bondibene. 2014. "A Study of Patent Thickets," *Intellectual Property Office Research Paper No. 2.*

Heller, M. and R. Eisenberg. 1998. "Can Patents Deter Innovation? The Anticommons in Biomedical Research," *Science* 280: 698–701.

Hopenhayn, H., G. Llobet, and M. Mitchell. 2006. "Rewarding Sequential Innovators: Prizes, Patents and Buyouts," *Journal of Political Economy* 114(6): 1041–1068.

Hopenhayn, H. and M. Mitchell. 2001. "Innovation Variety and Patent Breadth," *RAND Journal of Economics* 32(1): 152–166.

Jaffe, A. 2000. "The U.S. Patent System in Transition," *Research Policy* 29: 531–557.

Jaffe, A., M. Trajtenberg, and R. Henderson. 1993. "Geographic Localization of Knowledge Spillovers as Evidenced by Patent Citations," *Quarterly Journal of Economics* 108(3): 577–598.

Jensen, K. and F. Murray. 2005. "Intellectual Property Landscape of the Human Genome," *Science* 310(5746): 239–240.

Katz, M. L. 1986. "An Analysis of Cooperative Research and Development," *RAND Journal of Economics* 17(4): 527–543.

Katz, M. L. and C. Shapiro. 1987. "R&D Rivalry with Licensing or Imitation," *American Economic Review* 77(3): 402–420.

Kirkwood, J. B. and R. H. Lande. 2008. "The Fundamental Goal of Antitrust: Protecting Consumers, Not Increasing Efficiency," *Notre Dame Law Review* 84(1): 191–243.

Kitch, E. W. 1977. "The Nature and Function of the Patent System," *Journal of Law and Economics* 20(2): 265–290.

Klemperer, P. 1990. "How Broad Should the Scope of Patent Protection Be?," *RAND Journal of Economics* 21(1): 113–130.

Kremer, M. 1998. "Patent Buyouts: A Mechanism for Encouraging Innovation," *Quarterly Journal of Economics* 113(4): 1137–1167.

La Manna, M., R. Macleod, and D. deMeza. 1989. "The Case for Permissive Patents," *European Economic Review* 37: 1427–1443.

Lemley, M. A. 2007. "Should Patent Infringement Require Proof of Copying?," *Michigan Law Review* 105: 989–1084.

Lerner, J. and M. Schankerman. 2011. *The Comingled Code: Open Source and Economic Development.* Cambridge MA and London: MIT Press.

Lerner, J. and J. Tirole. 2004. "Efficient Patent Pools," *American Economic Review* 94(3): 691–711.

Lerner, J. and J. Tirole. 2002. "Some Simple Economics of Open Source," *Journal of Industrial Economics* 52: 197–234.

McFetridge, D. and M. Rafiquzzaman. 1986. "The Scope and Duration of the Patent Right and the Nature of Research Rivalry," *Research in Law and Economics* 8: 91–120.

Merges, R. and R. R. Nelson. 1990. "On the Complex Economics of Patent Scope," *Columbia Law Review* 90: 839–916.

Merton, R. K. 1973. *The Sociology of Science: Theoretical and Empirical Investigations.* Chicago: University of Chicago Press.

Milgrom, Paul and Sharon Oster. 1987. "Job Discrimination, Market Forces and the Invisibility Hypothesis," *Quarterly Journal of Economics* 102: 453–476.

Murray, F., P. Aghion, M. Dewatripont, J. Kolev, and S. Stern. 2016. "Of Mice and Academics: Examining the Effect of Openness on Innovation," *American Economic Journal: Policy* 8(1): 1–43.

Murray, F. and S. Stern. 2007. "Do Formal Intellectual Property Rights Hinder the Free Flow of Scientific Knowledge? An Empirical Test of the Anti-Commons Hypothesis," *Journal of Economic Behavior and Organization* 63: 648–687.

Nagaraj, A. 2015. "The Private Impact of Public Maps – Landsat Satellite Imagery and Gold Exploration," MIT Sloan mimeo.

Nordhaus, W. 1969. *Invention, Growth, and Welfare: A Theoretical Treatment of Technological Change.* Cambridge MA and London: MIT Press.

Phelps, Edmund S. 1972. "The Statistical Theory of Racism and Sexism," *American Economic Review* 62(4): 659–661.

Polansky, A. 2007. "Is the General Public License a Rational Choice?," *Journal of Industrial Economics* 55(4): 691–714.

Reinganum, J. 1989. "The Timing of Innovation: Research, Development, and Diffusion," in R. Schmalensee and R. Willig (eds.), *Handbook of Industrial Organization*, Vol. 1, pp. 849–908. Amsterdam: Elsevier.

Reinganum, J. 1982. "A Dynamic Game of R&D: Patent Protection and Competitive Behaviour," *Econometrica* 50: 671–688.

Reinganum, J. 1981. "Dynamic Games of Innovation," *Journal of Economic Theory* 25: 21–41.

Roberts, Caprice L. 2010. "The Case for Restitution and Unjust Enrichment Remedies in Patent Law," *Lewis & Clark Law Review* 14(2): 653–685.

Robson, Arthur J. 2001. "Why Would Nature Give Individuals Utility Functions?," *Journal of Political Economy* 109(4): 900–914.

Robson, Arthur J. 1996. "The Evolution of Attitudes to Risk: Lottery Tickets and Relative Wealth," *Games and Economic Behavior* 14: 190–207.

Rossi, C. and A. Bonaccorsi. 2005. "Intrinsic vs. Extrinsic Incentives in Profit-Oriented Firms Supplying Open Source Products and Services," *First Monday* 10(5). Available at http://pear.accc.uic.edu/htbin/cgiwrap/bin/ojs/index.php/fm/article/viewArticle/1242.

Rowe, M. P. 1990. "Barriers to Equality: The Power of Subtle Discrimination to Maintain Unequal Opportunity," *Employee Responsibilities and Rights Journal* 3(2): 153–163. Revised and extended from a series of papers called "Saturn's Rings" and "Glass Ceiling" written

1973–1989. Available at http://ombud.mit.edu/sites/default/files/docu ments/barriers.pdf.

Rowe, M. P. 1976. "Rings of Saturn Phenomenon." Available at http://mrowe.scripts.mit.edu/docs/Other/The%20Saturn's%20Rings%20 Phenomenon.pdf.

Sakakibara, M. and L. Branstetter. 2001. "Do Stronger Patents Induce More Innovation? Evidence from the 1998 Japanese Patent Law Reforms," *RAND Journal of Economics* 32: 77–100.

Sampat, B. and H. Williams. 2015. "How Do Patents Affect Follow-On Innovation? Evidence from the Human Genome," *National Bureau of Economic Research Working Paper 21666.*

Sarsons, Heather. 2015. "Gender Differences in Recognition for Group Work." Harvard University. Available at http://scholar.harvard.edu/ files/sarsons/files/gender_groupwork.pdf?m=1449178759.

Schumpeter, J. 1942. *Capitalism, Socialism, and Democracy.* New York: Harper & Row.

Shapiro, C. 2006. "Prior User Rights," *American Economic Review* 96: 92.

Shapiro, C. 2001. "Navigating the Patent Thicket: Cross Licenses, Patent Pools, and Standard Setting," in A. Jaffe, J. Lerner, and S. Stern (eds.), *Innovation Policy and the Economy*, Vol. 1, pp. 119–150. Cambridge MA and London: MIT Press.

Simcoe, T. and M. Rysman. 2008. "Patents and the Performance of Voluntary Standard-Setting Organizations," *Management Science* 54(11): 1920–1934.

Spence, A. M. 1984. "Cost Reduction, Competition, and Industry Performance," *Econometrica* 52: 101–121.

Trajtenberg, M. (1990) "Patents as Indicators of Innovation," in *Economic Analysis of Product Innovation.* Cambridge MA: Harvard University Press.

US District Court. 2003. *Heary Bros. Lightning Protection Co., Inc.* v. *Lightning Protection Institute*, 287 F. Supp. 2d 1038 (D. Ariz.).

US Federal Circuit. 1998. *State Street Bank & Trust Co.* v. *Signature Financial Group*, 149 F.3d 1368.

US Supreme Court. 2014. *Alice Corporation* v. *CLS Bank International*, 134 S. Ct. 2347.

US Supreme Court. 2012. *Mayo Collaborative Services* v. *Prometheus Laboratories, Inc.*, 132 S. Ct. 1289.

US Supreme Court. 2010. *Bilski* v. *Kappos*, 561 U.S. 593.

US Supreme Court. 1948. *US* v. *Line Material Co.*, 333 U.S. 287.

US Supreme Court. 1926. *United States* v. *General Electric Co.*, 272 U.S. 476.

US Supreme Court. 1912. *US* v. *Terminal Railroad Assn.*, 224 U.S. 383.

US Supreme Court. 1853. *O'Reilly* v. *Morse*, 56 U.S. 62.

Vermont, S. 2006. "Independent Invention as a Defense to Patent Infringement," *Michigan Law Review* 105(3): 475–504.

West, J. and S. Gallaghcr. 2006 "Challenges of Open Innovation: The Paradox of Firm Investment in Open Source Software," *R&D Management* 36: 315–328.

Williams, H. (2013), "Intellectual Property Rights and Innovation: Evidence from the Human Genome," *Journal of Political Economy* 121(1): 1–27.

Wright, B. 1983. "The Economics of Invention Incentives: Patents, Prizes, and Research Contracts," *American Economic Review* 73: 691–707.

Index